Can Russia Modernise?

Sistema, *Power Networks and Informal Governance*

In this original, bottom-up account of the evolution of contemporary Russia, Alena Ledeneva seeks to reveal how informal power operates. Concentrating on Vladimir Putin's system of governance – referred to as *sistema* – she identifies four key types of networks: his inner circle, useful friends, core contacts and more diffuse ties and connections. These networks serve *sistema* but also serve themselves. Reliance on networks enables leaders to mobilise and to control, yet they also lock politicians, bureaucrats and businessmen into informal deals, mediated interests and personalised loyalty. This is the 'modernisation trap of informality': one cannot use the potential of informal networks without triggering their negative long-term consequences for institutional development. Ledeneva's perspective on informal power is based on in-depth interviews with *sistema* insiders and enhanced by evidence of its workings brought to light in court cases, enabling her to draw broad conclusions about the prospects for Russia's political institutions.

ALENA V. LEDENEVA is Professor of Politics and Society, School of Slavonic and East European Studies, University College London. Her previous books include *How Russia Really Works* (2006) and *Russia's Economy of Favours* (Cambridge University Press, 1998).

Can Russia Modernise?

Sistema, Power Networks and
Informal Governance

ALENA V. LEDENEVA

CAMBRIDGE
UNIVERSITY PRESS

CAMBRIDGE
UNIVERSITY PRESS

University Printing House, Cambridge CB2 8BS, United Kingdom

Published in the United States of America by Cambridge University Press, New York

Cambridge University Press is part of the University of Cambridge.

It furthers the University's mission by disseminating knowledge in the pursuit of education, learning and research at the highest international levels of excellence.

www.cambridge.org
Information on this title: www.cambridge.org/9780521125635

© Alena V. Ledeneva 2013

First published 2013
3rd printing 2013

Printed in the United Kingdom by Clays, St Ives plc.

A catalogue record for this publication is available from the British Library

Library of Congress Cataloguing in Publication data
Ledeneva, Alena V., 1964–
Can Russia modernise? : sistema, power networks and informal governance / Alena V. Ledeneva.
    pages   cm
Includes bibliographical references and index.
ISBN 978-0-521-11082-2 (hardback) – ISBN 978-0-521-12563-5 (paperback)
1. Putin, Vladimir Vladimirovich, 1952 – Friends and associates.   2. Putin, Vladimir Vladimirovich, 1952 – Political and social views.   3. Social networks – Political aspects – Russia (Federation)   4. Power (Social sciences) – Russia (Federation)
5. Political culture – Russia (Federation)   6. Social change – Russia (Federation)
7. Russia (Federation) – Politics and government.   8. Informal governance – management.   9. Informal leadership.   10. Informal power – sociology.   I. Title.
DK510.766.P87L43   2013
303.30947 – dc23   2012030784

ISBN 978-0-521-11082-2 Hardback
ISBN 978-0-521-12563-5 Paperback

To my daughter Maria Ledeneva

Contents

Figures

Tables

Boxes

Acknowledgements

First and foremost, I would like to express my gratitude and admiration for my respondents. They remain anonymous but it is them that I owe most. Not only have they mastered *sistema*, they have articulated its complexity, pinned down its ambivalence and shared their insights. Without their expertise, experience and generosity with time this book could not have been written.

I want to acknowledge with appreciation my anonymous reviewers at Cambridge University Press and esteemed readers of the early drafts of the manuscript who have offered valuable comments: Harley Balzer, Tony Giddens, Phil Hanson, Geoffrey Hosking and Elizabeth Teague. I am grateful to John Crowfoot, Nina Fahy and Benjamin Woodgates for their excellent line editing. My CUP editors, John Haslam and Carrie Parkinson, and the copy editor Barbara Docherty have been professional, patient and positive.

For permission to reproduce visual materials I am grateful to Evgeniia Albats and *The New Times*, Valentin Dubinin and Cari-catura.ru, Irina Demchenko and Ralph Gibson at RIA-Novosti, Zhenia Vasiliev and Petr Cheryomyshkin.

A number of research projects have contributed to the writing of this book. I am grateful to the British Academy for the support of my 2006–7 project on *Informal Influence in Judicial Systems: 'Telefon-noe pravo' in Russia* (SG-43818) and the 2009–10 research project on the *Defects of the Russian Judicial System: Evidence from Russian Cases in the UK courts* (SG-51440). I thank the EU-Russia Centre, Fraser Cameron and Maria Ordzhonikidze for their support of the 2010–11 survey on *Telephone Justice in Russia: An Update*. Alexei Grazhdankin and the team at the Levada Centre gave me help and advice with the surveys over the years. I was able to conduct my 2007 fieldwork thanks to the invitation and support of the Higher School of Economics (HSE), Moscow. I thank my colleagues Svetlana Barsukova, Vadim Radaev, Andrei Yakovlev, Rozalina Ryvkina and especially my hosts Nikita Pokrovskii and Natalia Shushanian for their warm welcome at the HSE. Masha Lipman, Nikolai Petrov and Lilia Shevtsova, at the Carnegie Endowment for International Peace have given me advice and inspiration. I am indebted to the UK Leverhulme Trust that funded my Leverhulme Fellowship and enabled me to spend my 2010 sabbatical at the Centre for International Studies and Research (CERI) and the Paris School of International Affairs (PSIA) at Sciences Po, Paris. My colleagues at Sciences-Po, Gilles Favarel-Garriques, Beatrice Hibou, Christian Lequesne, Marie Mendras, Kathy Rousselet and Lilia Shevtsova, also a visiting professor that year, were wonderful. I was made exceptionally welcome in Paris by Natalia Polenova, Florence Weber and Valery Yakubovich.

Back at home, many thanks go to my colleagues at the School of Slavonic and East European Studies (SSEES), Robin Aizlewood, Pete Duncan, Seth Graham, Sean Hanley, George Kolankiewicz, Svetlana Makarova, Tomasz Mizkiewicz, Eugene Nivorozhkin, Slavo Radosevic, Maria Rubins, Alex Titov and Andrew Wilson, who have all helped in various ways with my project. I thank Maria Widdowson and the School's administrators for their help with research grant applications and technical support.

I have benefited from the help of my research assistants, Oliver Carroll, Licia Cianetti, Costanza Curro, Piotr Drozd, Elena Tsirlina and Aglaya Snetkov. My graduate students have been wonderful in helping me in the final stages of the manuscript: Conal Campbell, Tim Cook, Aneurin Jones, Anna Rosenberg and Kiril Tasev.

I am grateful to my colleagues who have helped shape various aspects of research: Tim Colton asked me a question leading to research on informal power, Karl Karp noticed that my research was in fact aimed at *sistema*, Vladimir Gelman stated he did not know what *sistema* was, Gerald Mars' admiration for Mary Douglas made me go back to her writings, Peter Reddaway drew my attention to the importance of the *Three Whales* case, Vladimir Pastukhov led me to Richard Pipes' memoirs and other sources, Karen Dawisha invited me to the most stimulating Havighurst Centre 2011 symposium. I thank Alexei Trochev for his invaluable digests about the Russian judiciary; and Serguei Oushakine and Kim Scheppele for their hospitality and ideas. I thank Kathryn Hendley, Ekaterina Mishina, Ella Paneyakh, Georgy Satarov, Peter Solomon and Vadim Volkov, who helped with their comments on my paper at the Institute of Law Enforcement at the European University at St Petersburg, under the 'ash cloud' of 2010.

A lot of people have helped me through the period of writing this book. I am grateful to my doctor Eric Leclercq, who has been gentle and flexible, to Matthew Alfred, Karen Clarke and Lea Harris. I owe my calm to Paul and Valery Canarelli, Robin Hayward, Karen Russell, Jim Perrichon, Reyna Halunajan, Nhita and Tania. For their endless support and friendship I thank Ellen Dahrendorf, Irina Davydova, Margaret Mathieson, Elena Ragozhina, Peter and Lorna Rogan, Houshang Argavan, Valery Belousov and John MacGinnis.

My special thanks go to someone who read every line of this book and has been utterly supportive but wanted to remain unnamed. Finally, for her generosity and team spirit, I want to thank my daughter Maria Ledeneva, the coolest girl I know, to whom this book is affectionately dedicated.

Domain de Murtoli, Corsica
September 2011 and September 2012

Abbreviations and acronyms

ATS-1	Automated Telephone Station-1, an elitist secure telephone network of 1,000 users
ATS-2	Automated Telephone Station-2, an elitist secure telephone network of 5,000 users
BEEPS	Business Environment and Enterprise Performance Surveys
CBI	Confederation of British Industry
CEO	chief executive officer
CPS	Crown Prosecution Service
CPSU	Communist Party of the Soviet Union
ECHR	European Convention of Human Rights
ECtHR	European Court of Human Rights
EU	European Union
FAPSI	Federal Agency of Government Communications and Information
FAR	Federation of Automobilists of Russia
FCPA	Foreign Corrupt Practices Act 1977 (US)
FGUP	Federal State Unitary Enterprises
FSB	Federal Security Service, successor to KGB
FSKN	Russian Anti-narcotic Service
FSO	Federal Protective Service
GOK	mineral processing production plant (*gorno-obogatitel'nyi kombinat*)
GR	government relations
HR	human resources/executive search
IC	Investigative Committee
INDEM	Information for Democracy, think tank
IPO	initial public offering
KGB	Committee for State Security
KPS	Government Communications Commission
LDPR	Liberal Democratic Party of Russia

MChS	Ministry of Emergency Situations
MGIMO	Moscow State Institute of International Relations
MID	Ministry of Foreign Affairs
MVD	Ministry of Internal Affairs
NGO	non-governmental organisation
NGPF	non-governmental pension funds
NMG	National Media Group
OGPU	State Political Directorate
PA	Presidential Administration
PACE	Parliamentary Assembly of the Council of Europe
PATS	Priority Area Telecommunications System
PGO	Prosecutor General's Office
PR	public relations
PS	presidential telecoms network (*presidentskaya svyaz'*)
PSU	Primary Sampling Unit
QC	Queen's Counsel
RAO EES	Edinaya Energeticheskaya Sistema, United Energy System
RF	Russian Federation
RFE/RL	Radio Free Europe/Radio Liberty
Rosimusch-estvo	Federal Agency for State Property Management
SK	special switchboard (*spetskommutator*)
SSU	Secondary Sampling Unit
VAS	Supreme Arbitration Court
VAT	value added tax
VChK	Cheka, state security organisation
VGTRK	All-Russian State Television and Radio Company
VTB	Vneshtorgbank, state bank
VTsIOM	All-Russia Centre of Study of Public Opinion

Introduction: *modernising* sistema

From the power of networks to networks of power

Sistema is an open secret in Russia that has a powerful grip over the society. It represents common, yet not articulated, perceptions of power and the system of governance. My ethnography of *sistema* is an attempt to articulate, assemble and cross-check such perceptions with insiders of the corridors of power, as well as to explore the daily functioning and mundane practices of Russia's 'state machine'.[1] The perceptions of *sistema* are elusive, context-bound, obscured by self-deception and often resist articulation but the daily patterns commonly associated with the power of *sistema* can be identified.

This book is a sequel to *Russia's Economy of Favours* (Ledeneva 1998). There I applied the bottom-up perspective to analyse *blat*, networking and informal exchange at the grassroots level. Here I look at the workings of power networks and methods of informal governance. I explore both enabling and constraining aspects of belonging to power networks and delve into the nuances of how they can be managed. I rely on my respondents to articulate the 'secrets' of *sistema*. *Sistema* rules are taken for granted by insiders, and their misrecognition of *sistema* is part of the story. The best sources are once-an-insider respondents, who broke *sistema* rules and were marginalised, or those who distanced themselves from *sistema* due to their career movements, personal development and global outlook.

---

[1] An analogy can be drawn with 'political machines' in the USA, and the spoils system aimed at the distribution of official positions among members of the winning party. William 'Boss' Tweed is known to have created a 'political machine' of the Democratic Party who set up a charity fund, Tammany Hall, that controlled key appointments in the State of New York and 'allocated' state orders. See J. H. Knott and Gary J. Miller, *Reforming Bureaucracy: The Politics of Institutional Choice* (New York: Prentice Hall 1987: 18–19), quoted in Yakovlev (2012).

Sistema victims, as well as critics of Putin's *sistema*, are emphatic about the negative features of his system of governance, but it is not exclusively dysfunctional.[2] The network-based governance is complex, diffuse, unpredictable and seemingly unmanageable, but at the same time it serves to glue society together, to distribute resources and to mobilise cadres, to contribute to both stability and change and to ensure its own reproduction. The central argument of this book is that Russia cannot modernise without modernising the network-based governance patterns referred to as *sistema*. It might be tempting to assume that there are obvious reform measures that can be undertaken to replace *sistema* with a market economy and the rule of law (*pravovoe obshchestvo*). But the point about *sistema* is that it enables Russian society to cope with its problems while at the same time undermining it. There is no obvious way of tackling *sistema* without weakening the various kinds of social cohesion that enable Russian society to function. The key question, therefore, is how to modernise the informal networks behind *sistema* without losing their functional potential while limiting their dysfunctional implications. In what follows, I highlight *sistema*'s open secrets and the paradoxes that tend to remain unarticulated.

Paradoxes of modernisation

The paradox of modernising Russia is that it is already in some ways modern, or even post-modern. Russia is one of the largest IT outsourcing supply markets and, though far behind India and China in volume, it is dominant in the top range of software.[3] Russia was the first country to launch a man into space, has remained a champion of sputnik launches and runs projects on space tourism. Its economy is open to the global economy, the number of initial public offerings (IPOs) is growing and its financial services are developing rapidly. Its commercial disputes are considered in international courts and its civil

---

[2] Whereas Latynina (2009) and Loshak (2010) emphasise *sistema*'s absurdity, Belkovskii and Golyshev introduce numerics to differentiate the economy of r–o–z (*raspil, otkat, zanos*) that was functional (at levels of 25–10–2) from the economy of r–o–z that became dysfunctional (at levels of 60–30–10), Editorial, *Forbes Magazine*, 21 October 2010, www.forbes.ru/svoi-biznes/ predprinimateli/58657-otkat-raspil-zanos.

[3] 'Outsourcing to Russia: country profile and statistics', www.sourcingline.com/ outsourcing-location/russia: 'Russia is a leading nation for the outsourcing of complex and advanced IT application development.'

cases have dominated the European Court of Human Rights (ECtHR) in Strasbourg since the year 2000. Russians are known for their culture, education and 'cynical reason' (Yurchak 1997). While largely apolitical, the younger generation is adroit at cyber-creativity and cyber-activism.

Yet the modernisation discourse presumes that Russia is in some way pre-modern, and not only in terms of Russia's dependence on natural resources.[4] In a social sense, the modernisation of Russia means 'a very simple thing', as suggested in a novel by Viktor Pelevin:

> that trains in Russia would follow the timetable, bureaucrats would not demand kickbacks, judges would ignore telephone commands, natural resource traders would not take their money to London, traffic policemen would live on their salary, while *Rublyovka* residents would move to *Chistopol'skaya krytaya* [a prison].[5] (Pelevin 2008: 176–7)

What does all this have to do with modernisation? The characteristic common to all these problems is the gap between the way things are formally declared to be and the way in which things get done in practice – in the order listed above, these are: timetable, code of conduct for state officials, civil and commercial legislation, corporate code and property rights, law enforcement and equality before the law. In this context, to modernise Russia means to minimise these gaps.

In academic literature 'pre-modern' institutions are associated with traditional forms of governance such as patrimonial power. They are also associated with patterns of informality that rely on personal relationships to compensate for the failure of organisations and on personal trust to substitute for the low levels of impersonal trust in public institutions. Since such patterns of informality personalise, subvert and soften the 'iron cage' of bureaucracy, they are obstacles to Russia's social and institutional modernisation. In Pelevin's story, the reaction to the modernisation scenario is quiet laughter and a knowing smile, followed by an explanation of the madness of the suggested doctrine and references to the PR nature of the modernisation campaign, the

---

[4] Dmitri Medvedev has formulated the 'four *is*' (*institutions, infrastructure, innovation, investment*) of Russia's economic programme, followed by the fifth '*i*' for *intellect* (knowledge-intensive projects).

[5] *Rublyovsko-Uspenskoe shosse* is the site of elite residences just outside Moscow. The author suggests that the elite should be sent to prison because of the means by which they raised the money to acquire property there.

social myths supporting it and the use of administrative resources (Pelevin 2008: 177).

Experience shows that top-down efforts to modernise Russia can be partially effective, yet overcoming its 'pre-modern' features and 'catching up' with other modern societies is by no means a linear process. In this context, one has to take modernisation as a multi-dimensional concept. The aim of my study is to gain an understanding of the workings of the power networks that account for the failure to implement leaders' political will and the unfortunate outcomes of well-intended modernisation programmes. One should not think about power networks simply in terms of 'personalisation of bureaucracy' or 'patron–client relationships' penetrating formal structures of governance throughout Russia's history and diverting it from its course. Power networks serve to control resources and to mobilise cadres. They constitute *sistema* – a pattern of governance that works but simultaneously presents an obstacle for change. Former Soviet President Mikhail Gorbachev has given revealing testimony about the Soviet *sistema*:

I was in charge of the Stavropol region for 10 years . . . 55 years in politics overall . . . I knew our system inside out. I saw it all. I understood. But for a long time, I couldn't admit that it was the System. I used to think it was all about people. I assumed that cadres could be changed. My own Stavropol experience showed that a radical change of cadres, their rejuvenation, provides an opportunity to solve many problems. If one could achieve it in every region, I thought, the same thing could be achieved in the whole country . . . When I came here [to Moscow] it turned out things were not that simple. Here it was impossible to move even a single person. I knew then that I was in trouble. And not just me. Signals came from everywhere: people wondered what was happening. Unsolved problems everywhere but information was restricted, people under pressure, say a wrong word and that's it (*piknul i vsyo*).[6]

A close Gorbachev ally of that period, Eduard Shevarnadze, also a member of the top Soviet leadership, has said that by the beginning of the 1980s the 'system' had gone rotten. When asked to clarify whether he meant that the Communist Party apparatus was corrupt, he said:

No. *Sistema*. The system had gone rotten. Then, ten years ago, I didn't say it but from the very beginning it was created on the basis of wrong principles.

[6] TV interview with Vladimir Pozner, summer 2009.

I felt as if we were in a dead-end, lost without a compass. (Timofeev 1993: 181)

When the USSR collapsed, so did the political system whereby the Communist Party directed affairs from behind a facade of bogus institutions. During the presidency of Boris Yeltsin (1991–9), these highly personalised arrangements were supposed to be replaced by new, transparent institutions and market mechanisms. However, the new institutions proved to be weak and ineffective. It was not long before informal networks, inherited from the Soviet period while differing from them in important respects, sprang up to bridge the gap. In Putin's Russia, the reliance on power networks for governance became known as 'manual control' or 'Putin's *sistema*'.

Russian elites continue to talk about *sistema* – it is the third most frequently used term after 'business' and 'money' (Oleinik 2008a). Putin is commonly seen as effective in overcoming the legacy of Yeltsin's inner circle and appointing his own people to key positions. Once he had left the Presidential office, however, he too admits to the pressures imposed by *sistema*. In a way not dissimilar to Gorbachev, Putin points out the difficulty of firing people as follows:[7]

To sack someone is a serious problem. Sometimes it looks like a person has to be simply kicked out. But I assure you that this is not always the case ... I know all too well that these cases are tied up with a complex political struggle. It seems, perhaps, as if a criminal case can be opened on anyone ... But once you look closer, there are no real foundations. And if not, then one is innocent.[8]

Some commentators see Putin's article as important to understand what is happening in Russia's power structures, others doubt if Putin even wrote it himself.[9]

---

[7] Originally published in *Russian Pioneer*, http://ruspioner.ru/news/557.html, subsequently http://ruspioner.ru/columns/putin/613.html; see n. 9 below.

[8] Quoted from 'Svoi biznes: Chinovniki biznesmeny', *Forbes Magazine*, 20 October 2010 13:24, www.forbes.ru/svoi-biznes/58524-chinovniki-biznesmeny.

[9] Putin acknowledged the ownership, see the discussion of *Okolonolia [gangsta fiction]* by Natan Dubovitsky (also published in a special edition of *Russian Pioneer*, Moscow: Media-Group Zhivi, July 2009, rumoured to be authored by Vladislav Surkov, First Deputy Chief of Staff of the Presidential Administration), *NATO Research Review*, October (Rome: Research Division, NATO Defense College 2009).

It is worth noting that the leaders reflect upon the pressures of *sistema post factum.* Living under *sistema* can best be understood when the pressure of it is gone. Just as the role of *blat* networks – the use of personal contacts to get things done – could be fully articulated and conceptualised only after the collapse of the late Soviet economy of shortage, the role of power networks in *sistema* will be best understood once they become less central. When bidding farewell to the literary censorship of the Soviet era, the writer Fazil Iskander grasped the spirit of living within the *sistema* in his cruel but witty description of the post-Soviet literary situation.

Imagine that you had to share a room with an aggressive madman all your life. Moreover, you also had to play chess with him. On the one hand, you had to play so that you would not win and anger him with your victory; on the other, you had to play so subtly that he would not suspect that you allowed him to beat you. When the madman disappears, this precious skill and life-long experience of survival with a madman turns out to be redundant. (Quoted from Genis 2002: 29)

Such an explanation of the psychological stupor experienced by Soviet writers once the censorship of the Soviet regime had disappeared chimes with the experience of post-Soviet judges, who are reported to be uncomfortable with the lack of informal guidance. The ambivalence of pressures of *sistema* and the necessity to read between the lines and to comply with informal signals competently have been grasped in linguistic idioms and folk wisdom. The affirmative resolution on the document can mean anything from 'do it immediately' to 'don't do it no matter what' (Zhvanetskii 2009, first performed in 1986). The colloquial advice 'to avoid falling out of the system' includes: 'don't complicate life for yourself or others'; 'don't play with fire' (*ne igrai s ognem*); 'don't look for trouble' (*ne lez´ na rozhon*); 'don't overtake the steam engine' (*ne begi vperedi parovoza*); 'don't be holier than the Pope' (*ne bud´ svyatee papy rimskogo*); 'don't make a circus' (*ne ustraivai balagan*); 'don't insist if you don't have to' (*ne obostryai tam gde eto ne nado*).[10] All of these formulae imply the skill of distinguishing between 'where necessary' and 'where not necessary', the sensitivity to perceive threats and signals unnoticeable to outsiders and the tacit knowledge of 'how to survive with a madman'.

---

[10] I have assembled the list of idioms from the novels by Pavel Astakhov.

My study of *sistema* began with an analysis of grassroots informal networks in the late Soviet period (Ledeneva 1998), continued with an analysis of their transformation in the 1990s (Ledeneva 2006) and is completed by an analysis of power networks in the 2000s. I have argued that the power of the grassroots networks that somewhat balanced the rigidity of the authoritarian regime in Soviet Russia has not been sufficiently channelled into the production of a robust civil society in the post-Soviet period. The lack of checks and balances and of trust between the State and society has resulted in a disproportionate influence of power networks. The power networks have benefited from their links to the 'vertical of power' (*vertikal´*) but have also embraced opportunities provided by the market and globalisation, thus producing new types of exposure and vulnerability for *sistema* (Ledeneva 2008b). This book scrutinises the power networks of Putin's two terms as President; conceptualises their role in the formation of the network-based system of governance, best known as Putin's *sistema*; and contrasts them to the Soviet *sistema*. Where data are more recent than 2008, I assume that the model of governance has not changed under President Medvedev, unless specifically stated. Before I approach the issues of modernisation of power networks, I need to register the considerable changes that have occurred in *blat* networks.

The power of informal networks

The power of informal networks was such that *blat* – the use of personal networks for obtaining goods and services in short supply and for circumventing formal procedures – can be effectively conceptualised as the know-how of the Soviet system and the reverse side of its over-controlling centre. On the one hand, the Soviet regime was penetrated by widely spread informal practices, depended on them and allowed them to compensate for its own rigidity. On the other hand, informal practices served individual needs and facilitated some personal freedoms and choice. The power of networks to tackle the economic, political, ideological and social pressures of the socialist system effectively meant that the system worked against its own proclaimed principles. Yet paradoxically, by subverting the socialist system, the power of networks also supported its existence.

Thus, research into *blat* has helped solve a double puzzle in the history of authoritarian regimes: how people survived in an economy of shortage, and how the regime survived under similar constraints. But it also opened an avenue to explore the nature of political and economic regimes from a new perspective – the perspective of informal practices. Informal practices have become an important indicator in assessing models of governance. In *How Russia Really Works*, I identified the informal practices that replaced *blat* in the functioning of the political and economic institutions of the 1990s (Ledeneva 2006). What has happened to *blat* since the 1990s?

There is no satisfactory answer to that question. If you claim that the influence of *blat* has declined and the term has become obsolete, people overwhelm you with examples of its relevance. But if you argue that *blat* continues to operate, they reply that the term is long out of fashion and it is money that matter most. In fact, both tendencies can be seen. Change is happening to a varying degree in different sectors and contexts. As a term, *blat* emerged to designate Soviet practices characteristic of state-centralised regimes and economies of shortage. Once the economy of shortage has given place to markets of goods and capital, *blat* loses its relevance for everyday consumption but is still important to get access to jobs, healthcare, education and so on. Consider the data collected in a national representative survey conducted toward the end of Putin's Presidency by the Levada Centre – Russia's most respected polling agency. When asked to define *blat* nowadays by choosing as many prompts as necessary, 18 per cent of respondents indicated that the term was no longer used, while 5 per cent noted that the word *blatnoi* meant criminal, and that it had returned to its original pre-revolutionary meaning. At least one in five respondents associated *blat* with an exchange of favours (22 per cent) or best described by the proverb 'I scratch your back, you scratch mine' (*ty-mne, ya-tebe*) (15 per cent). With regard to formal constraints, the responses were: 'circumvention of formal rules and procedures' (17 per cent), 'problem-solving' (12 per cent), '*blat* is necessary in order to give a bribe' (6 per cent) and access to administrative resources (4 per cent). Tellingly, people were familiar with both the term and the practices. Only 7 per cent of respondents found it difficult to answer the question, and some respondents offered their own definitions, including '*blat* is higher than Stalin' and '*blat* is the price to pay for socialism' (*izderzhki sotsializma*), as well as '*blat* is the corrupt system, the whole industry' and '*blat* is life'.

Table I.1 *Use of* blat *in 2000–7*

'What did you use your contacts for in the last seven years?' (Multiple choices possible, percentage of those admitting the use of contacts)

Contacts used for	%
Healthcare services:	
Access to local surgery	15
Hospital bed	6
Reducing the cost of operation	4
Solving problems with traffic police:	
Registration of vehicles	10
MOT registration	8
Finding a job Education:	12
Places in primary-secondary	7
Higher education	5
Legal services	2
Help in courts	3
Avoiding army conscription	4
Everyday services:	
Better quality	3
Better price	1
Repairs of housing, garages, dachas	3
Tickets for events, theatre, concerts	2
Hobbies	1
Consumer goods	1
Foodstuffs	1

In response to a question about the uses of *blat*, the hierarchy of needs presented above is the reverse of what it was in the Soviet days. Then, *blat* was essential for obtaining foodstuffs, consumer goods, books and theatre tickets and was more or less an omnipresent practice. Now these items are at the bottom of the list and mentioned by 1 per cent of respondents each (see Table I.1). At the end of 2007, services that still required *blat* were healthcare, education, employment and dealing with the traffic police.

This hierarchy of needs is not specific to Russia; the middle class uses contacts for medical or educational purposes in many societies. The impact of informal networks on an institutional environment is one of degree; what distinguishes the Russian case is the scale of the use of

Table I.2 *Use of* blat *in regions in 2007*

'In your opinion, how widespread is *blat* in your city or region now?' (One response only)

	Frequency	%	Cumulative %
Widespread	454	28	28
Rather widespread	613	38	66
Not very widespread	208	13	79
Practically absent	63	4	83
Difficult to answer	264	17	100
Total	1,601	100	

informal practices. In response to the question, 'In your opinion, how widespread is *blat* in your city or region now?' (Table I.2), two-thirds of respondents said it is widespread or rather widespread in December 2007 (note the difference with low percentages of personal experience in Table I.1).

However, if one interprets these data on the basis of *blat* in its Soviet sense (as serving the economy of shortages of food and services) one misses a crucial point. A new shortage emerged in post-communist Russia – money – and *blat* practices adjusted to it. In Soviet society, money played only a small role and access to goods and services meant everything. Now that the capital and commodity markets work and goods and services are available, it is access to money, secure investment and getting a well-paid job that have become the new terrain for personal networks. Not only have networks re-oriented themselves to serve this new type of shortage, the use of contacts has become 'monetised' in the sense that money is not excluded from personalised transactions. This is particularly pronounced in the private sector that emerged in post-Soviet Russia and significantly shifted the use of networks towards the needs of business. According to data from the INDEM think tank, ways of 'beating the system' formerly associated with *blat* amount in today's Russia to 10 per cent of the overall corruption market. About 90 per cent of bribes in Russia are paid by businessmen for export licensing and quotas, state budget transactions, tax transfers, customs duties, privatisation deals and servicing debts to the federal budget (Satarov *et al.* 2005). New informal practices, such as tax evasion and creative accounting, have emerged to compensate for the institutional defects of the economic transition (Ledeneva 2006).

Informal networks: a problem or a solution?

It used to be assumed that once the centralised system ceased to exist, there would no longer be a need for alternative currencies or extensive use of informal networks. Markets would take care of the functions that used to be performed by informal networks. However, research shows that the use of networks has not only not diminished, it has actually increased, especially in newly emerging sectors (Miller *et al.* 2001; Rose 2001). Often the legacy of socialism is blamed, and the Soviet grip is indeed part of the story. But one must not dismiss the rationality of informal practices and their effectiveness for problem-solving. In a transitional period, the defects of markets were compensated for by informal networks, by what Michael Burawoy called involution, whereby low levels of impersonal trust in state institutions were balanced by strong interpersonal trust.

My research into the 1990s found that informal practices, serving the emergence of democratic and market institutions even if sometimes in a semi-legitimate way, are not automatically detrimental (even creative PR campaigning and compromising materials in the media are arguably preferable to the non-competitive elections of the 2000s). In any case, the view that informal practices have a negative impact is in itself a normative judgement and cannot be merely assumed without detailed research. I have argued against the stigmatisation of informal practices and suggested the importance of distinguishing between their supportive and their subversive effect on political and economic development. The ambiguity of informal practices is an important theoretical assumption that allows us to differentiate between the functions of networks and to analyse their multi-vector functionality: from sociability, safety nets, survival kits and forms of social capital to means of access, diversion of resources, bridging formal organisations and subverting formal procedures, thereby blocking the effectiveness of governance (Ledeneva 2007). In empirical terms, it is much more important to identify the various levels/sectors of the economy and society in which informal networks are particularly problematic.

Yet the reasons for the emergence of informal practices (survival strategies) are not the same as the reasons for their reproduction (vested interests) – this accounts for the fundamental change in the use of networks in the post-Soviet period in Russia and elsewhere. What once was thought of as a solution can become a problem. Hernando de Soto's analysis of the Latin American informal sector suggests that policy should integrate the perspective of informal practices and legalise them or give them institutional status where possible (de Soto 2002).

The comparative analysis of the role of *blat* in Russia and analogous practices of networking in China (*guanxi*) seems to indicate that the informal practices that have proliferated among elites in both regimes tend to exclude ordinary people from the rights and opportunities that markets are supposed to have opened. Comparative studies of informal practices show that many features of social behaviour are universal, especially in terms of networking and informal exchange, but that there are huge differences between their functionality and implications in different regimes (Ledeneva 2008b).

An interdisciplinary approach is essential for understanding the workings of informal networks: one has to grasp the history of *blat*, its political significance and the ideological nature of bargaining powers, the economic functions, social skills and divisions behind *blat*, as well as the anthropological aspects of the informal exchange of favours – not exactly an exchange of gifts, but not one of commodities either. Favours of a specific kind – favours of access – are a concept relevant for regimes with state-centralised distribution systems, but they may become relevant in other types of regimes where the state plays a central role in the bailout of private financial institutions (the 2008 financial crisis certainly put the oligarchs in a new queue for a bailout).

Studies of informal networks have helped to develop the post-Communist (or post-socialist, as anthropologists refer to it) academic field. *Blat* research has been relevant for studying social capital, consumption, labour markets, entrepreneurship, trust, mobility and migration, shortages, barter, survival strategies, alternative currencies, shadow economies, redistribution and remittance economies and democracy. All these developments illustrate efforts to re-integrate social dimensions into studies of politics and economy. Where the literature tends to focus exclusively on political and economic aspects, the 'informal' perspective contributes insights into the social forces at play. The use of informal networks does not admit to quantitative analysis as readily as other phenomena, but it does provide explanatory tools for social scientists and analysts attempting to understand

Russian behaviour (Rose and Mishler 2007). It is time to look into the use of informal networks by the power elites.

Sistema *as a new puzzle*

Lilia Shevtsova defines the Russian system as 'a specific type of governance structure whose characteristics include paternalism, the state domineering over the individual, isolation from the outside world, and ambitions to be a great power. The heart of the system was the all-powerful leader, above the law and a law unto himself, concentrating in his hands all powers, without a balancing accountability, and limiting all other institutions to auxiliary, administrative functions. The Russian system did not need fixed rules of the game; it needed fixers' (Shevtsova 2003: 16). The notion of fixers is reminiscent of the pushers in the planning system – *tolkachi* and *blatmeisters* – whose purpose was to lubricate the rigid constraints of *sistema*, but also points to the theme of leadership, central to understanding informal governance. It is crucial, however, to see that *sistema* constrains the leader, too, as Gorbachev's account implies. What is this *sistema*? What makes it so powerful? If *sistema* is an obstacle for change, then why is its reform not on Russia's modernisation agenda?

Power networks operate on principles similar to other informal networks and impose certain norms of reciprocity and informal constraints on people in official positions: (a) blurred boundaries between friendship and the use of friendship; (b) helping friends at the expense of public/corporate resources or access; and (c) recruitment into networks according to a particular logic – it could be loyalty, dependence, or compliance based on transgression/compromised recruiting – rather than the logic of competition and professionalism. Although there might not be significant differences in patterns of informal constraints at the grassroots and among the elites, there are implications for the process of research. The workings of the federal Russian state or the workings of regional administrations are difficult for outsiders to research, let alone the Kremlin administration and their ties to business, media and judiciary.

To capture the operation of power networks, a researcher should have personal exposure to the Russian leadership, including in-depth interviews with members of the political elite. Published interviews and existing research should be combined with innovative ethnographic research in order to solve the puzzle of how power can be channelled in non-transparent settings. Kremlinological accounts of '*bulldogs fighting under the carpet*' have certain explanatory power but they excessively personalise the workings of the state. Given the dependence of Russian governance on pro-*sistema* compliance with unwritten rules, attempts to restructure the rules of the game by changing the formal rules can have only a limited effect. This is partly because top-down efforts are difficult to sustain, and partly because any change in the formal rules introduces, and is perceived as, yet another constraint to be dealt with informally. This often results in readjustment and a reconfiguration of the informal workings of the system around new constraints, rather than a decline in the significance of unwritten rules.

The reproduction of *sistema* is based on its non-transparency: (a) networks of insiders are tied together by following an unwritten code; (b) members are recruited on the basis of loyalty; (c) members are initiated and 'compromised' (compromising material is collected to ensure compliance); (d) rewards and punishment are distributed on the basis of extra-legal criteria; (e) the foundations of belonging to networks of power are hidden behind formal appointments and are non-transparent, feeding back into the reproduction of *sistema*.

Every ruler who aims to modernise Russia faces the obstacle of *sistema*, presumed to be a collective outcome of the pre-modern ways of governance – the so-called 'governance puzzle'. Its essence is a vicious circle generated by the ruler's dependence on informal leverage. Informal power is an attribute of any formal status. Russia's specifics are in its unarticulated nature, political culture of informality and lack of accountability. These features, identified in Soviet times, seem to be reproducing successfully in an environment of ineffective 'checks and balances' and help sustain the workings of *sistema*.

Just as occupying a formal position is not the same as having real power, the existing legal framework is different from the mastery of the rules of the game. The complexity of the rules and the selective nature of their enforcement – grasped in a formula of 'over-regulation and under-enforcement' – compel the majority of Russians, willingly or unwillingly, to violate them. The whole economy operates in the mode of 'legal nihilism', so that everyone is bound to disregard at least some laws. Anybody can be framed and found in violation of rules. While everybody is under the threat of punishment, the actual punishment is 'suspended' as it is not feasible to prosecute everyone. Accordingly, law enforcement is not impartial and is often mediated by informal leverage or informal command. To establish the rule of law would require reducing the use of informal governance and therefore incur a certain loss of manageability of the formal institutions required to control powerful clans. Means of informal governance for such control reproduce the gap between the rule of law and the existing rules of the game.

The 'legal nihilism' of the followers leaves no option to the rulers but to rely on extra-legal criteria in distributing punishment and to exercise discretion in applying informal leverage where necessary.[11] Consequently, Russia-watchers are preoccupied with understanding the power networks behind the facade of politics and figuring out an 'informal pyramid' hiding behind the formal hierarchy in the 'vertical of power'. I contest this assumption not simply on the basis of the network-based approach and the impossibility of the vertical in a country the size of Russia, but also on the basis of a new conceptual framework for understanding the workings of *sistema*. I would argue that the informality of existing ties with a certain individual in a high position should not be confused with the informality of the *use* of these ties that stands for intervention and diversion of the operations of formal institutions. The analysis of power networks is not about tracing friendships or close relationships of people in politics but about the forms of undue influence they imply. Power networks serve in a re-distributive capacity based on undue influence, but to separate them from the operations of formal institutions or to tag them as 'corrupt' is to miss the point about the nature of governance in Russia. The most conspicuous example of undue influence is the political pressure on the judiciary, resembling the Soviet practice of 'telephone justice' (*telefonnoe pravo*, see Chapter 5). Crossing the boundaries of the formal separation of powers through informal channels constitutes the public–private crossover, whereas people knowing each other and communicating informally in private sphere does not. Political control of the media is another instance in which the formal separation of powers is blurred.

---

[11] Note the myths about Russia (Medinskii 2008) and the 'legal nihilism' of people (*narod*) as depicted in Petr Lutsik's film *Okraina* (1998) and Alexei Balabanov's *Trofim* (1996).

A great deal of pressure from *sistema* comes from within the same institution. It has been reported that the pressure on judges internal to the judicial system is stronger and more systematic, so much so that the political authorities have to intervene with an informal command to tell judges to rule by merit.[12] Similar internal pressures within the state bureaucracy, exercised through appointments and promotions, effectively helped to reproduce *sistema* and blocked administrative reforms for over fifteen years.

The inner workings of *sistema*, its unwritten rules, informal codes, and power networks constitute a puzzle for a number of reasons. First, there is the problem of access – physical access to the 'sites' of the workings of the state does not entail exposure to the workings of *sistema*. Second, the formal sites of the state workings lose their relevance because of the 'network' character of the state that emerges through the personal contact between state officials in various branches of public administration and/or between them and their counterparts in politics and business, law enforcement, the judiciary and the legislative system. Third, the hidden nature of the workings of *sistema* leaves no trace or record, making it difficult for researchers to substantiate their findings.

To date, 'elite studies' have focused on the quantitative and qualitative analysis of discourse (Drobizheva 1996; Gudkov *et al.* 2007, 2008; Oleinik 2008b); formation of clans (Kosals 2007; Kryshtanovskaya and White 2003, 2005, 2011; Mitrokhin 2008; Mukhin 2005; Wedel 2003); anti-modern networks (Rose 2000, 2009); the network state (Kononenko and Moshes 2011; Steen 2003); the network society (Castells 2000); and the association of state networks with the middle class (Brym and Gimpelson 2004; Gudkov *et al.* 2008). Little research has focused on the inner workings of *sistema*.

Anton Oleinik claims that the network dimension is missing from the 'Models of power relationships in post-Soviet societies', a special issue of the *Journal of Communist Studies and Transition Politics* (Oleinik 2008a). The ethnography of power networks in public administration can be approached at the point of contact between public administrators and their counterparts – friends, patrons and

---

[12] Report: 'The judicial system in Russia: its present state and issues' (Moscow: CPT 2009). The report was commissioned by the Institute for Contemporary Development, run by Igor Yurgens and chaired by President Dmitri Medvedev.

clients – in politics and business, law enforcement, the judiciary and the legislative system. The 'network state' concept has been used to indicate that state institutions have been penetrated by networks that diffuse, dissolve and diversify their operation (Kononenko and Moshes 2011; Steen 2003). This point is also valid in the global context – the state still attempts to function as a gatekeeper of network interaction, providing some stability for a particular configuration of overlapping power networks, yet it itself becomes superseded by global networks (Castells 2009).

Conceptually, most accounts of Russia's systems of governance miss out the non-hierarchical, network-based aspects of *sistema*. In political analyses the 'formal' or 'vertical' dimensions of power predominate (Sakwa 2011 on the power 'vertical'). Even when informal influence, connections, clans, cliques, clusters and other types of informal alliances within the elites are identified, the social networks that generate 'informal power' are not seen as intrinsic to the concept of governance. Moreover, it is often assumed that power networks shadow formal positions of power so that a 'map' of such a pyramid of informal ties and influences can be produced. The purpose of this book is to approach informal power from an ethnographic perspective, to collect evidence of the ambivalence of power networks and to explore the factors of and possibilities for their modernisation.

Methodology and fieldwork

In searching data on the workings of *sistema* I draw on interviews with *sistema* insiders conducted during the 2005–10 period, quoted anonymously, and on observations during Valdai discussion club meetings in 2005–7. Because the workings of power networks of *sistema* are hidden behind facades of official hierarchy, one has to rely on the willingness and ability of insiders to articulate the networks' capacity of circumventing the formal rules and/or enforcing the unwritten rules.

To approach a subject on such a scale, abstraction and secrecy, one has to be patient. Information is sensitive and tacit for its carriers. Observation, specifically participant observation, attuned to changes in slang and discourse, is essential. Imaginative methods are required for gathering stories, and time for assembling, cross-checking and interpreting. My primary sources are a few precious in-depth interviews with respondents who work in and with the administration (*rabotali vo vlasti*) and are able to articulate the pressures and paradoxes of *sistema*, as well as interviews with experts, all forty-two of whom will remain anonymous. I use published interviews of state officials and non-state players to illustrate the nature of my interviewing sample. Where possible, I rely on secondary sources such as memoirs, novels and articles by former and current officials, diplomats, advisors, investigative journalists and other researchers. I also find inspiration in the existing ethnographies of clans and mafias, psychological experiments, studies of organisations, corporations and leadership. I try some novel approaches, such as the ethnography of the material culture of power networks extended to embrace material objects – for example, the Kremlin's exclusive telephone network, known as *vertushka* (Buchli 2002; Kopytoff 1988; Prown 1982). The hidden aspects of hierarchies and networks revealed by access to *vertushka* have evolved with the technological developments in material culture and point to new privileges in the era of mobile phones. Borrowing from legal anthropology, I apply a counterintuitive technique to find out about the informal workings of power networks from formal documents – judicial rulings and witness statements received during questioning and cross-examination, available in the public domain. Finally, I use quantitative methods and devise surveys to complement qualitative data, where possible. The methods in this study are multiple, interdisciplinary and adjusted to the theme of each chapter. I include a description of my interviews, survey questions and sources in Appendices 1–3 (pp. 256–72).

1 | *What is* sistema?

Defining the contours of *sistema*

Sistema is an elusive term. Among its many meanings featured in the glossary (pp. 277–8), I am most intrigued by the one meant to allude to common, yet not articulated, perceptions of power and the system of government in Russia. My research is based on collecting such perceptions and exploring *sistema*'s open secrets (Ledeneva 2011a). The term is appropriately ambivalent to embrace *sistema*'s strengths and weaknesses, opportunities and pressures, as well as to refer to their origins as systemic, pointing everywhere but nowhere in particular. Academic outsiders tend to avoid such levels of obscurity, abstraction and immeasurability. Insiders are not ordinarily bothered with definitions of *sistema* – they intuitively 'know an elephant' when they come across one. One of my respondents explains the unarticulated nature of *sistema* by the lack of distance of insiders from it:

This is not a system that you can choose to join or not – you fall into it from the moment you are born. There are of course also mechanisms to recruit, to discipline and to help reproduce it. In the Soviet Union, all people were corporate (*korporativnye*), nuts and bolts of the same machine, but some new features emerged in the post-Soviet period. In the Soviet Union there was more or less a consolidated state, whereas now it is impossible to disentangle the state from a network of private interests. Modern clans are complex. It is not always clear who is on the top. A *kompromat* attack [leak of compromising information – AL] can come from within the same clan. Perhaps this complexity is not a new quality after all. Perhaps it was also complex in the past, only we don't know it well so the Soviet *sistema* comes across as more consistent.

Although the connotations of *sistema* are ambiguous and often context-bound, a shorthand term for a 'system of governance' (*sistema upravleniya*) is the most common. In this narrow sense, it means *vlast´* – the authority of state institutions. In a wider sense, the term lends itself to a variety of interpretations and applies equally to the political system and the economy, to specifics of leadership and bureaucratic order. My focus is on the paradoxical ways in which things get done in practice – adhering to official rules and formal procedures but also following unwritten codes and practical norms. The ambivalence of the term allows me to explore the obscure nature of power emerging from the potency and complexity of Russia's power networks on the one hand, and the imperfections of state institutions, on the other.

Vadim Kononenko and Arkady Moshes introduce the notion of a 'network state' to describe the organisation of governance in Russia (Kononenko and Moshes 2011). They pursue the Foucault 'governmentality' approach and conceptualise the network state as focused on micro-practices, on 'techniques' of power, as opposed to portraying state power as a will to domination. 'Governmental technologies' are defined as 'a set of practices and strategies, governmental projects and modes of calculation, which operate on the something called the state' (Kononenko and Moshes 2011: 12–13). Putin's 'governmentality' is specific in at least three ways. First, it is too reliant on the profusion of personalised networks in governance, thus leaving institutions underdeveloped. In this sense the Russian state remains caught in patrimonial path-dependent patterns of governance. Second, resources are distributed through diffuse networks rather than following market principles, and benefit those who adapt and manipulate the blurred line between the public and the private, now known as bureaucrats-turned-businessmen (*chinovniki-biznesmeny*) or security officers-turned-businessmen (*oborotni v pogonakh*). Third, institutes of 'checks and balances' are not effective because of the compliance of the majority, the dependence of the judiciary and the weakness of civil society *vis-à-vis* the state:

The security bureaucracy can do anything. There is no right to private property. Those who clash with the system have no rights whatsoever. Even though they are enshrined in law, rights are not defended by the courts, because the courts are either afraid of or part of the system. Can we be surprised that rational people don't strive for self-fulfilment here in Russia? Who will modernise the economy? The prosecutors? The police? The *chekists* [security officers]?

This quote comes from the final statement at the second *Yukos* trial in November 2010 by a former tycoon Mikhail Khodorkovsky, who was jailed on fraud charges in 2005. He held *sistema* responsible for the impunity of the security bureaucracy (*silovaya byurokratiya*), weak property rights and dependence of the judiciary – in his view, incompatible with Russia's modernisation. He criticised the popular idea of authoritarian modernisation, pointing out that in a global context it leads to capital flight, brain-drain and withdrawal:

We've already tried this kind of modernisation. It didn't work. We were able to make a hydrogen bomb and even a ballistic missile, but we are still unable to manufacture our own modern quality television; our own inexpensive, competitive, modern car; our own mobile phones; and many more modern products . . .

. . . The country needs more than one Korolev [the inventor behind Russia's space programme] and one Sakharov [a nuclear scientist and the winner of the 1975 Nobel Peace Prize] under the wing of the all-powerful Beria and his million [secret police] troops. The country needs hundreds of thousands of Korolevs and Sakharovs, protected by fair and clear laws, by impartial courts that will allow these laws to live instead of gathering dust on a shelf like the constitution of 1937. Where are these Korolevs and these Sakharovs today? Have they left? Are they preparing to leave? Have they gone into internal emigration? Or have they hidden among bureaucrats so as not to be steamrollered by the system?[1]

Khodorkovsky highlights both the negative sanctions of *sistema*, forcing people to justify bureaucratic arbitrariness and lawlessness, and the positive sanctions, rewards and financial incentives for people: 'They are trading their reputations for a comfortable life inside the present system, for privileges and handouts.'[2]

The present-day *sistema* incites people to work, but does so in an ambivalent, even paradoxical, way. Richard Sakwa notes the duality of the Russian political regime's stated goals and its practices, a duality which perpetually subverts the principles it proclaims (Sakwa 2009: 5–7; 30). He suggests that a dual state reflects the 'bifurcated nature of the system in its entirety' (Sakwa 2011: 3). Lilia Shevtsova (2007) acknowledges the capabilities of *sistema*, its success, certainty and

[1] Text audio of Khodorkovsky's Final Statement, Khamovnichesky Court, Moscow, 2 November 2010, translated by Radio Free Europe/Radio Liberty, 2 November 2010, www.rferl.org/content/Text_Of_Closing_Statement_By_Mikhail_Khodorkovsky/2208523.html.
[2] *Ibid.*

stability, but points out their ambivalence. She speaks of the failure of success, the uncertainty of certainty, the instability of stability and the impotence of omnipotence as Russia's systemic paradoxes.[3] Thus, the economy functions in a dysfunctional way: the economic growth and stability of Putin's Russia is detrimental to Russia's development in the long term. Understanding *sistema*'s paradoxes is essential for shifting the analytical frame beyond dualities, binaries and dichotomies. I document the tensions that exist between conflicting or interacting power networks, explain how key players cope with the 'doublethink' emerging from the clash of their formal and informal capacities and show how subversive practices can support *sistema*. Although some of this ethnography may resemble the workings of governmental technologies in other societies, the features outlined below play out differently in different macro- (cultures, political and economic regimes, socio-historical circumstances) and micro-situations.

Embeddedness

Though formally defined by the law and institutions, the operations of power networks are equally dependent on the unwritten rules, social networks and informal norms widespread in society. The use of networks is not an individual choice but a testament to the institutional and social fabric of society: the use of personal networks outside the personal domain compensates for under-developed impersonal forms of trust.

Diffuse nature

Networks that penetrate formal and informal hierarchies ensure that both types of hierarchies have no fixed boundaries. For example, while the clan hierarchy tends to be vertical, controlled top-down and associated with a person in a high official position, networks can operate in a horizontal, de-centred mode and rely on very weak ties. Networks can thus serve as cross-clan bridges, just as they serve

---

[3] Lilia Shevtsova's lecture at Sciences Po, Paris, for the Shevtsova/Ledeneva course 'Can Russia modernize? Elite behaviour, network politics and leadership control', autumn, 2010.

as cross-institution bridges. Convergence of interests and resources or competition between clans produces overlapping boundaries and diffuse forms of operation.

Complexity

No single actor or institution can plan or predict *sistema's* outcome. Distributive and mobilising powers are organised according to the network principle as well as the hierarchical one. As a result, not even the leader, with both formal and informal powers, is powerful enough to change the system. The more 'enlightened' the leadership is about the implications of its governing practices, the more rule-abiding informal interventions become. For example, interventions from above might occur to persuade judges to follow the rule of law; such 'particularisation' in applying universal rules and 'personalisation' of institutional practices, however, preserve the pattern of following the order from above.

Anonymity

Power networks hide behind a 'collective (ir)responsibility'. They are based on the use of informal power, influence and leverage for manipulation of property rights behind institutional facades. The unwritten rules of *sistema* are neither transparent for outsiders nor easily articulated by insiders. Difficulties of articulation result from the blurred boundaries between the public and the private: 'I do not separate myself from the state. If the state says we must give up our companies, we will give them up', says Oleg Deripaska, 'owner' of the world's largest aluminium company (Deripaska 2008). 'What difference does it make whether something is state property or private property?' says Igor Sechin, deputy prime minister of Russia (quoted from Hanson 2009: 113). The anonymity of the state and its power networks are not without implications. Even if personalised channels of power networks might be effective in the short term and on a selective basis, their long-term effect is to create a gap between the real and the formal centres of power, ultimately undermining both the strength of institutions and their manageability.

Ambivalence

Where formal and informal values are contradictory, the disparity between the constraints of the formal hierarchy and the informal filters enacted by social networks generates compromised behaviour and double standards that cannot be associated exclusively with corruption or undue influence. Public perceptions of bureaucrats (*chinovniki*) reflect the ambivalence of power networks. Russian citizens do not like or trust public administrators, yet they seek employment with them. The army is the second most trusted institution after the Church, yet avoiding conscription seems to be a national obsession. Citizens say they fear the police more than gangsters, yet they call for the police when in trouble. Experts tasked with improving the image of public officials against the background of such survey data find it difficult to deal with these paradoxes.[4]

Open secret

The 'open secret' of *sistema* is that its power rests on people's compliance with it in exchange for opportunities to benefit from it. This paradox, whereby people fear the omnipresent power of *sistema* but also engage in everyday practices of 'beating the system', enhances the power of *sistema* and helps its reproduction.[5] Some people say, for example, that they find corruption quite useful, since it enables them to avoid hassle and buy better services than would normally be available. This is the 'open' part of the open secret. The 'secret' part is that people do not mind having this advantage at the expense of the others, the common good or the public resources. Open secrets make people smile knowingly: the knowing smile indicates cynicism about

---

[4] In March 2009, Dmitri Medvedev initiated a federal programme on 'Reforming and development of the system of public administration for 2009–2013' that included a project on positive image-making for bureaucrats. Y. Shestopierova, 'Chinovnik – drug cheloveka', *Izvestiya*, No. 195, 19 October 2010: 1.

[5] Tatiana Zaslavskaya coined a term 'cheating slave' (*lukavyi rab*) that grasps this paradoxical feature of *sistema*. Dmitri Bykov, the author of *Citizen-Poet* poetry and columnist of *Novaya gazeta*, defines 'our person' (*nash chelovek*) as someone who does not fear anything or anyone in particular, but lives in generalised fear: fear is his most comfortable state. D. Bykov, 'The end of the choir', *Profil'*, 22 November 2010: 88.

the common good, low participation in civic action and opportunistic behaviour.

The leadership trap

The leadership demonstrates some awareness of *sistema* but has no strategic plan or practical capacity to reform it. Economic growth and political stability are prioritised over matters of governance, while the political will to tackle *sistema* dissolves into numerous, yet seemingly ineffective, administrative reforms. The limitations of the leadership *vis-à-vis sistema* are created by their own opportune use of *sistema* potential, even if driven by the best intentions. By relying on governmental technologies to ensure state domination (Darden 2001; Wilson 2005) and instruments of informal governance, the leader gets caught in the web of power networks, as discussed in Chapter 7.

Changes and continuities of Putin's *sistema*

Before I tackle these paradoxes of Putin's *sistema*, I undertake the task of tracing its connections to the Soviet era. Putin's *sistema* has been characterised as neo-Soviet, with particular reference to its strong leadership, superpower ambitions and confrontational foreign policy. It has also been said to reproduce the tradition of 'stability of cadres' associated with the Brezhnev period of late socialism. In her empirical study of Soviet and post-Soviet political elites, Olga Kryshtanovskaya (2005) has suggested that Soviet leader Mikhail Gorbachev de-stabilised *sistema*, thus making its trends much more difficult to delineate. Boris Yeltsin's period was remembered as nightmarish by officials. Putin's 'vertical of power' therefore became known for re-introducing the stability of cadres. Most analysts and respondents agree that Putin 'does not betray his own people' (*ne sdayot svoikh*). There are exceptions when informal agreements are broken and people are willing to go against the *sistema*, but these are few.[6] There

---

[6] See the resignation of Veshnyakov and the appointment of Churov as Chair of the Central Electoral Commission in Natalia Morar´, 'Churov i Veshnyakov: two worlds – two chairmen of the Central Electoral Commission', *The New Times*, 2 April 2007, http://compromat.ru/main/mix1/churov_a.htm, and the discussion of the qualities that a public servant is supposed to have in V. Khokhlovskaya and E. Golovina 'The first law of Churov – Putin is always right!', *Profil'*, April 2007.

is also some continuity with the 'administrative-command' system of governance of late socialism: the use of administrative methods that served the post-Soviet masters in 'mobilising cadres' and 'distributing resources' according to their new targets and priorities.

Many analysts argue that the Soviet Communist Party provided the 'frame' and 'glue' that made the Soviet system work and that the Russian government has now lost both irretrievably. In a more nuanced picture, changes and continuities are observable. Lost are the Communist Party's enormous powers and the secret police that kept the state bureaucracy under control, but Putin's *sistema* has been tagged 'neo-Soviet' for re-creating United Russia, the 'party of power' and reinstating the role of security services in the economy. Like the Communist bosses, Putin has been criticised for the use of clan politics, with reference to both *siloviki*, referring to Putin's background in the security services, and *piterskie*, referring to his place of origin (Kryshtanovskaya 2005).

Can such resemblances be characterised as continuities? Can points of continuity in the governance model be traced back clearly to the Soviet era? Should not one consider pre-Soviet Russian legacies as well? In this case it is necessary to distinguish specific Soviet and Russian bureaucratic dynamics from universal ones, and to identify patterns of human interaction in social networks.

To invoke the parable on new wine and old wineskins, the subtleties of the wine will eventually unfold for those who can (1) decode the effect of its ageing in bottles, maturing in barrels, growing on particular vines and being nurtured by particular soils; (2) recognise the profound shifts in climate, technology and human choices, reflected in the wine; as well as (3) identify the right moment to open the bottle.

Correspondingly, the continuity and change within *sistema* reveals itself differently to those with expertise of Soviet 'bottling', Russian 'barrelling', universal principles of 'nurturing' and fundamentals of human nature. I accordingly organise the discussion of factors of continuity and change of *sistema* into ideal types, as shown in Table 1.1. The chapters in this book focus on these factors in detail.

Russian historians point to the 'pendulum' nature of the past political and economic regimes, whose features in the periods of stability differ significantly from those characteristic of the periods of instability (Gaman-Golutvina 2006; Prokhorov 2002). When considering factors of continuity with the Soviet *sistema*, I will not differentiate

Table 1.1 *Factors of continuity and change in* sistema

Factors of formation	Factors of continuity	Factors of change
Soviet administrative system	'Bottling': administrative culture	Monetisation: business integration
Russian patrimonial rule	'Barrelling': political culture	Technology/infrastructure: legal integration
Universal roots of informal power	'Soil and vine': social network culture	Globalisation: reflexivity

between the periods of stability (for example, late socialism) and the periods of instability (for example, Stalin's purges). For my purposes, I assume that different periods display different features but all of them are relevant for understanding the workings of *sistema*.

'Bottling': the Soviet administrative-command culture

The collapse of the Soviet Union provides a starting point for assessing continuity and change in *sistema*. Soviet *sistema* is associated with the theoretical tenets of socialism – no private property, centralised planning, political and ideological rigidity. This *sistema*'s inherent logic, its components and their interaction differ qualitatively and significantly from that of a market economy:

The traditional Soviet economic system is best described as one of centralised planning, implemented administratively through the issuing of direct commands and extensive, detailed coordinating instructions. Subordinates provide information and suggestions that may greatly influence commands, yet in principle they have little autonomy in determining what to do, or even how to do it; they are rigidly bound by commands once issued. (Ericson 1991: 11–12)

In practice, there were further distinctions associated with features of 'real socialism' such as the phenomenon of '*tolkachi*' (the brokers of the planned economy who made sure plans' ends were met (Berliner 1957); the economy of shortage (money played little role as there was nothing to buy in the shops that ordinary people could access, while the elite enjoyed exclusive access to shops that were closed to the general population); inefficiency of the command rule and limited individual rights. Some practices that emerged to compensate for the defects of the planned economy have outlived it and found uses in market contexts. The 'administrative-command system of governance' proved particularly resilient. The term emerged in the period of Gorbachev's reforms of restructuring the socialist economy and political openness (*perestroika* and *glasnost'*). Coined by the economist and then mayor of Moscow, Gavriil Popov, the 'administrative-command system of governance' referred to the Soviet style of governance: centralised, bureaucratised, administrative in distribution of resources and command-based in mobilisation of cadres. The term was used when the system came under attack, especially in the best-selling weekly newspaper *Argumenty i fakty* (at least fifty articles between 1985 and 1991), and subsequently spread to the whole central press in the late 1990s. Historians of the Soviet state supported such a diagnosis with archival evidence of the early Soviet period that identified: (1) the diminishing role of the soviets [local government bodies], distancing them from power, substituting the 'power of workers' slogan for 'power for workers' – in effect *personalising power*; (2) the *emergency nature* of the system, resulting from mass repression and the administrative mobilisation of resources; (3) the constant monitoring, instructions for and control of administrative bodies, the *bureaucratisation* of the state apparatus and its merger with the party apparatus, the result being known as the 'party state'; (4) the *nomenklatura* principle of appointments, whereby state officials were vetted, cleared, recommended and confirmed by Party committees at every level; (5) the *lack of professionalism*, insufficient experience and personal dependence of cadres [bureaucrats], since selection was based on the principles of 'fitting the system', loyalty and political credentials rather than talent, skills and managerial ability (Korzhikhina 1992: 4–26).

Perestroika allowed sociologists such as Tatiana Zaslavskaya, Rozalina Ryvkina (2011), Boris Grushin, Yuri Levada and others to reflect on, or rather to publicise, their research on the inner workings of the state apparatus – the informal mechanisms and practices supporting the administrative-command methods of governance. The personalised control of the *nomenklatura* and the network dimension of Soviet bureaucracy, or administrative market, featured prominently in many analyses (Kordonskii 2000; Naishul' 1993; Prokhorov 2002;

Timofeev 1993). Vitalii Naishul´ wrote on the bureaucratic market and customary rights, where every official in the *nomenklatura* received an allocated resource and power over it on conditions of declared (Communist Party membership) and/or undeclared (informal, personal) loyalty to *sistema*. Lev Timofeev argued that the *nomenklatura* was not a fixed structure with a rigid hierarchy and referred to it as a 'corporation':

Everybody who was involved in administrative and managerial activity was also caught in a net of *nomenklatura* connections, relationships and obligations. This net of contacts was thrown over the whole country and society – looser in some places, denser in others, with an occasional hole. (Timofeev, 1993: 6–7)

Violation of the ethics and betrayal of the interests of the *nomenklatura* corporation, in Timofeev's view, could be punished severely by exclusion from the *nomenklatura*, or redundancy without a prospect of another appointment, or criminal charges. Sanctions, however, were imposed selectively, upon the decision of the Party (Timofeev 1993: 6–7).

Fascinating accounts emerge from historians of the informal workings of the administrative-command system. An archive-based study of networks of regional elites provides insight into the Soviet *sistema* (Gorlizki 2010). Oleg Khlevnyuk identifies the following features of *sistema* in the period of the 'consolidation of Stalinist *nomenklatura*' in 1945–53: stabilisation of cadres; compromises in 'centre–regional' relationships; and informal relationships and practices that helped stabilise regional networks. The latter included the use of '*krugovaya poruka*' (collective [ir]responsibility) among regional elites for resisting control and orders from above. '*Krugovaya poruka*' was used to cover up for power excesses by regional officials or to protect an official when compromising information was leaked to the centre, and to punish the whistleblowers leaking such information (Khlevnyuk 2009; Hosking 2004; Ledeneva 2004, 2006).

In his studies of memoirs and in his interviewing project with the veterans of Brezhnev's *nomenklatura*, Nikolai Mitrokhin noted that, when remembering the past, officials disclosed their informal alliances rather willingly. They did not consider membership in an informal network as 'membership' but treated it as 'friendship' or 'relationship'.

Only occasionally did they admit to 'sharing the line' of some influential figure. At the same time they proudly reported some real help they had provided to their *alma mater*, professional group, region, or another client. They simply 'misrecognised' the fact that with hindsight such actions could qualify as lobbying, use of public office and even corruption, as well as appearing morally reprehensible. It was essential for them, however, that no group motive or calculation be attributed to their actions – these were actively denied (Mitrokhin 2008).

Opinions differ on the role of informality in the Soviet institutional framework. Merle Fainsod (1963) and J. Arch Getty (1986) viewed the significance of informal networks in the Soviet economy primarily as a hindrance to efficient governance. Building on the work of T. H. Rigby (1981, 1986), Graeme Gill (1990), Gerald Easter (1999) and Yorum Gorlizki (2010) in particular and other scholars viewed personal networks as central to the workings of the system. On the one hand, they showed how personal networks became embedded in the institutional order, personalised power and supported it. On the other hand, informal networks channelled the diversion of public resources into private use and thus subverted the planned economy, especially its ideological and moral foundations.

In Soviet times, oral and personal commands used to be much more important and were followed much more closely than written decrees (*ukazy*) and instructions (*rasporyazheniya*), and they remain important in the post-Soviet context (Colton, 2007: 325):

As it tended to be in the Soviet Union, the party boss's word was most conclusive when it was spoken, not written. If the two ever deviated, the verbal held . . . The primacy of the informal oral commands and handshake agreements reflected the weakness of the law, insidious secrecy and mistrust, and the need for authority figures to cut through the thicket of often conflicting administrative requirements. (Colton, 2007: 82)

It goes without saying that oral commands are delivered against the backdrop of detailed, documented, signed and stamped written instructions, themselves of some importance, so that traps in the minefield of written and oral commands are unavoidable. Whereas violations of written instructions create a situation of 'suspended punishment' (Ledeneva 1998: 77–9) oral commands serve as tests for loyalty, and both enhance dependence on *sistema*.

Requesting written instructions when an oral command is too risky
is a tactical means of non-compliance. One of my respondents, himself a former Communist Party apparatchik, explained the importance
of the process of the 'selection of cadres' (*podbor kadrov*), designed
to test character, compatibility and team qualities, which resulted in
independent-minded cadres not being recruited or promoted. Timothy
Colton also tells a story about a post-Soviet official who reproached his
subordinate for implementing his written instruction: 'If I had wanted
you to do something, I would have called you.'[7] The punch line of this
story offers not simply a commentary on the significance of oral communication in the top echelons of power in Russia, but also implies
that subordinates had to be alert to the status of various documents
and able to interpret them correctly. Such patterns of informality –
whereby the workings of formal institutions are backed up by informal relationships and alliances, and leverage and loyalties are created
by a personalised system of power and recruitment – are not uniquely
Russian, but their ubiquitous and taken-for-granted use in Russia has
important implications.

In the Soviet model of governance, oral commands functioned at
every level of the 'party state' to enact the supreme status of the
Communist Party and to achieve discretionary control and manageability on the basis of informal leverage. Even though the present-
day political regime formally declares itself in favour of constitutional
rights, separation of powers, independence of the judiciary and guarantees for property rights, compliance with informally received oral
commands or signals and the 'above-the-law' status of authority still
remain key features of governance. Moreover, when informality in
getting things done and inequality before the law is taken for granted,
sistema 'matures' to operate in an anonymous and seemingly automatic
regime. A respondent with a *nomenklatura* background explains the
current workings of *sistema* as follows:

When people in power are above the law, their influence is no longer a
matter of a direct telephone call or command. The system becomes much
more sophisticated than that. The multitude of stimuli and pressures are
organised in such a way that circumstances themselves push one in a certain

---

[7] Timothy Colton's comment on the paper that I delivered at the Post-Communist
Comparative Politics Seminar at the Davis Centre, Harvard University,
31 October 2005.

direction. Circumstances of course can be staged masterfully by our various services – security services and information services. Everybody understands that *kompromat* can always be found or produced in order to deprive one of a position in the system, and in such a way that there is no chance for recovery or retaliation. But on the surface the matters are in full compliance with the law.

'Barrelling': Russian political culture

Arguably, some of the features of the administrative-command system outlined above were not exclusively Soviet. After five years in power, Lenin expressed concern at the legacy of the old state apparatus and the threat of bureaucratisation, alienation from the people and the lack of checks and balances. He was also worried about the difficulty of reforming the state apparatus. In *Pravda*, Lenin pointed out that 'our state apparatus...is in effect the old state apparatus, principally unchanged...even if [it has] undergone slight cosmetic changes' (Lenin 1923). He also pointed out the particular difficulties of reforming power institutions and admitted: 'one could clearly see which fundamental changes might be achieved in five years and which ones would require much longer.'

Western scholars went even further in emphasising the role of the past political culture in Soviet governance. In his seminal article on 'Muscovite political folkways', Edward Keenan defined the features of the political culture of direct relevance to the Soviet *sistema*:

the operational basis of each setting is informal and traditional (lacking connection between real power and formal status);

decision-making is corporate and conspiratorial;

stability and risk-avoidance are favoured over innovation and progress; and

there is a reluctance to promulgate systematic codified law (as those who need to know the rules know them). (Keenan 1986)

In the post-Soviet period, the role of political culture in sustaining the specifics of Russia's governance model has also been emphasised (Brown 2005; Whitefield 2005; Kryshtanovskaya and White 2005). The model relies on non-transparency in decision-making, such as the forces 'behind the facades' of state institutions aimed at mobilising and redistributing resources (Prokhorov 2002) or the insiders' political market, characterised by the infighting of clans and clientelist clusters (*oboimy*) (Khlevnyuk 2009; Krystanovskaya 2005). As mentioned above, Putin's *sistema* has often been associated with *siloviki* and *piterskie* clans (Fedorov and Tsuladze 2003; Mazo 2003).

My respondents tend to use the term 'clan' (*klan*) more frequently than, say, the recent term 'gang' (*banda*), coined perhaps after Scorsese's film *Gangs of New York* (2002), retelling the story of violent fights for wealth and influence in the USA in the 1860s. The term 'team' (*komanda*) is also used for designating people of the 'inner circle' of a high official. In his analysis of the Brezhnev and Gorbachev power elites, Nikolai Mitrokhin uses 'team' on the grounds that it is a more neutral term, to avoid connotations of 'kinship' and 'territory' (*zemlyachestvo*) associated with the terminology of clans.[8] He defines teams as relatively small groups of followers around a high-status official, who move with him throughout his career. Yet he also introduces the notion of a 'super-clan', which unites a number of teams and clans under the patronage of one of the top people in the country. For example, Mitrokhin suggests that the super-clan of Nikita Khrushchev consisted of Muscovite and Ukrainian clans, and a team of his wartime friends, who became generals. They backed him up in power struggles and were rewarded with *nomenklatura* appointments. The super-clan of Leonid Brezhnev in the mid 1960s consisted of the 'Dnepropetrovsk clan' that was part of the Ukrainian clan of the 1950s, the Moldovan clan, professional lobbyists from the military–industrial complex and a number of regional clans from Uzbekistan, Azerbaijan and the Russian provinces. In 1965 Brezhnev acquired the support of the Stavropol clan, under the leadership of Fyodor Kulakov (Mitrokhin 2008). Putin's period similarly has been portrayed as a struggle between clans of *siloviki* and clans of liberals and their supposed lists of members have been scrutinised (Fedorov and Tsuladze 2003; Kryshtanovskaya and White 2005; Mazo 2003; Petrov 2011).[9]

In academic terms 'clan' is not the best term to use, even if the territorial principle and the non-open nature of power networks are also appropriate characteristics in this context. Although the so-called

---

[8] Rigby used to use the term 'Seilschaft', denoting an Alpine mountaineering team, climbing while roped together.
[9] 'Korporatsiia "Rossia": Putin s druz´yami podelili stranu', *The New Times*, 31 October 2011: 4–12.

'clans' can be linked to their patrons and/or territory and indeed can display some features of kinship, nepotism and consistency over time, they are not organised around a bloodline, not based on marriages or directly linked to resources as they are in clan-based societies (Schatz 2005; Collins 2006; Sharafutdinova 2011). This might be one feature where Russia is genuinely unusual. The network ties in Russia are more multi-vector than traditional kin- or clan-centred networks and thus are more opportunistic, less stable and less predictable for outsiders than, say, in China or Kazakhstan. In comparison to China, Sheila Puffer and Daniel McCarthy note that 'commitment and trust among network members in Eastern European business networks are typically low, the ties extremely weak, the network knowledge poor and participants few' (quoted from Aidis *et al.* 2008).

Lacking the strength and stability of clans, power networks in Russia are formed in periods of stability. They are more identifiable, predictable and manageable in stable environments, while instability and limited opportunities generate clashes between clans. In unstable conditions:

the rules of the game constantly change, new personalities emerge overnight and new spheres of influences are carved out for them, there are people who say 'We are friends and we can do anything we want', while those who could do anything yesterday, become suspect and charged with corruption. For business it means that the stable, if unfair, system of old connections gives place to a new one that does not deliver on the commitments of the old one. (Solov'ev and Zlobin 2010: 153).

Many respondents stand by the term 'clan' as adequate to describe Putin's *sistema*. Yulia Latynina uses the term in her analyses:

From the administrative point of view the country can be divided into Moscow, where nobody makes any decisions because different clans have interests that are too conflicting, and the rest of the country, where nobody makes any decision because you need to ask Moscow first. (Latynina 2009: aphorism 7.2)

I do not use the term 'clan' in my analysis of *sistema* in order to emphasise the reservations about it as discussed in this section. Specifically, I do not associate 'power networks' – the term I prefer – with pyramidal structures, personal loyalty to Putin or Putin's full control, even though Putin can act as arbitrator and/or guarantor of their power.

Unlike those who perceive clan politics as central to the workings of Putin's *sistema*, I argue that power networks can be deeply fragmented and ambivalent in whom they include or exclude. They are sometimes constructed by personalised conflicts between officials, though these conflicts do not actually stop negotiations among diverse and opposing social actors. As shown in the Introduction, even leaders of state, formally on top of the hierarchy and in possession of substantial constitutional powers, by their own admission find themselves under pressure from *sistema*. Every insider feels the pressure of *sistema* but its actual source is hard to identify. Even if the pressure occurs, say, in the form of a criminal case and all fingers point to somebody else's orders, it still remains anonymous, dissolved in the diffuse workings of *sistema*. It is an unintended consequence or collective outcome of the tight web of interests in power, economic resources and influence. Reconfigurations of power networks reflect changes in formal positions, interests and resources and it is not unusual that the same personalities can emerge in different so-called 'clans' at different times. An expert illustrates this point with the example of X:

X is an enigmatic Russian billionaire, characterised as a shrewd and successful investor. This is accurate but X also functions as a broker/intermediary [fronting person], acting for more powerful interests across a range of seemingly antagonistic power groups. Despite early and close links to the faction around the Yeltsin family, X has also moved smoothly into the sphere of the Putin-aligned 'St Petersburg group'. In the late 2000s X sold off a large part of his Russian assets and moved his investments into western banks. Some Russian media portrayed X [as] bailing out of Russia before the economic crisis, an unpatriotic act which may have irked Putin. Others suggest a different scenario, with X forced to sell, possibly as punishment for his interference in others' designs on Mikhail Gutseriev's Russneft [oil company].[10]

Sistema benefits from hierarchical control but also relies on the strength of networks, their flexibility, adaptability and capacity to self-configure, thus integrating both hierarchical and non-hierarchical dimensions of power. Some of its signals are communicated formally, through hierarchical channels, some informally, through networks. In

---

[10] A similar account can be found in C. Belton, 'The secret oligarch', *The Financial Times Weekend magazine*, 11–12 February 2012: 14–19.

other words, *sistema* is a networked 'extension' of power concentrated on the top and channelled by networks. Such networks are not entirely open; they are clustered around centres of power and recruit with caution, prioritising the sustainability of the formal hierarchy and also preventing the autonomy of its informal networks.

'Soil and seed': social network culture, or why comply with oral commands?

Compliance or non-compliance with informal codes is a well-researched theme in social psychology, associated with socialisation, behavioural disorders, peer pressure and ostracism. Given the impossibility to observe *sistema* settings without being an insider, I rely here exclusively on the ability of insiders to articulate their own stimuli for compliance. Evidence of manipulative use of the law and of the use of informal leverage in the interviews in this section and throughout the book comes not so much from cases, examples or anecdotes, as from the perceptions of the dangers of *sistema* and 'taken-for-granted' attitudes, from the feel for uncertainty and paradoxes and the culture of compliance. At any level in the hierarchy, the fear of pending sanctions or exclusion is cited as the reason behind listening to oral commands from above and engaging in informal relationships for back-up. I distinguish four ideal types of stimuli that induce compliant forms of behaviour from *sistema*'s subjects and thus constitute the core of governmental technologies. These types follow Weber's types of social action – traditional, affectual, value-rational and instrumental (Weber 1968).

The traditional type of compliance with authority is associated with habitual behaviour – 'I do it because it is the way it has always been done', 'I do it because everyone does it' – and presumes a lack of self-reflection. Such forms of behaviour occur in settings where individual resistance seems futile and irrational, or where there is a perceived lack of choice. A number of respondents made comments on the lock-in effect of *sistema*'s top positions:

Of course there are many people who simply cling to their positions of power. But there are people who do not cling to their seat, but simply can't imagine what else they can do. I have a colleague, who worked closely with the President for many years. He says, 'Listen, I feel like I can't do anything else'. I tell him: 'Come off it, you are a talented person, at the peak of your ability, perfect age, you can do anything you like...' But I know what he means. After you've done something for a long time, there is a sense of insecurity that this is the only thing you can do. On the one hand, it becomes a routine, but on the other hand, you get hooked on a job that is creative, not conveyer-belt boring anyway, something comes up every day.

The addictive nature of powerful jobs produces behaviour that combines traditional and affectual – determined by an actor's specific affect, feeling, or emotion – if not all ideal types. Emotions associated with fear and anxiety as well as charisma, adrenalin and addiction are important drivers for the behaviour of political elites. Olga Kryshtanovskaya describes this phenomenon with a metaphor of 'dizzying heights' – a sense of isolation that comes from breathing the air of power (Kryshtanovskaya 2005). An emotional attachment to privileges, specially equipped cars and offices and other rewards enhance a sense of belonging. Yet penalties are just as effective in making people work, and work well. It also has been suggested to me that *sistema* has a destructive effect (*sistema lomaet*) on its protagonists by blocking off options. Consider the following personal account about the destructive effect of *sistema*:

When I came into the administration, I thought for some time that I would work with the President for a while and then go into business, lobbying, working with people, or something like that. But when the first term was over in 2004, I understood that there was no demand for me in business, already no demand [laughs]. It was a difficult period as it dawned on me that there was nowhere I could actually go. So I had to adapt to this situation and it was not easy.

Just as talent and expertise stimulate dependence on high-powered jobs, so do mediocrity and incompetence. One respondent suggests that compliance with *sistema* is based on the 'hooks' of dependence:

To be appointed, one must 'hang' on a hook (*na krychke ili v kompromisse*). In other words, *sistema* has to have leverage to ensure that you are compliant and loyal, and preferably that you have a stake in the *status quo* personally too. One such hook is to appoint people not worthy of their positions. They constitute the type of state officials who *a priori* are not fit for office, but are keen to receive a place for whatever is required of them. The other hook is a system of *kompromat* – normally hidden from view – either *kompromat* is created when necessary or they appoint people that are already dependent, on whom *kompromat* already exists.

A number of respondents emphasised that the ascent to power is conditional on one's willingness to compromise oneself in order to create collateral against one's liberty in the future (see also Gambetta 2009 and Ledeneva 2006 on *kompromat*). In a way, the context of non-transparent governance requires that the majority of insiders have no stake in making the system transparent or changing it. Should such a stake emerge, compromising information ensures that the credibility of this person is ruined. Security matters make staffers misrepresent the state of affairs. Where it is not possible to use people blindly, they are put on the spot. I have been told stories about Kremlin officials being 'broken' by the Beslan hostage crisis of 2004:

X had become a different person when he returned from Beslan. He was made to report reduced numbers of children captured in the school and the terrorists responded to these reports by saying that they would shoot children to make the reported numbers correct.

Y was sent to explain why replacing the popular election of regional governors with their appointment by the President was an adequate response to the Beslan events. An unsolvable puzzle, because these were not related at all. He was pushed to give that silly interview. Then he was pushed for giving it. Then he tried to push himself to mend his image, to come up with some great idea. Then he became misinterpreted and wanted to exit. But he soon realised there was nowhere to go and he burnt out.

Fear often features in respondents' accounts. For some officials the fear of losing their positions is associated with fear of not being protected if they make a lot of trouble for a lot of people:

Take Z, for him it is a problem he must be thinking about right now. Okay, he is in Putin's shadow now, for cover-up and for protection, but once he is in the street, or Putin forgets about him, he has a lot to answer for... It is one thing when a matter is political and quite another when you send someone to prison and take over his business. This is serious and people will not just forget it or forgive it. It is not that simple... and one has to have bodyguards... vengeance catches up with you in different ways.

Needless to say there are various rational and irrational underpinnings that support the *status quo* behaviour of state officials and their compliance with *sistema*. As one respondent wittily noted: 'everyone has his own relationship with his chair. It is not necessarily a will to power, everyone has one's own reason to stay in it.'

As for the value-rational type, a sense of mission, hard work and personal loyalty have been brought up in interviews as essential values of *sistema*. A former insider who left the Kremlin and was particularly well positioned to comment, said:

The job there was truly very interesting. Especially in my time it was particularly exciting – a change of eras, a transition from the revolutionary stage to evolution. This is how I saw my mission there: to help transform the period of revolution into evolution in a smooth way. I don't like revolutions generally, and in my time, thank God, the task was to organise the evolutionary process. With all the costs and heartburns of that time, one has to say that we turned the corner (*naladilos'*).

The same respondent, as well as some others, emphasised the importance of reputation for hard work and professionalism:

Officials understand that the most valuable thing they can acquire in public administration is a reputation as a clever and decent person, as well as a good manager. Then you can go into business, you are invited into business. Some might like the contacts in your phonebook, some might like your intellectual, human and managerial qualities.

Interestingly, the importance of contacts translates into its material symbol – a phonebook – thus pointing to the 'material culture of power networks' line of inquiry that I undertake in further chapters – the use of the *vertushka* telephone network and mobile phones by officials, and the practice of giving oral commands or sending signals, known as 'telephone justice' (*telefonnoe pravo*).

The most important value referred to in interviews was loyalty – loyalty with Russian, Soviet and post-Soviet specifics. It implies that under the contradictory constraints imposed by formal rules and informal norms, relationships matter more than rules for individual survival. Loyalty has developed connotations of personal loyalty to a patron that goes well beyond corporate values or team spirit and carries a promise of 'protection'. Personal loyalty also implies 'personalised' service – inclusive of display of emotional attachment, personal attention and friendly favours – and compliance that prioritises informal commands over formal instructions.

Another touch of continuity is associated with the sanctions, rewards and privileges reserved for loyal members. Rational economic behaviour – the instrumental type – in Soviet days especially focused on the privileges entailed by belonging to *sistema*, since it was coupled with the impossibility of a successful career outside the Communist Party:

The old system was all about sanctions: 'give up your Party membership and that is it.' It was a source of pressure and a threat, given that everything in life hinged on that membership. If you give up, you go back to work carrying coal (*kochegarom*). In the 1990s, this system disintegrated, but it was restored by [the] oligarchs. They replaced the Party membership system and its entitlement to privileges with a direct supply of material wealth. For example, they created a system of dependency for journalists by paying them an income, providing them with lifestyle opportunities and giving them loans and accommodation to keep them under obligation.

Distributing opportunities to borrow, to earn and to invest constitute the neo-Soviet 'hooks' of *sistema*. Post-Soviet pragmatism associated with material wealth, consumerist experience and a global lifestyle constitutes a new rationale for staying within the *sistema* remit. Yet the ties that bind people to *sistema* are still Soviet-like. One respondent describes it as *verbovka*, a term historically used for involuntary army recruitment (Klyuchevskii 1987: 85) but that acquired the connotation of recruitment into security services in the Soviet period:

What it means is that you establish a personal relationship, not just for one night, but for life. Only there are different ways of making someone do what you want (*oblomit' cheloveka*). This is recruitment (*verbovka*). It is almost an art, and the secret of success [is] that you are to love your recruits, support your agents, build up the dependence that compels them to do what you want them to.

The provision and sharing of informal income has become a way of creating such dependence. Other respondents noted the importance of kickbacks for the functioning of *sistema*:

Kickbacks – a man's [got] to live! Through kickbacks officials make a living for themselves, for their boss, for the whole economy. Even law enforcement organs operate on the basis of additional pay for performing their official duties. The same principle applies to the controlling organs – not a single person finds oneself there by chance, they mostly represent certain corporate interests. The consensual or agreed/coordinated relationship between the leadership and rank-and-file officials serves private material needs, and this is what makes the current *sistema* different from the Soviet one.

Apart from kickbacks material 'hooks' include black-cash salaries, bonuses, property acquisition at discounted prices and lifestyle privileges. At the same time, such 'monetisation' of privileges and possibilities of wealth creation outside *sistema* represent a clear departure from the past. Just as it has become possible to leave the government for business, possibilities have emerged for exporting business proceeds out of Russia. Arguably, these have been the most important factors of the post-Soviet transformation, as well as the reason behind the state's efforts to stay in control of business. Strengthening property rights in Russia entails weakening ties within power networks. On the other hand, sustaining insecure property rights is instrumental for preserving the power of *sistema*. It was exposure to business and the global environment that made it possible for *sistema*'s insiders to reflect on its workings.

Factors of change: business and monetisation

There appears to be a clear difference between the *modi operandi* of *sistema* and business. An official who spent over a decade in the government and left it for business defines the difference in a compressed formula: 'business focuses on the result, government focuses on the process.' Asked about the 'process' characteristic of the workings of *sistema*, he observes:

Decision-making at the level of top ministers and deputies generates a giant flow of documents. It splits into and multiplies by ten, like in a computer game – one project or idea that may occur in a ministry requires dozens of reviews and approvals in other ministries. All ministers are under the tremendous pressure of document flow and tend to react in a 'bat away' fashion (*na otboi*). But if there is a personal interest against a decision – and often there is a personal interest – one can block it by allying with some reviewing ministry, say to block a pension reform through an unexpected FSB angle. The minimum effect will be to delay the process, the maximum to kill it.

The unpredictability of the workings of *sistema*, in which informal interests can be pursued through formal affiliations and official positions, adds to its complexity:

Complex decisions that touch upon the interests of many are therefore confronted by many objective and subjective constraints. Such man-made and/or accidental blocks take a lot of effort and resources to undo. Even without evil intentions. With evil intentions, the process can go on for years.

The final outcome of this process is a decision, formulated in a memo, or fixed in a normative document. However, even then the process does not stop. Other decisions need to be taken, the majority of which are urgent. The incentives are such that meeting a deadline is much more important than the quality of the document or decision produced:

In other words, you are punished more severely for the delay than for the poor quality of a document (decision, project, normative document), whereas a good substantive decision is not necessarily rewarded. Moreover, if your decision is substantive you are likely to come into confrontation over it with other groups.

The 'Eureka' test for finding a substantive solution in the debris of *sistema* is resistance. The same respondent explains:

Toward the end of my government career, I came to realise, and said it openly, that if, in a conciliatory meeting (*soglasitel'noe soveschanie*), I see many displeased people I know that I have done something good. If people do not confront my views, I know it's trivial.

The complexity of *sistema* as depicted by its insider also suggests that informal influence helps to navigate the labyrinths of governance structures and can be exercised in both hierarchical and network dimensions.

Representative of the nature of the state–business relationship in Russia but also of the diffuse nature of *sistema* in general, the pressure of *sistema* is not exclusive to government officials. Mikhail Gutseriev, a businessman whom the UK had refused to extradite to Russia on the grounds that he would be at risk if he returned, eventually negotiated the closure of the Russian criminal cases against him and returned to Russia (see Chapter 6). Having experienced the pressure of *sistema*, he estimated it as follows:

While in London, I suddenly realised that I spent 50 per cent of my time on business and 50 per cent on myself . . . whereas in Russia, I spent 20 per cent on business and 80 per cent on confrontation. (Reznik 2010)

In other words, in London Gutseriev was free of *sistema* and of confronting its pressures linked to both state hierarchies and business networks. Yes his return testifies to the limitations of such freedom. *Sistema*'s runaway rules keep the players on their toes and turn them into its prisoners. Another Moscow-based businessman explains:

In order to be part of *sistema*, one has to live in it. You can't just come and go. You have to be here every day. Moreover, you need . . . [sighs] . . . every key official has as a minimum . . . five meetings and attending all of them gives you an overall perspective on your situation, on where it is going. But if you drop out, go on a trip, especially on a long trip, say for a year, you won't understand anything: neither the balance of forces nor the influences involved (*ni rasstanovku sil, ni rasklad*) . . . Then the officials are all made of flesh and blood, so you observe relationships, monitor attitudes toward issues. You 'read' positions and influences. Also you watch the boss and how he disregards one and favours another, so you forget the former, run to the latter at the right time . . . The balance of forces doesn't change radically every day but there are tendencies and they have to be monitored carefully.

Monitoring the dynamics of *sistema* for its insiders is just as important as monitoring financial markets for traders. The parallel also stands for markets' fluidity, complexity, unpredictability and anonymity – it is misleading to think of *sistema* as a consolidated entity. The importance of monitoring – watching the changing rules and boundaries – comes across in another hypothetical example given to me to illustrate the routine workings of power networks:

Everything is divided; the web of interests among competing clans is so tight and personalised that you have to constantly watch out. Say, there are several media structures and each one has a patron, an owner or a Kremlin official. Say, [Kremlin official Alexei] Gromov oversees one information agency, Vladislav Surkov another [Kremlin department]. Personal relationships, hatred or dislike, between patrons and media bosses are represented by the staff on the ground. If, say, a call or request comes from the wrong side, the staff should ignore it. Not every time of course, but if such calls become repetitive, or if their tone changes from a request to an order, or they encroach on our territory in other ways, it should be reported to the boss.

Factors of change: globalisation

As a result of monetisation and globalisation, *sistema* has changed in various ways. In the Soviet economy, where money played a limited role, informal exchanges were largely non-monetary, embedded in pre-existing social relationships, widespread among the less well-off. Under market conditions, ties have become weaker, private settings more prominent, boundaries between the private and the public more pronounced. Social networks have become less accessible for the poor and have been appropriated by the rich and powerful – as people say, the society in which one was connected at the bottom and lonely at the top has changed into one in which one is lonely at the bottom and connected at the top. In Pierre Bourdieu's terms, *social capital* has become less accessible but its volume has increased dramatically. He argued that 'the volume of the social capital possessed by a given agent ... depends on the size of the network of connections he can effectively mobilise and on the volume of the capital (economic, cultural or social) possessed in his own right by each of those to whom he is connected' (Bourdieu 1986: 249; Bourdieu and Wacquant 1992: 119).

Opportunities provided by markets in post-Soviet Russia and captured by networks made *sistema* more complex. While contacts still help to provide an introduction to a gatekeeper, they do not secure a solution to one's problem. Given the danger that hierarchies may depend on networks more than networks depend on hierarchies, *sistema*'s governance model preserves the weakness of the rule of law, so that the application of formal rules can be selective and allow manipulation of the balance between hierarchies and network resources. In theory, monetisation of informal exchanges is expected to enhance competitiveness and openness of networks. In practice, informal networks remain 'closed' and turn into clans, clubs and circles. And yet they are challenged by globalisation (Wedel 1998). In the late twentieth and early twenty-first century, globalisation and advances in communication technology have affected the operations of networks. In later chapters I illustrate how globalisation has transformed the power of *sistema* technologically and challenged its sovereignty in the legal sphere.

In his book *Communication Power*, Manuel Castells (2009) emphasises that in the global history of human societies the period of early technologies and the time-lag of the feedback loop in the communication process amounted to a one-way flow of the transmission of information and instruction. The relative indifference of the historical accounts to the importance of networks in the structure and dynamics of society is thus linked to the actual subordination of these networks to the logic of vertical organisation, whose power was inscribed in the institutions of society and distributed in one-directional flows of command and control. Under those conditions, networks were an extension of power concentrated at the top of the vertical organisations that shaped the history of humankind: states, the religious apparatus, war lords, armies, bureaucracies, and their subordinates in charge of production, trade and culture (Castells 2009).

It is only in the context of the global age, Ulrich Beck argues, that we have to start from networks to understand institutions (Beck 2005). The globalisation effect as formulated by Giddens can be illustrated by the dynamics and frequent appearances of the Russian Federation in international courts (Giddens 1999). *Sistema* is 'pushed down' in increasingly numerous court cases brought to the European Court of Human Rights (ECtHR) by Russian citizens. It is 'pulled up' by the cases initiated by the Russian Federation, such as extradition cases, where *sistema* has to defend itself on unfamiliar territory. There are also 'sideways squeezes' of commercial disputes in European commercial courts that often reveal the presence of *sistema* interests behind those represented in court cases.

The global integration of Russia has somewhat ambivalent implications. On the one hand, such institutions as the London Stock Exchange (LSE) or London law courts are powerful instruments of information-gathering about *sistema* operations, as shown in Chapters 5 and 6. On the other hand, the 'West,' and especially Britain, becomes in a sense part of *sistema*. Russian oligarchs enjoy tax havens, rather lax financial regulation, easy terms for registration on the LSE, and global companies are content to make a profit from what could be construed as an outcome of lawlessness. As Philip Hanson suggests, 'Britain, along with other Western countries, is not well placed to preach to Moscow about the business environment when some of its own institutions are complicit in the dubious Russian practices that we deplore' (Granville *et al.* 2012: 15–16).

Reflexivity: why do good people do bad things?

Just as one has to question the origins of continuity and change in order
to be able to disentangle a web of influences of administrative, political
and network cultures it is essential to raise the question of reflexivity.
How can people partake in *sistema* and not reflect on it? Experimental
evidence suggests some lines of analysis. In his famous experiment
imitating prison, Philip Zimbardo observed how good people engage
in evil actions when considering them legitimate – the so-called 'Lucifer
effect', named after God's favourite angel, Lucifer, who fell from grace.
Whereas the focus of Zimbardo's experiment was the 'Lucifer effect' on
all its participants, central to my study of *sistema* is the effect of 'being
blinded to reality' that Zimbardo experienced on himself. He noted
the 'negative power' on which he had been running, throughout the
week-long experiment, as superintendent of a mock prison (Zimbardo
2007: 179).

   I use Bourdieu's term 'misrecognition' to refer to such a capacity for
'being blinded to reality' – the 'misrecognition effect', as I am going
to call it (1990: 105). I observed it, to a varying degree, among my
respondents, when discussing boundaries of doable actions and other
sensitive aspects of incremental moralities. In experimental conditions,
with forms of violence involved, the misrecognition effect serving to
preserve self-identity is demonstrable:

> If you were placed in a strange and novel cruel Situation within a powerful
> System, you would probably not emerge as the same person who entered
> that crucible of human nature. You would not recognize your familiar image
> if it were held next to the mirror image of what you had become. (Zimbardo
> 2007: 180)[11]

Individual differences in the capacity for 'misrecognition' and self-
reflection while playing by the rules, result in different degrees of
involvement with the System. In debriefing the experiment and exploring the moral choices that have been available to the participants and
the ways in which they dealt with them in this 'us v. them' game,
Zimbardo identifies those who hated being part of the system. One of
the prison guards thought of asking to become a prisoner. Between the

---

[11] The Russian prisons Lefortovo and Matrosskaya Tishina are detailed in
   Andrei Rubanov's novel, *Plant, and It Will Grow* (*Sazhaite i Vyrastet*) (2002).

'bad' and the 'good' guards were those who had gone 'by the book', done their job, played their role and punished infractions, but were rarely personally abusive toward individual prisoners. Some guards were ready to apologise openly for having gone too far, for fully enjoying their power. Others felt justified in what they have done, seeing their actions as necessary to fulfil the role they had been given. The main problem was making them recognise that they should be experiencing guilt for making others suffer.

A similar spectrum of attitudes is observable in my study of *sistema*, with a caveat that de-briefing is only possible with those who have dropped out of it, while the current subjects of *sistema* hold conflicted, if not paradoxical, views on it. The same respondents who hate *sistema* also depend on and benefit from it. Apologetic or self-critical accounts are rare in comparison to self-legitimising, 'blame-it-all-on-*sistema*' narratives.

Zimbardo's findings about the human failure to reflect on wrongdoing and to stop abuse while complying with the rules and routines of the experiment informs our understanding of the foundations of systems, both legitimate and illegitimate. He emphasises the anonymity, temporality and autonomy of the System:

> The System includes . . . extensive networks of people, their expectations, norms, policies and, perhaps, laws. Over time, Systems come to have a historical foundation and sometimes also a political and economic power structure that governs and directs the behavior of many people within its sphere of influence. Systems are the engines that run situations that create behavioral contexts that influence the human action of those under their control. At some point, the System may become an autonomous entity, independent of those who initially started it or even those in apparent authority within its power structure. Each System comes to develop a culture of its own, as many Systems collectively come to contribute to a culture of a society. (Zimbardo 2007: 179–80)

Such systems can rely on a symbolic violence that accounts for the tacit modes of social domination and inequality but also relates to violence *per se*. Weber (1968) has theorised the monopoly of legitimate violence exercised by the state. Foucault has pointed out the grey areas between 'liberties – the strategic games that result in the fact that some people try to determine the conduct of others – and the state of domination, which [is] what we ordinarily call power.

And, between the two, between the games of power and the states of domination, you have governmental technologies' (Foucault 1979: 19). Whereas governmental rationalities are revealed by the systems of imprisonment and control, their dysfunctional aspects reveal 'systems within systems', that is the grey areas, associated with the patterns of illegitimate violence and their links to authority.

Ethnographic studies based on participant observation provide further insights into why good people do bad things in circumstances that do not involve direct violence. Apart from 'the system made me do it' and 'everyone does it', conditions associated with shortages and other material constraints, relative deprivation and unfairness often become incentives for 'cheating the system'. In both violent and non-violent settings, moral choices are shaped by an environment that is alien or even shocking for outsiders, but which has become the working framework for inmates. In his best-selling ethnographic study, *Gomorrah: Italy's Other Mafia*, Roberto Saviano highlights a symbiotic relationship between organised crime and the high fashion industry (Saviano 2007: 42–4). He refers to the *Secondigliano* System, or the System, as follows:

System – a term everyone here understands, but that needs decoding elsewhere, an obscure reference for anyone unfamiliar with the power dynamics of the criminal economy . . . The word clan members use is System – 'I belong to the Secondigliano System' – an eloquent term, a mechanism rather than a structure. (Saviano 2007: 38)

Saviano reveals the ways that the System is integrated with the legitimate high fashion industry that turns a blind eye towards this dialectics of commerce. The locals make no secret of it, but the *Secondigliano* System has issued a death threat to Saviano for publishing his book. The diffuse nature of the System, reaching out beyond Mafia clientele, is an example of the fluid boundaries of *sistema* and its functional ambivalence.

Are violent institutional settings, such as prisons and organised crime groups, indeed relevant for the analysis of Russia's *sistema*?[12] The

---

[12] Note the unprecedented assimilation of criminal, or *blatnoi*, jargon into common use in the Soviet Union, and an even stronger wave of 'criminalisation' of the vernacular in the 1990s (Applebaum 2003; Hosking 2004; Oleinik 2003; Solzhenitsin 1973; Varese 2001; Zinov'ev 1978,); see also *Gentlemen of Fortune* (*Dzhentelmeny Udachi*) (Mosfilm, 1972), directed by

generic patterns of human transgression identified in Zimbardo's psychological experiments with legitimate power are certainly part of the explanation of how *sistema* achieves the compliance of its subjects. Studies of illegal systems, such as the Mafia, global outlaws and other informal institutions, reveal their symbiotic relationships with legitimate hierarchies and formal institutions (Gambetta 1993; Varese 2001; Volkov 2002).[13] This symbiotic relationship can be seen as a consequence or as a cause of the authorities' inaction, with both sides locked into each other. Symbiotic relationships between legitimate and illegitimate systems also have been identified in research on hazing, a fairly universal practice in rigid institutional settings, as well as in research on international profiteering from wars and conflicts (Nordstrom 2004).

A. Seryj, who had then come out of prison. Georgi Daneliya assisted
him with the script. Seryj used his prison experience and criminal slang (*fenya*)
in the movie. The most characteristic terms can be found in the glossary
(pp. 273–80); (see also Ledeneva 1998: 183; Ledeneva 2006: 237–9).

[13] Interaction between formal and informal institutions and their links to
political regimes are considered in (O'Donnell 1996; Lauth 2000; Helmke and
Levitsky 2004; Gel'man 2007).

2 | *Putin's* sistema: svoi *on top*

Technically, the term 'Putin's *sistema*' is a contradiction in terms. One should not personalise the logic of *sistema*, it is a collective outcome even if the President sets an example. The logic of *sistema* informs daily routines, exercised at all levels of leadership, and dictates the so-called 'practical norms' (Blundo and Le Meur 2009; de Sardan *et al.* 2006). According to one much-respected insider of *sistema*, the so-called 'scissors' between the strategic views and daily tactics of its protagonists is the ultimate obstacle to modernisation in Russia:

If you speak with a minister, with the PM, with the President, you are totally convinced you are on the same wavelength. They all say reasonable and sensible things. But when these strategic conversations turn to practical problems that have to be solved here and now ... How do they solve them? By increasing state influence, by a telephone call to a judge or else ... because ... like ... strategy is strategy; but we have to survive today and deal with these problems. There are many problems, important ones. In a big country, with huge responsibility ... one has to solve them. We cannot wait until everything works automatically. Today we manually have to 'help' judges not to get lost 'between three trees' ... Not out of self-interest but for the common good (*v interesakh dela*): if you don't strengthen the anti-monopoly legislation you are then cornered to increase state influence. And so on. And of course you have to have an extraordinary political will to be able to monitor the strategy dimension on a daily basis, to be self-aware and reflect on your every move: whether it is in line with the strategy or goes sideways. For this you need not only political will but also an inner 'compass' – and that is catastrophically [lacking]. This is the problem. Say, for example, the President is convinced about the strategy of attracting some private capital, or private investment, into the defence industry but the next day at some meeting when discussing some concrete problem at a concrete defence enterprise, what kind of reflex does he have? To increase state influence! So what do we have here? Strategy is one thing, we understand how

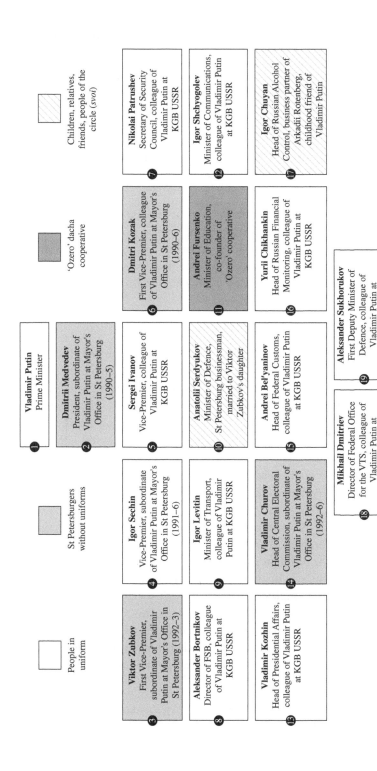

Legend:

People in uniform (white box)

St Petersburgers without uniforms (light grey box)

'Ozero' dacha cooperative (dark grey box)

Children, relatives, friends, people of the circle (*svoi*) (hatched box)

1. **Vladimir Putin** — Prime Minister

2. **Dmitrii Medvedev** — President, subordinate of Vladimir Putin at Mayor's Office in St Petersburg (1990–5)

3. **Viktor Zubkov** — First Vice-Premier, subordinate of Vladimir Putin at Mayor's Office in St Petersburg (1992–3)

4. **Igor Sechin** — Vice-Premier, subordinate of Vladimir Putin at Mayor's Office in St Petersburg (1991–6)

5. **Sergei Ivanov** — Vice-Premier, colleague of Vladimir Putin at KGB USSR

6. **Dmitri Kozak** — First Vice-Premier, colleague of Vladimir Putin at Mayor's Office in St Petersburg (1990–6)

7. **Nikolai Patrushev** — Secretary of Security Council, colleague of Vladimir Putin at KGB USSR

8. **Aleksander Bortnikov** — Director of FSB, colleague of Vladimir Putin at KGB USSR

9. **Igor Levitin** — Minister of Transport, colleague of Vladimir Putin at KGB USSR

10. **Anatolii Serdyukov** — Minister of Defence, St Petersburg businessman, married to Viktor Zubkov's daughter

11. **Andrei Fursenko** — Minister of Education, co-founder of 'Ozero' cooperative

12. **Igor Shchyogolev** — Minister of Communications, colleague of Vladimir Putin at KGB USSR

13. **Vladimir Kozhin** — Head of Presidential Affairs, colleague of Vladimir Putin at KGB USSR

14. **Vladimir Churov** — Head of Central Electoral Commission, subordinate of Vladimir Putin at Mayor's Office in St Petersburg (1992–6)

15. **Andrei Bel'yaninov** — Head of Federal Customs, colleague of Vladimir Putin at KGB USSR

16. **Yurii Chikhankin** — Head of Russian Financial Monitoring, colleague of Vladimir Putin at KGB USSR

17. **Igor Chuyan** — Head of Russian Alcohol Control, business partner of Arkadii Rotenberg, childhood friend of Vladimir Putin

18. **Mikhail Dmitriev** — Director of Federal Office for the VTS, colleague of Vladimir Putin at KGB USSR

19. **Aleksander Sukhorukov** — First Deputy Minister of Defence, colleague of Vladimir Putin at KGB USSR

'Russia is their home': Putin's networks

Source: The New Times, 25 October 2011: 6.

the modern world is organised and we want to adjust. We even do so, intellectually, but our skills, reflexes and instruments are still Soviet (*sovkovye*) – an axe, a saw, a stone. They are on the desk and [to] hand... The scissors between strategy and tactics are the key to understanding why people sometimes perform actions opposed to what strategy dictates. Our leaders do not want to have a corrupt and manipulated judicial system. And they devise the changes in strategy accordingly, but tactically, today, they have an emergency and their hands reach out for the phone.

I am more interested in the phenomenon of *sistema* in general than Putin's particular power networks, but I rely on the vast evidence and research available on the latter in order to integrate the logic of *sistema*, its practical norms and the role of power networks in its *modus operandi*, into the story of Russia's modernisation.

Integrating the network dimension into the model

Let us start with an example of loyalty, viewed to be the key value in Putin's *sistema*. In her study of political elites, Kryshtanovskaya proposes a scenario of a trade-off between patron and client where the patron provides a certain formal capital to an appointee in exchange for competence and loyalty that would ensure the patron's ability to capitalise on this appointment. She finds that 'formal capital is given to an insider by the system, while informal capital is accumulated by oneself, thanks to competence, communication skills, intuition and circumstances' (Kryshtanovskaya 2005: 61). However, from a network perspective (Bourdieu 1986; Coleman 1988; Granovetter 1973; Putnam *et al.* 1993) informal capital is relational. One's standing in the patron–client hierarchy is of crucial importance, being born in the right family makes all the difference. Loyalty to a boss in a formal hierarchy should not be assumed. In public administration, norms of a 'good bureaucrat' or 'good employee' may clash with social norms of being a 'good brother, son, or friend'. In the corporate sphere, the term 'parachuters' (*parashyutisty*) refers to appointees sent 'from above'. They are treated with caution because of their link to someone above the level of their formal boss.[1] Under the clash of constraints, loyalty

---

[1] See 'Luchshii "parashyutist" Aleksandr Rodnyansky', head of the Expert group of National Media Group (NMG), yet he defines NMG policy, No. 2 in the top 10 best-remunerated corporate leaders. 'Stakhanovites of capitalist labour', *RBK*, July 2010: 70–3.

becomes personalised and ensured by networks. How can a patron ensure that an appointee's part of a transaction – loyalty – will be completed? The answer is by appointing tried and tested people (*svoi*), whose networks are not significantly different from the patron's. There are also rewards and penalties, further enforced by networks, for making *svoi* people remain loyal. Reliance on networks is a fairly universal feature of governance systems, whereas their particular features are defined by the specifics of networks. For example, when asked about the specifics of Putin's *sistema*, a respondent-lobbyist concludes:

The key question about *svoi* networks is how closed these networks are and how people are recruited into them. For Putin, for example, the entry barrier is steep – he only trusts people he has known for a long time. But once in a network, it is fairly safe, he doesn't ruin people. But he keeps people on a rota, allowing them closer when they get brownie points.

Personal networks channel the practices, strategies, values and tacit knowledge that hold *sistema* together and thus produce that seemingly omnipresent yet unidentifiable *sistema* pressure. This is not to say that *sistema* can be deciphered outside of formal hierarchies or economic processes; rather that the functioning of formal hierarchies and economic processes can only be understood if the network dimension of *sistema* is integrated into the analysis. The omission of the non-hierarchical negotiation process that takes place within power networks in the contexts of mediating appointments and channelling resources would render any understanding of *sistema* and its reproduction radically flawed.

Given the importance of network rewards (what networks can do for you) and network penalties (what networks can do to you) reported by respondents, I distinguish four ideal types of power networks and their key functions in *sistema*.

Ideal types of power networks

By 'networks' I understand social ties between people – relationships with kin, friends, acquaintances and colleagues, as well as the large numbers of people, groups and institutions that have connections with each other and work together in some way (Wellman and Berkowitz 1988).[2] The strength of such social ties can be measured by frequency

---

[2] The term 'network' is used differently. Thus, Manuel Castells (2000) advances the idea of a network society based on the new technologies and

of contact (Granovetter 1973). Social ties operate in both private and public settings – large families, just as large companies, may have stronger and weaker ties within them – but also serve to transcend the private–public divide. For the purposes of identifying the power networks operating within *sistema*, I offer a typology that helps to pin down their pervasive and constantly changing presence. Ideal types of networks are based not on dichotomies – strong or weak, private or public – but on *scales*.

As mentioned above, the scale from *strong* to *weak* ties is defined by the *frequency* of contact (Granovetter 1973). Strong ties are associated with family, inner circles and most regular contacts. Weak ties have a low frequency of individual contact and are characteristic of institutional affiliations, such as profession (for example, *siloviki, yuristy*), a firm (for example, people from Yukos or Gazprom, *yukosovtsy, gazpromovtsy*), membership (*okhotniki, veterany*), alumni associations (*odnoklassniki*), or compatriots (*zemliachestva*). The boundaries between strong and weak ties are blurred. Strong ties can weaken. Weak ties can develop into strong ones, especially in the world of politics. Time is an implicit factor in judging the strength of ties, especially when it comes to the assessments of leadership styles. Yeltsin was particularly unpopular, for example, for turning his back on loyal people, thus making the transition from strong to weak ties sharp and painful. Putin, by contrast, has been criticised for his reluctance to sack and a lengthy testing period over a number of years, thus developing strong ties slowly. Thinking about strength of ties as a scale rather than a dichotomy takes such factors into consideration to some extent.

The other scale, from *private* to *public* domains, represents a range of *contexts* in which networks operate, from exclusively intimate to those associated with institutional settings. It is worth pointing out that the boundaries between the public and the private are blurred, too. There tend to be no clear-cut divisions between public and private domains in societies with a Communist past. Communist societies used to be known for their omnipresent 'state property' and minimal privacy for individuals: the 'state property mentality' is particularly prominent in societies with the longest periods of Communist rule. In the

communicational networks characteristic of the information age, while Dirk Messner in *The Network Society* (1997) focuses on social networks and excludes electronic networks, media networks, intra-firm networks or even production networks (Perkmann 1999).

INDIVIDUAL	Strong ties		
Private settings (centred)	1 'Inner circle' Sharing life (family and the most trusted, private affairs)	3 'Core contacts' Sharing career (patrons and clients, public affairs)	**Public settings (de-centred)**
	2 'Useful friends' Sharing leisure (sport, dacha)	4 'Mediated, or periphery, contacts' Sharing affiliation (alumni, associates, co-members)	
	Weak ties		INSTITUTION

Figure 2.1 Types of networks

economy of shortage friendship was difficult to distinguish from the use of friendship – friends were meant to help each other unconditionally and it resulted in excessive reliance on personal networks outside private contexts. In a post-Soviet context, Krystanovskaya (2005) discovered a lack of private–public divisions at the very top of the political elite. Private lives, timetables and lifestyles are fully determined by their belonging to the elite group with top responsibilities. When the division between public and private is more clear-cut, networks fall into those predominantly operating in private domains and serving private needs and those predominantly operating in public domains and serving public needs. Yet the lack of clear boundaries between public and private allows networks to serve both domains.

Generally speaking, social networks can be characterised by centrality, i.e. the extent to which individuals are linked to the same centre(s) and by the strength (frequency) of ties between individuals in the network. In networks of a de-centred nature (low centrality), where all the nodes are tied up between themselves within a network, one can identify the core of the network by its most frequent contacts. Power networks are centred around people in the top positions of hierarchies.

In Figure 2.1, the intersection of the proposed scales provides us with four ideal types of personal networks. In terms of ideal types, centred networks are associated with individuals, strong ties and private settings, de-centred networks with institutions, weak ties and public settings.

The types of power networks in Figure 2.1 are ideal. If we consider an actual network, say, members of dacha cooperative 'Ozero' to which

Putin belonged in his St Petersburg days, we can assume that they shared some leisure activities then and trace their career trajectories since Putin became the President; we find them in all four groups, each performing designated duties but also 'servicing' the power network and making sure it remains operational. This point is well illustrated in the depiction of Putin's networks in *The New Times* journal (see pp. 51, 57–8), and in the attempts to map out the Putin inner court, initiated by Kryshtanovskaya and White (2003, 2005). Putin's people can be traced in every sector or industry. *The New Times*' research identifies these in the banking and financial sector, gas, oil and oil-related industries, railways, navy and infrastructure, autotransport, construction and road building, energy, military–industrial complex (VPK), metallurgy, chemical industry, media, telecommunications, alcohol market, sport, tourism and services. On p. 51 one finds the co-founders of 'Ozero' in governmental structures. The same people appear in different sectors in different positions – the flex net described by Janine Wedel (2001, 2003, 2009). Putin's contacts in Figure 2.2 show the banking and financial sector and Figure 2.3 in the gas and oil-related industry, also inclusive of people in uniforms, St Peterburgers, and '*svoi* people'.

The fluid and criss-crossing nature of networks, attempted in *The New Times* becomes explicit as one sees the same people featuring differently in various classifications of Putin's elites. Nikolai Petrov's analysis of these elites before the 2012 Presidential elections provides us with an opportunity to see the various efforts to pin down Putin's power networks. I will briefly cite the models referred to as the 'Kremlin towers', the 'Politburo' and the 'Planets' (Petrov 2011).

The 'Kremlin towers' model, suggested by Vladimir Pribylovsky, derives from the Russian aphorism that 'the Kremlin has many towers', a comment not just on its architecture but on the insider rivalries that pervade the regime.[3] Pribylovsky distinguishes nine essential power blocs in a circle. At least two of them are associated with the security services from St Petersburg (*piterskie yuristy*).

The first one is the *piterskie chekists*, associated with Igor Sechin. It includes Alexander Bortnikov, Vladimir Ustinov, Viktor Zubkov, Mikhail Fradkov, Anatolii Serdyukov, Andrei Belianinov, Sergei

---

[3] C. Clover, 'Russia: shift to shadows', *Financial Times*, 16 December 2009. See also Mukhin (2005).

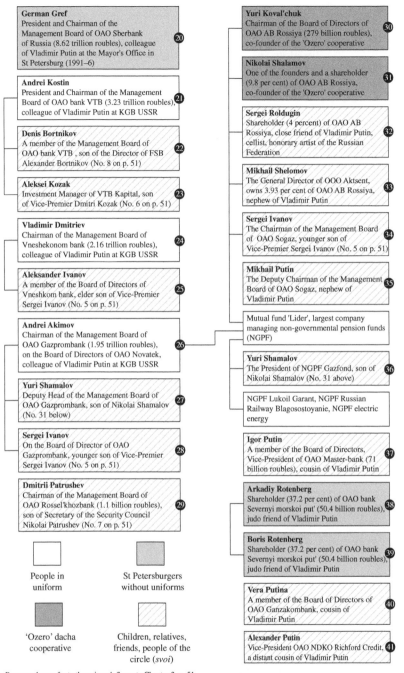

German Gref
President and Chairman of the
Management Board of OAO Sberbank
of Russia (8.62 trillion roubles), colleague
of Vladimir Putin at the Mayor's Office in
St Petersburg (1991–6) **20**

Andrei Kostin
President and Chairman of the Management
Board of OAO bank VTB (3.23 trillion roubles),
colleague of Vladimir Putin at KGB USSR **21**

Denis Bortnikov
A member of the Management Board of
OAO bank VTB , son of the Director of FSB
Alexander Bortnikov (No. 8 on p. 51) **22**

Aleksei Kozak
Investment Manager of VTB Kapital, son
of Vice-Premier Dmitri Kozak (No. 6 on p. 51) **23**

Vladimir Dmitriev
Chairman of the Management Board of
Vneshekonom bank (2.16 trillion roubles),
colleague of Vladimir Putin at KGB USSR **24**

Aleksander Ivanov
A member of the Board of Directors of
Vneshkom bank, elder son of Vice-Premier
Sergei Ivanov (No. 5 on p. 51) **25**

Andrei Akimov
Chairman of the Management Board of
OAO Gazprombank (1.95 trillion roubles),
on the Board of Directors of OAO Novatek,
colleague of Vladimir Putin at KGB USSR **26**

Yuri Shamalov
Deputy Head of the Management Board of
OAO Gazprombank, son of Nikolai Shamalov
(No. 31 below) **27**

Sergei Ivanov
On the Board of Director of OAO
Gazprombank, younger son of Vice-Premier
Sergei Ivanov (No. 5 on p. 51) **28**

Dmitrii Patrushev
Chairman of the Management Board of
OAO Rossel'khozbank (1.1 billion roubles),
son of Secretary of the Security Council
Nikolai Patrushev (No. 7 on p. 51) **29**

Yuri Koval'chuk
Chairman of the Board of Directors of
OAO AB Rossiya (279 billion roubles),
co-founder of the 'Ozero' cooperative **30**

Nikolai Shalamov
One of the founders and a shareholder
(9.8 per cent) of OAO AB Rossiya,
co-founder of the 'Ozero' cooperative **31**

Sergei Roldugin
Shareholder (4 percent) of OAO AB
Rossiya, close friend of Vladimir Putin,
cellist, honorary artist of the Russian
Federation **32**

Mikhail Shelomov
The General Director of OOO Aktsent,
owns 3.93 per cent of OAO AB Rossiya,
nephew of Vladimir Putin **33**

Sergei Ivanov
The Chairman of the Management Board
of OAO Sogaz, younger son of
Vice-Premier Sergei Ivanov (No. 5 on p. 51) **34**

Mikhail Putin
The Deputy Chairman of the Management
Board of OAO Sogaz, nephew of
Vladimir Putin **35**

Mutual fund 'Lider', largest company
managing non-governmental pension funds
(NGPF)

Yuri Shamalov
The President of NGPF Gazfond, son of
Nikolai Shamalov (No. 31 above) **36**

NGPF Lukoil Garant, NGPF Russian
Railway Blagosostoyanie, NGPF electric
energy

Igor Putin
A member of the Board of Directors,
Vice-President of OAO Master-bank (71
billion roubles), cousin of Vladimir Putin **37**

Arkadiy Rotenberg
Shareholder (37.2 per cent) of OAO bank
Severnyi morskoi put' (50.4 billion roubles),
judo friend of Vladimir Putin **38**

Boris Rotenberg
Shareholder (37.2 per cent) of OAO bank
Severnyi morskoi put' (50.4 billion roubles),
judo friend of Vladimir Putin **39**

Vera Putina
A member of the Board of Directors of
OAO Ganzakombank, cousin of
Vladimir Putin **40**

Alexander Putin
Vice-President OAO NDKO Richford Credit,
a distant cousin of Vladimir Putin **41**

People in
uniform

St Petersburgers
without uniforms

'Ozero' dacha
cooperative

Children, relatives,
friends, people of the
circle (*svoi*)

Page numbers refer to the epigraph figure to Chapter 2, p. 51.

Figure 2.2 Putin's networks in the banking and financial sector
Source: The New Times, 25 October 2011: 7.

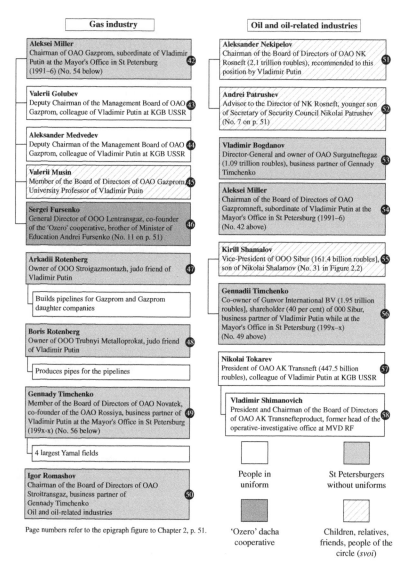

Figure 2.3 Putin's networks in gas- and oil-related industries
Source: The New Times, 25 October 2011: 8.

Chemezov, Nikolai Tokarev, Gennady Timchenko, Vasily Titov, Vladimir Strzhalkovsky and Vladimir Artyakov.

The second one is the *piterskie chekists,* associated with Viktor Tokarev and Nikolai Patrushev. It consists of Boris Gryzlov, Oleg

Safonov, Rashid Nurgaliev, Sergei Smirnov, Valentina Matvienko, Andrei Kostin, Mikhail Kuzovlev and a variety of St Petersburg–Karelian and St Petersburg–Afghan *chekists*.

Other *siloviki* include the Zolotov–Cherkesov group, also associated with Sergei Ivanov and the Rotenberg brothers (Arkadii and Boris). The group of Orthodox *chekists* consists of Vladimir Yakunin, Georgii Poltavchenko, Vladimir Kozhin and Vladimir Dmitriev.

Some financial and power brokers fall into Alexander Voloshin's group: Roman Abramovich, Alisher Usmanov, Igor Shuvalov, Natalia Timakova, Arkadii Dvorkovich, Oleg Deripaska and some into the group of St Petersburg economists led by Aleksei Kudrin: Sergei Ignatiev, Alexei Ulyukaev, Elvira Nabiullina, Anatolii Chubais, Arkadii Dvorkovich (until 2009) and possibly German Gref and Vladimir Kogan.

Also from St Petersburg, the group of *piterskie yuristy* (lawyers), associated with Dmitri Medvedev includes Konstantin Chuichenko, Anton Ivanov, Elena Valyavina, Nikolai Vinnichenko, Dmitri Kozak, Artur Parfenchikov, Ilya Yeliseev, Alexander Konovalov, Yuri Chaika, Vladimir Pligin, the Zingarevich brothers, Zakhar Smushkin, Georgii Kozhokar and possibly Viktor Vekselberg and Alisher Usmanov. The lawyers associated with Medvedev are sometimes referred to *civiliki*, as opposed to *siloviki*, a pun referring to the faculty of civil law at the St Petersburg State University. The Reiman group is associated with Leonid Reiman, the former Minister of Telecommunications, and his clientele (*piterskie svyazisty*). There are also St Petersburg physicists (*piterskie fiziki*): the Koval'chuks, the Fursenko brothers and Viktor Myachin.

The 'Politburo' model, suggested by Evgenii Minchenko, is based on following eleven members: Vladimir Putin, Dmitri Medvedev, Igor Sechin, Alexei Kudrin, Sergei Naryshkin, Vladislav Surkov, Sergei Sobyanin, Yuri Koval'chuk, Gennady Timchenko, Roman Abramovich and Alisher Usmanov.

Similar to the uneven cast of the 'Kremlin towers', the 'Politburo' candidates come from different walks of life as well: vice-premiers (Igor Shuvalov, Viktor Zubkov, Vyacheslav Volodin, Dmitri Kozak, Sergei Ivanov); *siloviki* (Anatolii Serdyukov, Viktor Ivanov, Nikolai Patrushev, Alexander Bortnikov, Mikhail Fradkov, Sergei Shoigu); state corporations (Sergei Chemezov, Vladimir Yakunin, Alexei Miller, Anatoliy Chubais, Alexander Voloshin, Petr Aven, German Gref);

formal leaders of the ruling parties (Boris Gryzlov, Sergei Mironov/Valentina Matvienko); Presidential Administration (PA) (Alexander Beglov, Boris Gromov) and the Patriarch.

The 'Planets' model, suggested by Evgenii Gontmakher, depicts Putin as the sun surrounded by three circles of planets. The first, and the nearest, circle includes planets of Koval'chuks (Mikhail, Boris and Yuri), Vladimir Kogan, the Rotenberg brothers (Arkadiy and Boris), Gennady Timchenko, Alexei Kudrin, Andrei Fursenko, Vladimir Strzhalkovsky, father Tikhon (Shevkunov) and Roman Abramovich. There are also smaller planets – Igor Sechin, Sergei Sobyanin and Vladimir Litvinenko, which are supposedly the largest. Silvio Berlusconi and Matthias Warnig also appear in the list. The second circle consists of Alexei Miller, Vladimir Evtushenkov, Petr Aven, Oleg Deripaska, German Gref, Viktor Zubkov, Vladimir Yakunin, Sergei Chemezov, Nikolai Tokarev, Anatoliy Chubais, Vladimir Yakovlev and Sergei Fursenko. The third circle includes Sergei Mironov (before leaving the Federation). From the Federation Council are Boris Gryzlov, Vladislav Surkov, Vyacheslav Volodin, Dmitri Kozak, Valentina Matvienko, Ramzan Kadyrov, Alexander Tkachev, Sergei Darkin, Tatyana Golikova, Viktor Ivanov, Anatolii Serdyukov, Alexander Bastrykin, Sergei Ivanov, Alexander Bortnikov and Rashid Nurgaliev (quoted from Petrov 2011). By implication, each 'planet' has its own 'orbit' (sector of economy or society), 'satellites' (essential networks of the planetary persons) and 'populations' (those whose well-being depends on their planets being on the right side of the Sun).

My approach in this book is different. Instead of mapping Putin's personal networks, I map the types and the functions that networks have in Putin's *sistema*. In other words, rather than describing the network-based model of Putin's *sistema*, I offer insights on the nature of power networks and their workings that would help assess any system.

Ambivalence of power networks

Relationships between an individual in a high official position and his contacts, as depicted in Figure 2.1, change over time. For example, it is not unthinkable that a long-time friend or a weak-tie acquaintance, once appointed to a trusted position, would advance to the inner circle. Such changes of position in a network are based on the dynamics in the strength of ties and shifting contexts (a private relationship can lead to an appointment and a formal subordination or, conversely, a formal subordination can lead to an informal relationship that lasts longer than the formal relationship). These changes are impossible to reflect in a model but they can be tracked down through a temporal monitoring of networks.

My ideal types, based on analytical distinctions of strong and weak, private and public, individual and institutional, serve to frame the fluid, blurry and ambivalent nature of real-life situations that play such a key part in the workings of *sistema*. For example, under the conditions of Soviet socialism and the economy of shortage, the boundaries between public and the private were particularly hazy. Social ties and their instrumental use became blurred. Kin and friends, and in late social-ism even acquaintances, were expected to provide each other with access to goods and services in short supply and help out in other ways, too. 'Networking' acquired connotations of the pragmatic use of networks, not necessarily self-serving but serving the interests of a network. Along with social back-up, personal networks also provided unauthorised access to institutional resources, thereby forming pat-terns of mediation between individuals and institutions, private and public domains, society and the state. There was no Soviet word to denote 'networks' or 'networking' (a post-Soviet term *seti* is used in academic contexts). However, related idioms in common use were *blat*, 'people in one's circle' (*svoi lyudi*), 'one of us' (*svoi*) and 'circle of joint responsibility' (*krugovaya poruka*), all of which carry connotations pointing to an exclusive (closed) nature of networks and their calcu-lated use. Once personal relationships cease to be distinguished from their use, friendship effectively means the use of friendship; practices of 'mutual help' penetrate the public domain and make use of public resources, thus perfectly fitting the definition of 'misuse of public office for private gain'. For socio-historical reasons, however, the boundaries between the public and the private in such contexts are blurred, and many such exchanges are perceived as legitimate.

The omnipresent use of networks accounts for the acceptance of, or at least ambivalent attitude towards, such a practice. It is often said that societies differ mainly in the reaction provoked by corrup-tion rather than its actual occurrence (Johnston 2005). This approach highlights the ambivalence of the Russian public: people resent cor-ruption but also believe it is inevitable, thus resulting in tolerance, if not acceptance of, corruption and nepotism in the corridors of power. An investigative report 'Power of families – 2011: the government' identifies about fifty families that embody a symbiosis of institutions, organisations, businesses and networks.[4] State–business relationships are often mediated by the children of top state officials. Corporate archives of state-owned companies are full of examples.[5] The senior partner of human relations/executive search (HR) firm Ward Howell, Anton Derlyatka, interprets the appointments of top state officials' children to the top corporate executive positions as a form of state intervention in business. They also signify the importance of the state, and the related importance of government relations (GR) for the corporate sector.[6]

While such alliances may emerge in any society, their frame of reference and their implications are different[7] – the embedded expectations from kinship in Russia are huge. Extending help to children is rarely questioned. Some comparative studies of entrepreneurs in Russia and China show that social networks play a major role in explaining entrepreneurship in both contexts (Aidis *et al.* 2008). Thus, researchers find that in Russia having a father who was a Communist Party member increases the likelihood of becoming an entrepreneur: even when the Communist Party has lost its influence, the informal networks it established remain powerful. Kinship networks in Russia are not normally large and tend to be of a centred type – with a patron

[4] The named families include Patrushev, Kudrin, Levitin, Shuvalov and Skrynnik. For more details see M. A. Litvinovich, 'Vlast' Semei – 2011. Pravitel'stvo'. Part 1, *Monitoring Expert Group*, 2011, http://election2012.ru/reports/1/.

[5] See, for example, the appointment of Andrei Patrushev, son of the former head of the FSB. Ekaterina Drobinina, 'Rossiiskie goskompanii: kak zanyat' vysokii post v 25 let', *BBC News Russia*, 21 February 2012, www.bbc.co.uk/russian/business/2012/02/120220_officials_children_top_managers.shtml.

[6] See also A. Limanov, N. Ahakrinskaja, D. Dokuchaev and V. Protasevich, 'Nasledniki rossiiskoi elity poluchat'luchshie chasti strany', *The New Times*, 20 June 2011, p. 14, on the jobs of Denis Bortnikov, Stanislav Chemezov, Petr Fradkov, Dmitrii Gryzlov, Alexander Ivanov, Vladimir Khristenko, Alexei Kozak, Sergei Matvienko, Yulia Serdyukova, Andrei Yakunin, Petr Zhukov, etc.

[7] For example, the Director of the World Bank has been forced to resign over an improper correspondence recommending a pay-level increase for his girlfriend, who had to move jobs so that they would not work in the same organisation. Although practices may look similar, the context and the reaction of the public, as well as the generally legitimate framework of electoral, media and other public institutions, providing checks and balances, make an enormous difference.

member in the centre of a network, defined by wealth or position in the government or a private firm (Aidis *et al.* 2008).

These individuals are integral to the kinship network, not because of active involvement in everyday exchanges but for their symbolic presence, which entitles the members of the network to expect support. The size of a network can increase through marriages and other alliances. Necessary links between government structures and commercial banks, insurance companies and other sectors tend to be mediated by kinship as well as by other social networks.

The theme of expectations is closely linked to the theme of double standards. People may object to particular cases of nepotism (*kumovstvo*), but also assume that good parents do whatever is necessary to help their children, even if it involves morally reprehensible practices such as soliciting exemption from army conscription (Nesmachnaya 2009).[8] For those working in public administration, the social norm of being a 'good parent, relative or friend' comes into conflict with the norm of being a 'good bureaucrat', thus resulting in a double standard in the treatment of people of the circle (*svoi lyudi*) and the general public. In a society where the written rules contradict the unwritten norms and being a good brother is incompatible with being a good bureaucrat, those in charge of administrative positions have to compromise their bureaucratic duties in a carefully calculated way, so that they can keep both their jobs and their social circles. In Soviet times, the rules of the game were determined by the Communist Code, the Party discipline, the fear of the secret police and the wider socialist ideological framework that downplayed the role of materialistic incentives and private property. In post-Soviet Russia, the incentive to be a good bureaucrat is weakened due to the demise of party discipline and the change in incentives as such. The new 'vertical of wealth' undermines the morals and integrity of officials: experience of systemic corruption has made them pragmatic and cynical. The monetisation of the economy has given the formerly unspecified difference between what is to be done for '*svoi*' and for the 'others' a financial equivalent: a kickback (*otkat*).

The double standards applied by bureaucrats are mirrored by double standards in the public's attitude toward them. The public expects more integrity from the public administration than from itself. On

---

[8] Army conscription is avoided by corrupt mechanisms.

the other hand, the public is not surprised to hear about incidents of nepotism, corruption, or about the revealing outcomes of income declarations enacted according to Russia's anti-corruption legislation of 2010.[9] Personal obligation and loyalty tend to be taken for granted and viewed as acceptable regardless of the context, even if they make one bend some formal rules. Public complicity in understanding peer pressure from family, friends and the institutionalised system of informal kickbacks (*otkaty*) creates low expectations of public officials consistent with generally low levels of trust in public institutions in Russia (World Values Surveys,[10] 2011 Russian Public Opinion[11]).

When reported in the Russian media, the abuse of office by the public administration is often linked to corrupt incentives and the negative qualities of human nature: dishonesty, shamelessness and greed. Associating corrupt practices with greed conceals the reverse side of the coin: the embeddedness of corruption in trust, personal loyalty, close relationships and altruistic incentives. In the same way, the grassroots practice of giving a bribe for a hospital bed qualifies both as corrupt behaviour and an expression of care for someone in need of an operation. Giving a bribe or a kickback to an official, say, for his permission for a pharmaceutical firm to import vaccine with no trouble from customs is justified by one's responsibility to one's countrymen as well as family, business and employees. This dual nature of motivations underlying corrupt behaviour, the actual squeeze between loyalty to the law (universal rule) and loyalty to a personal network (particular situation) reflects the ambiguity of social networks.

Supportive yet subversive: the functions of power networks

The ambiguous nature of networks means that the 'positive' implications of networks enjoyed by some private parties – flexibility,

[9] See Federal Law No. 273-FZ, 'On Counteracting Corruption', 25 December 2008, the National Anti-Corruption Plan approved by the President of the Russian Federation on 31 July 2008 No. PR-1568, the National Anti-Corruption Strategy, Approved by Decree of the President of the Russian Federation No. 460, 13 April 2010; *President of Russia* website, http://eng.news.kremlin.ru/ref_notes/8.

[10] World Values Surveys, 1989–2012, www.wvsevsdb.com/wvs/WVSData.jsp.

[11] Levada Centre, *Obshchestvennoe mnenie: ezhegodnik* (Moscow: Levada Centre Publishing 2011): Trust in state institutions, 1994–2011, Figures 8.1.1 and 8.1.2: 89.

	Strong ties		
	'Back-up'	'Safety net'	
	FREE-RIDING	LOCK-IN EFFECT	
Private settings			**Public settings**
	'Survival kit'	'Buffer effect'	
	LIMITED RIGHTS	PATH DEPENDENCY	
	Weak ties		

Figure 2.4 Functional ambivalence of networks

psychological support, reduced risks and transaction costs – may at the same time have 'negative' implications for the others, for the network and for the economy.[12] Woolcock (1998: 165) finds that: 'a high level of social capital can be... "negative" in that it also places high particularistic demands on group members, thereby restricting individual expression and advancement; permits free riding on community resources; and negates, in those groups with a long history of marginalization through coercive non-market mechanisms, the belief in the possibility of advancement through individual effort' (see also Burt 1997; Portes 1998).

I summarise these functions of power networks and their ambivalence – each function has enabling and constraining implications – in Figure 2.4, on the understanding that they are ideal types and the boundaries between strong and weak ties are blurred, as are the boundaries between public and private contexts (at least in the perceptions

---

[12] The 'positive' and 'negative' implications are referred to in inverted commas because their evaluation depends on whether the interests of networks are consistent with the interests of the economy and on the perspective from which the assessment is made. For example, limits that the group or community puts on individuality cannot be seen as outright negative. Studies of stress levels indicate that stress is much higher in so-called 'atomised' societies than in network-based societies where individuals might be subject to certain restrictions imposed by networks.

of network users). There seems to be a reverse side to each of the functions of networks, as discussed below.

I distinguish four types of manifest functions of networks and identify their latent functions as follows:

(1) Networks are conducive to *social comfort* or '*back-up*' – human cooperation and mutual help, providing sociability, emotional support and assistance for routine domestic needs. The latent, or reverse, side of the back-up function is the *high cost of the implicit contract*. Even if one 'inherits' a network, rather than building one's own, the network does require maintenance and investment. Maintaining social ties (satisfying reciprocal demands and thus reproducing trust) generates cost. In other words, belonging to the network creates obligations towards the other members of the network, or an implicit contract. Therefore, whatever advantage one receives from being embedded in a network (incurring fewer transaction costs) is counterbalanced by the obligations of the implicit contract (Bourdieu 1986). These obligations, imposed by the relationships of trust and reciprocity, may result in excessive exploitation of one's resources (or access to resources) by other members of one's network, which can turn into a *free riding problem*.

(2) Social networks constitute a '*survival kit*' – a basis for survival strategies or achieving access to resources for private use in crisis situations. Cooperation is a way of coping with daily problems, hardships and challenges. According to Wellman (1999), the use of social networks is one of the five basic means by which people and institutions acquire necessary resources – along with market exchanges, state distributions and, to a lesser extent, self-provisioning and coercive appropriations. 'Just as people use their financial capital to purchase things on markets and their human capital to gain better access to markets and state distributions, they also use *network capital*, their connections with people and organizations. Such network capital can assume many forms, such as altruistic, long-lasting and multipurpose relations; short-term instrumental relations; asymmetric patron–client relations; corrupt, exploitative unequal exchanges' (Sik and Wellman 1999, emphasis added). On the one hand, the use of networks is less costly, more effective and more easily accessible than any other alternative, such as market purchases or acquiring state

redistributions (Polanyi 1957; Wellman and Wortley 1990). On the other hand, benefiting from social networks has a reverse effect of *limited rights in individual decision-making, in responsibility for and ownership of the outcome.* Membership in a closed social network (with consequent sanctions to enforce the implicit contract) can subject members to restrictive social regulations and limit their individual action. All kinds of levelling pressures keep members in the same situation as their peers (Ledeneva 2004) and strong collective norms in communities may restrict the scope of individuals (Portes and Sensenbrenner 1993). Non-compliance with the demands of membership can also result in a loss of reputation as a reliable member of the network.

(3) Networks can be used as a resource, or '*safety net*', to achieve certain goals in the public domain, to avoid risks or to enhance chances in competition, or to bend the rules in one's favour. Appointing trusted people is an effective method of monitoring, control and policy implementation. Investing in and maintaining networks of partners constitutes routine management strategy. The reverse side of a safety net function is the *lock-in effect*, especially within closed networks. It is the 'belonging' to closed networks, rather than networks in general, that reduces adaptive capacity and carries the dangers of lock-in effects (the inability to break out of a network). These lock-in effects may be strengthened by processes of cognitive dissonance in tight groups: individuals who make up a dense network tend to develop a commitment to one another and to their group (Grabher 1993; Meyerson 1994). Information that disturbs the consensus of the group's perception of reality is likely to be rejected. Belonging to a network seems to yield positive results up to a certain threshold. Research identifies lock-in effects at the levels of sectors, localities and regions. Especially for de-industrialised regions, part of the problem is that they are locked into institutional structures that are relevant to an earlier phase of successful economic development but which now constitute a barrier to moving onto a new path of development.

(4) Social networks tend to produce a '*buffer effect*': they protect against the environment and reduce the rigidity of constraints. In high-risk environments where impersonal systems of trust are not sufficiently developed, people are compelled to cooperate and to 'beat the system'; they rely on interpersonal trust, even where

ties are weak and contexts are public. In low-risk environments, where personal networks cease to be instrumental, networks serve civic associations, non-governmental organisations (NGOs) and pressure groups. In the context of blurred boundaries between the public and the private, by providing what hierarchies cannot, power networks, however loose, offer an instrument that enables one to recruit and ensure cooperation. The reverse side of the buffer effect of networks is the so-called *path-dependency effect* (Stark and Bruszt 2001a, 2001b). For example, networks that have been used to solve business problems (many studies of social capital emphasise that networks help to circumvent restrictions in starting up businesses) can later become a serious obstacle for a further development of the business environment (skills of maintaining networks may not fit the context of competition, transparency and market values).

Overall, the functional ambivalence of networks, as argued above, is in tune with Portes and Landolt's findings that social capital should be viewed from both positive and negative sides (Portes and Landolt 1996). Portes and Sensenbrenner further argue that 'it is important not to lose sight of the fact that the same social mechanisms that give rise to appropriable resources for individual use can also constrain action or even derail it from its original goals' (Portes and Landolt 1996: 1320–50). In other words, networks do not only distribute and mobilise, they also divert and misappropriate the structures organising the economy's dominant functions and processes.

Conceptually, an important assumption is that the use of personal networks is a perfectly rational response for both individuals and organisations. Informal networks generally should not be viewed only as detrimental to Russia's development. Power networks function with an ambivalent effect: they are both supportive and subversive of institutional environments. Their types and functions should be differentiated and analysed accordingly. Therefore *sistema* cannot simply be associated with the 'negative' or latent four functions of networks – it also makes use of their 'positive' or manifest potential. Before considering the network dimensions of Putin's *sistema*, let us say a few words about the 'vertical of power' and the hierarchical underpinnings of *sistema*.

Putin's vertical of power

Under Putin's Presidency (2000–8), Russia saw a dramatic strengthening of the state's rule-making capacity. Enhancing the so-called 'vertical of power' became central to regional reforms: synchronisation of federal and regional laws, improving the judiciary's financial standing, a simultaneous strengthening of the executive branch of power and the weakening of the independence of the legislative branch and the media (Sakwa 2008, 2010). Despite the unprecedented approval rates enjoyed by Putin during his Presidency in that period, doubts persisted about the independence of the judiciary and the competence and probity of the state institutions, including the police. Considerable concern surrounded the fundamental integrity of the state bureaucracy.[13] The notion of 'state capture' by private interests, associated with oligarchs of Yeltsin's period, gave place to a phenomenon of 'business capture' by state officials. Business capture constituted a dramatic increase in the formal state share in the ownership of strategically important enterprises, including media outlets; formal and informal supervision of businesses by *siloviki*, usually associated with the security services and colloquially known as curators (*kuratory* or *smotryashchie*); widespread rent-seeking behaviour of officials (*koshmarit´* or *otzhimat´ biznes*); as well as 'authorised' corporate attacks (raids). State officials became associated with kickbacks for allocation of resources and the abuse of administrative power (*administrativnyi resurs*). In addition, one can also think of many examples where so-called informal activities did not clash with formal rules but used them manipulatively – i.e. violated not the letter of the law but its spirit or, worse, aimed at creating formal rules that served informal interests – the phenomenon known as 'state capture' in the 1990s or more recently 'legal corruption' (Hellman *et al*. 2003; Kaufmann and Vicente, 2005). By 2008 it had become clear that the World Bank-backed administrative reforms, which aimed to reduce and restructure the role of the state, had proved ineffective against the network-driven growth of bureaucracy.

Experts suggest that the duality of state governance structures, serving the President and the government separately at the federal level, was to be blamed (see Figure 2.5). No reform to date has managed

---

[13] G. Satarov, 'Nedovarennaya lapsha na razvesistykh ushakh. Vertikal´ vlasti', *Ezhednevnyi zhurnal*, 21 October 2010, http://ej.ru/?a=note&id=10484.

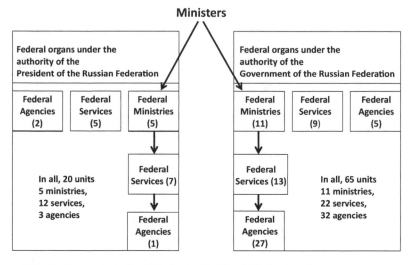

Ministers

| Federal organs under the authority of the President of the Russian Federation | Federal organs under the authority of the Government of the Russian Federation |

| Federal Agencies (2) | Federal Services (5) | Federal Ministries (5) | | Federal Ministries (11) | Federal Services (9) | Federal Agencies (5) |

| In all, 20 units 5 ministries, 12 services, 3 agencies | Federal Services (7) ↓ Federal Agencies (1) | Federal Services (13) ↓ Federal Agencies (27) | In all, 65 units 11 ministries, 22 services, 32 agencies |

85 federal organs including 16 federal ministries, 34 federal services, 35 federal agencies

Figure 2.5 Structure of federal organs of executive power: duality of state governance structures

to address the issue sufficiently (Mironov 2005). In particular, efforts to reform the PA – often seen as a source of duplication and informal supervision – only resulted in staff re-shuffles and the curtailing of administrative reform. According to Olga Kryshtanovskaya, members of the PA (in her estimate, over 2,000 employees) perceive themselves as king-makers, who manipulate politics and control the media (Kryshtanovskaya 2005). Yet the power of the PA is not only a feature of the dual executive, it is also an indication of the lack of balance between the branches of power.

Although the divisions in the jurisdictions of the Presidential and the governmental federal structures are more or less clear, the governance structure and the administrative capacity of the Russian state depends strongly on cross-institutional networks and coordination mechanisms that often undermine possibilities of reform (Brym and Gimpelson 2004). The numbers of top officials were reduced in Putin's round of administrative reform in 2004 but bounced back in 2006 (see Table 2.1).[14] Since 2006, the state bureaucracy has been large and

---

[14] According to the state statistical service, the number of bureaucrats at all levels of government in Russia grew by 143,500 in 2005 to a total of 1,462,000, or

Table 2.1 *Dynamics in numbers of top officials in 2003–6*

Number of	2003 before administrative reform	2004 after a year of administrative reform	2006
Vice-premiers	6	1	3 (5 in 2007)
Ministries	30	16	16
Federal service	18	33	35
Federal agencies	3	28	32
Max number of deputy-ministers	16	2	8

Source: E. Shishkunova, *Izvestiia*, No. 189, 12 October 2006: 3. Information for 2008 is from 'Duties of vice-premiers in the government of the Russian Federation', *RIA-Novosti*, 12 May 2008, 17:45, www.rian.ru/mainline/20080512/107171747.html.

growing at all levels. From 2008, there was an additional intake of 20,000 officials at the federal level, an increase of 60,000 in regional administrations and 50,000 at the municipal level. The latest available figure amounts to at least 510,000 officials at the federal level (including the judiciary). There has been another call to reduce the number of federal officials by 20 per cent by 2014.[15]

According to experts, none of the reforms conducted in Russia in the post-Soviet period, on both federal and municipal levels, were as tightly coordinated with international advice and global expertise as administrative reform (Leksin *et al.* 2006; Manning and Parison 2003). The same experts, who worked closely with EU experts and consultants and senior government officials, acknowledged that due to the specifics of the institutional framework in Russia the number of state officials and intermediary agencies had increased (from 59 to 85 agencies at the federal level) and that the structure of the federal executive organs remained too complicated (Mironov 2005).

approximately 1 bureaucrat per 100 residents. Bureaucrats as a share of the overall workforce have increased from 4.55 per cent in 2000 to an estimated 4.92 per cent in 2005. In the Russian draft budget for 2007, the amount of money spent supporting public servants was set to rise 50 per cent to 821 billion roubles. R. Orttung, 'Causes and consequences of corruption in Putin's Russia', PONARS Policy Memo No. 430, December 2006.

[15] V. Kuz'min, 'Minus 100 tysyach: predlozheno sokratit' federal'nykh chinovnikov', *Rossiiskaya Gazeta*, 23 September 2010: 2, www.rg.ru.

Putin inherited formal power structures and a complex web of cross-ministerial networks that made straightforward bureaucratic following of written instructions impossible. It left Putin reliant on the 'administrative resource' and informal networks, unwritten rules and oral commands in order to pursue his reforms. The phrase 'administrative resource' (*administrativnyi resurs*) was originally coined to describe unfair advantages for incumbents in post-Soviet elections, but since then has become widely used to denote the abuse of administrative power in spheres beyond its formal subordination (Panfilova and Sheverdiaev 2005b: 9–15). In Putin's era, the term came to denote the top-down use of the distributive and mobilising capacity of administrative power to achieve manageability of the economy.[16]

Putin's networks

Given that the vertical of Putin's power has been well researched (Sakwa 2008, 2010, 2011), I complement these relevant analyses with an examination of its network dimension. To illustrate the workings of Putin's *sistema*, let us consider his networks according to the ideal types suggested above, with their functions and implications. The assumption of a fluid, temporally sensitive, overlapping and complex nature of actual networks *vis-à-vis* their ideal types applies fully here.

'Inner circle'

The inner circle in a narrow sense includes people who are in contact with each other on a daily or regular basis. In a private setting, the term mainly applies to family. But in politics, the private and the public are hard to separate, so the inner circle includes a wider circle of people.[17] In electoral democracies, the inner circle of an elected President is based on the core group of his electoral campaign. Its

---

[16] The phrase is also used of those in possession of contacts or support in administrative organs, which constitute a resource for getting things done.

[17] For example, the former deputy minister of property relations, Zumrud Rustamova, left for a position in business after her marriage to Arkadii Dvorkovich, former Deputy Minister of Economic Development and now head of experts in the presidential administration (Karpov and Salakhitdinova 2007).

nomenklatura analogy is a 'team' that follows the patron from one position to another.[18] Given the rapid career of President Putin, he was originally considered to have no team but after just over a year the majority of sources associated with the President's inner circle were *siloviki*, those with backgrounds in the security services. Yet this inner circle cannot be seen as cohesive. There are a number of networks *within* Putin's inner circle. For example, Igor Sechin's network was thought to include Federal Security Service director Nikolai Patrushev, FSB deputy director Aleksander Bortnikov, Putin aide Viktor Ivanov and Aleksander Bastrykin, head of the Investigative Committee.

Another network included Viktor Cherkesov, chief of the Federal Drug Control Service, and Viktor Zolotov, head of the President's personal security service (the experts said), and was meant to counterbalance Sechin's group (Latynina 2008, see Chapter 6 for the details of this conflict). The third group within the inner circle is believed to include Prosecutor General Yuri Chaika, who enjoyed good relations with the then Chief of Staff Dmitri Medvedev and Finance Minister Aleksei Kudrin (Mereu 2007).[19] According to a source in the security services, the group also has ties with Putin's long-time friend Yuri Koval'chuk, who controls Bank Rossiya; Gennadii Timchenko, owner of the oil trader Gunvor; one-time Kremlin Chief of Staff and now Mayor of Moscow Sergei Sobyanin; billionaire Roman Abramovich; and former Kremlin Chief of Staff Aleksander Voloshin (Mereu 2007; Petrov 2011).

The inner circle of people who 'speak for the President', however, should not be confused with those who have the President's ear. In this wider sense, the inner circle can be defined as people invited to a birthday party: in 2000, when he became President, Putin is reported to have had twenty-one guests. Some of them must have been guests of honour but some of them are those 'significant others' that one shares leisure activities with or turns to informally for information. Stories from this birthday party serve as an epigraph and an epilogue of Boris Mazo's book on who is who in Putin's personal circle. Its ethnographic epigraph says:

[18] 'Seilschaft', in Rigby's terms.
[19] Another cleavage within the inner circle was linked to the arrest of the Deputy Finance Minister Sergei Storchak, interpreted as an attack on Finance Minister Aleksei Kudrin.

For Vladimir Putin's birthday – the first of the recently elected President, which was pointedly spent in St Petersburg – his former judo teacher gave him a small statue of two fighting boys. Nothing special, not made of gold. But while giving the small sculpture, the coach turned the attention of those gathered to the fact that although the boys were fighting seriously, they were both smiling. 'And you and I know why they are smiling', the coach finished his toast, addressing the President.

The guests nodded in agreement to show that they understand, too: because the rules of battle are clear and transparent, because victory is unattainable, and one can only enjoy the process. Other truthful and wise sentiments were expressed, but the President and his ex-coach only smiled. (Mazo 2003: 5)

The epilogue offers further details of the birthday party that could be of interest to an ethnographer of power network birthday rituals as a way of 'servicing' networks (Mazo 2003: 235). Birthday rituals are like the consummation of a relationship, members of the circle have an obligation to attend. The effort and resources that go into the organisation of elitist birthday parties can be paralleled to wedding spendings and are estimated in the number of guests: the fewer guests, the more exclusive is the circle. One of the corporate respondents described an average birthday party, organised by a vice president of some energy-related state company for his wife. It was set up in one of the most exclusive family palaces in France, with a twenty-four-course meal (six sessions of four courses each), the orchestra of the central television channel and a variety of celebrity performers for the twenty-eight guests.

'Useful friends'

In contrast to kinship, networks based on the ties of friendship have the 'advantage' of being harder to trace and to prove. Given that many friendships are formed at a young age, sport and education outlets are important foundations of future social networks and relationships. Putin's 'old friends' are reported to benefit from 'authorised' access to resources. *Forbes* magazine conducted journalistic investigations of businesses owned by Putin's judo partners Arkadii and Boris Rotenberg and identified their multi-faceted assets: from a judo club and alcohol business to banks, coal, gas pipes, shipping, construction and development (Kosyrev and Abakumova 2009). *Vedomosti* reports Arkadii Rotenberg as a business presence in road construction, as well as Yuri Koval'chuk, a friend associated with the dacha cooperative 'Ozero'.[20] The dacha cooperative was set up in 1999 and most of its personalities have made spectacular careers in both the private and the public sector. Some of these personalities have become public figures and will be considered under 'core contacts' below. Here we focus on 'friends' in the sense of their private access to the body: 'they can enter Putin's office though a private room or they don't even have to come to the office – they solve their problems (*reshat' voprosy*) by phone or in informal settings.' Because their telephone calls are returned, they quite literally have the President's ear. Some useful friends remain unnamed but are rumoured to be serving as 'fronts' for Putin's wealth. Thus, in December 2007, the Russian political commentator Stanislav Belkovsky told the *Guardian* that Putin had secretly amassed a $40 billion fortune. Putin was the beneficial owner of '75 per cent of Gunvor', he claimed, adding that Putin's ownership was concealed through a 'non-transparent network of offshore companies'. Putin denied the claim three months later (Harding 2009).

Gennady Timchenko, the 'secretive Russian billionaire' in charge of Gunvor, also denied the association. Indeed, he even initiated a libel case against *The Economist* after the magazine suggested he had benefited from his close relationship with Vladimir Putin. He originally claimed that 'while he and Putin knew one another, their relationship was one of casual acquaintanceship rather than friendship' (Harding 2009), but after a while has abandoned his libel case and agreed a settlement with *The Economist* in the High Court in London. *Private Eye* suggests that *The Economist*'s long defence document unearthed some data and new lines of inquiry, while the efforts of Timchenko's lawyers at Shillings, a firm specialising in cases of reputation risk, 'merely produced an anodyne "clarification" in the current issue of *The Economist*, which offers no apology and makes no mention of

[20] *Vedomosti*, 20 September 2010: 16. See also Forbes (*Russia*), 1 November 2012. According to *Le Figaro*, the wealth of Gennady Timchenko is estimated at 1.4 billion Euros, Yuri Koval'chuk, 685 million, Boris Rotenberg 504 million, Arkadi Rottenberg 504 million and Sergei Pougachev 1.73 billion, 9 November 2010: 10.

paying a penny in costs or damages.[21] In a carefully worded statement, *The Economist* just disowns allegations it had never made.'

Although the 'friendship' between an official and a businessman is hard to prove, the 'use of friendship' is more accountable. Whereas it might be difficult to document the frequency of accessing an 'administrative resource' by a businessman, and especially to establish how such access converts into business advantage, to register the reverse favour – say, access to a businessman's private jet for an official – is relatively easy. Investigative materials on the flight itineraries of government officials can be found in *Novaya Gazeta*, compromat.ru and legal cases. The head of the Kremlin property department, Vladimir Kozhin, was aboard Timchenko's private jet flying from Moscow to Sochi via Prague, together with Timchenko himself and a State Duma deputy, Alina Kabaeva, who has been linked to Vladimir Putin. The itinerary was used in a legal case as evidence of his friendship with Putin. In an interview with *Kommersant Daily*, Kozhin commented on the flight and the nature of his relationships:

Well, you know my take on it. When it concerns people like the President and the Prime Minister, only they themselves can call someone their friends or comrades. The rest is rumour and gossip. As for me and Gennady Timchenko – we have known each other for a long time, from the times not even of St Petersburg but of Leningrad, when life was different, the country was different, he was different and I was different. I repeat, we have known each other for a long time and in this sense a personal relationship between us exists. Yet where I flew, with whom, and in which jet – this is my private life. And if someone somewhere stole or found something... oh well, help yourself. (Korobov and Kashin 2011: 1)[22]

The last sentence must be related to the illegitimate source of the flight itinerary. The quotation raises an interesting point about the protection of a top official's private life from public curiosity, especially against the background of the blurred boundaries between the relationship

---

[21] See the full text of the *Private Eye* article of 7 August 2009, and *The Economist*'s article under the headline 'Grease my palm, bribery and corruption are endemic in Russia', *The Economist*, 27 November 2008, at Edward Lucas' blog http://edwardlucas.blogspot.com/. See also 'Gunvor: riddles, mysteries and enigmas', *The Economist*, 5 May 2012.

[22] See the full text in Korobov and Kashin (2011: 1). Oleg Kashin, a journalist with *Kommersant.Daily*, was brutally attacked in the city centre in November 2010.

and the use of the relationship in patron–client contexts. Finally, it is essential to note the reverse trajectory of such relationships. The client is assumed to structure the relationships in such a way that a top official in the hierarchy, just like any gatekeeper in it, is willingly or unwillingly compelled to serve as a patron to their friends, followers and clients (Schmidt 1977). Yet, the patron becoming a client of his useful friends is also part of the equation. Useful friends can be put in charge of the patron's needs.

'Core contacts'

Patrons need support in order to conduct their policies, and they resort to network resources to implement their will in institutional settings. The dynamics of Putin's regime are often linked to the waves of appointments of his trusted people to key positions in Moscow. It is possible to see these appointments as Putin's appointments, yet from a network perspective it is significant that these trusted people were not part of Putin's personal network but part of a power network of which he was a part, most notably from his period of work with Anatoly Sobchak, the mayor of St Petersburg until 1996. Before his appointment as Prime Minister in 1999, Putin himself could be considered to be part of the personal network of Anatoliy Chubais, who had left for Moscow years before Putin, though not perhaps part of his power network.[23] However when Putin became President, he also became the centre of his power networks, relying on them to achieve his main targets: economic growth, stability and control of the Russian regions. As early as 2001, *Vedomosti* awarded the title of 'Politician of the year 2001' to 'collective Putin'. The nomination has been described as follows:

Putin appointed his St Petersburg contacts to these key posts: Minister of Defence – Sergei Ivanov; Interior Minister – Boris Gryslov; he 'helped' Sergei Mironov get elected to the post of Speaker of the Federation Council; he 'made' Alexei Miller become the head of Gazprom, Russia's largest company. And this is just the tip of the iceberg. St Petersburg appointees are now in charge of Sheremet´evo Airport, the nuclear complex 'TVEL' and a number of non-political but strategically important structures. All these

[23] Anatoly Chubais has been rumoured to have blocked Putin's first job offer in Moscow, whereas Kudrin gave Putin a place to stay in the city.

northwest migrants represent a political unit known as 'President Putin'. People with neutral appearances, sad eyes, quiet voices and cautious judgements work in a coordinated way and without much publicity. Maybe this is the secret of success, and we will witness some positive changes analogous to those taking place at Gazprom.[24]

In many ways, appointing 'executors' of policies and personally loyal people is a common management tool. Leadership implies a team, trusted and tested in electoral, *nomenklatura* or business fights. Putin's economic policies and legal reforms are sometimes associated with the power networks of liberals and sometimes with the power networks of *siloviki*. But such a distinction is nominal from a *sistema* point of view. 'This is a system where no one is allowed to have his point of view', Kryshtanovskaya (2005) said, 'Gref and Kudrin are the so-called liberals, but they were just given the task of being liberals. If the Kremlin asked them to be conservatives, they would act as conservatives' (quoted from Mereu 2007: 1).

The perpetuating role of networks as a 'safety net' has been established as essential in the context of radical change. David Stark argues that network ties are a resource for both navigating the uncertainties of post-socialism and for managing the new uncertainties of the internationalisation of the economy. In their capacity as 'safety nets', power networks represent a third dimension to the existing dichotomy of the vertical (hierarchies) and the horizontal (markets) ones (Stark and Bruszt 2001a, 2001b). Networks are neither vertical nor horizontal. Their 'safety valve' quality resides in their ambiguity and their 'navigational' capacity. They compensate for the defects of vertical and horizontal structures, and also turn these defects to the advantage of the network.

The 'safety net' of *sistema* is embodied by curators (*smotryashchie*) – the supervisory role assumed by authorised agencies in the Russian economy. Putin's Presidency saw the role of the security services in the economy increasing, state shares in large companies going up and the curators' functions being performed by government ministers (Pastukhov 2010). Detailed analyses of state holding dynamics, state corporations and other aspects of state capitalism are available (OECD 2006). Kryshtanovskaya and White number the companies directly subordinated to the Russian government at 68 and publish the list of

---

[24] *Vedomosti*, 29 December 2001, www.vedomosti.ru.

22 officials on the boards of major state companies in 2010 (2011: 30–1).

On a smaller scale, tried and tested people are appointed to take charge of projects. Vladimir Kozhin told one such story about a former head of the FGUP 'Kremlin',[25] Vladimir Kiselev, who had featured in a scandal about misappropriation of funds raised in charity events. As is clear from the quotation, Kiselev's professionalism helped him in getting the job, but his inability to comply with instructions from above made him lose it:

I knew Vladimir for a long time, from Leningrad times. We never had a close personal relationship. This is what enabled him to come to work here, because I believe that when two friends work together, especially when one is subordinate to the other, it always ends badly. We organised FGUP and we offered the top job to Vladimir because it was his specialty: he organised the White Nights festival at St Petersburg – this is how I got to know him, saw him work and remembered his skills. Overall his work with us started well but at some point some unacceptable things happened. They started working largely for themselves: they didn't seek approval of their actions from us, they conducted some independent PR actions, they attracted sponsors – regardless of whether we agreed on them or not. So I had to tell him that it's not going to go on like that. He can do anything – invite anybody he likes, of any orientation, fame or reputation, but not under the umbrella of my department (*upravleniya delami*). That was it. The enterprise was liquidated, shut down and he went into the open sea (*pustilsya v svobodnoe plavanie*).[26]

Needless to say, it is difficult not to step over the public–private boundary in the context of commercial use of Kremlin property. Kremlin guidance occurs in corporate contexts as well, however. An investigation of Putin's contacts in Gazprom by *Novaya Gazeta* provides a list of thirteen people. It includes names such as Victor Khmarin, Alexander Grigoriev, Vladimir Musin, Valerii Golubev, Nikolai Shamalov, Mikhail Putin and Mikhail Shelomov.[27] Some of these might qualify

---

[25] FGUP 'Kremlin' was an enterprise organised to capitalise on the large specialised premises and concert halls in the Kremlin, in Staraya Ploschad´, in large hotels and in sanatoriums that were under-used and expensive to keep. Kiselev was invited to produce events on these premises and to market them for the Kremlin property department (*upravlenie delami*).

[26] Korobov and Kashin (2011: 1).

[27] R. Shleinov, 'Druz´ya prem´era', *Novaya gazeta*, No. 143, 23 December 2009: 12–13.

as 'useful friends,' some as 'front' persons, some as 'parachuters', while some might be representative of the 'safety net' power network.

'Mediated contacts'

Finally, there are networks that are associated with Putin through weak ties and institutional associations: they refer to Putin's place of birth, *alma mater* institutions or army service.[28] Kryshtanovskaya's analysis of political elites shows that territorial origins have been an important factor in appointments under Putin's administration, as well as corporatism associated with his background in sport and the security services (2008).[29] Moreover, as we saw, it became common to refer to appointments at any level as '*piterskie*' (Petersburgers), '*yuristy*' (lawyers), or '*siloviki*' (security service people). Even if an appointment has nothing to do with Putin's personal networks, such references reflect the effect of *sistema* on people's mindset. They assume that there is a network principle operating behind the vertical of power – officials appointing and recruiting their own people at every level – even when it is not always there. Anecdotal evidence suggests that people with 'familiar' surnames enjoy whatever advantages they can get.

Weak ties – party membership, corporate contacts, clubs and hobbies – are complemented by 'personalising' these contacts, or engaging in exchanges of access to gatekeepers with colleagues, friends and family. Belonging to any territorial or educational community, party, or association facilitates personal bonds and ensures preferential appointments, property acquisition, state support for business

---

[28] A surge in hits on the Facebook-type website odnoklassniki.ru that allows people to trace their classmates produced interesting professional and marital dynamics in 2000s, as well as an interest in an informal exchange of favours.

[29] Olga Kryshtanovskaya, Director of the Applied Policy Institute and a scholar on Russian leadership, said that Putin remains a 'shadow tsar' whose allies dominate the executive branch. In a country where the ability to lead often depends on manipulating feuding factions and rewarding loyalty, only two of Medvedev's cabinet members are considered 'his men' – Justice Minister Alexander Konovalov and Nikolai Vinnichenko, Director of the Federal Bailiff Service. The President has two key allies in his administration – Konstantin Chuichenko, head of the Audit Office, and Sergei Dubik, head of the State Service Office. 'There is no balance of power between President Medvedev and Prime Minister Putin. Medvedev is still much weaker. He doesn't have a team of his own. He remains a member of Putin's team' (Kryshtanovskaya 2008).

ventures, jobs and assistance in problem-solving with law-enforcement agencies. There is a curious coincidence associated with Putin, Sechin and Zubkov: they all submitted their doctoral theses at the Mining Institute at St Petersburg. Recent research has revealed the connection of ruling elites in Russia to three of the most prestigious higher education institutions: Moscow State University, the Moscow Institute of International Economy and International Relations (MGIMO) and St Petersburg State University. It has also been revealed that the most prestigious positions among school graduates are those associated with tax and customs agencies and other forms of gatekeeping positions.

The name of this type of power network is not accidental: *mediated* contacts have been essential for Putin's presidency. Putin has been referred to as a 'media President' (*mediinyi*), his leadership style is associated with 'media effects' and his management tools with 'manual' and 'remote' control. Media and the Internet are crucial for Putin's 'managed democracy', media campaigns and media rule (Belin 2004; Fossato and Lloyd 2008; Gehlbach 2010; Hutchings and Rulyova 2009; Lipman and McFaul 2005; Oates 2007; White 2008).

Power networks based on mediated contacts serve as a 'buffer': as communicators and policy 'intermediaries' (Yakubovich 2005). For the leadership, the power networks are the channels of informal governance. Intermediaries perform the essential function of linking social networks – they fill networks' structural holes (Burt 1992a). Intermediaries, or brokers, function at all levels – from securing social benefits and insurance payments at the grassroots, making contacts with media, law enforcement and licensing agencies at the middle level, to obtaining access to the offices of the Prime Minister and the President at the top level. The role of intermediary involves circumventing formal rules and restrictions, overcoming institutional obstacles, speeding up formal procedures, providing introductions and recommendations and, most importantly, anonymity. Just like offshore companies, the intermediaries serve to hide the link between nodes or networks, sometimes legalising that link.

In the 'through-the-looking-glass' logic of *sistema*, lawyers have acquired a specific function, somewhat inverse to their legal expertise. The market of 'legal services' starts from the local police office and mediation in bribing police officers (to have certain documents withdrawn, to commit deliberate errors in the charges so that they will be dropped in court, or to ensure release on bail) to more serious cases, where an intermediary continues to provide assistance with opening and closing criminal cases, with investigation, prosecution and court proceedings (Parshikov 2008). Intermediaries demonstrate a great mastery of power networks – from serving as corrupt channels to officials to manipulating the law and compromising professional standards in the interests of a client (Ledeneva 2006). The use of power networks to direct the workings of institutions or to ensure that they function as designated is an obstacle to the emergence of impersonal systems of trust and creates the path dependency that impedes Russia's modernisation.

Prospects for change

The post-Soviet monetisation of the economy has transformed the workings of power networks in a number of ways. People of the 'inner circle' whose privileges were provided by their position in the hierarchy became interested in creating material wealth outside it. The needs of 'useful friends' have increased from obtaining jobs and items of personal consumption to opportunities for making financial fortunes. The 'core contacts' became less locked into *sistema* and therefore less motivated to pursue the network's interests. 'Mediated contacts' became available for rewards of various kinds and thus less predictable in the outcome. Informal leverage has to be sustained in order to ensure desired outcomes. It may be suggested that Putin's power networks play a wider variety of functions than, say, the power networks of Yeltsin or Gorbachev (see Chapter 7). Identifying trends in the functions of networks, in my view, is more essential to understanding *sistema* than concentrating on personalities and their networks. I argue that the four ideal types of networks operate in different modes or capacities. The inner circle serves to back up a leader and to 'programme', 'filter' and 'develop' the power network. Useful friends benefit from 'authorised' business opportunities, outside the power vertical, and generate resources for the survival of the power network and/or increasing its financial base. Core contacts are more likely to benefit from public appointments within the power vertical and serve as safeguards of both the hierarchy's and the network's interests. The mediated contacts are used for outreaching, 'switching' to a different mode and channelling changes. These functions, with their inherent ambivalence discussed above, are linked to the key features of *sistema*:

- The operational basis of the inner circle is informal and traditional, i.e. based on time/space proximity to the centre of power (the inner circle is defined on the basis of loyalty/strength of ties with the leader)
- Access to resources is decided on a corporate and conspiratorial basis, i.e. patrons provide clients (useful friends) with opportunities or allocate resources in exchange for corporate participation and undisclosed returns
- Core contacts prioritise personal loyalty, stability and risk-avoidance over professionalism and innovation, thus securing a binding force and ensuring the reproduction of *sistema*
- Mediated contacts benefit from affiliation with power networks and contribute to sustaining the dependence on and compliance with the unwritten rules. The non-transparency of *sistema* generates possibilities for rent-seeking, manipulation of rules and unfair advantages for insiders, as well as fear and dissatisfaction among them.

As much as these features seem characteristic of Putin's *sistema*, sometimes referred to as 'neo-Soviet', they are relevant for the late Soviet *sistema*, as well as for the governance patterns in other periods of stability in Russian history (Keenan 1986). Yet one should not underestimate the universal features of network-based governance (see, for example, Christiansen and Piattoni 2003).

The necessity of informal governance is linked to the criss-crossing and overlapping hierarchies – the lack of clarity in the pecking order – associated with the non-hierarchical negotiation process. Decisions require extensive consultation involving private and public actors before any draft proposals are made. Putin's *sistema* – formally highly institutionalised but at the same time requiring continuous negotiations among the actors involved – contains a fundamental tension: policy-making has to follow the rules of formal decision-making rules (and thus obey institutional boundaries, as outlined in Figure 2.5), while at the same time overcome institutional divisions in order to negotiate outcomes. The resort to informal networks has been one important way to resolve this tension. Power networks are established among those involved in particular policies, cutting across institutional affiliations and positions at different levels of policy-making. The presence of networks can help to narrow substantive disagreements among institutional and business actors, exert influence on decision-makers to agree on compromised solutions and facilitate the acceptance of emerging policies in a variety of different domains. Power networks prepare the ground on which formal institutional mechanisms operate in the decision-making process. Much of the work of power networks is informal, in that the contacts among actors are fluid, responsive to the requirements of the situation rather than following formal procedures. Networks come into being mostly through personal relationships – activating common interests, shared views and mutual recognition – and generate valuable resources such as knowledge, solutions and visions.

Power networks have a decision capacity that can move matters forward but can also involve exchange based upon gatekeeping mechanisms and 'favours of access' (their functional ambivalence illustrated in Figure 2.4). Admission to a decision-making network tends to be exchanged for conformity with existing practices, thus making the decision-making more rigid, as well as for concealment of policy-sensitive information, thus making the decision-making more secretive. Reliance on a select circle of implementing power networks is coupled with neglect for procedural correctness for insiders and exaggerated demand for procedural correctness for outsiders. These phenomena then border on practices of clientelism, usually seen as inefficient and illegitimate (Christiansen and Piattoni 2003). Compromising decisions and goal diversion are inevitable consequences of such practices, but fraud and corruption can also be the outcome. Is it possible to 'modernise' the clientelist patterns within power networks? In order to answer this question, I consider logics of recruitment, operation, reproduction and exit from *sistema* in Chapter 3.

3 | *The inner workings of* sistema: *from* blat *to* otkat

Putin on *sistema*: 'manual control'

At the meeting of the Valdai discussion club with President Putin in September 2005, the author of this book posed a question on corruption. Not corruption in Russia in general, but corruption within the Kremlin walls. Previous heads of the Russian state were known to rely on their security services for gathering and keeping sensitive information (*kompromat* files) on their staff, peers and enemies, so I asked the President what information he sought and used on a regular basis with regard to corruption. I also wondered whether there was an anti-corruption strategy at the Presidential level.

The immediate answer was a smile. A knowing smile, I thought. His following remarks, especially the reference to his KGB work experience with information and its ineffectiveness, made other Russians in the room smile too. As with the majority of questions, Putin took time answering it. According to my notes, he expressed some surprise that I asked about the Kremlin, as budget matters were decided elsewhere. He also pointed out that the problem of corruption resides not in people, but in the system. Therefore, targeting people with *kompromat* is ineffective. One must target the system, and that can only be done against the background of economic growth and political stability. Naturally, I was intrigued by his reference to *sistema* and pondered over his answers and their possible interpretations in the context of *sistema* vertical and *sistema* power networks (see Box 3.1)

The systemic nature of corruption was similarly distinguished from corruption in power networks in an interview with another senior Kremlin insider:

I have worked *vo vlasti* [in the PA – AL] for some time. I can tell you, corruption there is not a total evil, absolutely not total, not at all. To say that people who work in the PA, or in the government, think about how to earn money or to get a bribe or something – of course not. It's full of people

Valentin Dubinin, 'Power' (Vlast´), http://caricatura.ru/parad/dubinin/10939/
and www.valdub.ru

Box 3.1 Corruption within the Kremlin: Putin's answers and possible interpretations, 2005

Putin said	'Vertical' interpretation	'Network' interpretation
The Kremlin does not allocate funds (budget)	There is little corruption in the Kremlin as such because federal resources (the budget) are distributed elsewhere (kickbacks for favourable allocation of resources are implied but are associated with formal hierarchies in charge of distribution of resources)	Most high-level corruption occurs in the government (i.e. centres of distribution of the state budget) but the PA is part of the formal hierarchy of funds allocation and operates on the basis of indirect forms of involvement and influence
Corruption is in the system and not in people	It is insufficient to punish people on a selective basis; one has to create a framework in which corruption is punished universally, and we are working on it	We turn a blind eye to what the people with whom we work are forced to do as a result of systemic pressure – otherwise there would be no one to work with
I worked in the KGB for fifteen years and can tell you that personal files, documents and confidential information are not effective	We have all the necessary information. We know everything there is to know about corruption in the Kremlin, and elsewhere; the problem is that corruption is	We are aware of the capacity of informational pressure and apply it in a selective manner in order to control people who have lost their sense

(*cont.*)

Putin said	'Vertical' interpretation	'Network' interpretation
instruments – they simply do not work	systemic and selective measures do not change the system: therefore, they do not work	of proportion; however, to punish everybody is ineffective
We will target the system	We need to create a framework in which people respect the law and learn to live by it, but you cannot change their behaviour overnight; it's an incremental process which requires economic growth, effective law enforcement and political stability: we are moving in this direction	We do not target people and do not punish those we know until the time is right; we have to be realistic about the targets we can achieve Elimination of corruption at this stage is not realistic; we do not have a strategy/business plan to address it; it is not a priority in our political agenda before 2008; it will be the next president's priority[1]

who either have come from business, made a lot of money already and now are getting a kick out of working, or the other way around: they plan to go into business and make money later. This is normal. Of course, things happen, and there is corruption. I am not saying there isn't. But I am saying that it is not a total evil. In some sectors of course, corruption is systemic,

[1] The priority of corruption for the next President was discussed at the 2006 Valdai discussion at Novo-Ogaryovo.

for example, in the traffic police... But when people say 'all *chinovniki* are corrupt' this is a projection and the rumour mill (*sarafannoe radio*). In reality people have no personal experience beyond [the] municipal level, militia and traffic police. They judge on the basis of legends, myths and hot journalist stories about corrupt politicians... This tells us that, at the level of people's experience, the level of corruption is the worst.

Separating *sistema* from its officials, officials from people, collective perception of corruption levels from individual experience of it and media stories from daily routines, as in the quotation above, are all important points to balance the one-sided negative coverage that Russia often receives. Yet such a divide also helps 'misrecognise' one's own role in day-to-day connivance with the workings of *sistema*. *Sistema* insiders tend to operate in a practical rather than a reflexive mode and resort to denial narratives if pressed to reflect on their practices. Just as in the *blat* misrecognition game, where the use of *blat* is 'misrecognised' as friendship in one's own case but 'recognised' as *blat* in others', the misrecognition of *sistema* officials, as discussed in Chapter 1, is central to its workings and reproduction. In accordance with Putin's line on incremental change of the system, requiring improvement in economic growth, effective law enforcement and stability of the political system, the respondent above emphasised that currently Russia cannot rely on either the institutions of civil society or any institutionalised system of checks and balances:

Before those institutions develop in Russia, we have to hope that those in power will exercise self-restraint, which of course does not always work but which evolves slowly and gradually. In [the] majority of cases those in power are guided by best intentions... and they have to think of the people, because Russia is governed on manual control (*v ruchnom rezhime*).

Deciding whether institutional defects create the demand for 'manual control', or whether manual control restricts the development of institutional capacity, is the chicken-and-egg dilemma. In Putin's Russia, 'manual control' is guided by best intentions but the 'right' outcomes are achieved by the use of the administrative resource and informal governance, especially when it comes to the issues of political stability, party politics and control of the media:

People have no set political preferences, television decides everything. A party's popularity can be boosted from zero up to 30 per cent. We need time for these political preferences to develop but, while they are emerging, it's manual control. What does Putin think? There are no assets that belong to no-one (*u nas nicheinogo ne byvaet*): if the state does not control the media, big business will control them. Putin thinks, yes, it does cost us (*izderzhki*), yes, this is unfortunate politically, and yes, I get criticised for it (*s gryaz´yu za eto meshayut*). But for the time being, I have no other way... What else can I do if people are ready to vote for a populist?

Putin's 'manual control' is in some way consistent with the *modus operandi* of the Soviet administrative system, where media executives were a key part of the *nomenklatura*. The same applies to other branches of power, including judicial, political and legislative, because they turn into 'personalised bureaucracies' and comply with oral commands.

Corrupt implications of a 'personalised' bureaucracy

In her monograph *The System Made Me Do It*, Rasma Karklins approached the subject of *sistema* through corruption (2005). Most contemporary definitions of corruption are based on the assumption that the transition to rational–legal systems of rule is complete and that corruption can be understood as 'the abuse of public office for private gain' (Alatas 1990; Johnston 1986; Kaufmann 1997; Rose-Ackerman 1999; Tanzi 1998; UNDP 2004). Although the precise wording varies, most conceptual formulations of corruption can be understood as involving the 'twisting' (betrayal, diversion, misuse, abuse, manipulation, exploitation) of something public (office, duty, good, trust, funds, resources, power, influence) into something private (gain, profit, benefit, advantage, interest). Most definitions refer or allude to deviance from the normative view on how things should be done – a move away from the public (communal, institutional, formal) and toward the private (personalised, unauthorised, informal). In other words, corruption is a modern concept, associated with the transformation of what Weber described as 'patrimonial power structures', where decisions are taken on the basis not of institutionalised rules but of personal relationships and traditional forms of authority (Weber 1968). Transformations of this kind lead to rational–legal and legal systems, where rules are institutionalised to such an extent that corruption can be conceptualised as a deviation from them. In historical terms, the practices inherent in patrimonial power turn into corrupt practices within a modern framework. Thus, the modernisation of bureaucracy initiated by Peter the Great in Russia undermined the custom of paying tribute to officials, eventually criminalising what had previously been regarded an acceptable practice (Klyuchevskii 1987: 209–10; Lovell *et al.* 2000). Its subsequent codification as an act of bribery allowed the tsarist state to make some attempts to combat the practice, albeit fitfully and not very successfully. Similarly, the 1990s transformation of post-Communist societies and efforts to harmonise their legislative and institutional frameworks with those of advanced market democracies have resulted, with varying degrees of success, in increasingly sophisticated instruments aimed at fighting corruption.

When Weber set out an ideal type of bureaucracy, he associated it with a hierarchical division of labour, directed by explicit rules that are impersonally applied; staffed by full-time, life-time professionals who do not in any sense own the means of administration, their jobs or the sources of their funds, and live off a salary rather than from income derived directly from the performance of their job. These are all features found in public service, in the offices of private firms, in universities and so on. Weber contrasted the bureaucracy to 'prebends' or 'benefices', meaning an office with some income-yielding property, e.g. a farm or tax-gathering rights from which the office holder lives. The notion of corruption made little sense in patrimonial systems where jobs were given away to loyal kin in order to feed their holders. The prebend officially owns his job and expects tribute for performing it, as opposed to a modern bureaucrat who is paid a salary for following the official rules reliably and is not allowed to charge fees for himself or to accept gifts (as this constitutes the misuse of public office for private gain).[2]

Not many post-Communist countries, let alone Russia, meet the modernity standard set out by Weber. In Weber's terms, the public

---

[2] Some governments have sold offices to raise money, such as judicial positions in eighteenth-century France and commissions in the army and navy in most European countries in the nineteenth century.

administration in Russia could be pictured as 'prebends' – feeding off the job – through their social networks and institutionalised practices of kickbacks and/or unofficial payments. Boundaries in perception of public and private spheres in post-Communist countries are blurred and routinely crossed through the use of personal networks for achieving goals in public domains. This generates forms of expediency that are not conducive to modernisation and that present an obstacle to the rationality of the 'rule of law'. Richard Rose describes state institutions in Russia as 'pre-modern' (Rose 2000). Kets de Vries *et al.* emphasise both a supremacy of friendship and 'bureaupathology' in the Russian national character that determines the operations not only of state institutions, but also private firms (Kets de Vries *et al.* 2004: 24–7).

Grounded in both Soviet and Russian legacies and a routine everyday occurrence, corruption tends to be 'misrecognised'. It is characteristic that the existing typologies of corruption are unlikely to be used by 'participants' (Karklins 2005; Knack 2006). If those involved in corrupt practices are at all present in such analytical frameworks, more often than not these 'deviants' are not conceptually given a voice. Most anthropologists object to such approaches and take pains not to follow the economists' path of evaluating actual practices against abstract models, but have instead sought to describe and analyse the activities actually taking place. The findings of anthropological research on post-socialism indicate that what, from the political science perspective, appear as instances of corruption are, in fact, new and interesting hybrids of Communist and post-Communist forms of exchange that may not add up to 'market democracy' or 'capitalism', and are understood best on their own terms (Caldwell 2004; Grant 1995; Ries 1997; Rivkin-Fish 2005). These bottom-up accounts focused on networks or practices are sometimes hard to distinguish from the revisionist accounts that emphasise the 'functionality' of corrupt networks and practices in overcoming institutional defects and in lubricating overly rigid political or bureaucratic regimes (Kaufmann 1997). For example, Michael Johnston (1986: 460) identifies the practices that link people and groups into lasting networks of exchange and shared interest as 'integrative' corrupt exchanges. From my perspective, the bottom-up accounts are important as they give voice to those capable of explaining the demands and pressures of *sistema*, of identifying tensions between formal duties and informal commitments and of understanding the driving forces behind the 'economy of kickbacks'.

Sistema recruitment: who can belong?

To point out the importance of social networks, *The Economist* business travel blog warns outsiders that Russians devote much energy to relationships and friendships, and that the concept of professional ties without personal contact is alien (*The Economist* 2008). Insiders learn about the personalisation of governance structures differently – the socialisation in *sistema*'s initiation rites, sanctions, criteria for appointment and promotion creates incentives for loyalty and compliance with the 'rules of the game'. In her analysis of the anatomy of the Russian elite, Olga Kryshtanovskaya remarks:

The rules of the game, never fixed or articulated, looked like a puzzle for outsiders but were clear and transparent for insiders. Esoteric norms regulated all spheres of elite activities but were revealed only if they were violated. A novice, who found himself inside the system, had to resort to his own devices, [as] in Kafka's *Castle*, in order to decode the hidden meanings and to understand the unwritten rules. He remained in the group if he solved the puzzle and was excluded if his intuition was not tuned to read between the lines. (Kryshtanovskaya 2005: 88)[3]

A former senior insider, who came to work in the Kremlin from the outside, as did Putin, recalls:

I ended up at the Kremlin by chance... I was never a career official like Kas´yanov, for example, who graduated from the right institute and went through all the stages: deputy head and head of sector, head of department, etc., then a deputy minister, first deputy minister, minister, vice-premier, first vice-premier, acting PM, PM, and then... then it's the end of the world [being sacked – AL]. I didn't have anything like that. Before I came to work in the Kremlin, I was there only once, on a school trip, and then after some time [laughs] came to take up a job. I was in two minds over taking it for quite a while but then like everybody else I was drawn into it (*vtyanulsya*),

---

[3] In the preface to her monograph, Kryshtanovskaya also uses the metaphor of the Kafkaesque castle. Such references militate against an argument for uniqueness: that a game must be learned is a universal principle of mastery of the game. The nitty-gritty of those rules constitutes their uniqueness.

things happened, I settled in (*prizhilsya*) . . . although in the beginning it was hard psychologically, many things irritated me. Those things made it easier for me to leave.

I failed to follow up on the 'many things' in this interview. Secondary sources highlight informal pressures, especially at the top level of managers in Presidential and federal administrative structures. In the context of that conversation, it could be specific human qualities associated with 'groomed appointments'. Another respondent, a lawyer experienced in dealing with *sistema* officials, makes a comment to that effect:

> Appointments might seem haphazard but often it is a long-term process of 'raising one's own people' (*rastyat svoikh lyudei*). In order to get an appointment or to be promoted to a certain position, one should demonstrate compliance – this is the way to get there. *Svoi lyudi* can be tied up by emotional ties of friendship, camaraderie, or loyalty. But they are also tried and tested people, who are supposed to be efficient and have a reputation for reliability and getting things done.

Values of loyalty and obedience do not always predominate over qualifications and professionalism – the criteria for an appointment may include both formal requirements and informal filters. Both are essential for understanding the inner workings of public administration in Russia, yet informal filters are often hidden and informal codes of conduct left unspoken. The generic paradox of *sistema* is that of 'open secrets' – shared yet unarticulated experiences. Let us look into *sistema*'s criteria for recruitment more closely, starting at the top.

The logic of *sistema*'s appointments seems to have survived the collapse of Communism and the upheavals of electoral democracy. Analysts suggest that the criteria of the (s)election of President Medvedev by Putin were not much different from the criteria of Yeltsin's choice of Putin and were generally similar to the logic of appointing weak, dependent Soviet leaders (Solov´ev and Zlobin 2010: 40). They distinguished the following criteria, in the order of importance: lack of Presidential ambitions; lack of candidate's own team; lack of serious back-up from the military and security forces (*siloviki*); lack of significant personal financial resources (Solov´ev and Zlobin 2010: 41–3); and, I would add, lack of experience and expertise for the job and lack of personal charisma, at least at the time of appointment.

It should be noted that hidden criteria are formulated in negative terms and applied as filters. *Sistema* filters out qualities that are dangerous for it – essentially, independence, in terms of both personality and resources. It can be suggested that negative filtering is related to the idea of 'negative identity' of Russians, conceptualised by Lev Gudkov (2004). In 'positive' terms, the informal criteria that I came across included: loyalty in personal relations; capacity to read and decipher *sistema* signals;[4] and understanding of and compliance with unwritten rules (*ponyatiya*) (Solov´ev and Zlobin 2010: 43, 51, 53).[5] In pragmatic terms, Yeltsin needed someone who would protect 'the family', and Putin had demonstrated his loyalty in the Mabetex affair, concerning the kickbacks to Kremlin officials from the Swiss-based company that renovated the Kremlin.

Where outsiders are recruited into *sistema*, criteria of personal loyalty are substituted by other ways of 'personalising' appointments. A bank owner involved in serving the key corporate clients in the country gives an example:

Personal vouching or recommendation (*lichnoe poruchitel´stvo*) is essential. For example, a minister wants to appoint somebody and invites him for a friendly chat, normally to establish whom he knows and how, and my name comes up in the conversation. The minister calls me and asks if I would recommend this person. I speak very generally: 'as far as I know he is *korporativnyi chelovek* [a person who follows the corporate rules of *sistema* – AL].' So the appointment goes through. But the funny thing is that if there is any problem with this appointee, I will be asked to step in to solve the problem informally.

Informal leverage is part and parcel of personal loyalty. Compliance can be generated by fear of responsibility, by a prospect of financial and/or legal implications of falling out with *sistema*, as well as by an 'acute sense of subordination'. This characteristic featured in a description of a staffer in the PA by a colleague:

---

[4] The Russian pun, coined by the Chief of Staff Alexander Voloshin, is a play on a successor (*priemnik*), or receiver (*priyomnik*) being unable to be so without a predecessor, or a transmitter of signals (*peredatchik*) (Solov´ev and Zlobin 2010: 51).

[5] Thus, Putin is known for not sacking any of 'his own' people and rewarding personal loyalty (Solov´ev and Zlobin 2010: 53).

Well, people tend to demonise him but he is not a menace. He has an acute sense of subordination and never prompts or pushes the boss. Such compliance is an outcome of his 'adjustment process'... Originally he didn't plan to stay in the PA, but having gone through all these torments he adapted. Nothing big happened. There are a lot of people up there who had ideas, but had to adapt somehow and stay on the lead... But they are all normal people. If not today then tomorrow, they will occupy high places, and there will be more and more of them. It's not all bad.

Being dissolved in social interactions within networks, informal criteria of recruitment are not always transparent, even to those who apply them. When articulated by experts and analysts, they sound crude, unfair and thus impossible for insiders to admit them, even if they see the point. For example, 'in a nutshell, both Putin and Medvedev became presidents by acquaintance – how very Russian!' (Solov′ev and Zlobin 2010: 49) is a pointed comment on the electoral culture in Russia. Michael Waller concludes more generally that in countries where democracy is new or weakly rooted, personal relationships and networks are readily used and accepted as substitutes for a democratic electoral process (Waller 2005: 36).[6]

In times of 'virtual politics', members of the 'inner circle' become 'appointed' to an elected position or given high positions with status and legal immunity (Wilson 2005). In the private sector, 'useful friends' become 'appointed millionaires' and are given opportunities to make fortunes. In the public sector, 'core contacts' are 'appointed' with an entitlement for 'feeding' opportunities (those who don't benefit from kickbacks are reported to be compensated with cash bonuses). 'Mediated contacts' benefit from the workings of *sistema* and are themselves instrumental for channelling its power and for manipulating the public. Putin's appointments of St Petersburgers exposed such informal criteria; even then, respondents struggled to define them. This peer pressure is taken for team spirit by a former insider, now London-based:

There are certain agreements at the time of appointment that of course can be broken at a later stage, so there are also mechanisms to keep [them] in

---

[6] Up to a point Waller is right, but in Britain Tony Blair and David Cameron both brought *svoi lyudi* into Downing Street and the civil service and manipulated the media indirectly. Cameron's network is now partly unravelling. In France the strong personal ties created at educational institutions such as Sciences Po dominate government. State officials have personal ties to business, finance, and media magnates.

place. If some agreement has been broken for some reason (or if one says 'no' in a situation where one is supposed to say 'yes') then psychological factors start [to work]. It is not even an individual choice, it's just [that] you are a member of the team, of a network, and a certain code prescribes that you can't deviate from it without breaking out of the team spirit. Reliance on such practices backs up the lack of accountability (*bespredel*) of the state bureaucratic machine.

Russian academics conceptualise the informality of the Kremlinate politics in terms of Russia's '*sistema*-centric genotype' that opposes the 'individual-centric genotype' (Chesnokova and Chesnokova 2007; Obolonskii 1994; Prokhorov 2002; Sergeeva 2008; Timofeev 1993; Yanov 2007, 2008). *Sistema* effectively blocks any personality, process or tendency that would threaten the existing *sistema*-centric pattern of social interaction. One has to credit *sistema* – it has a perfect self-preservation instinct, it is exceptionally sensitive to anything that can be a potential threat to it. The reaction is always to extinguish, to stamp out and to destroy at an embryonic stage (Obolonskii 1994).

The ways of *sistema* recruitment do seem to be changing – international assistance with administrative reforms, the presence of head-hunting firms and expanding human resource services have benefited the public sector. The problem however remains that, even when – as with the Skolkovo project to build a high-tech research and development hub – *sistema* is forced to prioritise professionalism under pressure of the rapidly developing market economy or the impact of globalisation, the grip of informal filters remains strong, thanks to their elusive nature and their role in sustaining the operation of power networks. When I inquired in interviews whether informal filters had more traditional or more pragmatic origins, one respondent called it 'genetic informality', another referred to it as coming from nature (*prirodnoe*) and yet another called it 'normal'.[7] *Sistema*'s unarticulated informal filters originate in traditional ways of getting things done, but also serve pragmatic purposes. In a Moscow interview, a respondent with experience of many government departments emphasised the difference in *sistema*'s recruitment depending on the kickback potential of the position:

---

[7] In the Russian *LiveJournal*, one comment on my 2009 article on *blat* and informality was: 'What if informal relationships are the norm, and it is their formalisation that is a deviation from norm?'

It happens differently these days: sometimes by *blat* (*po znakomstvu*), sometimes by resumé. There are many young interesting people, but there are also corrupt types. As a rule, primary recruitment does not involve money. It is later, in various ways and in the process of adaptation (*pritirki*), that people get subjected to a more subtle tuning, or get tested in deals, and then get fixed in certain positions, where there could be corrupt opportunities. In a department with kickback potential, cash could be paid for an appointment, but we are talking [about] a very limited range of positions – those associated with [rapid] income opportunities. In those positions, however, there are no occasional people, they know exactly whom they are recruiting, they select people more or less professionally qualified, but not on the basis of professional criteria.

In pragmatic terms, where rewards are distributed through a system of informal kickbacks, an independent professional with whistle-blowing potential would be unemployable. Therefore, in addition to professional expertise and institutional competence, the kin and social networks of the candidate ensure his or her 'fitness' for *sistema* and compliance with the informal ways of getting things done. Intermediaries can be used for such purposes.

Economy of kickbacks: *sistema*'s control of informal financial flows

The benefits of belonging to *sistema* can include access to corrupt income. Informal payments, or kickbacks (*otkat*), have become the core *modus operandi* of *sistema*, where informal income is shared – 'delivered' or 'lifted' – and to networks, through which such income can be received, hidden, invested or consumed. According to Alexander Chepurenko of the Higher School of Economics, state officials accumulate significant economic resources by combining rent-seeking behaviour and the so-called 'administrative rent' (*administrativnaya renta*), with entrepreneurial activities and profits received by their family, relatives or associates. In his view, the income drawn from the use of the 'administrative resource' is the hidden foundation of the growing middle class in Russia. As a result, the social stability associated with the middle class is rather specific, since it is based upon the shadowy rental incomes that state officials squeeze out of their positions in formal hierarchies and informal networks – 'in other words, bribes and kickbacks' (Iusupova 2007).

At the top end of the spectrum of kickbacks are those associated with state capture. Experts estimate that 'state services' include: the introduction of a false entry into the budget – from 4 per cent of the allocated sum; the signing of additional export quotas – from 10 per cent of market value; kickbacks for the signature of a state order – 20 per cent of the sum; the transfer of a budget allocation – from 5 per cent of the sum; kickbacks for the export of cheap gas – 50 per cent of the difference between the market and agreed price (Davydova 2006).

Actual numeric estimates are not as important as the identified patterns of services – the informal practices that penetrate all branches of power. In the legislative branch, so-called deputies' services include: custom-made legislation – from $0.5 million; introduction of draft legislation for consideration in the State Duma – from $0.5 million; introduction of amendments to legislation – from $0.2 million; adoption of legislation on tax, customs tariffs and customs regulation – from 10 per cent of the potential profit; a vote in favour of a certain outcome – from $2,000 (per vote); organising a deputy request to the Prosecutor General's Office (PGO) – from $50,000 (Davydova 2006; Nemtsov and Milov 2008).

In mature democracies, such services are associated with lobbying. They are regulated by both legislation on lobbying and preventive measures to protect legislative, judicial and law enforcement institutions from lobbyism. So far there has been no progress on such legislation in Russia, despite the efforts and initiatives of various think tanks.[8] Efforts by groups of individuals or entrepreneurs to influence the country's legislature in their own interest – state capture – entail significant cost and expertise (Pavlenko 2002: 79–96). Typically, such networks of acquaintances strive to push through amendments to certain laws or new legislation that would bring economic advantages. A range of legitimate and shadow technologies of lobbying in the Russian State Duma by ministries and agencies is described in a book on such lobbying practices (Tolstykh 2006: 140–9).

At the bottom end of the spectrum (as estimated by a member of the public on one of the anti-corruption websites) kickbacks are collected

---

[8] See the anti-corruption analysis of forestry legislation in Krasnov *et al.* (2004). Authors propagate legislation that would not only forbid public administrators to get involved directly or indirectly with entrepreneurial activities or to receive covert rewards for pushing through certain decisions, but also restrict the number of loopholes in the legislation that allow for arbitrariness and lobbying.

and 'lifted' monthly from small firms at the level of $1,000. They serve to establish contact with various controlling organs (technical safety, sanitary inspection, police, fire inspection, local authorities, etc.). The actual sum depends entirely on the size of the company and its location. But multiplying an average of $1,000 by the number of firms registered in Moscow, a very rough estimate amounts to about $200 million monthly, or $2.4 billion a year (Forumfontanka.ru 2007).

Where informal payments are impossible to discuss with the bribe-takers directly, bribe-givers tend to be more willing to talk. Research by the Russian think tank INDEM assesses payments to officials by the business sector. Although half of the businessmen approached refused to answer the question about the share of bribes in the monthly turnover of their firms, 25 per cent of companies indicated that they pay state officials up to 5 per cent of their turnover, 13 per cent of firms from 5 to 10 per cent, 5 per cent of firms from 10 to 20 per cent and 2.5 per cent of firms as much as 20–50 per cent (Satarov *et al.* 2005). This research shows that kickbacks vary from 10 per cent on deliveries of IT equipment to 50 per cent on orders for scientific research. A new employee of a state IT service, Ivan, who has come from business, says:

I used to be sceptical about state officials. But now I feel much worse about them. [An atmosphere of] denunciation, set ups, incompetence and unwillingness to work – [pervades] not just our organisation but most state structures. If people knew the scale of theft that is going on, they would simply come and set fire to it all. (Iusupova, 2007)

By 2010, the estimate of kickbacks in the IT sector reached up to 75 per cent. The president of a large software firm, Cognitive Technologies, identified the following trend in kickback dynamics. In her view, in 1996–9, kickbacks amounted up to 10 per cent of the contract value; in 1999–2003, up to 20 per cent; in 2003–5, up to 35 per cent; in 2005–8, up to 40 per cent; in 2008–9, up to 60 per cent; in 2009–10, up to 75 per cent (Uskova 2010). She also said that the scale of impunity, childlike naïvite and lack of boundaries was striking: for example, 'an official of one of the largest ministries suggested paying him 75 percent of the contract'.[9] The insurance for

---

[9] The firm Cognitive Technologies was created in 1993 and employs 683 people (Uskova 2010).

builders on state contracts is reported to hit the 80 per cent mark for kickbacks, although building firms quote a maximum of 30 per cent, and only on very large contracts.[10]

The formal side is preserved: there are open competitions and tenders. Behind the facade, state officials might delegate writing the IT specification to a computer firm that will eventually win the tender and reserve the right to request the appropriate kickback in the event of allocating budget funds to that particular firm. The task of the IT firm is to complete the project within the budget allocated. Other schemes in public procurement ensure that companies win public tenders because their owners or managers are related to (or financially associated with) officials in charge of tender commissions or to members of these commissions (NEWSru 2008b). Satarov's study (2005) finds that the majority of IT contracts to state-run companies such as Gazprom or RAO EES are loss-making. The benefits come from their affiliation with the big names, rather than their actual contracts with them.

Measurements of business corruption are an important indicator of the power of social networks in public administration. Business Environment and Enterprise Performance Surveys (BEEPS) showed that businessmen claim considerable expenditures on interactions with corrupt officials (BEEPS 1999, 2002, 2005, 2009). My own research has identified informal practices, particularly those based on interaction between public administration and business, that are essential for operation of both the formal and informal economy and for compensating for the defects of impersonal systems of trust in Russia (Ledeneva 2006; Ledeneva and Shekshnia 2011). It goes without saying that every bribe requires a support network to provide information, introduction, delivery, security and performance, and the bribing practices become more and more sophisticated.

Commercial structures serve the needs of *sistema* as institutional intermediaries. Russian banks tend to play a dual role *vis-à-vis* the state tax organs – they are both taxpayers to, and agents of, the fiscal organs (Hainsworth and Thomson 2001).[11] Since a substantial share of tax revenues is collected via the bank payments system, the tax authorities

---

[10] A. Rozhkov and A. Filatov, 'Otkat-80%', *Vedomosti*, 24 September 2010: 7.
[11] That would be true not only for banks but for all organisations, as all employers collect income taxes.

rely heavily on banks not only to provide information about clients' finances, but also to cooperate in tax collection (Tompson 2007). This practice creates an incentive for firms to conduct transactions in cash. However, the use of 'black cash' strategies by firms is limited, and typically requires the banks' help in obtaining large quantities of cash in violation of restrictions on the use of cash for inter-company transactions. Hence, banks play a critical role in so-called 'tax optimisation' strategies. The centrality of banks in managing informal financial flows is the key to understanding the scale and the *modus operandi* of the informal economy in contemporary Russia.

The relationship between the taxpayer and tax collector normally is not based on negotiation but in Russia, as Hainsworth and Thompson (2001) indicate, 'The bargained tax bill is no more a paradox than was the bargained plan' (Tompson 2007). Unlike the use of 'black cash' or bribes (*tenevye skhemy*), many tax schemes are grounded in legal loopholes and can be more properly described as tax avoidance/tax optimisation than tax evasion. Taxpayers exploit the defects in tax legislation that, according to some respondents, may have been deliberately left in place. The centrality of law in such creative scheming, however, is a noticeable and positive development (Berenson 2008). At the same time, practices of speeding up return of VAT (from 10 per cent of the returned sum), paying for the withdrawal of a tax claim (from 10 per cent of the sum of the claim), or for setting up a tax inspection for a competitor (from $50,000) are commonly known and used. A FSB-linked businessman in the energy sector emphasised the need to have contacts in the right places in order to make such contexts negotiable:

Good contacts [in the FSB] can help one receive a warning of a planned tax inspection visit, and an intelligence of how much they expect to collect, so that when they come you are ready to negotiate peacefully and to find a mutually agreeable way to settle the bill. Both sides understand the demands and the costs of staying in line with *sistema*.

Such negotiations are reminiscent of nuances in the Soviet connotations of '*svoi*' highlighted by anthropologists. In her study of the Russian soul, Dale Pesman defines the term '*svoi*' as confidence to speak openly without fearing that what one says will be used against one (2000: 165) *e svoi* is relevant predominantly for private settings. Alexei Yurchak defines '*svoi*' in public settings more inclusively as 'normal people' – those who also understand the norms of public settings and how they differ from private ones. For example, the norm of paying the Komsomol membership fee on time had to be observed as a ritual; everyone had to participate in these routine rituals so as not to cause problems either for the *komsorgs* (Komsomol leaders) or for themselves (Yurchak 2005: 110). Similarly, paying kickbacks in the post-Komsomol Wonderland keeps one on '*svoi*' terms with *sistema*. When I asked whether there were rules or codes of behaviour around kickbacks, one respondent, a businessman, came up with a new normality code for an official:

One should take kickbacks openly so that others know about it. Moreover, one should give advance warning to one's superiors and ask for feedback [presumably some form of consent and approval for the percentage – AL]. One should also share the spoils with subordinates. One should never think of [the] spoils as one's own. Easy come easy go. We do not have private property. It's only a facade. In reality, everybody is fed up with Putin's *sistema*, but there is no way out of it.

The kickbacks' percentage will depend on the network one belongs to. There are instances when contacts in high places are used to lower the percentage of kickbacks on a state contract, and there are instances where clients compete for the opportunity to pay kickbacks, the size of which is not even negotiable. Entering the informal kickbacks' payroll can be read as a sign of recognition and as evidence of a working relationship. A media-related respondent sums it up as follows:

For us, it is about US$100,000 monthly. Every month we deliver and we distribute. This is very important. This is the basis of good relations. To suck up, not to let down, to display loyalty is crucial.

How could the Russian economy afford to carry such a burden of kickbacks in the 2000s? Analysts attribute it to the unprecedented growth of oil prices during Putin's two Presidential terms. The pattern of rent-seeking behaviour by state officials is typical for petrol states generally, where brokers' services become sophisticated and well paid (Hertog 2010). Yet Russia is different because there is little foreign investment and its 'governmentality' carries traces of an imperial past. Statism plays a role in supporting *sistema*, where business networks are expected to serve state priorities rather than their own business agendas. Even where kickbacks may have been initiated by businessmen, bureaucrats have grasped the initiative and abused their monopoly for extortion. It has been suggested that the 'state capture' practices of the 1990s, where businesses were predominantly the initiators of informal payments, have given place to 'business capture', where the initiative has been seized by state agencies. An OECD 2006 report notes that the Russian state significantly expanded its role in the economy in 2004–6, particularly in 'strategic' sectors such as oil and gas. It goes on to argue that 'the expansion of state ownership in important sectors will probably contribute to more rent-seeking, less efficiency and slower growth' (OECD 2006: 33–8). There subsequently emerged new 'grey areas' of conflict of interest and informal influence, associated with the practices of the government's supervision and representation on boards of large state-controlled companies.[12]

Back in 2008, Dmitri Medvedev said he was against the practice of placing state officials on the boards of major corporations: 'I think there is no reason for the majority of state officials to sit on the boards of those firms' (Elder 2008). Nearly all the country's top officials – from the then deputy head of the PA turned Deputy Prime Minister, Igor Sechin, who chaired the oil major Rosneft, to Finance Minister Alexei Kudrin, who chaired the boards of the Vneshtorgbank (VTB) and the diamond monopoly Alrosa – also headed the boards of state companies (see the 2010 list of officials on the boards of major state companies in Kryshtanovskaya and White 2011: 31).

In 2011, President Medvedev stated again that government officials should not serve on company boards, demanding that cabinet ministers step down by the end of June. He said the move would lead to better management of state-run companies and improve the investment climate in the country.[13] Now top officials are replaced by 'truly independent directors, whom the state would hire' to implement its plans. In terms of corporate governance, it is hard to see how directors hired by the state can be independent, but the formal dissociation from the government and the Kremlin is a step forward. From the network

---

[12] Even more interesting in this respect, coordinated with the existing legislation, are the state corporations created toward the end of Putin's second term in office (Volkov *et al.* 2011).

[13] 'Kudrin vows to quit boards of VTB bank, diamond firm Alrosa', *RIA-Novosti*, 16 April 2011, http://en.rian.ru/business/20110416/163553909.html.

perspective, 'truly independent directors' will continue to channel signals and represent informal affiliations and loyalties, but their actions are likely to become even less transparent.

The independence and personal integrity of state officials are undermined by the necessity for them to work in the context of systemic corruption and power network in-fighting. A particularly high-profile case, sometimes interpreted as an attack on the then Minister of Finance, Alexei Kudrin, was the arrest in November 2007 of Kudrin's deputy, Sergei Storchak, who was accused of embezzling in a large-scale fraud scheme. He was eventually released, with all charges dropped against him in January 2011. Scandals surrounding the governor of Amur Region, the mayor of Kaliningrad and the mayor of Togliatti reflect developments at the regional and local level. The governors of Nenetsk Autonomous District, Vologda Region, Smolensk Region and Tver Region have been sentenced for embezzlement and abuse of public office (Vyzhutovich 2006). Legal charges are expected to be pressed against the former Mayor of Moscow, Yuri Luzhkov, who was sacked by President Medvedev for 'loss of trust' after seventeen years in office.

Given the scale of kickbacks, there is little wonder that public officials feature prominently in court cases while administrative reform in Russia is stalled. Yet the attitudes to kickbacks are not straightforward: those who pay kickbacks complain about their extortionate size, yet are satisfied to receive resources and benefits from *sistema* without having to compete for them. One respondent, a lawyer, emphasises the ambivalence of officials' attitudes:

Officials themselves hate *sistema* and what it does to them, but they depend on it for their survival and well-being, for their ambitions and careers, for achieving their goals. In this sense *sistema* is like life itself: you might not like everything about it, but you go on living.

Institutionalised kickbacks are instrumental in accessing state funds and resources and in advancing networks' vested interests, thus sustaining businesses and families. It is the enabling functions of kickbacks that are essential to the reproduction of *sistema*. *Sistema* agencies involved in the re-distribution of resources enjoy control and informal leverage over contractors, and even introduce elements of competition informally. I have been told of instances where informal payments were linked to performance and facilitated the quality of service!

The role of informal payments is intrinsically ambivalent. They support individual entrepreneurial activities and ensure success in the short term, but they also produce anti-social patterns of behaviour that in the long term create an environment where competition, innovation and entrepreneurial spirit do not endure. More generally, informal practices are at least partially responsible for the success of the Russian transition, but also have a corrupting effect on both the people and the economy (Ledeneva 2006: 2). On the surface, kickbacks might not look different from the 'facilitation payments' used by firms in modern societies, but the legal framework, social norms and the scale of their use make them 'pre-modern'.[14]

The social norms surrounding informal payments in society at large also constitute a legitimating factor. For example, 'forced payment' in the health and education sectors is considered normal by 27 per cent and 23 per cent of the population, respectively; a further 59 per cent are prepared to pay to ensure quality (Gudkov *et al.* 2008: 37). So far, social norms prescribe that trust should be placed in very small communities – there is little trust in impersonal systems, although the situation is improving. The latest data show that the majority of Russians acknowledge their defencelessness in the face of arbitrary power exercised by state institutions – courts, police and tax authorities – while 53 per cent of 'middle-class' respondents rank 'arbitrariness and extortion by state officials' as the second most acute problem (Gudkov *et al.* 2008: 38). A June 2009 poll by the Levada Centre asked: 'Do you feel protected against arbitrary actions by the police, tax inspectors, courts, and other government structures?' In response, 43 per cent said 'not really' and 29 per cent said 'definitely not'.[15]

Kickbacks paid to state bureaucrats effectively work as in Weber's model of 'prebends' whereby office holders are allocated fields (colloquially denoted as *polyany*, grazing grounds) where they can 'feed' at the expense of their clients, and also pump further resources into their social networks. As one of the respondents testified:

---

[14] The UK Anti-Bribery Act, which entered into force in July 2011, is a harsher version of the US FCPA 1977, enacted to outlaw payments to foreign goverment officials to assist in obtaining or retaining business. Its adoption is the biggest change in British bribery legislation in over a century. The bill, which ran into trouble from the Confederation of British Industry (CBI), a lobbying group, was finally passed after twelve years of debate.

[15] Medvedev's police reform has resulted in improving poll results.

A single official cannot handle cash, they need to have their own trusted people: lawyers, solicitors, bankers, managers, intermediaries in London who will use their names to legalise it. Whether an official controls this network or the network controls the official is hard to tell. In the latter sense, it is the system of economic relationships that exploits officials and their capacity to extract cash, although [the] officials themselves might be willing to be exploited.

The transition to modernity means that bureaucrats should stop 'feeding' from their jobs and receive compensation for performing their duties in the form of a salary instead. In theory, the problem of kickbacks is solved. Officials' salary should be substantial enough to render informal earnings unnecessary (Johnston 2005). Officials' services should be de-monopolised (Rose-Ackerman 1999); their undesirable behaviour should be made costlier for them (officials should fear the loss of their official income, of their job, status and reputation), whereas desirable behaviour should be rewarded (Huskey 2004). In practice, however, such measures of 'modernisation' of the bureaucracy in Russia are unlikely to curb officials' unhealthy appetites, excessive consumption, obsession with money, a luxury lifestyle, education and travel abroad that no salary, however high, could satisfy, and that no penalty is going to prevent.[16] Thus the institutional framework requires a fundamental change in morals, social norms and individual incentives, if *sistema* is to change.

Alternative mechanisms of governance should be in place before the informal constraints can be loosened. In the meantime, communicated either through formal hierarchies or through informal networks, such constraints constitute an effective mobilisation tool both within the state sector and elsewhere. Thus, the Russian leadership is known for imposing levies of 'corporate responsibility' that extend to include support of towns and regions.[17] An illustration of the point is caught on tape in an infamous scene of 'bending an oligarch' over the situation in a Russian Northern town of Pikalyovo. President Putin made Oleg Deripaska sign an enterprise-saving contract, the terms of which he had not even seen. Other oligarchs were

---

[16] The death penalty for corruption in China serves as a deterrent, but does not eliminate corruption.

[17] See Mr Putin vs Oleg Deripaska: *'Idite i Podpishite'/'Come Here and Sign'*, www.youtube.com/watch?v=VrRHM-oSHlw.

given villages to support after the fires of summer 2010.[18] Informal control can be used to promote the modernisation agenda and to achieve strategic goals. But the governance mode of *sistema* based on informal control and tactics undermines the strategic goals of modernisation – separation of powers, working state institutions, innovative (and investing) business, secure property rights, equality in the face of the law and a capable civil society. This is the 'modernisation trap' of informality: one cannot use the potential of power networks without the consequences they entail. Whereas *sistema* networks enable the leadership to mobilise and control resources effectively in the short term, they also create long-term lock-in effects and raise the issue of control mechanisms of networks that may grow too powerful. Social networks have an in-built capacity to reproduce. Maintaining informal control through power networks, rather than creating a climate in which such control is redundant, is the major obstacle to Russia's modernisation.

How *blat* networks are different from *otkat* networks

Depending on how you look at it, the use of personal networks is associated either with trust relationships, mutual obligations and informal norms, or with the betrayal of trust by agents who bend or break the formal rules set out by the principal. The bottom-up approach to the study of grassroots networks highlights *blat*, effectively, as 'beating the system' by outsiders with a set of strategies for accessing resources and diverting the workings of central distribution systems though personal contacts, or as technologies of gatekeepers and brokers exchanging favours of access. The purpose of *blat* networks was to access privileges enjoyed by insiders. The story of *sistema* is about kickbacks and privileges for insiders. The purpose of power networks is to channel, distribute and mobilise resources concentrated within *sistema*. If *blat* networks subvert the existing rules of the game bottom-up, power networks do so top-down, by its insiders, on its own field, by its own rules, without checks and balances.

---

[18] 'Oligarcham razdali sgorevshie derevni', *RBK-daily*, No. 146, 17 August 2010: 1-2, www.tbcdaily.ru.

Both *blat* and power networks are to some extent open for recruitment. Both are used for extracting benefits; both undermine competition. However, the reliance on networks serves a range of purposes: from survival and decent living at the grassroots level to the enrichment and luxury consumption of the elites. There are serious implications of such reliance on networks. First, where acceptance of the use of networks for getting things done is embedded in society, it is not surprising that power networks are routinely perceived to exist for enrichment (*vlast' sushchestvuet dlia obogascheniya*).[19] Society does not call its leaders to account because the use of networks is a common practice.[20] Instead, morality becomes incremental and is associated with unwritten codes prescribing what it is fair to take. The leadership becomes bound by the ability to sustain privileges for power networks. Understanding the pressure of power networks on the leadership provides an insight into the types of leadership that would work.

On the one hand, there are differences in how personal networks are used at grassroots and power elite levels. It appears that grassroots networks are more open and opportunistic – one can initiate relationships and use them for accessing resources from the central distribution system, whereas power networks are more closed, filtered out and controlled. The difference also stems from the political and economic frameworks in which networks operate. As the Soviet system was not economically viable due to the rigid ideological constraints, economy of shortage and the limited role of money, *blat* networks served individuals as the 'weapon of the weak' in oppressive conditions and to some extent served the economic needs of the central distribution system. In Putin's Russia, power networks operate without those constraints and benefit from the post-Soviet reforms, while effectively undermining the key principles of market competition – equality of economic subjects and security of property

[19] A. Konchalovsky, 'Russkaya mental'nost' i mirovoi tsivilizatsionnyi protsess', *Polis*, 5, 2010.

[20] Perceptions of *blat* as an initiative or alternative currency that constituted an element of the market in centrally controlled economies may have produced a preconception that these networks contribute to the operations of the market in a favourable environment. A similar take on civil society implied that networks were viewed as embryos of such a society, but in fact they stifled its development because networks were based on the 'two-tier people' principle: *svoi* and *chuzhie*. These double standards are reflected in a popular saying 'for friends we have everything, for enemies we have law' (Parshikov 2008).

rights – and the key principle of the rule of law – equality before the law.

An alternative to *blat* appointments

Although the 2008 (s)election of President Medvedev can be seen as yet another *sistema* appointment made on the basis of personal loyalty and the required vulnerability of the appointee, some of his initiatives can be interpreted as challenging to Putin's *sistema*. In his four years in office, there has been a tremendous change in the public discourse about key features of *sistema* initiated from above – corrupt practices in public appointments have never before been publicly acknowledged at the Presidential level. Mikhail Gorbachev (2010), in the article '*Perestroika*, 25 years later' says:

I sense alarm in the words of President Dmitri Medvedev when he wonders, as he has in recent public remarks: 'Should a primitive economy based on raw materials and endemic corruption accompany us into the future?' Can we be complacent when 'the government apparatus in our country is the biggest employer, the biggest publisher, the best producer, its own judiciary, a party in its own right, and ultimately a nation unto itself'? You cannot say it any more strongly. I agree with the President. I agree with his goal of modernisation.

Medvedev raised concerns over appointments through personal contacts or by payment – '*blat* appointments' – shortly after his inauguration in July 2008. Medvedev called for an integrated system for the reproduction and renovation of the professional elite and suggested the creation of a national reserve of cadres (Viktorova 2008). The first hundred nominees on this planned 1,000-strong 'Golden' list of candidates were published in February 2009; and a further 500 were announced in 2010. Most of them are young, dynamic and have proved themselves successful managers outside the government apparatus who could benefit the public administration. Yet the initiative remained unpopular. Critics rightly pointed out the lack of transparency in the creation of the list. Specialists considered it arbitrary in criteria and unusable. The intelligensia saw continuity with the practice of administrative 'listing', wittily described in Dmitri Bykov's novel *Spisannye* (*Listed In and Out*, which could also be translated as *Signed Off*). Sceptics argued that Medvedev's initative was not going to change the practice, if only because he had no real power over *sistema*. From the *sistema* point of view, the 'professionalisation' of top appointments pursued by the 'Golden' list can be interpreted as a weakness of the President's own network of cadres. Besides, it turned out that Medvedev's political will was not sufficient to change Putin's sistema, so the main outcome was merely a certain shift in public discourse on corrupt appointments.

Recognition of the systemic nature of *blat* and paid appointments at the Presidential level has reduced the 'misrecognition' of *sistema* and delivered new facts and figures. Thus, in response to this initiative, the leader of the Liberal Democratic Party of Russia (LDPR) faction in the State Duma, Vladimir Zhirinovskii, claimed in an interview with *Komsomolskaya pravda* that the trade in appointments was a common national practice and volunteered a price list. With the notable exception of the price for a place on a party list for election to the Duma, his list included the following tariffs: from €5 to 7 million for a position of governor; from €5 to 7 million for a seat in the Federation Council; and between €3 and 4 million for a position as head of a Federal Service or head of a department (Viktorova 2008). A member of the Anti-Corruption Committee in the State Duma, Anatolii Golubev, said the figures were realistic, but added that the price depended on the level of contact through which an appointment had been lobbied (Viktorova 2008): the higher the contact, the lower the price. Contacts are the key dimension of appointment procedures, and the figures are indicative of the expectations of a 'return on investment' by an appointee by whoever secured the appointment.

There has been a change in the meaning of 'contacts' as well. If in the 1990s the entire business sphere worked on the basis of *a priori* existing relationships and trust – what used to be called *blat* – the development of markets since then has resulted in the need to expand contacts, which implies networking skills rather than *blat*.[21] Instead of *blat* appointments, analysts now speak of 'clan' appointments (Russia Today 2008). The adjectives '*setevoi*' (networked) and '*ne setevoi*' (not-networked) have also come into use. In tune with Solov'ev and Zlobin's account of the Presidential choice of a successor, discussed on p. 194, an informed source also described the 2008 presidential candidates as *nesetevoi*:

---

[21] Opinions differ on the impact of *blat* on job markets, see Nesmachnaya (2009); also Yakubovich (2005); Yakubovich and Shekshnia (2012).

[Sergei] Ivanov is not a networked person (*chelovek nesetevoi*). It is normally clear from early on. Those who worked with Putin years back – Patrushev, other people – had already followed him then. Sechin was already there. Then Putin worked in Internal Affairs and Chemezov joined in. Ivanov or Medvedev had nobody like that. One person maybe.

From a network perspective, it is perfectly legitimate for a leader to have a team, the 'inner circle' and private friends and core contacts, as well as the periphery, or mediated, contacts one cannot help developing throughout one's career. It is not the contacts *per se* but the specific characteristics of these contacts (in Putin's case, their link to the security services), their mutual instrumental use, and in particular the scale of their use that cause concern. Even more strikingly, when private assets and closed tenders awarded to Putin's 'useful friends' are debated in the press, it causes little public outcry and Putin's approval rates remain high. His 2012 electoral success is not simply an outcome of the rigged elections. It is an indication that his power networks are only the tip of the iceberg of *sistema*'s economy of kickbacks benefiting its supporters at all levels. It is a sign of *sistema*'s grip on society.

Exit from *sistema*

When individuals fall out with *sistema*, they often, as evidence in this book illustrates, find it easier to speak about it. The more insiders leave *sistema*, the more we learn about it. There are no exit terms and conditions: at the stage of recruitment to *sistema*, people are meant to remain loyal for life, dependent on handouts from *sistema* and satisfied with *sistema*'s status games. One could envisage *sistema* as inclusive of the *nomenklatura* and its personal networks, exploited under relatively lenient political and economic conditions. Under the Soviet system, one had no other way but to become a dissident. As Kryshtanovskaya has put it:

To be compromised – is essential from *sistema* point of view. That part of [the] citizens that didn't want to play the game offered by [the] authorities (*vlast'*) had a choice: to become a passive member of society without any prospects or to challenge *sistema* and step on [the] thorny way of dissidents. (Kryshtanovskaya, 2005: 107)

In post-Soviet Russia, in many ways, the Russian state continues to have an upper hand over selected targets. From time to time it uses environmental regulation, taxation and natural resource licensing to exert administrative pressure and wrest control over a company away from its previous owner: prominent examples are Russneft from Mikhail Gutseriev (as discussed in Chapter 6); and Sakhalin-2 from Shell, Matsui and Mitsubishi (Hanson 2009; Granville *et al.* 2012).

Why do people (or companies) get forced out of *sistema*? If one looks for a single reason for exit from *sistema*, it can be more or less grasped in a truism: one ceases to be the 'right subject' for *sistema*. Like the majority of unwritten rules, the meaning of this know-how or, literally, 'know-who', is context-bound. Who are the 'right' people for *sistema*? When and why do they stop being 'right' for *sistema*? Is it simply about compliance, and what does compliance involve at different stages of careers or development? And, crucially, how does the exit from *sistema* differ from the exit from a formal hierarchy? Can these questions be answered solely on the basis on dissociation from (or re-connection to) informal financial flows?

More often than not, the exit from *sistema* is unintended – that is, caused by professional errors and personal mistakes *vis-à-vis sistema*: losing a 'feel for the game' and a 'sense of proportion', misreading or ignoring *sistema*'s signals. Unintended exit is further preconditioned by external factors, whereby a person, who ceases to be 'right' for *sistema*, is forced out by pressure (sacked or forced to submit their resignation) or provoked to exit by circumstances (being set up or occurring by chance). The 'who is behind a set-up?' (*kto zakazal?*) question is often asked, but does not always have a clear answer. Being 'out of joint' with *sistema* is in itself sufficient to lose one's position both in the public and the private sector. As a rule, all the elements described above have to be present to account for a 'loud' exit. On rare occasions, exit can be initiated by oneself, when an individual for personal reasons willingly dissociates from *sistema* and from its values, ties, penalties and rewards.

In his critique of Putin's *sistema*, Mikhail Khodorkovsky defines individual strategies of exit on the basis of the degree of dissociation from *sistema*: being forced to emigrate, emigrate voluntarily, being ready to emigrate, going into internal emigration, or staying hidden among bureaucrats pretending to be one so that not to be steam-rollered by the system (see Chapter 1). Hiding among bureaucrats

often surfaces in a widespread bureaucratic sabotage, in itself consti-
tuting a mode of *sistema* operation. According to evidence assembled
by Andrew Monaghan, the vertical of power, defined as the ability to
ensure the fulfilment of the leadership's instructions and goals, is sabo-
taged. 'As one newspaper editorial noted in early 2010, the handpicked
officials are not effective and often "quietly sabotage the orders of the
prime minister and president". If the shortcomings in the vertical of
power could be ignored before the financial crisis (a good indication
that it did not work under Putin either), the inefficiency of state officials now not only dissatisfied Medvedev and Putin but posed a threat
to the budget'[22] (Monaghan 2011: 9).

Exit options in today's Russia are also more attuned to modernity,
with its complexity, uncertainty and global diversity. They include the
possibilities of expressing criticism without being prosecuted, acquiring work in an (fairly) independent private sector, leading a wealthy
and comfortable life in Russia or abroad upon exit and even of participation in oppositional activities. Technological advances and the
spread of the Internet are essential in this respect. Acts of individual
courage acquire supporters, anti-*sistema* campaigns are made public.[23]
The network-based foundations of the new media and technology mirror the potential of *sistema*'s power networks but facilitate non-*sistema*
logics and norms; orchestrate anti-*sistema* protest in a decentred fashion; and have the potential to develop into collective action and resistance, such as the Internet-based campaigns against *migalki*, discussed
in Chapter 4.

[22] 'Vertikal' loyal'nosti', *Nezavisimaya gazeta*, 24 March 2010.
[23] For a notable fight with *sistema*, see Yana Yakovleva's column at
www.slon.ru; see also G. L. White, 'Once-jailed Russian executive pushes law
changes', *The World Street Europe*, December 30, 2009.

4 | Sistema's *material culture: from* vertushka *to* Vertu

'One searches in vain for a book that gets the story right', sighs a senior Kremlin official:

In 2005 I went to Moscow's biggest bookshop to browse for books in the politics and history department. I looked at what was written about us. As an insider, I knew how the things were and wanted to see how they were interpreted. I was shocked! Books covered every angle: kind, evil, clever, silly. I looked through piles of them, but none of them had got it even close. What I saw was that people wrote categorically about things they could not possibly know about. For example: 'Kasianov came to Putin and said:... Putin replied:... Kasianov objected.' Was the author there? No. How did he know? Who told him that? Putin or Kasianov? Had he said something like 'according to a source close to Putin'... But no. Not at all. Many facts were simply wrong and actors' motivations were misrepresented. Since I knew most of the people depicted in that book well, I was pretty sure that this particular person could not have said what was attributed to him, especially since I knew what he did say. In some instances I was in the middle of the events and I knew that what was described in the book simply didn't happen... And then I thought, 'If there is so little resemblance to reality in the books describing a fairly recent period, when the witnesses are still alive and can remember what happened, what about history books? How much of them is likely to be true?' It's a scary thought. Perhaps the best we can hope for is a more or less smooth narrative. Who needs to know what really happened, apart from a narrow circle of academics? Is it even important?

I immediately suggested that perhaps a book could be written by an insider, not an academic, but my interviewee would not consider that on the grounds of loyalty. When asked if there is a book that approximates his vision, he recommended an American novel *Hard Line*. It is written ten years after resignation by a former White House official Richard Perle, who found it possible to tell an insider story of the deployment of medium-range missiles in Europe in the early 1980s, in his view, misrepresented in academic accounts, in a literary form (Perle

Putin and his *vertushka*
Source: © RIA Novosti.

Putin's mobile power
Source: © RIA Novosti

1992). Aware that my academic account is unlikely to satisfy insiders, I have nonetheless attempted to construct 'ethnography' of power networks. The culture of hidden signals, unwritten rules and tacit knowledge is elusive – it evades articulation and dodges the research methodologies that seek to pin it down. Relying on participant observation is a limited option. One cannot see the way insiders see until one becomes an insider oneself – at which point articulation is no longer an option. In her book *Sex in Big Politics*, Irina Khakamada reflects on her experience as a cabinet minister and offers a 'synchronic translation from Kremlinean'. Her perceptive account of the dynamics within the government includes reading seating plans and their changes, decoding the reactions of the Prime Minister, deducing priorities from the order on the agenda, decoding signatures, resolutions, body language and greeting rituals (Khakamada 2006: 14–17). Finding common ground between different accounts reduces the respective subjectivities of the respondents, but introduces a researcher's subjectivity into the selection of material. Besides, the most sensitive and, therefore, the most interesting stories do not make the final cut since anonymity must be sustained and a 'shared' narrative created.

The obvious weaknesses of methodologies for the study of sensitive subjects prompted me to explore new approaches. This chapter takes an unusual turn on *sistema* and focuses on the ethnography of its 'material culture' – 'material' in this context meaning substance and standing for the objectification of the process change. This is a developing field in anthropology that redefines 'material' by revealing its relationship with immaterial concepts (Buchli 2002; Latour 2005; Miller 2008; Tilley *et al.* 2006). The idea is to make *things* present in the description of social relationships and to provide an ethnography of elite artefacts as a 'backdoor' to accessing subjects that sociology is unable to penetrate because of their secrecy and elusiveness. I extrapolate this method to illuminate new facets of the intersection of power hierarchies and networks, in this case, through the access of my respondents to secure telephone networks. I view the use of telephones as a tool for the analysis of construction and reconstruction of power networks. I apply the 'biography of material things' approach in researching the transition to the use of mobile phones by officials, and I focus on how persons make things and how things make persons (see Appendix 2). I argue that there has been a certain shift in the 'material culture' of the elite from the use of material objects and privileges inseparable from their positions to the material objects they possess.

If one had to come up with one material artefact of the Soviet *sistema*, it would be the secure communication network for Kremlin insiders, referred to as *vertushka*. Even though *vertushka* is a telephone *network* that is technologically 'horizontal' for its members, the idea of *hierarchy* is written into its operations. *Sistema* reveals itself in the ways in which the hierarchy configures and reconfigures the network, organises power relations and transforms the latter into an instrument of control and domination. *Vertushka* is a perfect case to illustrate the 'material culture' of Soviet governance. It was based on the creation of an isolated piece of infrastructure, it was controlled by the security services, it revealed the formal hierarchy of privileges and concealed the informal power of networks.

In what follows I analyse the power dimensions of *vertushka* from Soviet times onward and argue that the so-called 'neo-Soviet *sistema*' associated with Putin's period in power and his re-instatement of the 'power vertical' is not a return to, but rather a departure from, the Soviet *sistema*. Insiders of the Soviet *sistema* familiar with the workings of the present-day institutions insist that Putin's *sistema* is not a *sistema* in the old sense of the word. In this chapter I demonstrate the key differences between the two from the perspective of material culture and consider the implications of technological changes in communication within power networks. The title of this chapter – 'From *Vertushka* to Vertu' – points to the global aspects of this technological change: from a home-grown, security-focused telephone network to a Vertu – a luxury mobile phone with global services, fashionable among the elite in the early 2000s. Capturing this shift in the material artefacts of power networks allows me to illustrate Russia's technological modernisation and to identify trends in the operation of these networks – their mobility, global integration and wealth. If *vertushka* stands for the Soviet culture of privileges, associated with hierarchical access to local infrastructure, security and isolationism, the ownership of Vertu mobile phones indicates and symbolises new values, associated with wealth, global outreach and security of property rights. The implications of such changes for *sistema* are three-fold. In what follows I illustrate how wealth and secure property rights undermine the workings of *sistema* and can redefine its nature, even if the culture of privileges continues to persist. Second, I emphasise the impact of technology in subverting the grip of *sistema* over individuals. I show how the predominance of '*svoi*' infrastructure, whereby privileged access is bound up with specially constructed, securitised pieces of infrastructure, gives way to the new and increasingly accessible technologies – such as mobile communication networks and the Internet, thus bringing the idea of common good and equal access to the public consciousness and spreading over a wider range of infrastructure, such as roads. Third, I argue that the global nature of mobile communication and the 'informalisation' of contexts in which mobile phones can be used replace the culture of official seclusion and ritualised formality of *vertushka*, thus significantly changing *sistema*'s operations and dynamics.

Vertushka paradox: privilege or security trap?

Belonging to *sistema* directly through a formal position in the hierarchy or through a network link almost automatically provides access to a whole variety of resources available 'for people of the circle', in a country where a wider social infrastructure is under-developed, unwelcoming and even hostile. In Soviet days, access to the telephone was such a resource. *Vertushka* has its roots in the time of Lenin (see the Chronology in Box 4.1).

Box 4.1 Chronology of *vertushka*
1876 — Alexander Graham Bell patents the world's first telephone
1881 — Tsarist government reaches agreement with Bell Telephone company to develop urban telephone networks in St Petersburg, Moscow, Warsaw, Odessa, Riga and Lodz[1]
1898 — First St Petersburg–Moscow cable laid, making it the longest inter-city line in Europe[2]
1899 — Ericsson opens its first foreign factory in St Petersburg; later, in Soviet times, the factory is nationalised and renamed Krasnaia zaria ('Red Dawn')[3]

(cont.)

1917 March	February Revolution precipitates the abdication of Nicholas II; initially, Petrograd's telephone exchange continues to serve all parties; by July, however, lines are reportedly cut off to the Bolsheviks on the orders of the Provisional Government, who feared an imminent coup
September	Lenin writes *Marxism and Insurrection*, which outlines the importance of controlling telephone networks in an uprising Bolsheviks take power, having first seized the telephone exchange
1918 March	Government and party apparatus transfer from Petrograd to Moscow **Manual switchboard installed in the Kremlin; there are initially 25 lines, but in September, a newer switchboard increases capacity to 100.**
1921 May	Sovnarkom establishes a dedicated cryptography department within the VChK (Cheka)
1922 January	**Work on the Kremlin's new automated switchboard is completed; unlike the previous operator-directed system, users now connect with each other using radial dialers**
1929	New department for government communications established within OGPU
1930	**First high-frequency inter-city lines laid between Moscow–Leningrad and Moscow–Kharkov**
1931 January	OGPU (State Political Directorate) issues decree on the creation of a modern inter-city government telephone network; construction of overhead telephone lines and regional exchanges continues throughout the decade
1941 June	Hitler begins Barbarossa offensive; by the time of the invasion, high-frequency government telephone networks had already been established between the Kremlin, military commands, the Russian regions and Soviet capitals Main government exchange is transferred underground to Kirovskaya metro station; the

	Krasnaya zarya telecommunications factory is also moved from Leningrad to Ufa
1943 January	Special 'Government Communication' troops established, tasked with developing and protecting lines of communication between Command HQ, armies and front lines
1951	Number of high-frequency government telephone exchanges increases to 223 (24 of which are stationed outside the Soviet Union); there are a total of 2,904 network users (439 outside the Union)
1954	New decadic dialing system increases network capacity to 3,500
1960s	Secure government telephone networks developed across Eastern bloc; encryption codes are prepared in the Soviet Union and dispatched to destination countries via diplomatic courier.
1978	**Dedicated government telephone network introduced for 1,000 high-level users; this elite network was named ATS-1, and the existing 5,000-line automated system was renamed ATS-2**
1980	ATS-2 capacity increased to 6,000 lines
1982	**Capacity of ATS-1 telephone network increased to 2,000 lines using imported quasi-electronic technology**
	Native quasi-electronic technology developed for the ATS-2 network; the new exchange increases network capacity to 7,000 lines in Moscow and 10,000 lines nationally
1991 August	KGB-led coup fails in its attempt to unseat Gorbachev; the same month, Gorbachev strips the KGB of its responsibility for government telephone networks: these transfer to a new body, the Government Communications Committee (KPS)
December	Russia secedes from the Soviet Union; President Boris Yeltsin institutes a new Federal Agency

(cont.)

	of Government Communications and Information (FAPSI), which takes over responsibility for government telephone networks
1993 February	A new law 'on Federal organs of government communication and information' stipulates that special networks of communication and information should be allocated to the highest organs of the state power of the Russian Federation, its federal subjects and the Security Council: 'Commercial structures can only have access to the network on commercial conditions' defined by the Ministry of Finance
1997	**ATS-1 and ATS-2 networks now have some 20,000 users, spread across nearly 300 urban centres and strategic objects; ATS-2 has been privatised**
2003	FAPSI restructured, with responsibility for government telephone networks transferred to the newly established Federal Protective Service (FSO)

Sources:
[1] S. L. Solnick, 'Revolution, reform and the Soviet telephone system, 1917–1927', *Soviet Studies* 43 (1) (1991): 157–76.
[2] www.3dnews.ru/communication/mgts_istoriya_v_detalyah/print.
[3] www.artlebedev.com/mandership/91/.

As early as 1918, Lenin insisted on introducing a small automated telephone exchange so that switchboard operators would not be able to listen in on the conversations of Communist Party leaders. Since the disk-dialling telephones that accompanied the new system were somewhat of a novelty they took the name *vertushka*, from 'to dial', 'to rotate' (*vertet´*). As a *nomenklatura* respondent explains:

The name *vertushka* relates to disk-dialling. Originally, phone calls went through an operator who managed the switchboard (*spetskommutator*) and connected people manually. ATS-1 was the first automatic telephone switchboard that made it possible to dial a number directly so that there was no operator to overhear the conversation. The disk-dialling phones later became

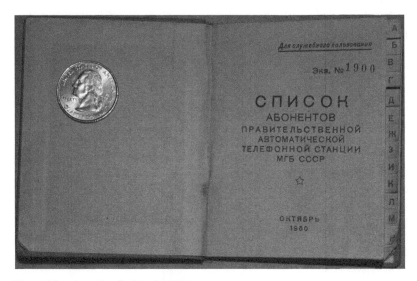

Для служебного пользования

Экз. № 1900

СПИСОК
АБОНЕНТОВ
ПРАВИТЕЛЬСТВЕННОЙ
АВТОМАТИЧЕСКОЙ
ТЕЛЕФОННОЙ СТАНЦИИ
МГБ СССР

☆

ОКТЯБРЬ
1950

Vertushka phonebook dated 1950

commonplace, but the name *vertushka* remained attached to the original and specially secured communication network. Technically a *vertushka* phone was protected by a metal lining inside the phone, so that its parts did not give out any electric or magnetic waves. Parts were made from special materials, so such a phone was rather heavy.[1]

Vertushka is best imagined as a secure telephone network, access to which is indicative of status in the corridors of power. Given that the *vertushka* phonebook had a precise record of who was allocated a telephone number and at which network, gaining access to *vertushka* was a way to demonstrate not only formal status (top positions in the hierarchy entailed automatic inclusion in *vertushka* networks) but also informal influence (some lines were allocated by Party decree) of a member of the *nomenklatura.*

---

[1] *Vertushka* was supported from a dedicated underground switchboard on Moscow's Myasnitskaya Street. K-6, which was the prefix of the automated systems, was the responsibility of the secret services; as such it was maintained with great care and stationed separately from the main ATS in Moscow, which was far more unreliable and unsafe (telephone calls could be picked up, sometimes unintentionally). Codes: initially K-6, later 296, then split into 224 for Kremlin/Liubyanka, and 244 for the Ministry of Foreign Affairs (MID); 296 remained for the CPSU Central Committee in Staraya Ploschad´.

Another official with *nomenklatura* experience testifies along similar lines:

Vertushka was the ultimate attribute of power, the artefact of belonging. When one got ATS-1, wow, hats off! But there was also an atmosphere of fear and vigilance. Remember the posters 'Don't chatter' (*ne boltai*), 'Careful, you are being listened to' (*ostorozhno, vas podslushivayut*)...The security services lived off it. For them, it was a job creation scheme. They went out of their way to come up with all that security equipment, special cells, safe-boxes for switchboards, and masses of people were in charge of all that security. The scale of it all was ridiculous because nobody ever discussed secrets on the phone anyway. It was unusual to have meaningful conversations on *vertushka*. *Vertushka* was yet another element of status and privilege, similar to an official car, a round-the-clock driver, state dacha, fur tailoring service on Granovskogo Street, special food allowance and so on among those who received them. But it also gave work and control to the security services.

Vertushka had a fearful reputation for secrecy. Legend has it that not even all-powerful Beria, the longest-lived and most influential of Stalin's secret police chiefs, managed fully to subordinate the network to his command.[2] Stories of tapping the *vertushka* network have been recalled by diplomats and public officials alike (Voslenski 1991). In his memoirs General Brusnitsyn recalls a constant external threat to the security of *vertushka* and the interest of foreign intelligence, confronted by the ninth department of the KGB that used to be in charge of the Kremlin telephone network. He confirms the view of the respondent above that *vertushka* was not actually used for secret communication:

The prestigious *vertushka*, or *kremlyovka*, was the ultimate desire of all Moscow officials. Foreign security services hunted *vertushka* like a goldmine of secret information. Actually it was prohibited to have secret conversations on *vertushka*, but who can tell a high official what he can or cannot do? (Brusnitsyn 2000: 92)

Although *vertushka* had a second nickname – *kremlyovkya* – it was not exclusively a Kremlin network. It also linked the Kremlin to some parts of the outside world. Special secure lines were installed in all

---

[2] 'Prervannaya spetssvyaz', *Izvestiya*, 5 April 2000. All media sources in this chapter are accessible through the Eastview electronic database, unless stated otherwise.

capitals of the Eastern bloc. Indeed government villas (*osobnyaki*) in these satellite states were sometimes equipped with *vertushka* phones (Voslenski 1991).[3]

In the late socialist period, the naming of *vertushka* had acquired a more folkloric aspect, as many *vertushka* phones had no dialling disks, they made the holders of such telephones, *vertet´sya* – run around and work more efficiently – after receiving a call. *Vertushka* was thus seen as a channel for oral commands.

Being on the receiving end of commands from above, even if your *vertushka* phone did not have a disk-dialling capacity, made you a part of *sistema*. In Soviet times *vertushka* was cherished as the ultimate privilege. It was a super privilege to be on the list of the ATS-1 network, and exclusion from the list represented a major penalty. The switch-off procedure during which such exclusion could occur took place every two years. It combined regular testing and a users' re-shuffle. The late Soviet statistics of exclusions are as follows: in 1988, 61 lines were cut off; 1989, 48; 1990, 47; 1991, 18; while at the same time it appears that some officials retained their *vertushka* access when they retired from their official positions.[4]

The *vertushka* networks were used in a hierarchical and non-transparent way: officials were ranked by the number of phones on their desks and by varying rights of access. Top officials had multiple telephones – external, internal (via secretaries), direct lines (again external and internal), *vertushka* and inter-city lines. Brezhnev was said to be particularly proud of his telephones, which he apparently showed to foreign journalists.[5]

Yeltsin and the privatisation of *vertushka*

Yeltsin's reforms started with an attack on privileges. A government commission on privileges and benefits carried out an inquiry into the costs of *vertushka*. The report put the cost of an inter-city phone at 46,000 roubles, and for ATS-1 and ATS-2 lines at 16,000 roubles per year. Overall, the budget for government telephone networks was

---

[3] Voslenski (1991) (originally published 1980).
[4] 'Zatraty na aparat pravitel´stvennoy svyazi – 16,000 rublei: sko´lko stoit "spetsvertushka"?', *Argumenty i fakty*, 12 September 1991.
[5] Voslenski (1991).

estimated at 500 million roubles a year (just over US$ 100 million at the exchange rate of that time).[6]

While *vertushka* remained an attribute of status, by the end of the 1990s it had begun to be used differently. The use of mobile telephones became technologically feasible and made it possible for bureaucrats to keep more flexible office hours. Secretaries routinely answered *vertushka* phones. In a way, the *vertushka* networks were rendered obsolete by the users themselves, since *vertushka* was no longer the only guaranteed route to reach a desired contact. By 2000, officials began to treat *vertushka* networks somewhat lightly; 'So you have the same annoying secretary answering "please call back tomorrow"'... 'A deputy minister may still use it, but anyone higher up would not', states a source in *Literaturnaya gazeta*. The majority of calls were far from serious: people would call 'to arrange a drink after work'.

Under Yeltsin, Russia's declining international influence was reflected in the fact that the inter-state *vertushka* also began to lose its importance. Romania demonstrated its independence from Moscow by turning the system off.[7] Most other former Soviet states followed suit – all but Mongolia, Cuba, North Korea and Bulgaria.[8] The rules of allocation within Russia also have loosened. Historically speaking, *vertushka* was a lever in the state's relations with the fourth estate. In Soviet times when media outlets were *de facto* extensions of government bodies, *vertushka* was routinely used to agree the coverage of governmental policies. Employees at the Moscow TASS agency were allowed to use *vertushka* only with the written permission of their manager. Information had to be agreed with those who gave the commands before publication.[9] By the early 1990s, *vertushka* was to be found in the great majority of media outlets, including journals such as *Planovoe khozyaistvo* (Planned economy), *Sovetskaya zhenshchina* (Soviet woman), *Rabotnitsa* (Working woman) and *Krest'yanka* (Peasant woman), but not in the best-selling *Argumenty i fakty*.[10]

As the 1990s progressed, *vertushka* became used a means of rewarding favoured journalists. *Vertushka* lines were given as 'presents'.

---

[6] 'Zatraty na aparat pravitel'stvennoi svyazi – 16,000 rublei'.
[7] 'Prervannaya spetssvyaz''.   [8] *Ibid.*
[9] 'Reviziya. S vami budet govorit' president', *Kommersant˝ vlast'*, 11 July 2000.
[10] *Argumenty i fakty*, 12 September 1991.

For example, the All-Russian State Television and Radio Company (VGTRK), which was set up in 1990 and included seven major TV channels and four radio channels, was reported to have received eighteen such gifts from Yeltsin. Access to government networks became open to many reporters and media outlets.[11] It was sometimes 'the only way to access the high level newsmakers directly, without going through a secretary'.[12]

While ATS-1 reportedly remained a highly privileged network available to only a select few high-level officials even during the period of extensive governmental upheaval in the 1990s, ATS-2 itself became privatised and open to anyone ready to pay the subscription fee of a few thousand dollars a month.[13] *Novye izvestiia* sources claim that, by the beginning of the 1990s reforms, almost all large commercial structures had acquired access to the *vertushka* network. They would go to the head of government communications, pay the requisite sum, and a *vertushka* phone would be installed. A former employee of the Federal Agency of Government Communications and Information (FAPSI) claims that a check was always carried out to ensure that the recipient was loyal to the authorities: 'Various departments checked up on a prospective user. If the person was not reliable or insufficiently patriotic, his application would be turned down.' But the grip of the security services seemed to have loosened. Refusal was a rare occurrence and all the so-called 'oligarchs' appeared to have access.[14] One such respondent recalls:

When I worked at a secret research institute (*pochtovyi yaschik*) we had a *vertushka* and an internal communications network. The *vertushka* phone was the symbol of supreme power and only the general director could use it. He stood up while taking a call – that had been standard practice since Stalin's time. I got my own *vertushka* in the late 1990s when I made my way in the communications business. I was working closely with FAPSI and that became possible.

With the monetisation of the economy, a commercial element emerged in the distribution of *vertushka* phones. Yeltsin ordered a Duma committee to look for ways of 'improving the financial basis of secure communications networks' as part of the bill 'on improving the

---

[11] 'Reviziya. S vami budet govorit′ president'.   [12] *Ibid.*
[13] See *'Privatised ATS-2'*, *Kommersant Daily*, 26 October 2005: 20.
[14] Skogoreva *et al.* (2003).

health of government finances'. At that stage the price of *vertushka* was believed to be approximately $5,000 a month for commercial use and it remained more or less stable through to 2000.[15] Nikolai Glushkov of Aeroflot refers to *vertushka* in an interview on the Aeroflot affair: 'The first call I received was at the beginning of 1996 from [Yeltsin's security chief, Aleksander] Korzhakov, who stamped his foot and shouted into the receiver that he would kill me if I crossed the [KGB's] path.'[16]

Commercialisation meant that *vertushka* began to lose some of its mythical status. It was reported that access to ATS-2 network became a matter of semi-open trade, at least for those who could negotiate a price for it. By 2000, the number of *vertushka* subscribers had reached a level that threatened the exclusivity of the network. Sometimes the assignment of secret networks was bizarre. It was unclear why, for example, a *vertushka* phone stood in the office of the Chair of the Duma Committee on Women, Families and Children, or of the Federal Veterinary and Phytosanitary Inspection Agency.[17] This was, formally at least, Putin's pretext when, as acting President, he moved on his first day (1 January 2000) to reorganise the distribution of *vertushka* and cut down the number of users. However, it appears that the opportunity was also seized to settle some scores and remove the privilege from various uncooperative media outlets.

Putin's vertical and *vertushka*

A specially formed commission of the PA (not FAPSI) made the decision to withdraw *vertushka* from most editors-in-chief. The 'black list' included the following outlets: *Gudok, Literaturnaya gazeta, Sovetskii sport, Ekonomicheskaya gazeta, Sel'skaya zhizn', Za rubezhom, Kul'tura, Moskovskii komsomolets, Moskovskaya pravda, Vechernyaya Moskva, Sobesednik, Novoe vremya, Ekspert, Narodnaya gazeta, TV-Tsentr, Radiokompanya Moskva* and the Chairman of the Union of Journalists of Russia.[18] At the same time, the editors-in-chief of tiny *Pravda Ilion, Vek, Nezavisimaya gazeta, Rodina* and some other apparently insignificant outlets kept their privilege. The clean-up took place without transparent criteria. FAPSI refused to comment on

[15] 'Reviziya, Spetssvyaz' vremeni', *Kommersant" vlast'*, 11 July 2000.
[16] *Ibid.*   [17] 'Tainye oligarkhi', *Ryazanskie vedomosti*, 11 July 2008.
[18] Khinshtein (2000).

the criteria for allocation or withdrawal and attributed responsibility to the PA.

In 2000, the journalist, author and, later, Duma deputy, Aleksander Khinshtein had given an optimistic view on the media's exclusion from *vertushka* by saying: 'Well, now it will be difficult for them to chase us once we publish some "loud" story.' He did not seem to foresee then that no 'loud stories' would be published.[19] Other commentators emphasised the shift to mobile communication among government officials. The editor of *Sobesednik* said: 'It is easier to reach an official on his mobile; we use it [*vertushka*] less and less as time goes on – though we do still get several calls a month.'[20] The deputy editor of *Izvestiya* commented that: 'Now a call from the administration is interpreted as a reward . . . a sign of excellence. Familiar old types of media administrators crept out of the woodwork, ready to serve with trembling hands.'[21]

As in many other sectors of government, Putin's arrival signalled a change in the way that government communication networks were used and allocated: in the media, in business and in the regions. Generally, inclusion or exclusion in *vertushka* networks is at the discretion of a committee chaired by one of the deputy heads of the PA.[22] In 2003, this duty was performed by Viktor Ivanov.[23] Until 2003, FAPSI director General Matyukhin also had a decisive voice in decision-making.[24] In 2003 FAPSI was disbanded and some of its functions were absorbed by the FSB while others passed to the Federal Protective Service (FSO). Nowadays, the FSO is in charge of both ATS-1 and ATS-2 *vertushka* and regional systems, with special 'communications centres' combining this role with the monitoring of regional developments for the centre.[25]

By the end of the Putin's second Presidential term, the communication network of *sistema* included the Presidential network (*presidentskaya svyaz´*); a governmental inter-city network (*pravitel´stvennaya mezhdugorodniya svyaz´*) considered to be as

---

[19] *Ibid.*   [20] 'Reviziya. S vami budet govorit´ president'.
[21] 'Vertushechnye dela', *Izvestiya*, 29 March 2005.   [22] Khinshtein (2000).
[23] 'U krupnogo biznesa otklyuchayut vertushki', editorial, *Izvestiia*, 25 November 2003.
[24] 'Chinovniki i businessmeny ne khotyat khoronit´ vertushku', *Moskovskiy komsomolets*, 28 July 2008.
[25] L. Gadzhieva, 'Nadezhno, sekretno, operativno', *Tverskaja zhizn´*, 6 August 2007.

secure as ATS-1 and ATS-2; a military network; and the Rosa mobile
networks, all of which could be accessed only through operators.[26]
Putin was reported to have eleven telephones in his reception area and
four on his desk.[27] The *vertushka* handset itself plays on Soviet retro,
being still manufactured according to Soviet designs – a gaudy white
in colour with a hammer and sickle crest. They can also, however,
take on a more elegant look: Putin's phones, for example, are made of
ivory.[28]

An official's formal status in the hierarchy can be determined by
the degree of exclusivity of the communication networks to which
he or she is entitled. According to media reports, in the 1990s the
most exclusive Kremlin network for Presidential aides and other select
officials included just twenty-four people.[29] By 2000, the Presidential
network was reported to have about 100 select users.[30] Both numbers
may be wrong, if one believes the top official who has put the size of
the most exclusive presidential network as 40–50:

There is a Presidential line (*presidentskaya svyaz'*, PS), the narrowest network, four digits to dial, 40–50 phone sets altogether. I had it on my desk
with the sound turned down (*zaglushennym*). I didn't like the fact that it
was a direct line, bypassing the secretary. You know, not everyone calls on
important business; they are important people, but they call for trifles (*po
pustyakam*). This line is direct to everybody who has it, only the President
has a secretary replying to it. I turned the ring-tone off once with a little ball
and this set off a huge scare. Within two days, the security services were
onto me in panic: 'Somebody has inserted something into your phone.' I
said, 'Don't worry, I did it myself. But, while you are about it, please turn
the sound down.' After that, the phone just made a clicking noise when
it rang, and that was not so irritating. Oh, I didn't like that phone...50
people in a network and everyone can call directly...50 people is a lot of
people, you know; that may not be the exact figure, but it was thereabouts.

I asked how this phone related to others:

There's a second phone that is part of a larger network – special switchboard (*spetskommutator*, SK) – with a wider range of users that makes

---

[26] *Ibid.*
[27] 'Zachem Putinu chetyre telefona?', www.compromat.ru/page_16139.htm.
[28] *Ibid.*
[29] 'Viktor Chernomyrdin obyazal chinovnikov otvechat' na zvonki po vertushke',
    Izvestiya 23 April 1996.
[30] 'Vopros – otvet. Svyaz' s pravitel'stvom deneg stoit', *Trud*, 3 August 2000.

contact through a distant secretary, girls on the switchboard. When you pick up the phone they know who you are and which phone you are calling from, and they greet you by name: 'Ivan Ivanovich, *zdravstvuite.*' You say, '*Zdravstvuite*, I would like to speak with such and such'. They say, 'One minute please', and dial some other number, whatever it is. They can connect to the city line and to any other number. This network also has a limited number of subscribers, not even every Deputy Prime Minister had such a phone. In the PA, only the head of PA and the first deputy head had such a phone and maybe a few other really key people. I had one of these special switchboard phones at home and in the office and in other places . . .

As mentioned above, half of the so-called *kremlyovka* lines are reportedly located outside the official state offices. Their locations include departure lounges in airports and train stations, the Presidential plane, helicopter and cars; the *Rossiya* and *Kavkaz* ships; a special section within the Central clinical hospital in Moscow. Lines are also installed in the apartments and dachas of a select group of high-ranking officials.[31] Further concentric circles of communication networks include ATS-1 and ATS-2.

In terms of status, the ATS-1 network is higher than ATS-2. The ATS-1 network includes ministers and deputy ministers.[32] ATS-1 access is also enjoyed by the speakers of both chambers of parliament, their deputies, some chairmen of parliamentary committees, regional governors and mayors. The leading lights in the pro-Kremlin United Russia party enjoy access.[33] The leader of the Communist Party, Gennady Zyuganov, also acquired one, a fact that his colleagues announced with great pride.[34] Duma deputies do not normally have them.[35]

ATS-2 is more embracing than ATS-1 and includes the heads of ministerial departments and a wide range of middle-ranking officials and entrepreneurs. It also served as a hot line for the media.

---

[31] 'Tainye oligarchi'.
[32] 'Chinovniki i businessmeny ne khotyat khoronit' vertushku'.
[33] 'Fal'shivye vertushki – Lidery dumskikh fraktsiy ne mogut dozvonit'sya glave gosudarstva napryamuyu', *Nezavisimaya gazeta*, 30 March 2009, www.ng.ru/politics/2009–03-30/4_false.html; and 'Zachem Putinu chetyre telefona?'.
[34] 'Fal'shivye vertushki'.
[35] 'V Kremle delyat "vertushki" i "migalki". Startiruet samyi zakhvatyvayushii etap administrativnoi perestroiki: raspredelenie glavnyh arbitrutov vysshei byurokratii', *Nezavisimaya gazeta*, 12 April 2004, www.ng.ru/politics/2004-04-12/1_kremlin.html.

ATS-2 networks were installed at *Izvestiya, Pravda, Sovetskaya Rossia, Krasnaia zvezda, Glasnost´, Komsomol´skaya pravda,* and *Ogonek,* among others.[36] Even so, some press outlets seemed to enjoy better access than others. Some editors felt they could initiate contact, some expected to be contacted often; others were seldom interrupted. But ATS-1 and ATS-2 were not mutually exclusive, as another Kremlin insider explains:

People at the top had all of these phones. The PS and the SK phones were separate, but otherwise a number of lines – ATS-1, ATS-2 – were all on one dashboard. Big bosses tended to have them on a dashboard rather than a number of separate phones. Similar dashboards were at home, in the Kremlin, in Novo-Ogarevo, in Bocharov Ruchei in Sochi, and everywhere in the President's usual places, only working while he was there and easy to switch from one place to another (*s pereklyucheniem*) so, if he called you, you could never tell where he was.

Locations outside the office were important characteristics of status. The use of *vertushka* in a mobile mode (*s pereklyucheniem*) and the use of an official car, equipped with radio-*vertushka*, were assigned to the highest Soviet officials showing off their rooftop antennae.

Diplomat and politician Dmitri Rogozin recalls the saying 'The cooler the *vertushka*, the more powerful the bureaucrat' (*chem vertushka kruche, tem byurokrat moguche*), and shares his fond memories:

When I was a chairman of the Duma committee on international affairs, I was the first to have an ATS-1 direct line to the Kremlin. It is cool to have a *vertushka* with a dialling disk: an official can stick his finger in it and get in touch with the select few (*spetsabonenty*). But it is super-cool to have a SK phone, when you simply take the receiver and ask for 'Puppkine'.[37] When the call comes from above, it is absolutely clear whom it is from, and that you should carry out orders. If you haven't got a *vertushka*, or don't get called, you're nobody. Some governors have been known to give press conferences on the occasion of being called by Putin.[38]

The Russian bureaucracy works on the understanding that the real importance of officials is made apparent by the extent of their access to the symbolic attributes of power. In other words, real power is

---

[36] 'Vopros – otvet. Svyaz´ s pravitel'stvom deneg stoit'.
[37] 'Zachem Putinu chetyre telefona?'.   [38] *Ibid.*

reflected by where they sit, the Kremlin (aides of the President) or Staraia Ploshchad´ (where the majority of presidential advisors have their offices),[39] whether they have a permanent pass to enter the Kremlin, which dachas they have been assigned, whether they have a limousine,[40] what kind of number plate they have, whether they have a *vertushka*, and what kind of *vertushka* it is.[41] In a way, *vertushka* is just another way to measure the proximity to the 'body of the tsar'. The informal rules surrounding *vertushka* are not codified, but drawing on the recollections of *sistema* insiders and some written sources, I have gathered a few (see Box 4.2).

Box 4.2 The code for use of *vertushka*

- Users were expected to stand up and answer the call with their surname. When a boss was on a business trip, the aide was supposed to follow strict instructions and inform the caller about the return date.
- With the exception of the top officials, ATS users were obliged to take all calls. How much this was observed in practice, however, is another question. It seems to have been followed early on, when members of the Politburo routinely answered their phones.[42] But by the early 1990s, when Yegor Gaidar headed the Russian government, secretaries were regularly answering phones.[43] Gaidar's successor, Prime Minister Viktor Chernomyrdin, tried to reinforce the old rule. In April 1996, he declared that secretaries must answer the phone only if their boss was not in the room. Failure to observe this procedure was to result in the withdrawal of the line.
- It was considered a violation to use another person's *vertushka*.[44] The phone must never be left unattended, so officials had to lock offices even if they were to be out for only five minutes. Legend

---

[39] As of 2004, officials were divided into two groups: *pomoshchniki* (deputy heads of the PA) and *sovetniki presidenta* (Presidential advisers). *Pomoshchniki* had some say over personnel in their jurisdiction. Both *pomoshchniki* and *sovetniki* had *vertushki* and *migalki*.

[40] In the mid 1990s, European 'limousines' were provided to specially selected bureaucrats in the PGO, the Constitutional Court, FAPSI, etc.

[41] 'V Kremle delyat "vertushki" i "migalki"'.   [42] Voslenski (1991).

[43] 'Prozrachnaya svyaz ', *Izvestiya*, 23 July 2008.   [44] Voslenski (1991).

had it that a cleaner was given a flat by Party leader Khrushchev
after sneaking into an official's unattended office and asking for
it on *vertushka*.[45]

- Likewise, a member of the *nomenklatura* with *vertushka* might
  not use an ordinary phone without causing a suspicion of false
  modesty, apparent arrogance, or 'independent thinking'.[46]
- A loud siren accompanies any call from the President; other calls
  are hushed.
- Although in theory *vertushka* is supposed to be secure for the
  communication of state and military secrets, in practice it is rarely
  used for that purpose.
- Every year, users of the ATS-1 and ATS-2 networks would be
  given updated phonebooks. These contained the name and occasionally the affiliation of the user, but no address or rank.[47]
- Being cut off from *vertushka* was a serious event, and could be
  interpreted as an imminent threat.[48]

Not only did the top telephone networks include only a small number of selected users, most users had no direct line to the President[49] –
that was reserved for a few high-ranking officials, who could be
counted on 'the fingers of one hand'. In Soviet times, these included the
Minister of Defence, the Head of the PA and a few other bureaucrats.[50]
In Putin's period the list was expanded to include the Prime Minister,
Deputy Prime Ministers, the head of the PA and the speakers of both
chambers of parliament. Other officials had to negotiate a multitude
of other links in order to speak to the President. The President's most
frequent contacts appeared on his dashboard. An eyewitness official
suggests the following setup:

There are many important people on the President's dashboard: the prime
minister, the head of the PA, the deputy heads of the PA, aides of the
President, advisors of the CEOs of Gazprom and electricity giant RAO EES,
and the speakers of the two chambers of parliament. He can add anyone he
pleases to his dashboard if he contacts this person often . . . for the simplicity

[45] 'Reviziya, Spetssvyaz´ vremeni'.   [46] Voslenski (1991).   [47] *Ibid.*
[48] 'Chinovniki i biznesmeny ne khotyat khoronit´ *vertushku*'.
[49] 'Fal´shivye vertushki'.   [50] *Ibid.*

of communication – it's sometimes a faster way of communication, you press one button rather than going through a secretary . . .

Who else was there on a dashboard? People from the legislative branch, the General Prosecutor, a few key ministers with whom the President is in frequent contact, though not the complete cabinet. But I don't remember any Court chairmen on that dashboard. At least, not in my time. If somebody is on the President's dashboard, this means that this person has a phone on his desk that says 'President'. And if this person wants to call the President, he picks up the receiver and the corresponding button on the President's dashboard lights up and rings and, if the President is at his desk, he will see it. One shouldn't read too much into those buttons, though. One can have those names on the dashboard but call them rarely. It's also a formality: important positions and people in prominent roles in the state have to be there.

The last point is important since it illustrates that the gap between the formal and the informal power is an integral part of the mentality found in officials at all levels. The difference of behaviour in formal and informal contexts is sometimes striking. As one respondent described his colleagues in the White House: 'I know they are normal people but in formal contexts they start behaving like aliens.'

Big business re-shuffle

In the 1990s, the commercialisation of the ATS-2 *vertushka* network reflected a more general power shift away from the bureaucratic machine. Although ATS-2 numbers were still allocated according to an established bureaucratic procedure, there were no particular restrictions and no need for underhand ways of getting access – one simply wrote to FAPSI (or, as of 2003, to the FSO). Many leading businesses were connected to the Kremlin via ATS-2 networks, while only a few enjoyed ATS-1 access. For example, the management of RAO EES enjoyed ATS-2 access, and RAO's Chairman, Anatoliy Chubais, was reported to have an ATS-1 number as well.

This situation began to change in the early 2000s. During the *vertushka* re-shuffle, an RAO source said that the company was not afraid of losing access to the *vertushka* network: 'We are a state company with a strategic role for the economy of the country.' The President as well as a number of Vice-Presidents of Rosneft confirmed access to ATS-2. Gazprom did not confirm direct access to the government and the President, but the company is known to have always had it. Oil company Yukos apparently never had it.[51]

In 2003, *The Financial Times* interpreted a round of *vertushka* allocations as a sign of a new battle between the government and big business: 'Twenty-eight special telephone lines that connect Moscow's most influential private business tycoons to the Kremlin will be switched off... The question of retaining the *vertushka* telephone sets with the hammer and sickle stamped in the middle of the dialling ring' is said to be 'a strong indicator of who is in and out of favour'. The Russian press acknowledged that *vertushka* access was regularly switched off, but also noted that the procedure had become more frequent in recent years (the ATS-1 numbers are switched off seasonally, in autumn and spring) and pursued certain informal agendas.[52] Given the timing and the context, any outcome of a regular procedure is perceived as a signal. *Novye izvestiya* reported:

Formally, nothing unusual is happening. But a month since the arrest of [Yukos owner] Mikhail Khodorkovsky, the revision of the *vertushka* lists among big business is symbolic, aimed at establishing who is in and who is out. Experts interpret such steps as an indirect declaration of a new era for oligarchs where they will have to prove their loyalty to the Kremlin and show what they are prepared to do for it.

Access to *vertushka* is read as an indication that an individual is on the right side of the power networks, and those excluded feel very uncomfortable. This is not to say that important issues are decided on *vertushka*. According to a former employee of the now-disbanded FAPSI, *vertushka* has comparatively little practical use: 'It isn't used for having conversations with the President.' Rather, it is a sign of status, 'good for massaging the ego and boasting to friends'.[53] Another expert remarked that the sign is more ominous than that: network cut-off means 'expect investigation'. Withdrawal of *vertushka* was read as a threat that one would soon be joining Khodorkovsky in prison, or as a signal to move to a safer place. As one of the oligarchs joked to *The Financial Times*, the safest place in the Russian business world at that time was outside it. Whether driven by privilege or fear, *vertushka* holders were keen to maintain the status quo.

---

[51] 'Bankira Frenkelya vydala Liana Askerova', *Slovo*, 19 January 2007.

[52] Arkady Ostrovsky, 'Russia's nervous digarchs left hanging on by the Kremlin', *Financial Times*, 25 November 2003. 'U krupnogo biznesa otklyuchayut vertushki'.

[53] Skogoreva *et al.* 2003.

Svoya infrastructure as pattern of resource allocation, *svoya* network as a pattern of control

Vertushka was an exclusive network but its pattern – creating an infrastructure for exclusive use – spread wide, well beyond Moscow, and deep into the managerial culture. Anecdotal evidence from a high official who represented the Chuvash Republic in the Central Committee of the CPSU provides an illustration:

> In Soviet times, telecommunications worked badly. In Chuvashiya, they simply collapsed and it all came down to a colossal complaint . . . I went to attend to the problem . . . which was resolved by setting up a mini-switchboard at the level of the regional administration (*obkom*) and linking it to all the collective farms (*kolkhozy*) – in effect, they created their own *vertushka*. There was an operator who connected with a *kolkhoz* in a matter of half an hour, just like international lines used to work. Such telephone stations had a catalogue of numbers, some of them flagged red as important contacts. And this case was not an exception. This is how it used to be. *Istra* – the communication network that linked regions to Moscow – was designed according to the same 'chuvash' pattern. It amounted to the 'chuvashisation' of the whole country.

Since Soviet times, *sistema* dealt with shortages of infrastructure on the basis of 'ranks of privilege' and the 'exception', or 'emergency' principle, finding local and patchy solutions to problems (Ledeneva 1998: 79–80). A former deputy minister of telecommunication formulates the infrastructural basis of governance as follows:

> One can't govern without infrastructure . . . Because there was no developed infrastructure, special clusters were created, originally just for themselves (*dlya sebya*), and then for wider purposes. Lenin started the whole thing. He initiated the Kremlin telephone network; later it was followed by other types of privileged access – to Kremlin residences, dachas, canteens, shops, kindergartens, schools – everything for insiders (*vsyo svoyo*)!

The *vertushka* pattern was replicated at the regional level, both in the period of Yeltsin's de-centralisation and in the period of Putin's vertical. For example, a new communications device was created to reflect the post-2000 regional settlement. The 40 × 40 cm box was produced by a Perm manufacturer, Morion (formerly in charge of the Soyuz-Apollon and the communications for Moscow Olympics). Twenty-two boxes were to be made: one for the President, one for each of

Russia's seven (now eight) federal districts, while the rest would remain at FAPSI.[54] This technological device, referred to as '*vertushka* of the twenty-first century' is Internet-based. It functions as a modem with encryption and data protection: a special plate encrypts and translates the conversation in portions. The only way of decoding is to use its twin device, installed at the other end of the line. Receiving such a communication box without being in the formal position of Presidential envoy is an important symbol of being a '*svoi*', and the press expects a fierce fight among top officials for the remaining devices.

Contrary to the expectations that the role of *svoi* will diminish in privatised Russia, the governing capacity of *svoi* people, installed to control, monitor and keep *sistema* going, has actually grown under Putin's vertical. One can notice the logic of a Soviet unofficial social contract – Stalin's Big Deal and Brezhnev's Little Deal were indeed the open secrets of the Soviet *sistema* – in Putin's Sistema Deal, exchanging power, privilege and private wealth for personal loyalty. *Svoi* networks, just like *svoi* infrastructure, are essential for the workings of *sistema* because of their simplicity, security and personalised exclusivity (a *svoi* factor). The traps of personalisation are grasped perfectly by a *nomenklatura* respondent who has worked out that *sistema* depends on him:

Alas, there is a plethora of such *vertushkas*, everywhere . . . but they have their uses . . . four-digit numbers are easy, connection is good (telephone stations, batteries and cables are additionally secured), and you always know that a *svoi* (a person who belongs to a circle) is calling. The latter is important. I never used my *vertushka* for *blat* purposes. 99 per cent of calls are official and urgent. The city network is not good enough for that, it works badly and is not secure. Internal networks are the *modus operandi* of *sistema*, especially considering that in five years or so one becomes a true expert on how to solve problems. I knew everything there was to know and everybody who was worth knowing in communications. If they removed me, they would not be able to make head or tail of it, and the whole system would have suffered. The *svoi* factor is perhaps the most important – without addressing people by their first name (*po imeni ochestvu*), without knowing them personally, it is impossible to solve problems.

If one of many deputy ministers feels like this, the top jobs are even more prone to the personalisation trap. The personalisation of *svoi*

[54] 'Vesh' nedeli – "*vertushka* XXI veka"', *Vedomosti*, 17 November 2000.

telephone communication is a reflection of the personalisation of formal hierarchies and the consequent role of power networks in making things happen, or not. With the new technology of mobile phones, and the commercialisation of *sistema*, the *vertushka* basis of identifying *svoi* has changed. Putin's rule is associated with leading officials' switching to mobile phones.

From *vertushka* to Vertu

With hindsight, the *vertushka* perspective reveals three stages in establishing a modern communications system and the consequent breakdown of the Soviet *sistema*.

Before 1997, there was an era marked by the power of *vertushka*, the end of which was probably initiated by Vladimir Borisovich Bulgak [Russian Minister of Communications, 1991–7].[55] Yeltsin made changes in this period, but old habits and ways of solving problems died hard.

Then there was a transition period associated with the presence of international business players. According to Naum Marder, now Deputy Minister of Communications and Mass Media, the Russian Telecoms Ministry granted 1,260 licences through August 1994, with 627 of them for communications services. The market was said to be competitive, yet strategic decisions remained with the three major structures that dominated the Russian telecommunication market: the Telecoms Ministry, which determined policy and worked out regulations; the joint-stock company Rostelekom, the international and long-distance telecom operator; and the Telekom company, made up of 287 telecom equipment-producing factories.[56]

The real change – the sector's further commercialisation – came with the arrival on the scene of Putin's Minister of Communications Leonid Reiman. A respondent from the communications sector referred to Reiman's period as the one 'where state interests were completely replaced, or privatised, by [the] narrow interests of certain

[55] V. Bulgak, March 1997 to March 1998, Deputy Prime Minister; April 1998, appointed Minister of Science and Technology; September 1998, appointed Deputy Prime Minister responsible for industry and communications in Yevgenii Primakov's government.
[56] P. Polishuk (ed.), *Russian Telecom Newsletter*, 2 (1) January 1995 (Boston, MA: Information Gatekeepers, Inc.).

groups – influence and commercial interests are the new name of the game. If there was such a thing as a Reiman *sistema*, it worked completely and exclusively to serve private interests.'[57]

Another respondent characterised this change from the *vertushka* point of view:

With Reiman's arrival, everything changed radically. He never used *vertushka* and gave everybody his mobile phone number instead. He was very democratic in the beginning and always rang back. Interestingly, he kept his St Petersburg number from the company he had set up. It was probably less secure than *vertushka* – everybody assumed in the 1990s that all mobile phones were monitored – but so was *vertushka*... The Ministry then provided mobiles for all their staff and the practice became established.

The bureaucratic hierarchies as well as the power networks defined within the remit of *vertushka* were undermined together with it. The importance of networks and wealth acquired through mobile phones came to define the new *sistema*. The Ministry created telecom companies that owned little more than a licence and sold them for millions. When asked about the limits on what they could do, a number of eyewitness respondents noted the following forces at play. First, competition for influence among businessmen worked as an improvised system of checks and balances. But it was difficult to find a broker to balance Reiman's influence since he was recognised as a Putin man. It was also dangerous for the companies they represented. Some foreign investors used their political links at the top level to communicate the message of the minister's competitive advantage.

Secondly, the ministerial staff itself engaged in various practices of sabotage of the licences' sell-off. Rank-and-file ministry officials came up with creative ways of using regulations and procedures, leaked information, or organised an open tender despite an order to sell to a designated buyer. These resistance practices slowed down the reform and undermined the Minister's effectiveness; even so, the 'mobilisation' of the telecommunications sector that Reiman generated was truly impressive. A Kremlin veteran comments on the clear preference for

---

[57] Reiman was admitted to be a beneficiary of an offshore firm in a commercial court case in Switzerland, www.kommersant.com/p712380/Rozhetskin_arrested_MegaFon; see also 'Reiman: svyazist, ministr, podozrevaemyi', 17 February 2012, www.forbes.ru/sobytiya/lyudi/79318-leonid-reiman-dosie-svyazista.

mobile phones shown by government officials, in contrast to *vertushka* lines:

When I worked, I didn't have a mobile but I was never without a communication line. Round-the-clock bodyguards had a line. At home, next to my bed, there was a bedside table that had five phones on it. It was not so difficult to get in touch with me, the operator would put anybody who wanted in touch with me. My personal friends, acquaintances and family always called me on a normal city line and my secretary told me, 'Your mum asked you to call her, your wife . . . ' and I rang back. I didn't have a mobile. Now, I look around, and practically everybody has a mobile phone, they all seem to have one.

Some officials developed a reputation for being inseparable from their mobiles. Moreover, mobile phones became a fashion and a new symbol of wealth. Somewhat uncannily, the brand called 'Vertu' became associated with power in Putin's Russia. It has become a new *VERTUshka*, now a symbol of success, private wealth and global awareness.[58]

The Vertu deal

Vertu is a signal. It is a very expensive and special accessory. The fact that the phone is hand-made adds to its value and prestige. But socially the key to its prominence is not very different from what *vertushka*'s used to be: 'People who want to feel that they are set apart from the crowd buy these mobile phones.' As one of the respondents confirmed: 'It is an instant image-maker. But it also has unique global services.' For example, Vertu allows its owners to back up all the information stored in their Vertu phones (including a contact list, to-do list and calendar) securely and transmit it to the Vertu Fortress storage in the UK, an ex-military bunker. If the Vertu phone is lost, stolen or damaged, you will be able to recover all the information directly from Vertu's database. It has a 'concierge key' on the side that gives access to a round-the-clock team of assistants ready to help the Vertu owner

---

[58] All of these, including a subtle reference to their Soviet roots, are encapsulated in an advertisement for Gorbachev's eightieth anniversary Gala at London's Royal Albert Hall in 2011, which was sponsored by Vertu, and had its logo prominently on the ad.

with information about travel, entertainment, restaurants, events and news, adjusted to his or her lifestyle and travel.

High-profile clients' needs for security, luxury consumption and personal assistance are addressed at a global level. The concept of Vertu is parallel to a luxury watch manufactured by the likes of Rolex, IWC and Patek Philippe, a fascinating artefact for a study of Russian elites, as well as mansions and yachts.[59] Vertu – a British-based manufacturer, a subsidiary of the Finnish mobile phone manufacturer Nokia – pioneered the luxury mobile telephone sector. The first Vertu phone was internationally launched in January 2002 and almost immediately became a hit in Russia.[60] The cheapest Vertu phone has a price tag of about $5,000, the most popular Vertu Signature range costs up to $81,000, while the most expensive Vertu phone (Vertu Python, Vertu Cobra and Vertu Dragon) is around $310,000.[61] The Parisian jeweller the House of Boucheron collaborated with Vertu on this limited-edition series of eight Cobra phones, which include a two-carat pear-cut diamond, a one-carat round diamond, two emerald eyes and 439 rubies totalling 21 carats. In effect, the Vertu concept is an inversion of the idea of the mass-produced mobile phone provided for free with a contract. Vertu claims that it takes expert craftsmen some three years of training to learn to make their phones. The Signature model is assembled by a single individual whose signature is proudly concealed under the battery: it takes over 1,500 working hours and a further 500 hours of polishing. Every component of a Vertu phone is designed to last for at least twenty years, made from gold, sapphire (for the mobile screen), rubies (for the bearings) and fine leather. Each mobile is hand-made in Hampshire, UK. On the Vertu website, one can find a classic model of Vertu Signature that contains 943 diamonds on its bezel and 48 more on its keypad, each set in place by hand in Switzerland.

[59] Y. Latynina, 'Russia: a superpower if measured in mansions and yachts', *Putin's Russia Symposium*, 15–16 November 2011, Havighurst Centre, Miami University, Ohio; 'A quick way to become a superpower', *The Moscow Times*, 23 November 2011, www.themoscowtimes.com/opinion/article/a-quick-way-to-become-a-superpower/448417.html#ixzz1l77shsx9.

[60] 'New Nokia Phones for Richie Rich', Reuters, 21 January 2002, accessed December 2009, www.wired.com/print/gadgets/wireless/news/2002/01/49887.

[61] www.mobilephonescoop.com/blog/index.php/2009/05/07/9-vertu-facts-worth-knowing/ and www.vertu.com.

Vertu's link to the UK is intriguing and represents a wider spectrum of needs satisfied by the Russian elites there: family safety, children's education, dental treatment, nutritional and medical tourism, business and legal services, commercial jurisdiction, LSE listing and financial services, wealth and finance management, luxury consumption, sport, culture and entertainment on a global scale. Yet Vertu also provides an interesting angle on the Russian regions. Just as the Mars bar in a village shop was used as a tag for globalisation in the 1990s, in the 2000s the Vertu shop in a Russian region reflects a degree of the commercialisation of *sistema*: twenty-eight Russian cities with a population of over a million have a Vertu outlet (to name a few, Volgograd, Orenburg, Samara, Vladivostok, Ekaterinburg, Irkutsk, Kazan´, Novosibirsk, Kemerovo, Krasnoyarsk and Sochi), while Moscow has four Vertu outlets and ten authorised dealers.[62] These should be viewed in the context of nineteen flagship boutiques worldwide and at least one official dealer in every major city (Vertu reserves exclusive rights for retail and has around 400 boutiques in total).

Russia led the Vertu consumer market in the 2000s, with sales outstripping those of any country in Western Europe.[63] Vertu's President, Alberto Torres, explains the continuous growth of sales – 140 per cent in 2006 compared to the previous year – by booming sales in Russia, China and the Middle East. Analysts reckon that Vertu sells about 200,000 handsets a year at an average price of $8,000 each.[64] Apparently, even the 2008 global economic crisis did not affect Vertu's sales.

Russian companies serve their customers' needs not just for luxury[65] but also for security. Thus, the Russian data protection company Ancort offers a platinum-covered, diamond-studded (fifty diamonds,

---

[62] See the distribution network in Russia, www.vertu.com/in-ru/gifting/gifts-for-him#in-ru_where-to-buy.

[63] 'For Nokia, excess is a Vertu', *Europe*, 21 December 2007, www.businessweek.com/globalbiz/content/dec2007/gb20071221_951028.htm.

[64] *Ibid.* That works out at $1.6 billion, nearly 3 per cent of Nokia's $58 billion revenues.

[65] A Russian businessman bought GoldVish's Le Million phone for his wife in September 2007 at a luxury goods fair in Cannes, certified by the Guinness World Records as the most expensive phone in the world, worth 1 million Euros, or about $1.45 million. The odd-shaped device is made out of 18 carat white gold and features 1,800 diamonds totalling 120 carats. 'The 10 most expensive cell phones in the world', 3 December, 2007, http://theforrester.wordpress.com/2007/12/03/the-10-most-expensive-cell-phones-in-the-world.

ten of which are blue) Diamond Crypto smartphone that sells for
$1.3 million![66] Designed by diamond encruster *extraordinaire* Peter
Aloisson, the Diamond Crypto Smartphone is sometimes quoted as
the world's most expensive cell phone (depending on exchange rates).
In response to specific needs, the JSC Ancort has developed a Windows CE-based smartphone ready for Aloisson's bejewelling that
employs 'powerful encryption technology' to provide 'secure protection of information against kidnapping, technological blackmail, financial racketeers and corrupt state officials'. What does this tell us about
sistema?

Just as the privilege-based culture of *vertushka* has led the Russian
elite into the open arms of the luxury brands of mobile phones, Soviet
restrictions on consumption and property resulted in the 'Pavlov-
ian dog' reproduction of privilege-based habits in other areas. Even
the younger members of today's Russian elite have acquired a taste
for privilege. In an anecdote about the sons of two leading members
of the Russian elite, Dima asks Sergei whether it is cool to have a
diamond-studded Vertu phone. 'Obviously, it isn't cool!' 'So what is
cool then?''Cool is when a platoon of soldiers are running behind you
with a field phone!'[67]

This anecdote reflects the importance of items that cannot be bought.
For the Russian elite, what is important is not how much something
costs; what is important is to project an image of privileged access,
contacts, status and exclusivity that no purchased commodity could
provide. Other anecdotes refer to the importance of shortages for the
national psyche: 'Everything should be available in the shops but some
things should be in short supply' (*pust´ vsyo budet, no pust´ chego-
nibud´ ne khvataet*).[68]

These privileges seem to be preserved by special efforts, because
they function as signals of belonging to the inner circle. 'The cooler
your car number plate or your passport number, the more you are on
the inside', states one respondent and tells a *blat* story of present-day
Russia, where shortages are almost artificially created and cherished:

I went to change my passport, as one does at 45. Looked at the line…and
called the head of federal service asking for a favour. I brought him a box

[66] 'For Nokia, excess is a Vertu'.
[67] The Russian version can be found at http://compromat.ru/page_27882.htm.
[68] 'U krupnogo biznesa otklyuchayut vertushki'.

of vodka, produced at a factory near Rublyovka that was famous in the old days for supplying vodka for Brezhnev. The factory no longer exists, its land has been developed into a cottage settlement (*kottedzhnyi posyolok*), but a friend of mine, a former co-owner, got hold of 40,000 boxes of that vodka. I exchange his boxes of vodka for my boxes of Borzhomi water, now a rarity that I have a channel for.[69] So I brought this famous Kremlin vodka, and people understood. We started drinking while I was waiting for my passport to be done. His aide asked me if I wanted a *blatnoi* passport number. I said, what? He explained with a smile, 'you know, the one with a good number that our people would know and recognise'. I was pleased as the figures were easy to remember. But this is it: one part of the population is divided from another. The situation increasingly feels as if one is in a castle with a moat around it, and the drawbridge has already been pulled up.

There are multiple implications of this divisive culture of belonging. It may give you immunity for speeding, allow you to become rich and powerful, with the caveat that your property rights remain insecure, and even put you above the law.

Informal rewards: privileges and the culture of belonging

The culture of privileges, stemming from the economy of shortage and evident in the *blat* mentality and the economy of favours serving the needs of grassroots networks, reproduces itself within power networks through the symbolic value and status implications of non-monetary privileges that are impossible to buy. Once *vertushka* loses its actuality, its place is taken by the distribution of other forms of privileges. In the busy streets of Moscow in the 2000s, sirens and flashing lights (*migalki*) allowing privileged use of roads became a privilege of key importance:

Yes, we had green lights everywhere. When I worked for the Administration, all the cars stopped, so we just started moving and ended up where we needed to be. When I left, I simply moved out of the state residence and the phones stayed there. And I certainly don't miss them. Not even *migalka* for that matter. If it irritates someone, it's my driver and my bodyguards who are struggling with traffic jams. I understand their problem, because they are at work whereas for me it's fine, I am happy reading books in the car. Sometimes it's a problem if I am late for a meeting, but the main thing is

[69] Borzhomi is a mineral water from Georgia, embargoed after the 2008 conflict.

that there should be enough literature in the car. Sometimes I speak on a mobile phone in the car but I don't like long chats on the phone (*trepat'sya*). Periodicals and books are what I prefer.

Referring to the infrastructure as a common good, one respondent remarked on telecommunications in Russia, 'Communications are like roads', and roads are in doubly short supply in Russia. 'From the transport point of view, Russia can be divided into Moscow where nobody can go anywhere because of constant traffic jams, and the rest of the country where nobody can go anywhere because of the absence of roads' (Latynina 2009: para 7.2). The Russian transport system is indeed a good metaphor for Russian society. In the 1990s, bending the traffic rules was used to explain the logic of informal practices (Ledeneva 2006). In the 2000s, the transport metaphor helps to illustrate the workings of *sistema*. Latynina highlights the problem – the problem of privileges – for power networks:

Let us imagine an official who had stolen all the money allocated to repair the road and who solves his own transportation problems with *migalki*. The same thing happens to Russia's system of public administration. (Latynina 2009)

The culture of privileges is resistant to regulation. Back in 2000, the government decreed that the number of flashing lights on cars should be restricted to 700, but within two years the number had increased to 1,000. In 2006, it reached 7,500 and Putin decreed a radical reduction of the number of flashing lights for official cars and the elimination of specially designated 'flagged' number plates (Decree No. 737, 1 December 2006). The list of organisations entitled to an official car with flashing lights was also revised. As of 2007 the result was impressive – the number of lights had gone down from 7,500 to 977.[70] The leaders of the United Russia Party launched a campaign against flashing lights but within a few months they began to reappear on their cars. The overall number of lights has also been rising. So another decree enacted on 8 April 2010, and another campaign, this time attempted to bring the number down to 966.[71] The lists of organisations were revised again. The Ministry of Interior is said to have lost fourteen lights in that revision but regained them within a few

---

[70] However, according to a count conducted by Duma deputies and independent experts, the number of real users is at least 1,500. Krasil'nikova (2010).

[71] R. Ukolov, 'Domigalis'?', *Profil'*, 12 April 2010: 30.

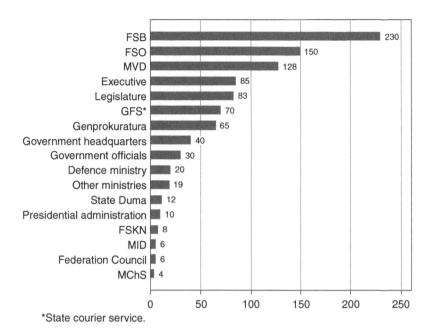

*State courier service.

Figure 4.1 The number of *migalki* allocated to state agencies
Sources: www.government.ru, *Kommersant-Vlast'*.

days – their general number is 142. Twenty-six *migalki* are allocated to the federal government.[72] Another source suggests that the federal government has twenty-five, while the government apparatus has forty. The PA has twenty, the State Duma has twelve and the FSB has 230![73] The distribution of lights among governing bodies, as presented in Figure 4.1, is indicative of their importance. State corporations are not on the list.

Apart from the allocations designated in the governmental decree, there are top state officials who are entitled to a car with lights under the law on state security. Some thirty people are entitled to a car with lights because of their 'protected' status under a Presidential decree. But the latter is a classified document.[74] The Vice-President of the most active civic movement, Federation of Automobilists of Russia (FAR),

[72] Krasil'nikova (2010).
[73] A. Kornia and N. Kostenko, 'Chinovniki ot biznesa', *Vedomosti*, 26 November 2009.
[74] *Ibid.*

Leonid Ol'shanskii, does not believe in the effectiveness of such decrees and points out the legal basis behind some of the *migalki*:

I don't think this PR campaign will be effective in any way. Three years ago, Putin signed a similar decree to reduce the number of cars with flashing lights down to 1,000, so now it is unlikely that there will be a further reduction. Besides, the Interior Ministry and FSB officials are entitled by law to a 'special regime of movement'.[75]

In an interview with *Kommersant*, Vladimir Kozhin offers a revealing interpretation of the problem as one that affects the elite but has no implication for the population in general, thus downplaying its significance while emphasising the hardship of bearing this kind of privilege:

If we went to a Moscow suburb now and asked people, flashing lights would not be their immediate concern. This is a problem specific to Kutuzovsky Prospect, the Garden Ring and, perhaps, the Rublyovsko–Uspenskoe highway . . . Imagine, we are sitting here and I get a call from the President who says, 'Come here'. He has a tight schedule and won't be waiting for me for three hours until I get to [his dacha] Gorki-9. Naturally, I drop everything, switch on this 'quack-quack-quack' (*kryakalka*) and get there faster than you will. I would enjoy the trip much more without that sound, you know and, when I can, I always ask the driver to switch it off. Because if you use it five times a day, you are not going to feel any better. It's a constant stress for both driver and passenger. It hits the brain so that you can't think or read: quack-quack-quack. Many of my colleagues would prefer to travel without it. Yet today this is not possible. To say that *migalki* are a serious problem for the traffic in Russia, or even in Moscow, is to turn the problem on its head.[76]

Society at large does indeed appear to perceive this not primarily as a traffic problem but as a matter of privileges for the elite. The 'Hunt for *migalki*' campaign, initiated by a radio station and the *Vedomosti* newspaper, counted a total of 1,236 vehicles with flashing lights in April 2010.[77] In the same month FAR launched a campaign against privileges on the roads with the slogan 'Servant of the people, take off your flashing light'. The campaign quickly extended to fifty cities. Drivers were urged to hoot their horns whenever they saw an official car flashing its lights and also to show resistance by not allowing them

---

[75] Shtykina (2010).
[76] Korobov and Kashin (2011).   [77] Ukolov, 'Domigalis'?': 30.

privileged passage through the traffic. This campaign to highlight the universality of the traffic code and the equality of all citizens before the law highlighted *sistema*'s fundamental flaw – the excessive privileges enjoyed by the 'servants of the people' – as well as the fear of popular unrest that underlies *sistema*.

According to a poll conducted by the Levada Centre polling agency, 78 per cent of the population expressed support for FAR's campaign. The keenest supporters are Muscovites (89 per cent), businessmen (87 per cent), students and people with higher education (84 per cent); 9 per cent opposed the campaign and 13 per cent did not have a view. Almost half (47 per cent) were confident that the campaign would be successful and inequality on the roads would be ended; 36 per cent did not believe it would be successful, while 17 per cent could not answer this question.[78] Popular support was enhanced by a silent campaign against road privileges for officials launched on the Internet. An Internet community calling itself 'Blue buckets' (named after the shape of the flashing blue light) organised a series of flashmobs, in Moscow in April 2010, in which protestors placed blue buckets on top of their own vehicles. Another Internet community called on its members to follow the example set by a Moscow businessman, Andrei Hartley, who had refused to give priority to a car bearing the Presidential advisor Vladimir Shevchenko; supporters were urged to videotape the violation of traffic regulations by official cars on their mobile phones and to publish the pictures on the Internet.[79]

Without romanticising the role of the Internet for the civic movement (Morozov 2011), I note the role of technology in the dissolution of the tacit boundaries of *sistema*, as the grassroots resistance against it is voiced in cyberspace. The awareness by society of the culture of privilege can help to promote the key principles of the rule of law: respect for the idea of common good as discussed in this chapter, equality before the law, as discussed in Chapter 5; security of property rights, which are kept unstable in order to keep people in control, as discussed in Chapter 6; and accountability of the leadership's informal governance, as discussed in Chapter 7.

[78] Shtykina (2010).
[79] A. Kolesnichenko and V. Iakov, 'Problesk pobedy nad migalkami', *Novye izvestiia*, 30 April 2010.

5 | 'Telephone justice' in the global age: from commands to signals

Women's power

When I was researching *Russia's Economy of Favours* (Ledeneva 1998), I was inspired by the personal story of a doctor, Natalia, who was an effective *blat* broker in her time. Her story exemplified the experience of the inner workings of the Soviet system at the grassroots level. In *How Russia Really Works* (Ledeneva 2006), it was the story of a banker, Tatiana, that best illustrated for me the business dynamics of the transitional 1990s, with its criminality, unlawfulness and unfairness. As I looked for a story to illustrate the profound changes that have taken place in Russia since 2000, I knew it should be associated with the increasing importance of the judiciary and Russia's integration into the international legal order. I was particularly keen to explore gender aspects – the majority of judges are women – and their relevance for the analysis of the key feature of *sistema*, 'telephone justice' (Swamy *et al.* 2001). 'Telephone justice' is a colloquial phrase to denote inequality before the law, selectivity in law enforcement and the consequent gap between law and justice.

The first decade of the twenty-first century produced a 'whistle-blowing' trend among the Russian judiciary, with a number of judges speaking out about the fear they felt and the administrative pressure they had experienced (see also Kaminskaya 2009). Several testified that, at a higher level, influence with judges and prosecutors can yield desired results in criminal, commercial and civil trials and that, even if unfavourable judgments are handed down, there are ways to ensure that they are not enforced (see interviews with Sergei Pashin).[1] In 2004, Olga Kudeshkina made headlines as the first Russian judge to speak openly about political interference in the Russian justice system. Dismissed from her position as a judge in the Moscow City Court for her

---

[1] *RFE/RL Newsline*, 17 October 2000, www.rferl.org/newsline.

150

non-compliance with informal commands, Kudeshkina took her case to the ECtHR in Strasbourg, and won.[2] Kudeshkina's conflict with the Chairwoman of the Moscow City Court, Olga Yegorova, may be unique, but it illustrates the workings of *sistema*,[3] as does systematic research conducted in Russia (Global Corruption Report 2007; Gorbuz *et al.* 2010; Hendley 2007, 2010; Huskey 1992; Mishina and Krasnov 2006; Sakwa 2010; Satarov *et al.* 2005; Solomon 2008, 2010; Trochev 2008; Volkov *et al.* 2011). According to a report entitled 'The judicial system in Russia: its present state and issues' published by the Centre for Political Technologies (CPT) in 2009,[4] the main problem is not corruption, levels of which do not exceed those afflicting society as a whole.[5] Rather, the principal cause for concern is the degree to which the courts are susceptible to administrative pressure by government officials and court chairmen and chairwomen, in charge of pursuing informal agendas and communicating informal commands. Judges are reported to fear the chairs, on whom they depend. Court chairs are in charge of 'administrative resources', they decide how a plea should be treated and which judge should take the case, arbitrarily transferring it from one judge to another who is more loyal; they award bonuses and can launch disciplinary proceedings against a judge. They 'have the know-how and are able to intercept and interpret hints dropped by the Kremlin, the local administration, or a influential official, politician or businessman', says the CPT report. As a result, officials have at their disposal courts that can be directed and managed, and use them as a means of punishment and as an instrument for supporting certain interest groups. Alongside Russia's so-called 'managed democracy', the Russian authorities, despite their efforts, have ended up with a 'managed judiciary'. Thousands of appeals are being sent from Russia every year to the ECtHR, while many commercial disputes

---

[2] ECtHR ruling No. 29492/05 *Kudeshkina* v. *RF*, 26 February 2009. For details, see Judge Olga B. Kudeshkina's speech, 1 March 2010, 'Deeds not words: the present failings of judicial reform in Russia', www.eu-russiacentre. org/eurc/judge-olga-kudeshkinas-speech.html.

[3] It would of course have been ideal to have heard the stories of both Olgas, especially since they both refer to *sistema* in their commentaries (see p. 154). When doing my fieldwork on 'telephone justice', I tried to contact Olga Yegorova, but was not successful.

[4] The report was commissioned by the Institute for Contemporary Development.

[5] Public perception of corruption among judges is leading among other factors but is on the decline (see Ledeneva 2008a, 2011b).

are taken to courts in other countries, signalling a *de facto* loss of Russia's sovereignty in the legal sphere. Experts believe that in future the number of complaints by Russian citizens to the ECtHR will continue to increase; meanwhile, the UK's legal community is the largest and the most expert in the world where Russia-related extradition and commercial cases are concerned. But let us hear Olga Kudeshkina's story in her own words.

Olga's story

The story starts with a sequence of events laid out in Olga Kudeshkina's formal speech to the All-Party Parliamentary Group on Russia at the UK House of Commons,[6] and continues with an informal interview:

In 2003 I had personally encountered violations of the independence of the judiciary when examining the case of Pavel Zaitsev, an investigator at the Ministry of Internal Affairs. He was facing criminal charges of abuse of office. The investigators considered that Zaitsev had committed such offences during his investigation of the smuggling of furniture for the *Grand* and *Tri Kita* (Three Whales) shopping centres.[7]

State Prosecutor Dmitri Shokhin behaved strangely in court . . . The chairwoman of the Moscow City Court, Olga Yegorova, openly interfered in the case. She demanded, in abusive terms, that I tell her who was posing which questions during the trial and why the judge took certain decisions and not others. In my presence the Court chairwoman phoned up the deputy Prosecutor General who had confirmed the charges in this particular case, and informed him that the judge had been summoned to explain what was happening in court. From her words I understood that she and the deputy Prosecutor General were working in tandem, and this explained the strange behaviour of Prosecutor Shokhin. Yegorova even went so far as to demand that the case materials be falsified by not including the announcement by the lay assessors who were assisting me that they were withdrawing from the case. In these texts they described the prosecutor's conduct as disgraceful, and having the aim of pressurising the court into reaching a decision that suited the prosecution. The chairwoman of the Moscow City Court further failed to take any decision in response to their statements. She would not

---

[6] The speech was presented to the All-Party Parliamentary Group on Russia and EU-Russia at the UK House of Commons, 8 February 2010, www.eu-russiacentre.org/eurc/judge-olga-kudeshkinas-speech.html.

[7] For details, see Chapter 6.

permit comment on the behaviour of the prosecutor to be included in the record of the proceedings and also made sure that the lay assessors no longer attended the trial.

I declined to carry out her instructions. In violation of the law, Chairwoman Yegorova took the case away from me and gave it to another judge. In my eighteen years working in the courts it was the first time I had come across such open and cynical pressure. It could only be termed a mockery of the law.

This was a moment when public interest outweighed considerations of professional solidarity. I spoke openly because it proved impossible to discuss these issues freely within the profession. This was because my fellow judges in Moscow find themselves dependent on the Moscow City Court chairwoman. My actions were intended, let me stress, to eliminate conduct that was unacceptable and incompatible with independence of the judiciary.

Because I called things by their true names and told people of the real situation within the judicial system, my powers to act as a judge of the Moscow City Court were revoked before I had completed my term of office . . . [Moreover] first the Judges' Council, then the Judges' Higher Qualifying Board of Moscow, and subsequently the Moscow City Court and the Russian Federation Supreme Court, all declared that everything I was saying was untrue. In their words I had deliberately belittled the authority of the judiciary and disseminated fabricated and offensive allegations about Russian judges.

As portrayed in this story, the logic of *sistema* is familiar: an individual has no choice but to comply or lose their job, to compromise or to be compromised. In modern Russia, however, *sistema*'s victims can receive the protection of international law. International law courts provide an exit, even if it is not an easy road to take. The number of cases concerning Russian citizens going to the ECtHR steadily grew in the 2000s; Kudeshkina herself took that route:

After failing myself to find truth and justice in Russia's courts, like many of my fellow citizens I was forced to seek those qualities at the ECtHR. On 26 February 2009, the ruling was issued on my complaint (No. 29492/05 *Kudeshkina* v. *Russian Federation*). It established that I did have grounds for criticising the work of the judicial system and, in particular, the pressure exerted on Russia's courts.

The ECtHR established that the chairwoman of the Moscow City Court had interfered in a fair and just hearing of a criminal case and also that I was prevented from taking part in a judicial hearing in my professional capacity. The arguments and facts I presented had been totally ignored by bodies representing the profession within Russia and by the Russian courts. They found full confirmation in the ruling issued in Strasbourg.

In the text of the ruling, the ECtHR commented that the pressure exerted on Russian judges was a problem 'demanding serious attention in order to ensure the independence of the judicial system and preserve public trust. In a democratic society the opportunity to openly discuss such subjects must always be preserved.' The Court established that by depriving me prematurely of my right to practise as a judge at the Moscow City Court, and by taking away recognition of my status as holding the First Qualification Class, my right to free expression had been violated, though it is enshrined in Article 10 of the European Convention on Human Rights.

... On 11 December 2009, I applied to the Moscow City Court for a re-examination of the decision made on 8 October 2004 by the Court's board for civil cases. My grounds were that new circumstances had emerged, i.e. the ruling by the Court in Strasbourg that established that there had been a violation of Articles of the European Convention on Human Rights (ECHR) in my case. Seven days later the Moscow City Court turned down my application, thereby negating the principle that the Russian Federation is obliged to observe the terms of such agreements, since this is an inseparable attribute of a constitutional, law-governed state. The public response given by the chairwoman of the Moscow City Court to the ECtHR ruling on my complaint must be seen to be believed. 'This struggle with the system recalls a certain person tilting at windmills', was one of Ms Yegorova's comments!

More than seven years after the conflict with Chairwoman Yegorova, I ask Olga Kudeshkina how she feels about it all now, having won her case in the ECtHR? She replies:

You know, time has passed and emotions have burnt out (*vsyo peregorelo*). And I understand that this is not her [Chairwoman Yegorova], this is *sistema*! If it had not been she, it would have been someone else. Maybe a different person, a bit better or a bit worse, but in the end the actual person didn't matter. Nobody could have worked differently there and then. Anyone not complying with commands of the Kremlin, Putin and the like would be removed.[8]

[8] See A. Politkovskaya, 'Diagnos: Absolyutno upravliamaya: Na meste predsedatelia Mosgorsuda nam nuzhen svoi chelovek, skazal deputat', *Novaya Gazeta*, 7 June 1999, especially the opinion of Pashin Sergei about Judge Yegorova, http://politkovskaya.novayagazeta.ru/pub/1999/1999–04.shtml. (Accessed 20 February 2012.)

Q: Before one gets removed, one has to be appointed. In the Sovietology days, the workings of *sistema* were decoded through appointments and promotions. How did the judges perceive Yegorova's appointment?

I can't say for other judges. There were rumours. I remember this because my appointment coincided with hers. I was appointed in November while her appointment took place on New Year's Eve, 31 December 1999. I didn't know what was going on there, what relationships or whatever. When I went to the Supreme Court for induction, I was told to expect a decision on the chairman of the Moscow City Court appointment but not to get involved into a fight over it. My mentor said, 'A decision will be taken and everything will get back to normal'. What was abnormal at the time was that not only she was appointed despite being turned down twice – once by the Judges' Council, once by the President (who at that time was Boris Yeltsin) – but also over the head of a candidate approved by the Judges' Council, nominated by the Chairman of the Supreme Court, and awaiting confirmation. The legitimacy of her appointment, therefore, could be questioned on the basis of a procedural violation. The nominee even appealed to the Constitutional Court but he was called in and told to stop his appeals if he didn't want trouble. As far as I heard, the chairman of the Judges' Higher Qualifying Board went personally to Putin to explain that the Board had approved Paukov, not Yegorova, but he was told off in a similar fashion (*chtoby ty zabral i bolshe ne bylo*). Many associated Yegorova's appointment with a FSB connection, with her husband, an FSB officer, and with the arrival of Putin, also a former FSB officer – 'once a security officer, always a security officer' (*byvshix ne byvaet*) – and also with her purpose of implementing the Kremlin's will. She set up a new order straight away. She treated judges as if they were her subordinates and launched purges from the very first meeting.

Olga Yegorova was appointed to head the Moscow City Court in 1999 by then-President Yeltsin over the objections of some senior city and federal judges. In her first year in office, seventeen judges resigned from the court, according to a report by the Independent Council of Legal Experts.[9] I raise a question of the FSB connection:

Do you know, my husband used to be a FSB officer as well. In my time we used to think that the best and the fittest went to serve there. For myself I

---

[9] 'Judge denies she colludes', *St Petersburg Times*, 21 June 2005, www.sptimes.ru/index.php?action_id=2&story_id=3926.

can say, I was an idealist and believed that we lived in the best country in the world and the like. Of course after *glasnost'*, we re-considered and re-thought many things. I wanted to believe that a true change is possible and that the new laws on the independence of the judiciary would work. We were romantics then. As soon as local competitive elections came into being, my husband then left a KGB Academy where he had studied and joined politics. We lived in the Kemerovo region [in south-west Siberia] then. Eventually he ended up in the Supreme Soviet and I went to Moscow after him. I then had two years without a job, [and] looked after the family. My husband worked in the Supreme Soviet until 1993 but then we went back to Kemerovo. I sat my qualifying exams and worked as a judge of the regional court for five years in a court of appeal in the Kemerovo region. When we came to Moscow for the second time, I was keen to get a job in Moscow, too. It is now that the General Prosecutor says that appointments occur according to the principles of planning and protectionism. But in the late 1990s I didn't have a problem getting a job.

Q: Have you experienced any changes during your career regarding the role of courts? Statistics show a tremendous rise in the use of courts; this seems somewhat surprising, given what you have said about the notion of dependence of judges and 'managed' court rulings?

When private property emerged and privatisation started in the 1990s, the capture and redistribution of property (*zakhvat i peredel*) became omnipresent. Initially, the courts had nothing to do with either capture or redistribution. Why not? Because to be considered in court, a case must be supported by documentation, and property has to be shown to have been acquired legally. In the early 1990s, such acquisitions took place according to unwritten rules (*po ponyatiyam*) and under the protection (*krysha*) provided by criminal gangs or security agencies (*silovye struktury*) such as the FSB and MVD. The unwritten rules of those providing protection determined the manner of acquisition. But in 1999, when Putin and his security services (*siloviki*) came to power, it dawned on them that most of the assets had already been appropriated by the oligarchs, while they [the *siloviki*] hadn't got their fair share. So another re-distribution began and Yegorova was part of it. Where judges didn't satisfy the authorities, they got pushed out.

Q: How widespread is 'telephone justice'? Is it specific to the Moscow City Court?

I do not remember experiencing such pressure when I worked as a judge in the Kemerovo region in the early 1990s. Well, the chairman could invite a judge to his office and say something like, 'You have such and such a case, be careful, pay attention to such and such circumstances'. Perhaps we were just lucky that our chairmen took the principle of judicial independence seriously. Things were different in other regions. For example, the Urals region was notorious in 1989–90 for the association of its judicial system with raiders' attacks. Many judges suffered the consequences if they refused to hand down the required rulings for the redistribution of property. Anna Politkovskaya wrote about it at the time. They appealed to the President, to the Supreme Court Chairman, but they were left defenceless in the face of the pressure.

In Novosibirsk, in 2002, judges rebelled against their chairmen, who used to intervene boldly and directly. It was reported in the press. Judge Zueva described the chairmen's interventions in detail. It took Judge Filatova seven years to be reinstated after those events, and it required criticism on the part of President Medvedev, the personal intervention of the Head of the Constitutional Court Zor´kin, and a decision of the Constitutional Court in 2008.[10] A number of judges appealed to the ECtHR, but it was a long time before their cases were accepted.

Q: There is talk of *krugovaya poruka* (collective responsibility), among judges, and the unpopularity of those who speak out or turn against their circle (*svoi*). Did you ever become *svoia* at the Moscow City Court and what does it take?

My first case was very tricky. The defendants – a group of investigators of drug dealing – had been in detention for over two years. They swore they were innocent and it looked as they had been set up, especially given that the drug dealer whom they were investigating had powerful parents. His mother alleged that the investigation team was corrupt, a bribe was planted in the flat of one of the investigators, and some documents in the case were falsified. The defendants were originally acquitted but after an appeal the case came back for re-consideration. No judge wanted to take it on, but I had just started, so I did. I remember the defence lawyer telling me then, 'Olga Borisovna, whatever your ruling is, we want to thank you for taking

---

[10] Postanovlenie Konstitutsionnogo Suda Rossiiskoi Federatsii ot 28 fevralia 2008g. N 3-P 'po delu o proverke konstitutsionnosti ryada polozhenii statei 61 i 121 Zakona Rossiiskoi Federatsii "O statuse sudei v Rossiiskoi Federatsii" i statei 21, 22 i 26 Federal´nogo zakona "Ob organakh sudeiiskogo soobshchestva v Rossiiskoi Federatsii" v svyazi s zhalobami grazhdan G. N. Beliusovoi, G. I. Ziminoi, Kh. B. Sarkitova, S. V. Semak i A. A. Filatovoi', *Rossiiskaia gazeta*, No. 55, 14 March 2008: 17, http://dlib.eastview.com/browse/doc/13612867.

this case'. At that point I understood I had got myself into something (*nu ya i vlipla*). Then I received my first 'informal inquiry over a prospective acquittal' in [the] chairwoman's office, and I was shouted at for the first time by Yegorova over the delay of the case. Generally speaking, this didn't have the same impact on me as it would have had on a younger judge. Not only was Yegorova younger than I, I also had more experience. I had been chairwoman of a small city court myself in Siberia, and so I had experience of management. So I was not afraid of Yegorova and I stood up for my views. That's what created the problem... To cut a long story short, she took me off the case requiring top qualification and assigned me to the understaffed court of appeal department where all the backlog was dumped on me.

Q: Do you think this 'load-test' was a signal or initiation?

The head of the appeal court told me later that she had wanted to test me and gave me all the backlog cases (*zavokokichennye dela*) just to see what I was like as a person. I spent nights there. It was hard but I didn't mind. I could see the head was principled and fair and I respected her. She was one of four judges who later on supported my story publicly and spoke in my defence.

I must have done something right because Yegorova asked me to take on the First Qualification Class cases again. I agreed. I like complicated cases, where one has to unravel the details – especially the 'set-up' cases (*zakaznye dela*) where you are not sure whether people have been detained on trumped-up charges. Or whether they are really guilty? You must never take anything at face value.

Q: Would you say that the *Three Whales* was such a case? A lot has been written about it. Some analysts have even depicted it as emblematic of Putin's Russia. What would be your opinion?

What can I say? It was clear that the clash of interests over smuggling was only the tip of the iceberg. When the case ended up in the State Duma Committee for Security, it was referred to as a 'riddle wrapped in a riddle'. Drugs, money-laundering, arms-trading, you name it. All 'roofs' [agencies] were involved as well, from Customs to the FSB and the Prosecutor's Office. When their interests clashed, a simple investigator was put on the spot. You know, he was a decent person, he was exceptional. No cars, no flats, a modest salary. His family lived according to his income. He did not abuse his position, and that's what he was punished for in the end.

Q: Would you say that *sistema* punishes its best people?

Not necessarily. His first sentence was also an acquittal. That was unexpected since, as a general rule, judges are known for their bias towards the prosecution (*obvinitel'nyi uklon*). The judge who made that ruling told me that she didn't have any instructions from Yegorova over the case. It looks as if at that point nobody had told Yegorova what to do. But that sentence was appealed by the [PGO], and the Supreme Court sent it back for re-consideration. Just as with my first case, no judge wanted to take it on, and the case ended up with me. In a way it was a coincidence because Yegorova was on vacation, her deputy called asked if I would take it. I was doing a court ruling and didn't really have time to think about it. I didn't know the case and so I agreed. Another judge came to me afterwards and said, 'Why did you agree to take that case? Do you know what's behind that case? You'll suffer for it (*namuchaesh'sya*).' Could I have known that it would be such a decisive case in my career and my life . . .

My survey data show that 30 per cent of the Russian population are aware of the existence of *krugovaya poruka* (collective responsibility) among judges, and that 35 per cent are aware of judges' fear of dismissal or sanctions and other forms of pressure within the judiciary. Thus, 15 per cent of respondents noted the dependence of judges upon their superiors; 12 per cent pointed to the existence of special telephone lines connecting government officials directly to legal institutions; and 12 per cent suggested that the courts are financially dependent upon local and federal authorities (see Appendix 1 for details of the survey).

'Telephone justice' in Russian courts

For outsiders, the idiom '*telefonnoe pravo*' means little, even when translated as 'telephone law', 'telephone justice', 'telephone rule', or 'telephone right'. It is a metaphor that describes the phenomenon by reference to what it is not – that is, it alludes to the practice of over-ruling legal procedures by informal commands as 'law'. It would be more precise, perhaps, to translate it as 'telephone command' or 'telephone over-rule'. However, this would be to misunderstand its true meaning and its ironic undertones. By using the translation 'telephone justice', I emphasise the existing gap in perceptions of law (*zakonnost'*) and justice (*spravedlivost'*), law and conscience, and law and morals, often viewed by respondents as the dichotomy of 'law v.

justice' (Ledeneva 2006). One respondent highlights the difference by suggesting that law is an 'averaged justice':

Our genetic memory is one of informality, informed by our instinct for individual justice. It would be great if people became more formal in relation to compliance with the law, as in Protestant countries. Law is also some kind of justice, but it is averaged out (*usrednennaya*). Here in Russia, everyone has one's own justice, and strives to attain it.

'Telephone law' is synonymous with exceptional powers and the status above the law enjoyed by a handful of Communist Party elites, 'whereby Communist Party leaders would pick up the telephone and call prosecutors and judges and tell them what outcome the Party expected in specific cases' (Karklins 2005: 14). Once Communist rule was over, the practice of exerting informal influence on legal institutions was adapted to post-Communist Russia (Solomon 2008, 2010). Following tip-offs from above, criminal cases were opened or closed, tax evasion charges were pursued or conveniently forgotten, law enforcement officials continued an investigation or abandoned it and arbitration courts arrived at a certain decision. The list could be continued with other variations on the theme of *administrative resource* such as the abuse of power for purposes going beyond official duties but not necessarily for private gain, and grounded in the lack of a *de facto* separation of powers and in inequality before the law (Pastukhov 2002).

While substantial reform has been initiated in the legal sphere, relatively little progress has been made toward resolving the problem of 'legal nihilism' (Solomon 2008, 2010). In a 2010 opinion poll, 26 per cent of respondents associated the existence of 'telephone justice' with the privileged status of the Russian authorities, who considered themselves 'above the law'– 'the law is not written for them'. In a thoughtful commentary in 2004, Valerii Zor´kin, President of the Russian Constitutional Court, noted that 'true legal awareness and respect for the law have not yet become integrated into a generally accepted system of values even among many public officials, who often believe that the interests of the state and of state-owned enterprises should by definition prevail over the interests of ordinary citizens'.[11] According

[11] Quoted from A. Brenton, 'Russia and the rule of law', EU-Russia Centre, 25 November 2010, www.eu-russiacentre.org/our-publications/column/russia-rule-law.html.

to an all-Russia national survey, 23 per cent believed that the Russian judicial system was used to demonstrate the government's position on specific activities or events through 'show trials' (see Appendix 1); 19 per cent perceived the judicial system as being used to dispose of political opponents. The same percentage of respondents was convinced that judicial power was being abused for the purposes of corporate attacks and business capture (Ledeneva 2011b).

Folk wisdom portrays the law as being only for the stupid: big people go above it, small people go under it and clever people go around it. Russian proverbs encapsulate popular perceptions of the law: 'The law turns wherever you steer it' (*zakon chto dyshlo, kuda khochesh´, tuda i vorotish´*); 'Where there is law, there is injustice' (*gde zakon, tam i obida*); 'Why bother about the law if you know the judges?' (*chto mne zakony, koli sud´i znakomy?*).

The extent of 'telephone justice' is impossible to establish precisely. While administrative pressure on the judiciary, corruption and selectivity in the enforcement of the law have featured prominently in the media, especially during the *Yukos* court cases (see p. 314), quantitative research shows an improvement in Russia's judicial system and increasing use of the courts by the public in the 2000s (Hendley 2007, 2009; Solomon 2010). Ambivalence surrounding administrative pressure on judges also emerges in my interviews. A balanced view of the situation is offered by one insider:

I am familiar with the judicial elite in Russia – I must say, they are exceptionally educated and decent people. I know some top judges very well – they are competent, serious. They are not scoundrels or tricksters. My impression is that they understand our society much better than our government does. There are many people in the government who got there by chance or by mistake (*vyskochki*), but it is virtually impossible to get into the judicial elite by accident. This praise does not mean of course that, if an official from the [PA] called one of those people, they would hang up or tell them not to call again. Of course not. Their lives are not easy either. But they care about the country and the state of its courts. They care about the system – it's not that they are some kind of leeches existing on handouts (*prisosalis´ k kormushke i zhivut*). No, of course not. Although there are different [sorts of] people there as well.

Legal experts whom I interviewed in Russia largely agree on the following formula: although it is ridiculous to suggest that every court case in Russia is decided according to directives from above, ways to influence a particular case can be found if needed. In other words, the pressure does not have to be pervasive to be fully effective.

The pressure imposed by *sistema* can be quite subtle. The form of influence, moreover, can be tailored to suit the personality of a judge. Court chairmen and women possess an arsenal of measures to deal with non-compliant judges, and can twist their personal integrity in a calculating way. Direct forms of influence may even be redundant when an atmosphere of 'suspended punishment' creates patterns of dependence on the courts' chairmen and women, induces self-censorship and rewards play by unwritten rules.

Legal scholars speak of a 'chilling effect' whereby informal norms and signalling devices make it clear what needs to be done without direct intervention. In systems characterised by what Philippe Nonet and Philip Selznick call a repressive law (as opposed to an autonomous law), law is subordinated to power politics, the rules of law and the judges who implement them serve the interests of the politically powerful, who personally are only weakly bound by legal constraints (Nonet and Selznick 1978: 16). Such conditions are conducive to self-censorship by judges.

In 2007, none of the serving judges whom I invited to comment on my data on 'telephone justice' agreed to do so anonymously. But by 2010 there was enough evidence in the public domain from judges to confirm the significance of such practices. Two judges of the Constitutional Court, Vladimir Yaroslavtsev and Anatoly Kononov, were forced to resign in 2009 as a result of speaking to the foreign press.[12] Their critique of the defects of the judiciary's inner workings is as poignant as Kudeshkina's. Such a change is one result of President Medvedev's efforts to publicise and prevent existing practices of putting pressure on judges.[13]

---

[12] Internal document of the Constitutional Court comparing statements of Judge Yaroslavtsev in his interview to *El-Pais* on the current legislation, 31 August 2009, http://elpais.com/diario/2009/08/31/internacional/1251669606_850215.html; see www.kommersant.ru/doc.aspx?DocsID=1285458; see also the information of the press service of the Chamber of Lawyers of the Russian Federation in connection with the resignation of Constitutional Court Judge Vladimir Yaroslavtsev and the redundancy of Constitutional Court Judge Anatoly Kononov, www.advgazeta.ru/newsd/90.

[13] Dmitri Medvedev urged the courts to make the practice of 'telephone justice' public, see E. Surnacheva, 'Telefonnoe pravo poluchit gromkuyu svyaz'',

There have been other significant changes, especially in the Arbitration courts. During an interview in 2005 with the newspaper *Parlamentskaya gazeta*, the Chairman of the Moscow District Federal Arbitration Court, Lyudmila Maikova, was asked how strong 'telephone justice' was in Russia. She dismissed the whole idea as gossip and myth. In 2008, Maikova herself faced suspension, charged with unethical behaviour associated with acquiring luxury apartments in Moscow, allegedly under the Mayor's patronage.[14] The journalist and author, Vladimir Solovyev, who drew attention to the practice of allocating Moscow apartments as a means of bribing the judiciary,[15] went on to accuse Kremlin official Valery Boev of 'giving orders to the Supreme Arbitration Court'. Boev sued for defamation but the case did not turn out as expected. For the first time, a high-ranking judge publicly admitted that the PA had tried to put pressure on her. The First Deputy Chair of the Supreme Arbitration Court of Russia, Yelena Valyavina, testified in court that Boev had instructed her how to decide a high-profile case,[16] and threatened that her career would suffer if she refused to comply. Her statements produced 'overwhelming evidence' now cited in extradition cases in London courts to illustrate that political pressure on the Russian judiciary is a reality (see Box 5.1)

The 2009 report to the Parliamentary Assembly of the Council of Europe (PACE) on politically motivated abuses of the criminal justice systems in its member states assessed four distinct families of criminal justice systems on the basis of fact-finding visits to London, Paris, Berlin and Moscow. Its section on Russia was entitled 'Still a system

Gazeta.ru, 10 May 2011, 21:59, www.gazeta.ru/politics/2011/05/10_a_3611653.shtml.

[14] 'Podpisano predstavlenie o lishenii polnomochii predsedatelia FAS', *Kommersant-Online*, 20 May 2008, www.kommersant.ru/doc/894029.

[15] V. Solovyev, 'Sudebnyi nigilism', *Analitika*, 27 September 2007, www.treli.ru/newstext.mhtml?Part=15&PubID=13898.

[16] The TogliattiAzot (ToAZ) joint-stock company is Russia's biggest producer of ammonia. In 1996 a state share of 6.1 per cent in the company capital was sold to a private company. In 2004 the Ministry of Property Relations challenged the privatisation deal in the Arbitration Court, arguing that it was made in breach of the then-current law. After two lower-court decisions upholding the deal, the third-instance Arbitration Court decided the case in favour of the state agency. An appeal to the Supreme Arbitration Court (VAS) followed. Valyavina took the case because no other VAS judge was willing to do so.

Box 5.1 Justice Valyavina's witness statement, as quoted in *RF* v. *Makarov and Makhlay*, 2009

In addition to Professor Bowring's evidence there is, unusually, overwhelming evidence to support his expert opinion. Judge Valyavina is a Judge of the Supreme Arbitration Court in Russia. In May 2008, she gave evidence before a Russian Court in relation to a defamation case. In the transcript of those proceedings, she said, 'At the beginning of my work in the summer of 2005, I received a case from the Presiding Judge of the Second Judicial Bench with the message that other Judges did not want to examine it because they feared being pressured, and so the only person that could examine the case was myself. The case was connected with the TolyattiAzot Corporation. I undertook the supervision of this case ... I then issued a ruling to request the case file and immediately afterwards a call came from Boev, then he came for a meeting. I thought this was connected with Human Resources and did not expect the conversation to turn out the way it did. It was a long conversation and he spoke at length about state interests, adding that I was probably failing to understand them correctly, and when we began to speak of this particular case, I reminded him that I was the Judge in this case and that he had no right to give me instructions. He was asking me to annul my decisions in this case. We did not discuss the details of the case – on the contrary, he said 'Yelena Yurievna, you still have to be reappointed!' Deputy Presiding Judges are appointed for six years and have a right to work for two six-year terms in a row ... Boev is a representative of the [PA] and can gather material and voice his opinions – including negative opinions. The speed with which Judges are appointed depends on objections from people like him, and Judges are afraid that they will not get what they should or what they have earned if they take such principled positions. (*RF* v. *Makarov and Makhlay* 2009: 7–8)

While the fact that Boev approached a senior judge did not automatically mean that the matter was politically motivated, British Judge Timothy Workman accepted it as such, following the Russian judges who had accepted Valyavina's statement as evidence of political pressure.

sui generis: the Russian Federation'.[17] The titles of the report's various sections are indicative of the problems of the Russian judicial system as viewed by international experts: (a) historical roots; (b) pressures on judges to convict; (c) views of the leadership of the Supreme Court of the Russian Federation; (d) jury trials – a key reform under threat; (e) defence lawyers – a high-risk profession; (f) lack of safeguards during the trial against irregularities at the investigative stage; (g) 'legal nihilism' – two emblematic cases (the *Yukos*-related cases: Mikhail Khodorkovsky, Platon Lebedev and others;[18] *HSBC/Hermitage Capital*: Sergei Magnitsky).[19]

The *Yukos* and *Hermitage* cases are covered in detail in the media and academic literature, but they could be seen as high-profile and unusual, so I highlight second-tier cases and turn to the evidence of 'telephone justice' assembled in foreign courts as an alternative source of information. It is perhaps counterintuitive to find evidence of informal commands and informal practices of 'telephone justice' in

[17] 'Allegations of politically motivated abuses of the criminal justice system in Council of Europe member states', 'Report to the Committee on Legal Affairs and Human Rights, Parliamentary Assembly, Council of Europe', June 2009. Rapporteur: Mrs Sabine Leutheusser-Schnarrenberger, Germany, Alliance of Democrats and Liberals for Europe.

[18] Khodorkovsky was convicted for tax fraud in 2005; his sentence was due to expire in 2011. However, he had been sentenced again, in December 2010, for stealing oil from his own company. His thirteen-year sentence (reduced, on appeal, from fourteen years) is running concurrently with his first and will keep him in jail until 2016.

[19] The company's CEO, American businessman Bill Browder, has been denied entry to Russia and his Russian associates have been subject to harassment and prosecution; see 'Hermitage CEO Browder: don't invest in Russia today', www.youtube.com/watch?v=84MsRuC-1l8. Three investigating officers from the MVD's Central Directorate, who embezzled $200 million from the state budget in a VAT return scheme with 'help' from the tax authorities, seem to be implicated in the case. Moreover, the investigation resulted in the tragic death of the company's lawyer Sergei Magnitsky in 2009. A bribe of $6 million was paid to keep him in prison illegally for a year where, held in solitary confinement, his health was fatally neglected: 'Glava MVD ne znal ob obogashchenii sledovatelei po delu Magnitskogo', *The New Times*, 4 August 2010, http://newtimes.ru/articles/detail/25380. Prison bosses were sacked following his death but the two investigating officers who arrested Magnitsky are still working for 'the good of their country'. The officers in question were awarded medals for good service in 2010, and this was interpreted as a signal of their impunity. 'William Browder o dele Magnitskogo, Putina and Medvedeva', *RBK-Daily*, 2 March 2012, 00:05, www.rbcdaily.ru/2012/03/02/focus/562949983114058.

judicial statements, but there are volumes of material confirming political pressure on the judiciary in Russia in extradition cases in the UK. Similar evidence surfaces in commercial cases. A wealth of data on the subject has also been accumulated in the ECtHR. Thus, in June 2010 the ECtHR asked Russia to hand over information relating to Moscow Mayor Yuri Luzhkov's tally of fifty-plus victorious defamation claims. Luzhkov had never lost a single libel case in a Moscow court during nearly two decades at City Hall, and his detractors alleged that the reason was that he controlled the courts.[20] In what follows, I consider the implications of such evidence for *sistema*, focusing in the first instance on extradition cases.

Defects of the Russian judicial system: evidence from extradition cases in the UK

Historically, extradition was a matter of diplomacy and extradition cases were rare. Today, globalisation has made the movement of people much more common. Increased possibilities for concealment have facilitated new forms of crime and, as a result, states have had to deal with the emergence of criminal havens. It is only relatively recently that extradition has become a matter of jurisprudence. The Russian Federation's membership of the European Convention on Extradition came into force on 9 March 2000. The UK has had extradition relations with the Russian Federation since April 2001. Since April 2001 and up to 11 February 2009, twenty-two people had been arrested pursuant to extradition requests received by the Home Office from the Russian Federation.[21]

Extradition requests in UK courts are judged on the basis of whether or not they circumvent the UK Extradition Act 2003 and the ECHR. Both pieces of legislation bar extradition in the event that a court decides that in any specific case a defendant would not get a fair trial in the country seeking his or her extradition.[22] Refusing to extradite

[20] R. Oliphant, 'Fall of the house of Luzhkov?', *Russia Profile*, 21 June 2010, http://russiaprofile.org/politics/a1277134075.html.

[21] 'Extradition requests received from the Russian Federation', 23 April 2009, 11:31:45, www.homeoffice.gov.uk/about-us/freedom-of-information/released-information/foi-archive-immigration/11234_extradition_request_russia?view=html.

[22] Where there is no bilateral extradition agreement between countries, they rely on the European Convention on Extradition of 13 December 1957.

Russian citizens to Russia is accordingly connected to the perceived defects of the Russian judicial system, both in general and in application to specific cases. My study of extradition cases in the London courts has shown that references to political pressure on the judiciary ('telephone justice') or political charges ('prosecution to order') often feature in cases involving Russian clients.

Russia has ratified the European Extradition Treaty, which means that it has only to present a *prima facie* case in order to secure extradition. It qualifies as a Category 2 territory – the European Union being Category 1 – and can submit extradition requests on this basis to all other signatories of the Treaty. In order to defeat the request, the defence must show that the case was politically motivated.[23] The debate is often also centred on whether the extradition of such a person would contravene their human rights under the ECHR, under the auspices of the Council of Europe (1950), which stipulates the right to free trial, bars arbitrary detention and argues for the preservation of human rights and freedoms. Article 18 relating to restriction of rights and freedoms, Article 5 on arbitrary detention, Article 3 on torture and Article 6 on fair trial are most frequently used by defence lawyers in objection to extradition requests.[24] The majority of extradition cases in the UK – such as *Zakaev* (2003); *Maruev and Chernysheva* (2005); *Azarov* (2007); *Izmaylov and Mikhaylyuk* (2008); *Nikitin and Skarga* (2008); *Dudko* (2009); and *Makarov and Makhlay* (2009) – all have references to the articles in the ECHR as well as the UK Extradition Act 2003. For example, in the case of Alexander Temerko, the barring of extradition was sought on the grounds that 'the request is made for the purpose of prosecuting him or punishing him on account of his political opinions' under Section 81(a) of the Act, and on the

---

[23] According to the Extradition Act 2003: 'A person's extradition to a Category 2 territory is barred by reason of extraneous considerations if (and only if) it appears that (a) the request for his extradition (though purporting to be made on account of the extradition offence) is in fact made for the purpose of prosecuting or punishing him on account of his race, religion, nationality, gender, sexual orientation or political opinions, or (b) if extradited he might be prejudiced at his trial or punished, detained or restricted in his personal liberty by reason of his race, religion, nationality, gender, sexual orientation or political opinions.'

[24] The European Convention forbids the extradition of persons prosecuted for their political opinions. Extradition is not allowed in civil cases and administrative legal cases. An extradition request is refused if a person has applied for and received refugee status.

grounds that 'he might if returned be prejudiced at his trial or punished, detained or restricted in his personal liberty by reason of his
political opinions' under Section 81(b), and that, under Section 87, his
rights might be violated under Articles 3, 6, and 18 (*Temerko* 2005: 2).
In the case of Tagir Izmaylov and Vladimir Mikhaylyuk, the judicial
statement argued that 'their extradition is in fact made for the purpose
of prosecuting or punishing them on account of their political opinion'
(*Izmaylov and Mikhaylyuk* 2008). Similarly in the case of Yuri Nikitin
and Dmitri Skarga, the judicial statement concluded that the 'prosecutions are motivated by political and economic considerations and
any deprivation of liberty would be arbitrary and unlawful' (*Nikitin
and Skarga* 2008). Politically motivated charges and the dependence
of the Russian judiciary, backed by documents and expert witnesses,
constituted the key themes in the defence against extradition.

Extradition was refused in twenty of the twenty-two judicial rulings in England and Wales where the Russian Federation has sought
extradition of a Russian national. The Head of Interpol-Russia, Timur
Lakhonin, has put these numbers in context:

> We have not yet had people extradited from the UK. The most famous
> cases [of refusal] are Boris Berezovsky and Ahmed Zakaev and Yulii Dubov,
> former Yukos managers, recently joined by Mikhail Gutseriev of Russneft,
> and . . . now possibly also Chichvarkin. Other countries have also barred
> extradition to Russia. For example, Sweden has refused to extradite three
> persons, two of whom were Chechens, charged with kidnapping, terrorism,
> banditry and smuggling. The reason for barring extradition is the same:
> politically motivated charges. About ninety people are currently awaiting
> decisions on their extradition in various countries . . . In 2008, fifty-eight
> people were sent back – both extradited and deported – to Russia. Russia
> has extradited eighteen people: six to Lithuania, three to Germany, two
> each to Latvia and Austria, one each to Estonia, Finland, Poland, Turkey
> and Croatia. In Europe, Spain holds the record for the number of those
> extradited and returned to Spain, amounting to a thousand people in 2006 –
> it is fairly simple within the EU countries.[25]

When countries outside the EU borders are involved, however, extradition is a long process. Lakhonin explains that, before an extradition

---

[25] In total, about 400 Russian citizens have been returned to Russia. M. Stepenin,
'Timur Lakhonin: k Berezovskomu prisoedinilis' Gutsriev i Chichvarkin',
Trud, 30 January 2009: 8.

request is issued, it is necessary to open a criminal investigation, decide on the charges and secure a court decision sanctioning the arrest. The approval of the PGO is also required. Once approved, Interpol officials around the world receive an arrest warrant that includes personal details, passport(s) and biometric data, as well as information about the legal charges and prospective sentences. Once the person is arrested and Interpol is officially informed about his or her location, the PGO sends an official extradition request to the government in question. An extradition request is received by a state official [the Home Secretary in the UK – AL] who forwards it to the appropriate organs of jurisdiction for consideration.[26] According to Interpol data, some eighty recent Russian extradition requests have been refused.[27] If this number is correct, a quarter of all cases have been decided in the City of Westminster Magistrates Court in London by the Senior District Judge and Chief Magistrate for London, Timothy Workman.

The Russian Federation as a litigant: the weaknesses of *sistema* in a global context

The weaknesses of the Russian Federation as a litigant feature prominently in judicial statements in extradition cases in London. These statements reveal problems of a procedural nature: (in)adequacy of evidence from the Russian Federation, (un)preparedness of extradition requests and (mis)understanding of the UK judicial process. Tracing the short history of extradition court cases in the UK, I identified some of the characteristics that have arguably got it off to a bad start.

From 2001 to 2003, the Russian government invested substantial resources in extradition requests for Boris Berezovsky and Akhmed Zakaev, sent expert witnesses and prepared evidence for the court hearings, yet were nonetheless unsuccessful. In the case of Zakaev, one of the leaders of the movement for Chechen independence, who had

---

[26] *Ibid.*

[27] Oleg Kiselyov, Rosnano's director of business strategy, has returned from London. In 2005, he was charged with fraud around Mikhailovskii GOK but the case was closed and he returned to Moscow in 2007. Mikhail Gutseriev won his extradition case in London but also returned to Russia once the criminal case against him was closed. See A. Zaritovskii, 'Pervyi zamestitel´ nachal´nika Sledstvennogo komiteta pri MVD Evgenii Timlev: Dela v 200–300 tomov – dlia nas normal´noe iavlenie', *Izvestiya*, 25 January 2008: 13.

moved to the UK in 2003, the British court did not reject the allegations made by Russian investigators about Zakaev's alleged involvement in illegal activity including murder.[28] Instead, the British judge ruled that Zakaev's case was based on ethnic and political grounds; Zakaev would not, the judge ruled, receive a fair trial and he would be at risk of being tortured were he returned to Russia. Summing up, Judge Workman noted: 'With some reluctance I have come to the inevitable conclusion that if the authorities are prepared to resort to torturing witnesses there is a substantial risk that Mr Zakaev would himself be subject to torture. I am satisfied that such punishment and detention would be by reason of his nationality and political opinions' (*Zakaev* 2003: 9).

The evidence of the witness Mr D was singled out by Judge Workman as particularly significant. According to the judge, the witness had made a statement to the Russian authorities implicating Mr Zakaev in December 2002 under pressure. The judge explained:

In giving his evidence before me, Mr D told me that he had been detained at a [Grozny] roadblock, held in a pit for six days, and subjected daily to torture in the form of beatings and electric shocks. He admitted making the statement but denied the truth of it. He told me that, having made the statement, he was told that he would have to repeat the allegations on television. This he did whilst he was still in custody. That interview was broadcast throughout Russia including Chechnya. He was detained for a further two months and released in February, when he realised that he could not return to Chechnya and he believed that he would be in danger if he remained in Russia. He therefore left the Russian Federation and made his home elsewhere, from where he contacted defence lawyers. (*Zakaev* 2003: 7–8)

Mr D was cross-examined. Challenging his assertions, the Public Prosecutor who had taken Mr D's statement asserted that Mr D had attended interrogations voluntarily, no one from the FSB had been present, there had been no visible signs of injury to Mr D and Mr D had made no complaint of ill treatment. Neither was there any record of anyone having been detained at the Grozny roadblock. In weighing the two

[28] Interpol received an order for his arrest on 25 October 2001. See the full chronology of the case in 'Why Denmark did not extradite Zakaev: text of the decision of the Danish Ministry of Justice on the case of Ahmed Zakaev', *Lenta.ru*, 4 December 2002.

sides of the story, the judge decided that it was more likely than not that Mr D's evidence was the more credible.

Another piece of evidence given by Russia's state official in the same case illustrates the somewhat manipulative way in which Russian authorities handle evidence. By signing up to the European Convention on Extradition, the UK acknowledged that there was 'at the very least a presumption that any trial in Russia will take place fairly'.[29] Therefore the Judge was prepared to accept that the trial process itself would be fair in terms of procedure. Yet in his examination of the pre-trial conditions for detention, the judge noted his hesitations over the official assurances:

The Deputy Minister responsible for Russian prisons gave evidence to me about the very considerable improvements that have taken place within Russian prisons in the past few years. They are commendable improvements made in difficult circumstances. He gave me an assurance that Mr Zakaev would come to no harm whilst detained in a Russian Ministry of Justice institution. I am sure that he gave that assurance in good faith. I do, however, consider it unlikely that the Minister would be able to enforce such an undertaking, given the nature and extent of the Russian prison estate . . . Although the Minister indicated that he would be detained in a Ministry of Justice institution, another witness eventually confirmed that the decision could be taken by the Prosecutor who could choose to place Mr Zakaev in an institution run by the FSB. (*Zakaev* 2003: 6)

Zakaev was subsequently granted political asylum and permission to remain in the UK. The case left a long-lasting impression on all parties. Judges' distrust of Russia's institutions and assurances are seen as biased in Russia. Whether this was because Russian officials assumed that the courts in England, like those in Russia, are politically influenced and therefore concluded – in a mirror-like thinking – that there was no point in expending resources on fighting a case that had been predetermined against Russia. Whether this was because the UK common law proceedings were unfamiliar territory, even with the guidance of the Crown Prosecution Service (CPS) representing the Russian Federation in the UK, but the Russian side put relatively little effort into subsequent cases. Thus, in the case of Temerko, Judge Workman noted that 'The Russian government chose not to call any evidence in

---

[29] Even if there is no jury trial at the present time in Chechnya, Mr Zakaev could be tried by a jury in a neighbouring state.

rebuttal' (*Temerko* 2005: 3). The same year, a similar issue was raised in the statement on Maruev and Chernysheva: 'All these witnesses gave evidence on behalf of the defendants, and the Russian government has indicated that they do not intend to call evidence in rebuttal' (*Maruev and Chernysheva* 2005: 2).

Three types of incompetence are recurrently referred to in judicial rulings on extradition cases, all of them related to modernisation: time discipline, substance discipline and 'fair process' discipline. It was these technical details that generated obstacles for the judicial process and highlighted the incompetence of the Russian Federation as a litigant.

First, as noted by Judge Workman in the cases of Nikitin and Skarga, timing was an issue. 'By the time the full hearing opened in November, the government of the Russian Federation had had over eight months in which to file any evidence on which it intended to rely. On the day before the hearing a letter was received from the Prosecutor General's Office offering certain assurances' (*Nikitin and Skarga* 2008: 2–3).

Second, materials provided by the Russian Federation are often inadequate; either too brief and insufficient or too long and detailed. Lawyers comment both on poorly constructed extradition documents, 'some of them 400 pages long and well-documented, but not really serving to persuade the court adequately' and on expert witnesses, 'the half-hearted individuals who do not believe in the cases they argue because they ultimately know and understand the falsity of these cases and may even be ashamed of the ways in which the legal system is used'. In the case of Andrei Azarov, District Judge Nicholas Evans stated in his ruling that the Russian side presented too much material and unnecessary paperwork, 'submitting (1) an eighteen-page opening note . . . (2) a four-page note . . . (3) a twenty-nine-page skeleton argument . . . I confess I did not find it a particularly easy document to follow' (*Azarov* 2007: 1).

Third, there are issues of 'fair process,' dialogue and participation. It has been said that Russians are 'not easy to work with, even if you represent them'. QCs representing the Russian Federation in extradition cases have had a hard time covering a clear imbalance in the preparation of cases. The efforts of defence lawyers who have prepared overwhelming evidence and summoned expert witnesses are mismatched against the almost total lack of input on the Russian side. Subsequently, the judge is left repeatedly to register the absence of input:

In the absence of any evidence being filed on behalf of the Government of the Russian Federation, Mr Baillie QC was obliged to test the defence evidence by way of cross-examination. (*Nikitin and Skarga* 2008: 3)

In the absence of any evidence to the contrary or explanation for the discrepancies, I accept Mr Wilcox's evidence, which demonstrates that the calculations on which the allegations are based are flawed. (*Nikitin and Skarga* 2008: 8)

And again:

I found Professor Sakwa's evidence persuasive, careful and well analysed. In the absence of any evidence to the contrary, I accept his conclusions. (*Nikitin and Skarga* 2008: 16)

Some of these issues result from differences in common law and civil law systems. Under common law, the judge is not involved in an independent inquiry but makes his decision on the basis of precedents and the evidence presented by both sides. In this context, the evidence of expert witnesses plays a key role. It seems that judges themselves are aware of this and of the impact that lawyers and expert witnesses have in a legal case. For example, Judge Evans commented in the *Azarov* case:

This defendant is by all accounts a very rich man. He is in a position to throw a great deal of money at experts and lawyers in his attempt to defeat this extradition request. It is necessary that the court be neither overawed nor impressed by the sheer volume of material produced by the defence (seventeen lever-arch files), nor the eloquence or skill of his lawyers. (*Azarov* 2007: 4)

Yet there is in reality little a judge can do about this imbalance. The judge is bound to rely on the arguments put forward by the defence if the claimant makes little effort or is unable to rebut the evidence provided.

I asked some of those involved with extradition cases about the lack of participation on the Russian Federation side, and received three interpretations. The political interpretation referred to a 'telephone justice' mentality and the resultant presumption that any participation is doomed and thus a wasted effort. The substantive interpretation, expressed by the majority of defence lawyers, suggested that the Russian Federation would not be able to rebut the evidence, even if it tried. The technical interpretation pointed to difficulties of timely translation of volumes of material produced by defence lawyers, dialogue 'lost in translation', and the incompetence of technical staff.

Experts are puzzled by Russia's passive position in extradition cases, especially in the context of the Prosecutor General's proclamations that succeeding in extradition cases is his top priority.[30] Some question whether extradition is actually the purpose of extradition requests, or whether they are instead intended as an instrument of pressure in order to achieve other goals, e.g. limiting freedom of movement or pushing for certain business decisions. Extradition requests can indeed be viewed as a 'global' addition to the range of sanctions used in business and political conflicts in Russia, as discussed in Chapter 6. Other commentators emphasise institutional problems within Russia's legal institutions – their complexity, internal divisions and lack of coordination; these undermine the ability of the Russian Federation to act as a successful litigant. It is odd that the Russian Federation has neither objected to Judge Workman as a judge, even though he has consistently ruled against extradition in Russian cases, nor ever appealed his decisions.

Only in two cases to date, those of *Tamarevichute* (appeal 2008) and *Dudko* (2009), have extradition requests been approved. Interestingly, these were both relatively low-profile cases by comparison to such well-publicised cases as *Berezovsky*, *Zakaev*, or the *Yukos*-related cases. In the case of *Tamarevichute*, the defence was rather weak and the case was subsequently also lost on appeal. Nevertheless, in this case the British judge ruled that it was insufficient simply to state that defects existed in the Russian judicial system, and that specific examples and links must be cited to show how such defects related to the cases in question. Lord Justice Richards went on to note in his ruling that 'the Russian Federation is a signatory to the ECHR and a member of the Council of Europe and the assumption must therefore be – in the absence of cogent evidence to the contrary – that it will honour its international obligations and will not act in violation of a requested person's human rights. In this case, the extradition request contains a specific guarantee that the Russian authorities will not breach the

---

[30] When Yuri Chaika became the Prosecutor General, he emphasised that succeeding in extradition cases would be his top priority. Addressing the State Duma, he announced a list of cases including the 'Berezovsky list' of five individuals and the 'Yukos list' of many more.

appellant's Article 3 rights and will afford her proper facilities for her defence' (*Tamarevichute* 2008).

In the case of *Dudko*, who stood accused of involvement in corruption and tax evasion in cooperation with a government official, the extradition request was granted. In this case, as in that of *Tamarevichute*, the judge concluded that while corruption exists in the Russian courts, a fair trial can still be held there. In his conclusion, Judge Purdy argued that:

I have reflected on all matters with care over some time. In my judgment, notwithstanding the clear findings of corrupt soliciting of bribes, there is nothing to support the contention that the trial process itself cannot deal properly with such issues as it would be required to do in this jurisdiction. Accordingly I reject the human rights challenge advanced. (*Dudko* 2009: 6)

This ruling may act as an important precedent for the future, both in narrowing the reasons for which an extradition request can be turned down, and in rebalancing the burden of proof so that more emphasis falls on the defence teams to demonstrate exactly how relevant defects of the Russian judicial system are in the specific case under consideration.

The future of informal commands

A striking shared element of the majority of Russian extradition cases in the UK examined here is that they begin by stating complete and implicit trust in the Russian Federation and its judicial system and conclude with pointing out political agendas behind defects in the Russian judicial system. In the *Temerko* case in 2005, Judge Workman highlighted the danger for lawyers involved in a defence of *sistema*'s victims that brought him to conclusion about its non-coincidental nature:

It is submitted on behalf of Mr Temerko that there was a substantial risk of discriminatory breaches in the right to a fair trial. In examining this evidence I have had particular regard to the evidence of Mr Schmidt and Miss Liptser. In particular, they told me of some of the events that occurred during Mr Khordorkovsky's trial and appeal. Mr Schmidt, an internationally respected human rights lawyer, gave evidence of the difficulties the defence team had in preparing Mr Khordorkovsky's case. He told me of attempts to interrogate Mr Khordorkovsky's lawyers, of their offices being unlawfully searched and of confidential and privileged documents seized. He told me of an incident in which he had been involved when prison guards seized documents from him and the Ministry of Justice then attempted to have him professionally disbarred by alleging that certain documents were being removed illegally from the prison. Mr Schmidt provided me with details of lawyers involved in the cases concerning Mr Khordorkovsky, Mr Lebedev and Mr Pichugin. Of 19 individuals, 12 have been the subject of application for disbarment. Five have been subjected to searches, two assaulted, one detained in custody and two forced to leave Russia. I share Mr Schmidt's view that this catalogue defies belief 'that so many lawyers could coincidently face so many misfortunes accidentally or by genuine due process of law'. I am satisfied that at least some of these lawyers suffered harassment and intimidation. (*Temerko* 23 December 2005)[31]

Before the UK signed the Extradition Act 2003, British courts would not extradite unless they were satisfied that the requesting state had supplied sufficient details of the case and that the case stood its ground. Since 2003, whether or not there is a case to answer has become irrelevant. Since the number of extradition requests globally has grown and since agreements exist between states, there is no need to vet each case that will be tried by another country's court. Thus according to the Extradition Act 2003 there is no need to verify whether the Russian Federation has a case or not; it is taken on trust that it does, and this matter is not what is contested in the British Court.

Further questions arise from the high number of Russian extradition cases being brought in the UK. It may appear that British courts provide a safe haven for criminals. It may also appear that only those who have money are given protection. Legal principles are now applied to cases that were traditionally political affairs and under diplomatic jurisdiction. The legalisation of what was formerly a diplomatic practice causes concern: how do international relations translate into the context of the rule of law? What implications do the differences between common law and civil law systems have? Judges are never truly independent: they tend to replicate and translate values of political regimes. In liberal societies, they are influenced by the liberal

---

[31] On 31 May 2011, the ECtHR ruled that Russia had violated the rights of the jailed oil tycoon and outspoken Kremlin critic Mikhail Khodorkovsky. In their unanimous ruling the judges in Strasbourg ordered Russia to pay him 24,543 Euros (£21,426) in compensation. However, the judgment stated that 'claims of political motivation behind prosecution required incontestable proof, which had not been presented'. See www.bbc.co.uk/news/world-europe-13600198.

agendas of human rights, property rights, prison conditions, public opinion and the media. Self-censorship is exercised to reinforce independence – a judge's status and reputation depend on his or her ability to create a precedent under the common law system or to stand up to pressure. In non-liberal societies, judges seem to be guided by considerations of compliance with the system, corporatism, loyalty and patriotism; self-censorship is conducive to dependence.

It is one of the outcomes of globalisation that the weakness of the rule of law in Russia is now exposed in foreign courts. Major commercial disputes are now resolved by English law: the ECtHR has been jokingly referred to as 'Russia's Supreme Court'. In 2009, 14,000 Russian nationals brought cases to the ECtHR, up from 11,000 in 2008.[32] These numbers cause load problems for the Court, the resolution of which remains at the top of its agenda. It should, however, be borne in mind that Russia has a larger population than many other member states of the Council of Europe; by proportion of population, Russia ranks fifteenth in the number of cases brought to Strasbourg. The number of extradition cases in the UK is small in comparison to the rest of Europe, and findings about instances of political pressure on the judiciary should be viewed in that context.

There are some positive trends in the Russian judiciary: the pecuniary factor of influence on judges such as 'personal gain, money, and bribes' was perceived to have declined from 55 per cent of respondents in 2007 to 46 per cent in 2010. The use of personal connections and informal relationships also decreased, according to respondents, from 47 per cent to 41 per cent, while the influence of informal commands and other forms of influence 'from above' fell from 24 per cent to 22 per cent (Ledeneva 2011b). When I asked a *sistema* insider whether an informal telephone call to a judge would cause a scandal in Russia in twenty-five to thirty years' time, his reply was optimistic:

I think, much sooner than that. Everything changes so quickly. It's hard to judge from the inside, as we are in the middle of it, and of course we wish it would change even faster. Especially since we have children and we all want them to live in normal conditions. Remember – ten or twelve years ago, Moscow was full of bandits. They sat in every restaurant, they drove the best cars and they behaved as if they were masters of the city. Where

[32] 'Soveshchanie po voprosam sovershenstvovaniia sudebnoi sistemy', 4 February 2010, Moscow and Gorki, 16:10, www.lenta.ru.

are they now? Gone. Faces have changed; a new generation has grown [up], altogether different. To us it seems slow but it fact it has happened fantastically fast. My estimate is that the generation that started school in 1991 will grow up as free people. When this generation is forty years old and takes over the dominant positions in government, state, business, academia [in 2025–30], this will change everything.

6 | 'Werewolves in epaulets': from doublethink to doubledeed

'Werewolves in epaulets'
Source: © Zhenia Vasilev.

In a novel by Viktor Pelevin, an English linguist, Muss, who specialises in Russian folklore, explains the changes of the past decade to her Russian boyfriend Styopa, a self-made banker:[1]

---

[1] See also Pelevin's perception of 'werewolves in epaulets' in the novel *A Khuli: Svyashchennaya kniga oborotnia* (Who gives a damn: the sacred book of a werewolf). Moscow: Eksmo 2004.

All fundamental social changes... are immediately reflected in folklore. What is happening now in Russia touches upon a deep-rooted, one could say, archetypal, foundation... Sociologists have not yet understood but folklore has already reflected the change. Such change is obvious in the joke about the Mercedes-600 and the black Volga....

Which joke? [Styopa asked]

At a crossing a Mercedec-600 crashes into the back of a black Volga with tinted windows. A gangster gets out of the Mercedes and starts bashing the windows of Volga with a gun. A window breaks and he sees... an FSB colonel... and then... he says, 'Comrade Colonel, I knocked and knocked but you didn't open... Where should we bring the money?'

Muss added:

What is particularly interesting about this joke is that one doesn't expect to hear any others. It is, so to speak, shared by all, as a victory.

That's no joke, sighed Styopa. – That's life...

He himself felt the wind of change though he could not find such remarkable words as Muss did. Life was changing. Gangsters were vanishing from business like rats who leave before a natural disaster strikes. From inertia the gangsters still ruled the roads in their vulgarly expensive cars; they also still sniffed heroin in their baroque palaces. More and more, however, serious disputes (*strelka*) were attended by people in uniform who made a joke of formally saluting each other – and this left it unclear whether such a meeting could in any sense be termed *strelka*. (Pelevin 2000: 36–8)

The renewed role of the security services in the economy, as they took over control and protection of business, as depicted in the novel, could be seen as positive. In contrast to the racketeering and gangsterism of the 1990s, it looked like the reinstatement of the state monopoly of legitimate violence over 'violent entrepreneurs' (Volkov, 2002, 2004). The agenda pursued by the security services, however, then moved beyond the 'control and protection' of business. By the mid 2000s, 'people in uniforms', the so-called 'werewolves in epaulets', became known not so much for demanding kickbacks and extorting payment for protection but for taking over assets and entire businesses on behalf of the state or particular power networks. They targeted the non-*sistema* businessmen (*nesistemnye biznesmeny*), businesses that grew too big or were not sufficiently defended. A revealing commentary on the logic of *sistema* in this respect was made by Evgenii Evtushenkov, the owner of the corporate group coincidentally named

'Sistema'. Explaining the raid on Mikhail Khodorkovsky's Yukos, he said:

I told him 'Misha, you'll lose your company'. And he said, 'that's fine, I have other plans' (this is a month or two weeks before his arrest)... But when you enter a new [political – AL] field (*polyana*), you should live by different rules, and these are even more difficult than in business. He was no longer in a class of businessmen. [The] size of business should correspond to the size of political influence of his owner. If it does, the owner can be confident that his business is safe. Because he has enough [administrative – AL] resource and energy to defend it.

If [the] business is significantly smaller than [the] political influence of its owner, the owner is called a politician. If [the] business is significantly larger, then it's hard to keep it safe, which is just what we've seen. The size of Yukos exceeded the size of Khodorkovsky's political influence... At some point he just got a big head (*pobronzovel*). And this is bad because you lose adequate perception of reality, while you must constantly watch your back (*obratku*) [monitor feedback]. If you don't, you start living in a distorted, virtual world, which is the most dangerous thing.[2]

In the 2000s, *siloviki* took it upon themselves to watch the size of others' businesses. Much evidence on the role of *siloviki* can be found in court cases inside Russia, and in international courts. These cases indicate an important trend towards the modernisation of conflict resolution and legal globalisation. In what follows, I draw on the *Three Whales (Tri Kita)* case, made famous by Putin's intervention and *siloviki* infighting, and on the examples of extradition cases related to commercial litigation in UK courts, against the managers of ToAZ and Sovcomflot (the state-controlled maritime shipping company). These can be seen as characteristic of *sistema* change: use of courts and global outreach. *Sistema* continuity is reflected in the personal appeals to the leadership by Evgenii Chichvarkin and Alexander Lebedev, targeting 'werewolves in epaulets', and the story of Mikhail Gutseriev, who has managed to fight legal battles successfully both in Russia and in the UK and to negotiate his return to *sistema*.

---

[2] Interview with Evgenii Evtushenkov, 'Evtushenkov: ruku Borodinu ne podam, vremia Chichvarkina proshlo', in conversation with Marina Zateichuk, *TV-Dozhd'*, 21 March 2012.

The 'Three Whales' affair: Putin's first term

Unfolding between 2000 and 2008, the *Three Whales* case is sometimes referred to as '*the* criminal case of the Vladimir Putin era'.[3] It
illustrates the emerging trend for the *siloviki* to displace criminalised
protection agencies and highlights the tendency of *piterskie siloviki* to
replace appointees of the Yeltsin 'family'. It underlined the importance
of infighting among the *siloviki* and unearthed unprecedented evidence as to how the power networks operated. 'Renovated' by Putin,
sistema has become, on the surface, associated with decorations and
adornment, with generals' epaulets and the luxury items associated
with the case – imported furniture and bathroom suites for the post-
Soviet style of refurbishment known as Euro-renovation (*evroremont*).
Yet ultimately, as the case also demonstrates, Putin's *sistema* remains
grounded in Russia's natural resources and major exports – oil and
arms – and the manual control of power networks.

The tip of the iceberg was an apparently low-level investigation into
a furniture smuggling network.[4] In 2000, both the Customs and the
MVD conducted parallel investigations into a contraband scheme, con-
cluding that luxury furniture from all over Europe was being imported
into Russia with counterfeit documentation. The latter under-reported
the weight and value of the goods in order to reduce custom duties.
The furniture was officially received by a shell firm Liga Mars and
then sold in the Moscow showrooms of *Tri Kita* (Three Whales) and
Grand. Subsequently the money was laundered in a complex scheme
involving the Bank of New York.[5] Captain Pavel Zaitsev, the inspector in charge of the MVD investigation, suspected that the scheme also
involved the smuggling of weapons and oil.[6]

The *Three Whales* affair received wide coverage in the Russian media
yet somehow it never resulted in a public outcry.[7] *Kommersant*, the

---

[3] Skoibeda (2007).
[4] The case has been researched by Licia Cianetti, 'Tri Kita: a political scandal or
an example of informal management of power in Russia. The role of political
scandals in Putin's Russia', BA dissertation, UCL, 2009.
[5] On the contraband scheme, see Skoibeda (2007).
[6] Burger and Holland (2008).
[7] See for example Y. Shchekochikhin, 'Otmyvanie graznykh deneg – ugroza
tsivilizatsii', *Novaia Gazeta*, 15 July 2002; A. Khinshtein, 'V moei smerti proshu
vinit magnata Zueva', *Moskovskii Komsomolets*, 29 May 2003; I. Bulavinov,
'Koloda Rossiiskoi Federatsii', *Kommersant-Vlast´*, 1 December 2003.

Russian daily newspaper, followed the affair for years, beginning in October 2000 when the customs officers on the case gave a press conference at which they explained how the smuggling network worked and hinted that the smugglers were being protected by the FSB.[8] These allegations referred to Evgenii Zaostrovtsev, co-founder of Three Whales, who was a retired FSB general and father of Yuri Zaostrovtsev, deputy head of the FSB with responsibility for the agency's economic security department. Before 1991, Zaostrovtsev, Sr had been the KGB superior of Nikolai Patrushev, head of the FSB from 1999 to 2008.[9] Consequent on the allegations, then-Prosecutor General Vladimir Ustinov, demanded that Captain Zaitsev pass the case to someone else and confiscated all the related files.

What appeared to be a routine smuggling investigation or, at most, 'an ordinary turf war between Mikhail Vanin, customs chief until mid 2004 and the man who once expected to replace him, Yuri Zaostrovtsev', was soon transformed into open conflict.[10] The PGO filed criminal charges, against Zaitsev (for 'exceeding his official authority by conducting twelve searches without the prosecutor's sanction and illegally detaining two suspects') and against two customs officers, Marat Faizulin and Oleg Volkov (for 'abuse of office and for trying to extort money from Sergei Zuev', co-founder of Three Whales).[11] The smuggling investigations were officially closed in May 2001 for 'lack of criminal evidence', and only the investigators in the *Three Whales* case at that point were prosecuted.[12] Faizulin and Volkov were acquitted on all charges, though they lost their jobs. Zaitsev's acquittal was repealed by the Russian Supreme Court, and he was eventually given a two-year suspended sentence. During Zaitsev's trial, a defence witness from the MVD revealed that his office had registered certain telephone conversations indicating that the PGO had received $2 million from Zuev to close the *Three Whales* case.[13]

After launching a parliamentary enquiry into the *Three Whales* affair, Duma deputy and journalist Yuri Shchekochikhin wrote directly

---

[8] L. Kadik, 'Tamozhenniki razobrali mebel'', *Kommersant*, 16 October 2001.
[9] Yasman (2006).
[10] Y. Latynina, 'New *siloviki* customs', *St Petersburg Times*, 27 July 2006.
[11] *Ibid.*　　[12] Yasman (2006).
[13] Yu. Shchekochikhin, 'Ordenonostsy: Kto i za skol´ko mozhet zakryt´ugolovnoe delo?', *Novaya Gazeta*, 18 February 2002.

to Putin, asking him to intervene.[14] As a result, the case was officially reopened by the PGO. It was the first recorded occasion on which Putin had officially taken control of an investigation and closely supervised it (by appointing a loyal 'independent investigator', Vladimir Loskutov).[15]

Some incidents in 2003 became linked to the case. The President of the furniture importers' association, Mikhail Pereverzev, who was a key witness in the trial against Faizulin and Volkov suffered a car accident and was subsequently shot dead in hospital. Yuri Shchekochikhin, who followed the case for *Novaya Gazeta*, died a few months later, aged 53. His death was officially attributed to a rare type of allergy but colleagues believed he had been poisoned because of the evidence gathered during the parliamentary inquiry that he was about to share with US prosecutors.[16] Another figure linked with the *Three Whales* affair, Andrei Saenko, the 'black broker' in charge of counterfeiting documents and registering front firms like Liga Mars, was seriously injured when an unidentified assassin opened fire on his car.[17]

Analysts interpreted the case as 'a reflection of the struggle between the [Yeltsin] "family" and St Petersburg's security personnel'.[18] The dismemberment of the Customs Committee, for instance, confirmed the total defeat of Mikhail Vanin: together he and the remnants of the Yeltsin 'family' had lost out to the so-called *siloviki*.[19] Vanin's departure opened a new era in the history of the Russian customs service, now 'transformed from an agency run by one specially trusted figure into an element in the economic regulation system'.[20] This transformation became even more evident in 2006. The customs service was transferred to the control of the Prime Minister, and Andrei Belianinov, Putin's acquaintance from the KGB (who had also worked in

---

[14] The minutes of the parliamentary discussion were subsequently reported in Iu. Shchekochikhin, 'Strana Trekh Kitov', *Novaia Gazeta*, 29 July 2002.

[15] O. Shkurenko, 'Istoria dela "Trekh Kitov"', *Kommersant*, 15 June 2006.

[16] The contraband scheme had ramifications in Europe and the USA, where parallel investigations were under way.

[17] For a complete list of the casualties and violent incidents associated with the *Three Whales* affair, see 'Sledstvie stoit na "Trekh Kitakh"', *Novaia Gazeta*, 27 March 2008.

[18] 'Tamozhennye politiki', *Kommersant*, 15 May 2006.

[19] About the 'fight among tigers' ('Family' v. *siloviki*) behind the *Three Whales*, see Rogov (2006).

[20] 'Tamozhennye politiki'.

Rosoboroneksport, the military import–export agency), was appointed its chairman. That meant 'the return of customs to the sphere of influence of the Kremlin security wing'.[21]

The *'Three Whales'* affair continued: Putin's second term

A series of high-profile dismissals and resignations among intelligence and law enforcement officers, who were accused of having either taken part in the *Three Whales* smuggling scheme or covered it up, stirred a new wave of public interest in the case.[22] In May 2006 three top FSB officers were fired, including General Sergei Fomenko, who headed the FSB's anti-contraband department.[23] It was only the beginning of a storm that claimed the jobs of a number of officials and precipitated the forced resignation of Prosecutor General Ustinov. He became Minister of Justice while, in a curious swap of posts (*rokirovka*), his office was taken by Yuri Chaika, until then the Minister of Justice.

Shortly after Ustinov resigned, Prosecutor General Chaika reopened the *Three Whales* criminal investigation. Suspects identified by the investigators as the organisers of the contraband scheme five years earlier were arrested. Of the 200 files Ustinov seized from the MVD Investigation Committee, only twenty remained intact.[24] None of the dismissed officials faced any criminal charge, moreover, although it looked as if the FSB and the PGO under Ustinov had indeed provided protection (*krysha*) to the smugglers.[25] The reasons why Putin forced Ustinov to resign were by no means clear. Some observers suggested that, with Igor Sechin's support, the Prosecutor General was becoming too powerful and might even be harbouring Presidential ambitions.[26] At least, this was what Viktor Cherkesov, head of the Russian anti-narcotic service (FSKN), allegedly told Putin.[27] The press also connected Ustinov's resignation to the undesirable publicity surrounding the *Three Whales* affair.[28]

---

[21] *Ibid.*   [22] Yasman (2006).

[23] R. Kupchinski, 'Russia: anticorruption drive touches the "Untouchable" FSB', *RFE/RL*, 2 June 2006.

[24] Yasman (2006).

[25] E. Zapodinskaia, 'Po delu "Trekh Kitov" sozrelo prestupnoe soobshchestvo: Chinovnikov v nem net', *Kommersant*, 12 October 2006.

[26] S. Charap, 'A rough selection campaign', *St Petersburg Times*, 11 July 2006.

[27] Latynina (2007).   [28] Burger and Holland (2008: 171).

Cherkesov becomes one of the main players during the second round of the affair.[29] He had the privilege of reporting directly to the President on developments in the case. It is believed that Cherkesov had the support of the new Prosecutor General Chaika, who also had direct access to the President.[30] On the other side in this 'turf war' between different *siloviki* factions were, according to many commentators, FSB head Nikolai Patrushev and Igor Sechin, Deputy Chief of Staff at the PA.[31] They lobbied Putin to create a joint Federal Investigative Committee (IC) that, albeit under the aegis of the PGO, would answer directly to the President and be a means of seriously reducing the PGO's powers of criminal investigation. Alexander Bastrykhin, who was affiliated with the Sechin clan, was appointed to head the new Committee.[32]

The IC's first action was the arrest by FSB agents at Domodedovo Airport in Moscow of four FSKN officers, including General Aleksander Bulbov.[33] Bulbov was a major figure in the FSKN-led investigations into furniture smuggling.[34] These arrests, allegedly for illegal wiretapping, are widely believed to have been retaliation for the 2006 wave of FSB dismissals linked to the *Three Whales* affair.[35]

In response to the arrest of four of his subordinates, Cherkesov published an open letter in *Kommersant* (9 October 2007). Referring to his earlier letter (*Komsomolskaia Pravda*, 2004), he praised the importance of unity among the security forces (*chekisty*) for Russia's well-being (they were the only force holding the country together, he said) and denounced clan wars that could potentially destroy the *chekisty*

---

[29] R. Shleinov, 'Skandal v prezidentskom gareme', *Novaia Gazeta*, 11 October 2007.

[30] Yasman (2006). See the discussion of direct access to the President in Chapters 4 and 7.

[31] See, for example, Latynina (2007) and B. Whitmore, 'Russia: uncertainty over Putin succession fuels "*siloviki* war"', *RFE/RL*, 9 November 2007.

[32] The Federal IC still remains much smaller than the MVD IC, which it has not absorbed. See Burger and Holland (2008: 181–4).

[33] The IC completed its investigation of the second criminal case against Lieutenant-General Aleksander Bulbov on 20 October 2010. The charges against him included fraud, falsification of documents and abuse of public office. Bulbov claims that the case against him was made on orders from above (*zakaznoe*).

[34] *RFE/RL Newsline*, 3 October 2007.

[35] E. Zapodinskaia, 'Iz-za "dela Gosnarkokontrolya" vybivaiut "Trekh kitov"', *Kommersant*, 12 October 2007.

corporation and, with it, Russia itself. [36] Cherkesov also suggested that the reason behind the arrest of his colleagues was to 'compromise the evidence' that Bulbov, in collaboration with Loskutov, had collected about the *Three Whales* affair.[37]

According to Latynina, Cherkesov had broken one of the golden rules of the secret services: 'Never appeal to the public. Appeal to the President.' By going public he signalled not only his disloyalty but also a lack of access to the Head of State.[38] One of my respondents suggested that Cherkesov spoke to the President about the letter and was given the go-ahead for its publication. Another suspected that it was a trap (*razvodka*) set for Cherkesov by Putin, who allegedly agreed that a letter be written, but after the interest prompted by its publication used it to punish the author. In the pages of *Kommersant*, Putin subsequently scolded Cherkesov for having 'aired dirty laundry' and publicly denied the existence of any such 'war of the clans' among the *siloviki*.[39]

Putin's role in the case was widely debated. He was depicted, at various times, as restoring order with a balanced and unbiased intervention;[40] sometimes as an impotent supreme leader, incapable of holding his power network together;[41] sometimes as a shrewd manager of a political game played by the *siloviki* much bigger than the *Three Whales* affair.[42] At stake in the conflict between the factions of *siloviki* seems to have been both control over the customs service (and the lucrative business it administered) and a favourable power position from which the factions could influence, if not the choice of Putin's successor at least their own post-succession status.[43] As Kirill Rogov

---

[36] Lilia Shevtsova refers to his 2004 letter as the 'Manifesto of the Cheka'. See Shevtsova (2007: 101).

[37] V. Cherkesov, 'Nelzia dopustit´, chtoby voiny prevratilis´ v torgovtsev', *Kommersant*, 9 October 2007.

[38] Latynina (2007). The reaction to police officer Alexander Dymovsky's public appeal to the President was largely negative, especially on the part of his colleagues, www.youtube.com/watch?v=R4vB2a15dOU.

[39] Bernstein (2007).   [40] See Skoibeda (2007).

[41] See Bernstein (2007) or Y. Latynina, 'A powerful President with little power', *St Petersburg Times*, 7 March 2008.

[42] See B. Whitmore, 'Russia: as elections near, rivalries in Putin circle heat up', *RFE/RL*, 15 October 2007.

[43] A. Konovalov, 'Monopoliya na demokratiyu. Predvybornaia bor´ba v Rossii est´, no vedetsya svoeobraznymi sposobami', *Nezavisimaya Gazeta*, 19 February 2008.

put it, 'it was indeed a matter of furniture: it was a matter of providing the right chair for the next President'.[44]

Essential to my analysis of power networks in the contemporary Russian model of governance is that the conflict between, on the one side, Sechin and Patrushev and, on the other, Cherkesov and Viktor Zolotov (head of the Presidential Security Service, SBP), illustrates both the range of unlawful methods – searches, confiscation and audio surveillance (*obyski, vyemki* and *proslushka*) – deployed on behalf of top state officials and the conflict resolution skills of the leadership (*razrulivanie*).[45] These instruments contribute to the process of informal governance and *reiderstvo* that often slip from view, ceding the limelight to its visible outcome, the restoration and expansion of the economic role of the *siloviki*.

Corporate raiding v. *reiderstvo*

In the Anglo-Saxon world corporate raiding is a perfectly legal activity (even though sometimes rules may be infringed). The basic idea is that a well-financed entrepreneur buys up shares in a target company, sometimes in a series of small-scale purchases so as not to alert the incumbent management and/or present strategic investor, until he gets control. The strategy is usually to reorganise and improve the company's performance with a view to selling it on in better shape some time later. There are arguments in favour of such corporate raiders, including those by private equity funds, because they keep incumbent managers on their toes and, when they do take over a company, the objective is to raise efficiency. It is one form of activity that characterises a 'market for corporate control', working through the stock market. It is correspondingly less of a feature of economies where banks rather than stock markets dominate (corporate raiding is much less characteristic, though not absent, in Germany and Japan). The difference between corporate raiding and *reiderstvo* – in scale but also in nature – is so great that I use a separate term for the Russian phenomenon, the key feature of which is theft of an asset followed by its more or less prompt resale.

[44] Rogov (2006).
[45] N. Gulko, 'Strained relations among the chekists', *Kommersant-Vlast'*, 15–21 October 2007.

Reiderstvo is driven by profit-making. According to the MVD, *reiderstvo* generates approximately 120 billion roubles (roughly $4 billion) in illegal profits.[46] 'Having invested a few hundred thousand dollars in such a raid, one can gain assets worth tens and hundreds of millions', says lawyer Pavel Astakhov, a member of the Public Chamber who is also a celebrity author and TV presenter.[47] A corporate raider, speaking anonymously to *The Guardian*, confirmed that the profits are enormous: 'It costs around $120,000–170,000 to bankrupt an average company. But you can then make $3–4 million profit.' Corporate raiders typically bribe officials in the Russian equivalent of the UK Companies House, he says, as well as bureaucrats in the agency for property registration and the bureau of land management. 'Basically raiding is robbing. The people who do it are educated and well dressed. They drive good cars. Most importantly, they have a calm head. They already have money but want more.' Asked whether he feels guilty, he replies: 'I feel sorry for the victims.'[48] In 2008 Vladimir Gusev, First Deputy Chairman of the Federation Council's committee on economic policy, entrepreneurship and property, claimed that at least 10 per cent of enterprises were engaged in fending off corporate raids. As a result they could not work to their full capacity, did not grow or invest, nor did they pay adequate taxes, and this had a knock-on effect for their employees (employment, housing, education and welfare). The phenomenon operates on such a scale, Gusev suggested, that it has amounted to yet another re-division of Russia's national wealth – the third in the last fifteen years.[49]

The full scale of *reiderstvo* is hard to establish. Between 2001 and 2008 major battles took place over re-dividing (*pilit´, po raspilu*) natural resources, the metallurgical sector and Moscow real estate. Some

---

[46] See Rosbalt Information Agency, 'Medvedev: Za Reiderstvo Nuzhno Bit po Rukam', www.rosbalt.ru/2008/02/27/460264.html; P. Aldrick, 'Exposing Russia's corporate "corruption"', 4 April 2008, www.telegraph.co.uk/finance/markets/2787471/Exposing-Russias-corporate-corruption.html; P. Astakhov, *Protivodeistviye Reiderskim Zakhvatam* (2007: 5–6) (quoted from Firestone 2010).

[47] In 2007 Astakhov's thriller *Raider* became not only a literary success but facilitated three criminal investigations. The novel ends sadly, with the anti-raider lawyer reflecting that those who helped him served the law '*IN SPITE OF* the System' (Astakhov 2007: 414).

[48] Harding (2008). Luke Harding was denied entry to Russia in 2010.

[49] Yudina (2008: 12).

assessments indicate there were 70,000 corporate raids a year.[50] Statistically, the bulk of raider activity is associated with 2006 and with Moscow, the Urals and the North-West. Outside Moscow, raiders tended to pursue either enterprises in large cities or agricultural land.[51] 'If in 2004–6 we were defending large enterprises such as the Orekhovo-Zuevskii chemical plant or the Podolsk cable plant', says Sergei Minaev, chairman of the anti-raider group of companies, 'in 2008 there was a certain decrease in the size of the attacks, and they largely targeted small and medium-sized business'.[52] Raids on a smaller scale still bring in about 300 per cent in profit.[53] According to data from the MVD Investigative Committee, the number of raider attacks has declined since the 2008 economic crisis: 512 criminal investigations were opened in 2007, but in 2008 the total was 352, with the majority still taking place in Moscow.[54]

Reiderstvo is a surprisingly low-risk business. In October 2005, the MVD made an investigation of complex economic crimes, including criminal corporate takeovers, its priority. Yet even then the numbers of raiders who were convicted remained low: of 346 criminal investigations, 51 cases were sent to court and 11 led to convictions and sentences.[55] In the three years since 2005, Pavel Astakhov estimates, tens of thousands of corporate raids resulted in less than a hundred convictions.[56] Only a handful of cases seem to have made it to the courts, which is an indication of defects in the legislation and of the complicity of corrupt officials, a 'managed' judiciary and weak law enforcement agencies.[57] Could such low risks indicate that some powerful interests are involved? The *modus operandi* of raider attacks speaks for itself.

---

[50] Harding (2008).
[51] Ermakov (2008: 2). See also www.navalnyilivejournal.com.
[52] M. Zhogleva, 'Okhotniki na reiderov', *Birzha* (13), 7 April 2008.
[53] Ermakov (2008: 2).
[54] A briefing by Yuri Alekseev, deputy head of the MVD, reported in M. Iurshina, 'Reiderov podkosil krizis', *Gazeta*, 20 May 2009: 2.
[55] *Ibid.* Compare this to the dynamics in the overall statistics of economic crimes in 2005: 438,000 registered cases, 324,000 investigated cases and 275,000 cases sent to criminal courts.
[56] *Ibid.* A source in the MVD department for combating economic crime suggests that 120,000 crimes relating to raider attacks were committed between January and October 2008.
[57] The Moscow City Deputy Prosecutor has confirmed that only a fraction of cases end up in the courts: in 2007 the figure was 2 out of 97; in 2006, 6 out of 81. Ermakov (2008: 2).

A standard method is for a company to be hit by a large invented tax bill. The owner is then arrested. While the owner is in prison, raiders use forged documents and falsified minutes of shareholder meetings to sell the bankrupted company to another firm. By the time the owner is released the business has been sold and re-sold numerous times. Michael Rochlitz scrutinised 110 corporate raids described in reports by investigative journalists. He calculates that more than eighty were instigated by corrupt officials in the state security services, the judiciary and the tax authorities (Rochlitz 2011).[58]

The arbitrary nature of *sistema* sanctions enables one official to engage in an illegal corporate raid and be rewarded, while punishing another for the honest performance of his official duties. Or vice versa. The purpose of such arbitrary treatment is to make everyone be constantly on guard and to avoid getting on the wrong side of *sistema*. A lawyer, involved in raiding court cases, who measures his own success by the number of acquittals he has achieved, by the official complaints he submitted (one of them led to the sacking of the Prosecutor's First Deputy), by the multiple attempts to revoke his status as a lawyer, as well as by his ability to organise a letter from Duma deputies in support of lawyers, says he was certainly targeted:

The real reason, of course, was that I was not 'sharing' (*ne delilsya*) [didn't pay] and did not give jobs to children of important officials simply because they are their children. So when we threw our weight behind the director of a defence enterprise facing a corporate raid, we exposed ourselves somewhat, and they got to us . . . Such was the pressure that I had to relocate my family and open an office in a different city.

For others, it had to be a different country.

From *reiderstvo* to *sistema* raiding

To distinguish *reiderstvo*, in which raiders bribe the officials, from those in which officials hire the raiders, I propose the term '*sistema* raiding'. The targets of *reiderstvo* may not differ from the targets of *sistema* raiding: both aim at state property, defence enterprises,

---

[58] Rochlitz offers a qualitative analysis of raids, such as those on the Mytishchinskii and Cheboksarskii electro-mechanical plants, the Tula and Sokolsky cellulose complexes and the like (Rochlitz 2011). Also see *Nezakonnye zakhvaty predpriyatii: Statistika ot MVD*, 28 June 2006, http://anticorr.ru/news/news674.html.

river ports, town-supporting enterprises (*gradoobrazuyuschie pred-priyatiya*), or national projects in health, education, agriculture and housing as the object of their activities.[59] Just as in other raiders' attacks, *sistema* raiding may result in a quick resale and commercial profit. The distinguishing feature of *sistema* raiding is that such raiders' attacks benefit not the raiders but the officials – who are the instigators (*zakazchiki*), the driving force behind raiding. They display certain instruments available to power networks in Putin's Russia: the use of the administrative resource in law enforcement, courts and the media. Let us consider an example.

Around 2006 there was a trend of the acquisition of land estates of about 200–250 hectares within a 150 km radius of Moscow, including the Moscow, Vladimir and Ryazan regions, and other administrative areas of the Central Federal District.[60] Since former *kolkhozy* (collective farms) and *sovkhozy* (state farm) had been reorganised into open joint-stock companies, the schemes used in raider attacks did not differ greatly in their technical aspects from any other corporate takeover (Allina-Pisano 2007). The distinction lay in the presence of high-powered officials behind the scenes. One informed source in the security services volunteered a true story, but without names or details:

A company bought some cheap suburban land near Moscow... Despite the privatisation of land and the reorganisation of *kolkhoz* into joint-stock companies, the peasants – who on paper were 'owners' of the land and shareholders – could not in practice do much with their 'property'. So when the company offered to buy shares from them for a small, but real sum of money, a queue formed of people ready to sell. By purchasing these shares the company managed to consolidate ownership of a variety of small plots of land. Then a successful and politically well-connected businesswoman cast covetous eyes (*polozhila glaz*) on this estate – well, the area is known for its beautiful landscapes. The directors of the company were put in prison and forced to sign property transfer documents (*otkaznye pis'ma*).

It can only be guesswork as to whether the prosecutor's office was paid off, or 'favoured' in other ways, in return for opening and conducting a thorough investigation of the company's business activities. The attack displayed a range of administrative resources that included a professional PR campaign

---

[59] Several 'National Projects' were launched in 2006. See the interview with the head of the MVD's economic security department, Major-General Yuri Shalakov, in E. Karachaeva, 'Reidery ukhodiat v regiony', *Vremia novostei*, 17 March 2008: 3; Barsukova (2009).

[60] *Nezakonnye zakhvaty predpriyatii. Statistika ot MVD.*

in the area, mobilising the people who had sold their plots to go to court and ensure that their transactions were reversed and the required court decisions taken. The investigation was portrayed as serving the interests of the people, which only added to the immorality of this story. After being used to recover assets from the previous owner, [the] ordinary people ended up with nothing – all they had done was to serve bigger interests.

This story illustrates how a desirable plot of land can be 'prepared' for purchase by a high-powered official. It shows how the courts deprive people of their rights instead of defending them (*ne zashchita prav lyudei, a ikh popiranie*), and how cops become the worst robbers (*samye bol'shie narushiteli*). 'Just as the traffic police become official "gangsters" with a state licence for organised robbery on the roads', ventures the same respondent, 'other state oversight agencies exercise their licence to exploit and attack businesses'.

The ambivalence between officials' public duties and their private interests is replicated in the ambivalence of hierarchies, which are served by and, at the same time exploited by, power networks. While some do the dirty work of the primary raiding, others in epaulets or sporting Camps de Luca suits, who have access to serious administrative resources, enjoy the fruits of their efforts. A legal aid activist explains such *sistema* raiding as follows:

Today, victims of raiders' attacks understand that they are confronted by a system they cannot overcome... because this is some kind of local know-how: there are connections between raiders and the corrupt authorities, the tax and law enforcement agencies and the courts. Investigations often point to corrupt officials who have either facilitated or initiated the raider attacks. At that moment, however, the pressure on the investigator becomes impossible to endure. At best the case will be taken away from him, at worst he will be sacked.[61] The whole corrupt system, based on *krugovaya poruka*, is weighted against the honest individual. If necessary this system uses the courts: some anti-corruption experts estimate that it costs \$30,000 to get a criminal case opened against a majority shareholder in a company that raiders find attractive.[62]

---

[61] Or under criminal investigation himself, as was the case with police inspector Pavel Zaitsev in Olga Kudeshkina's story above. Natalia Vasil'eva, a press clerk at the court where the second *Yukos* trial took place, said in an interview that judges faced a similar choice if they did not follow commands from above, www.gazeta.ru/politics/2011/02/14_a_3524202.shtml.

[62] S. Smirnov, 'Reiderov zakazyvali?', *Literaturnaya gazeta*, 28 January 2009: 13.

In other words, *sistema* raiding presumes a takeover of enterprises with the use of administrative resources and corrupt criminal prosecution, technologies of share-theft and a variety of fraudulent schemes. The formalities are diligently followed. The activities of most raiders are focused on the faking or manipulating of formal records, and this makes the participation of state officials almost inevitable. The editor-in-chief of the *Merger and Acquisition* journal, Anton Smirnov, identifies the following raiders' practices as particularly widespread in Russia: falsification of registration documents (*uchreditel'nye dokumenty*), double book-keeping, buying court decisions, conducting parallel shareholders' meetings, blackmail and other forms of pressure on the main owners and managers of companies. Pre-agreed court decisions and the illegitimate services of law enforcement agencies are the most expensive items in the raiders' budget.[63] In relation to *sistema* raiding, Smirnov's prediction is pessimistic:

The role played by administrative resources in this package will grow. Currently about 80 per cent of raiders' attacks are made with the help of officials. For larger assets, over and above $30 million in value, the proportion rises to 100 per cent. The modernisation of the Criminal Code in this sphere will eventually rule out 'black' forms of raider attacks and set up a trend towards 'whitening' the process. Yet this is not entirely a legal, or an economic, problem. The problem lies with the 'administrative resources'. It seems our leadership does not see any danger in property expropriation, while our local officials feed off raiders' attacks.[64]

The crossover of the public–private boundaries is observable both in raiders' technologies, relying on administrative resources and diverting state capacity, and in governmental technologies which rely on methods of informal governance and, where required, the raiding capacity of intermediaries.

'Werewolves in epaulets'

The catchphrase 'werewolves in epaulets', or 'werewolves in uniform' (*oborotni v pogonakh, oborotni v mundirakh*) reflects the tendencies

---

[63] *Ibid.*   [64] *Ibid.*

outlined above but also highlights the transgressional, if not surreal nature of Putin's *sistema*.[65]

Public-private crossover

'Werewolves in epaulets' are associated with 'moonlighting' by state officials, crossing the boundary between their public duties and their private (or affiliated) interests. By day the 'werewolves' perform their public duties; by night they engage in self-serving *reiderstvo* and extortion, empowered by access to both formal hierarchies and informal networks. In essence, any job can be turned to one's advantage, as Gerald Mars argues in *Cheats at Work*, and it is fairly common in all societies (1983). It is when the job turns into its opposite, and those charged with defending the public are widely perceived as abusing the public, that phrases such as 'werewolves in epaulets' emerge. The corrupt forms of the crossover are increasingly sophisticated: indirect participation in business that involves the children and intermediaries of state officials, and the various pet projects and charity funds associated with them. There are thus two forms of crossover: indirect business and indirect charity. They are also difficult to research: those who spoke about it openly were not the ones directly involved, whereas those involved firmly denied the practice, misrecognised it, or gave me a knowing smile. One general in charge of fighting organised crime suggested that I should stay clear of these subjects: 'You do not know and you sleep well. You want to stay sane, do yourself a favour and do not find out.'

Doubledeed

The misrecognition of the 'werewolves in epaulets' is reminiscent of the Soviet doublethink mentality that allowed a person to hold contradictory beliefs in public and in private settings. The difference is that in the 2000s the doublethink becomes the doubledeed: one can be a servant of two governors. One can hold a state position while enjoying the proceeds of affiliated businesses, personal wealth and the global lifestyle of

---

[65] Early mentions of '*oborotni*' may be found in *Trud*, 12 October 1997 and *Krasnaia Zvezda*, 6 July 1995 and 8 November 1998. For its current meaning, see *Novye Izvestiia*, 22 November 2000.

the super-rich. Helping themselves while serving the public and sharing their gatekeeping capacity with personal networks resembles the *blat* mentality. In the context of privatised assets, kickbacks-based deals and global finances, however, the implications are different, with the potential for subverting entire institutions.[66] Had the term '*blat*' not been so closely associated with the shortages of the Soviet distribution system, it would be appropriate to speak of '*blat* capitalism' in Russia, similar to '*guanxi* capitalism' in China (Ledeneva 2008a). Although different, both models of capitalism rely on the use of relationships, power networks and informal governance.

Werewolves' ability to resort to both extra-legal and legal methods – the doubledeed – is particularly damaging. Thomas Firestone has identified the following extra-legal strategies: blackmail, fictitious information and falsified documents, illegal corporate intelligence, physical threats and violence, financial resources to mobilise law enforcement agencies on the side of the raiders, deployment of administrative resources to organise other forms of pressure on the targeted enterprise, and use of collusive litigation. These define the difference between *reiderstvo* and a hostile takeover (Firestone 2008, 2010). Yet *reiderstvo* also relies on the letter of the law, court orders and lawyers (Firestone 2008: 1207). On the formal side of things, experts particularly note the link of *reiderstvo* with the bankruptcy laws and the law *On the state registration of legal entities and individual businessmen* (No. 129-NZ adopted on 8 August 2001, amended in 2003, 2004 and 2005).[67] By legislative measures, the state can defend its property from corporate raiders who are 'outsiders' as far as *sistema* is concerned. It is not so well equipped to fend off corporate raiders who are 'insiders', shielded by intermediaries and protected by their position.[68] At least, the state is not formally equipped to do so. Where the principal cannot delegate to its formal agents, however, it delegates to a trusted party.

---

[66] V. Pastukhov, *Opaque Institutions* (*Mutnye Instituty*), 2010, lecture given at St Antony's College, Oxford, 3 February 2010.

[67] Federal Law No. 129-Fz of 8 August 2001, 'On The State Registration of Legal Entities and Individual Businessmen' (With the Amendments and Additions of 23 June, 8 and 23 December 2003, 2 November 2004, 2 July 2005), http://legislationline.org/documents/action/popup/id/4376.

[68] To convey this spirit, Vladimir Sorokin refers to '*oprichshchina*' in post-modern Russia in his novel *Den´ Oprichnika* (Moscow: Zakharov Books, 2006).

Outsourcing

Outsourcing has been mentioned as a solution. One of my interviewees working on informal assignments from the government explains:

> How would I call what I do? Outsourcing. The Ministry of Justice does not have the mechanisms to enforce the decisions of the state – we have no institution similar to US marshals and our bailiff service is weak. So all the time the functions of state governance are given to private structures, especially where forceful solutions are necessary. The fact that these days many state officials came from the private sector is a help. For example, Rosimuschestvo [The Federal Agency for State Property Management – AL] takes a decision that the director of a state enterprise in which it owns 100 per cent of the shares should go. A new director is appointed, moreover, but this is not an easy decision to enforce, especially when the old director does not want to leave and employs raiders to take over. So the state agencies (*gosorgany*) hire counter-raiders. This is becoming an observable tendency and I perform in this capacity for the state.

It is indeed difficult to distinguish between a corporate raid and the recovery of state assets from a corporate raid. Correspondingly, while the lawful means of *reiderstvo* do not necessarily pursue public interests, the unlawful means do not always pursue the wrong target. Such ambivalence originates in the double standards of officials ('for friends we have everything, for enemies we have the law') and in the double-edged functions of power networks. As particular officials benefit from belonging to a power network, so the networks benefit from those particular officials – they serve as channels for advancing progressive pieces of legislation, for modernising the economy and for pursuing public interests.

The invisibles

The invisibility of the 'werewolves in epaulets' was part and parcel of the transformation that replaced the visible and identifiable gangsters of the 1990s with the invisible 'uniformed' officers. This has made cops-turned-robbers invincible, as if their corporate takeovers are empowered with a cloak of invisibility. The majority of raiders' attacks are conducted with the complicity of, if not on the initiative of, the law enforcement agencies. In extreme cases the police are known to have arrested property owners and released them only after they had re-assigned their assets to raiders. Under the circumstances, defence against raiders' attacks means defence against law enforcement agencies. Given that this defence can only be organised by law enforcement agencies, one becomes tied in certain power networks and trapped in *sistema* games.

Business capture

The 'werewolves in epaulets' represent the reversal of the capture of the state in the 1990s. In a sense the 2000s saw the return of a more customary and historically predominant model of governance in Russia, whereby the state captures business. The pre-Petrine rule of the aristocracy (*boyarstvo*), the rule of the new nobility (*novoe dvoryanstvo*) under Peter the Great, the nineteenth-century tsarist rule of the bureaucrats (*chinovniki*) and the Stalinist rule of the *nomenklatura* are all based on a model of governance under which membership formed the basis of property rights and those rights were rather limited (Gaman-Golutvina 2006, Soldatov and Borogan 2011). A similar model, known in English practice as 'trust law', separates ownership from control: an owner transfers legal rights to a trustee, who formally becomes a private owner and manager of the property but not its full beneficiary. As 'trustees' Russian businessmen of the 2000s do not enjoy secure property rights. They are allowed to run businesses on the understanding that they will reward their beneficiaries and, when requested, perform duties of corporate responsibility. Businessmen accept such terms because their businesses cannot function without the protection (lit. *krysha*, roof) of the beneficiaries and often because they did not create those businesses themselves. Where state contracts, profits and success come through networks, the proceeds are shared by the networks as well. Aware that they owe their fortune to the power network to which they belong, business displays compliance and convergence with *sistema*, coupled with fear and uncertainty. Insecurity *vis-à-vis* *sistema* is a key driver.

Insecurity forces

In tune with the ambivalence of *sistema*, the insecurity of property rights that empowers the 'werewolves in epaulets' to take over businesses also renders them vulnerable. In the same way that they benefit in their *reiderstvo* from insecure property rights, they may also find themselves exposed. When access to property and profits is determined by membership of some official's inner circle and loyalty to his/her power networks, formal property rights are of limited value. In practice, those in charge of resources and businesses are susceptible to methods of informal governance. While these may violate civil liberties they are legitimate in the eyes of the population, who remain dissatisfied with the outcomes of privatisation. When property is distributed through power networks, indeed, wealth is acquired through access to natural resources and when success is not self-made but rather 'granted' to people within the circle, then secure property rights would entrench unfairness. Fairness and justice is increasingly sought at the High Courts in London and other international courts, where the state officials often take the witness stand. According to Alan Riley, the High Court's commercial division has proved highly effective for Russian business and is awash with Russian cases, approximately half of them emanating from disputes involving the former Soviet Union. In part, this is linked to the unique flexibility of English common law, under which the doctrine of freedom of contract allows foreign parties to choose England as their governing legal forum.[69]

Globalisation of *sistema* raiding?

My analysis of extradition cases in London in Chapter 5 focuses on the defects of Russian judicial systems as presented in legal documents. Yet these cases may also be viewed in a wider context. In a narrow sense, an extradition request is a formal continuation of existing commercial disputes and related criminal cases in Russia. In a wider sense, an extradition request is a spill-over of corporate conflicts from the Russian and international commercial courts, where managers themselves may not be the primary target. They are the collateral damage in *sistema*-backed takeovers of their assets. Their extradition is instrumental for exhausting victims by litigation, undermining their morale and freezing their movements – it is the nearest one can get in an international context to keeping someone in prison so that they surrender their assets.

[69] A. Riley, 'Russia's courts of last resort', *New York Times*, August 4, 2011, op-ed section. See also (Gilinskii 2009).

Evidence of political pressure by the Kremlin administration on VAS in Russia, for example, in relation to the case of ToAZ, the producer of 8 per cent of ammonia (*amiak*) in the world (see Box 5.2), may also suggest a possible interest in commercial cases involving ToAZ (*Makarov and Makhlay* 2009: 7–8). A Duma deputy, Vladimir Gusev, himself a veteran of the chemical industry, describes the situation around ToAZ as absurd:

For its products, financial achievements and solid social policy, ToAZ and its general director Vladimir N. Makhlay were given Russian and international awards. Meanwhile, the enterprise was being stifled by inspections initiated by raiders and by unlawful demands...The staff stood up to the raiders. To escape unlawful court decisions, Makhlay had to leave the country and manage the company from abroad. He is certainly an effective manager. But it's absurd. Somebody should stop the raiders.[70]

Instead, in 2008 the Russian Federation made an official request for Makhlay's extradition, thus playing a role in the ToAZ raid. Yet it is not clear which power network in particular is behind the extradition request. Former Russian Finance Minister Alexei Kudrin, while in office, criticised the government for failing to work by the rules and for resolving key questions regarding mergers and acquisitions by instead considering the closeness of private businessmen to officials in power.[71] Evidence unearthed by defence lawyers in Sovcomflot-related extradition cases points in the same direction. Consider the account of the measures used in state-backed mergers, registered in the final statement of Judge Tim Workman with regard to the Sovcomflot manager Dmitri Skarga:

The recent history, as it relates to Sovcomflot, was that in May 2000 Mr Skarga was appointed to manage [the company]. He later became a Senator in the Federation Council serving in the Upper House of Russia's Parliament between October 2004 and September 2006. The general manager of Sovcomflot is appointed by the Russian Government, and Mr Skarga remained in post until October 2004 when he was replaced a year earlier than was stipulated by his contract. He was awarded substantial compensation...Mr Skarga's replacement then sought to use the prosecution of the former company leadership to pursue his own agenda, namely the merger of

---

[70] Law on corporate conflicts resolution is quoted to illustrate the case. Yudina (2008: 12).

[71] Belton (2011: 3).

Sovcomflot and Novoship. Mr Nikitin [of Novoship] was seen at the time to be building up a significant independent shipping company that would have challenged Sovcomflot's role as the country's primary commercial carrier. Seeking to use prosecution to force through a merger it was necessary to remove Mr Skarga from protection as a Member of Parliament. Mr Skarga was therefore removed as a Senator following what I was told was a midnight telephone call from the Kremlin. In January 2006, Mr Skarga and 10 Senators wrote collectively to the Russian Prosecutor General criticising the new management of Sovcomflot. (*RF* v. *Skarga and Nikitin* 8 December 2008, para. 29)

The commercial interests of the Russian state also surfaced in the extradition case:

One of the expert witnesses quoted in the ruling concluded that 'it is clear that there has been a concerted attempt by the state to use the *Yukos* and *Sovcomflot* cases to achieve certain goals of the Government and to enhance the perceived interest of the state ... The attack on Sovcomflot and its executives has been selective and there are grounds for believing that individuals in contemporary Russia are prosecuted because of political opinions expressed by these individuals and their role in broader political developments in the country. Similar motivations underlie the criminal investigations that have given rise to the extradition requests for Nikitin and Skarga ... There are thus, strong grounds for believing that their chance of a fair trial would be prejudiced.' (*RF* v. *Skarga and Nikitin* 8 December 2008, para. 30)

If the role of the government is obvious in extradition cases, it is rather less observable in commercial litigation, even if the state is a majority shareholder of a litigant company. However, the pressures of *sistema* feature prominently in the ruling of Justice Andrew Smith in the commercial cases against former Sovcomflot and Novoship group managers in London in 2010.[72] Three general observations made by the judge are relevant in this respect:[73]

---

[72] The High Court of Justice, Queen's Bench Division, Commercial Court, dated 10 December 2010, Neutral Citation Number: [2010] EWHC 3199 (Comm).

[73] The procedural position is that after the *Fiona/Intrigue* judgment the Sovcomflot group and Nikitin sought leave (i.e. permission) to appeal from the judge, which was refused. The parties therefore have applications for leave to appeal with the Court of Appeal. Those are likely to be heard in the autumn. Fiona is appealing part of Smith's judgment, Nikitin is appealing all on which he lost (i.e. the commission claims and findings of his dishonesty) and Intrigue

First, most of the central witnesses of fact were willing to give dishonest and untruthful evidence. In the case of those of the claimants' witnesses who live in Russia and particularly those who are employed by the Sovcomflot group or NSC group, I recognise the force of the defendants' submission that they are likely to have felt great pressure to support the claimants' case, and I am driven to conclude that sometimes untruthful allegations were made or supported by generally honest witnesses called by the claimants . . . Secondly, the claimants' witness statements were shown in cross-examination to be distinctly unreliable . . . Thirdly, witnesses manufactured an account of events, or supported a manufactured account of events, that was designed to build a fiction consistent with the documents, and the documents, as I conclude, inspired a false account rather than corroborate[d] a true one. (*RF* v. *Skarga and Nikitin* 8 December 2008, paras. 36–39)

The extradition requests for Sovcomflot and Novoship managers, had the extradition been granted in December 2009, would have undermined the major commercial trial in October–December 2010 that Sovcomflot initiated against them. If we assume that the Russian state is behind both extradition cases and commercial cases, their actions do not appear to be coordinated, unless the extradition request was not aimed at securing the actual extradition.

Personal appeals: Presidents v. 'werewolves in epaulets'

Despite the increasing incidence of legal battles in Russian and international courts, the practice of public personal appeals remains an effective means of resolving problems.

Making a personal appeal in May 2010 to President Medvedev, Evgenii Chichvarkin, the former owner of Russia's biggest mobile phone retailer Evroset, targeted a particular group of 'werewolves in epaulets'. Chichvarkin fled to London in 2008 and his extradition was subsequently sought on charges of kidnapping and blackmailing a former employee. In a video posted on the Internet, he urged Medvedev to look into his case, reiterating claims that Evroset, along with six other companies, had been attacked in corporate raids by a gang of eleven MVD officials. 'I blame this gang for raiding Evroset, so as

is appealing the costs decision as against Nikitin. If leave (i.e. permission) is given for any of the appeals there will then be a subsequent appeal. If the applications are refused, that will be that.

to confiscate the company, or at least minimise its value', he said.[74] He accused the MVD'S cyber-crime department of confiscating goods to the value of 1.5 billion roubles from seven Russian retailers in 2005, and organising a raid the following year to steal \$20 million of telephones from Motorola's Russian offices. Chichvarkin named and shamed ten individual officials at the Ministry, in addition to the supervisory officer (*smotryashchie*) at Evroset and two generals who provided protection (*kryshevali*) for the raids. They were to blame, he said, for the death of Sergei Kozlov, the former head of Motorola in Russia, who died of a heart attack in the months following the Motorola investigation, for the severe intimidation of Evroset employees, and for the list of other unlawful activities. In doing so, he gave a detailed account of the methods used in *sistema* raiding. In his appeal Chichvarkin alerted the President to the danger that Boris Levin, his former deputy now jailed for the kidnapping, might suffer the same fate as Magnitsky (see the US House of Representatives, Sergei Magnitsky Rule of Law Accountability Act, passed 16 November 2012).[75] Levin is said to have contracted hepatitis whilst in a pre-trial detention centre and is being denied medical attention, effectively a hostage to exert emotional blackmail on Chichvarkin.[76]

Rehabilitating Chichvarkin, analysts hurried to suggest, would help Medvedev salvage his liberal reputation, which had been undermined by the second Khodorkovsky trial, conviction and fourteen-year sentence (reduced to thirteen years on appeal).[77] Perhaps it was unrelated but in January 2011 the investigation of Chichvarkin, on charges of extortion and kidnapping, was closed.[78] In November 2010, nine other Evroset employees charged over the same incident were cleared in court by a ruling that no crime had taken place. The Supreme Court upheld the acquittal in January 2011.

---

[74] See Chichvarkin's blog, www.snob.ru.

[75] Moscow's infamous pre-trial detention centre Matrosskaia Tishina caught the public eye in May 2010, following the death of Vera Trifonova. Her kidney condition was deliberately ignored so as to coerce her into giving false testimony. *Russian Profile*, May 2010.

[76] In April 2010, Chichvarkin's mother was found dead in her flat. He was not able to attend the funeral.

[77] T. Balmforth, 'Throwing down the gauntlet of liberalism', *Russia Profile*, 12 May 2010.

[78] In 2008 Chichvarkin sold his stake in Evroset to Alexander Mamut for an undisclosed sum.

The charges were fabricated by corrupt police officials looking to take control of his business, Chichvarkin said, confirming that he wanted to return to Russia, and also saying he might sue for damages.[79] The closure of criminal cases in Russia is good news for Chichvarkin and his former employees. It flags the 'modernisation spirit', according to which a non-*sistema* entrepreneur should not be penalised, especially when the Evroset business had been sold in the meantime. It shows that personal intervention by the President works, but so do personal interventions of the officials facilitating criminal charges and extradition requests. Chichvarkin's evidence about 'werewolves in epaulets' will constitute additional proof of politically motivated charges and the role of state officials in *sistema* raiding, when subsequent extradition cases are heard in London.

Medvedev has taken substantial steps towards changing the legal framework. A package of anti-raider legislation was passed by the Duma in 2009 and 2010 (Firestone 2010). Falsifying the shareholders' register (list of shareholders) and registration documents will now be a separate offence under a specific article in the Criminal Code.[80] The main innovation in this legislation is that it specifies punishment for officials who take part in corporate raiding. If an official used his public office to make changes in documents, or secure their withdrawal or substitution, the penalty is up to four years' imprisonment; but if raiders' attacks have inflicted bodily harm, that sentence may rise to ten years. There have been significant efforts to modernise the Criminal Code in relation to economic crimes. The changes aim to close existing loopholes in the legislation and create new barriers for those accustomed to committing complex crimes and using sophisticated ways of 'beating the system' (Firestone 2010).

The question is whether such legislative changes will make any difference. Almost two years on, Medvedev admits the gap between what is on paper and the reality, but argues that things are getting better:

Because the law is not just a set of rules put down on paper. It is also the spirit of the law, the way in which legislation is executed. I can be perfectly frank: in our country, there is a gap between the letter and the spirit, between

[79] 'Chichvarkin case closed', *The Moscow Times*, 25 January 2011, www. themoscowtimes.com/news/article/chichvarkin-case-closed/429593.html.
[80] Editorial, 'Articles for raiders', *Ekspert* No. 24, 21–27 July 2010: 4.

how the law is formulated and how it is executed. I do not believe that this gap is dramatic in nature. On the contrary, I think that we are bringing closer the boundaries of the law and its execution. These problems exist in any state, but for us to walk this path – this is a serious task.[81]

Its seriousness stems from the difficulty in distinguishing between those government officials who are truly behind the anti-raider reforms and those who are themselves involved, however indirectly, in large-scale and globalised raids. The most recent appeal for protection from a 'bandit raid' came from Alexander Lebedev, the proprietor of the Russian newspaper *Novaya Gazeta* and the UK newspapers *Evening Standard* and *The Independent*.[82] Questioned about the alleged embezzlement at the bank that his business empire once controlled, he called on Prime Minister Putin to intervene in the investigation. It was being propelled, he claimed, by a criminal gang working with senior officials in the FSB and the MVD. 'I believe we are dealing with an organized mafia group which, under cover of orders from above, is making bandit raids on my business', he said in his open letter of 19 February 2011.[83] '[T]hese are the same people who went after Chichvarkin and Magnitsky', Lebedev claimed, reporting the mounting pressure on his relatives and on his bank's employees following an armed raid on the bank in November 2010 by the law enforcement agents.[84] The first-hand accounts of owners who have lost their businesses may be bitter and biased, just like witness statements by litigants in court, whereas judicial rulings include both sides of the story and are in the public domain.

It is worth noting that when appeals are made to the political leadership, the victims of raiders' attacks refer to their attackers as 'gangs' and 'bandits', while 'misrecognising' them as *sistema* raiders. In effect, it is an offer to comply with *sistema* if their particular case is resolved,

---

[81] President Medvedev's address to the 11th session of 'St Petersburg Dialogue', an annual Russian–German forum, broadcast live by the state-owned news channel *Rossiya 24*, 0824 GMT, 19 July, 2011.

[82] Belton (2011: 3).   [83] *Ibid.*

[84] As part of a separate probe into alleged embezzlement, police also raided the Moscow offices of Elena Baturina, Russia's richest woman and wife of the ousted Moscow mayor Yuri Luzhkov, in February 2011. The departure of Yuri Luzhkov is interpreted as an opportunity for reorganising spheres of influence and business interests in Moscow. No interpretation is final when it comes to *sistema*. In this sense, *sistema* is truly post-modern.

even on a basis of selective fairness, justice instead of court decisions and law enforcement and disregard for the institutions of the rule of law. In a way, personal appeals to the President are themselves testimony to the effectiveness of *sistema*'s means of informal governance: manual control, telephone justice and oral commands from above.

Sistema gives, *sistema* takes

One of most interesting examples of *sistema* raiding, apart from Yukos, is the case of Mikhail Gutseriev. There are cases where a state official (or a powerful broker of *sistema*) determines whether the existing owner of a business has to be forced out, and where a state-led forced takeover results in a new private owner, only one more acceptable to the Kremlin. The Russneft case is particularly interesting because it developed unexpectedly, with Gutseriev's rehabilitation and regaining of ownership. It also provides some insight into how personal appeals work their way through *sistema*.

The story first came to my attention at Valdai in 2005, when Putin seemed angered by a question about Russneft, Mikhail Gutseriev's company, and stated meaningfully: 'We know the Gutseriev brothers.'[85] In 2007, Gutseriev published an open letter titled *I Decided to Leave* explaining why he had to abandon Russneft and move to London (Hanson 2009).[86] The Gutseriev story is also a tale of the (usually) successful litigation against extradition, the traumatic experience of finding out 'who your friends are in times of trouble', and his (unusual) return to Russia.[87] Interviewed by *Vedomosti* on his return, Gutseriev claimed to be a non-*sistema* person (*nesistemnyi*), yet his views on exit and re-entry into *sistema* offer insights into its inner workings and its capacity to pursue its victims (see Box 6.1 and the discussion of informal sanctions in Chapter 7).

---

[85] Mikhail Gutseriev managed the state-owned oil and gas consortium Slavneft, and became involved in the battles around it, involving *kompromat* and the violent takeover of Slavneft's headquarters in 2002. The same year, Gutseriev's brother attempted to run for the Presidency of Ingushentia.

[86] M. Gutseriev, 'Ya reshil uiti', *Vedomosti*, 30 July 2007. Gutseriev was rumoured to have upset some powerful insiders by trying to acquire the Yukos stake in Transpetrol (Slovakia).

[87] Interview with Mikhail Gutseriev, see Reznik (2010).

Box 6.1 Excerpt from the interview with Mikhail Gutseriev, 2009

... Lots of people came to London and offered help with my return but I said the same to everyone: criminal cases against me should be closed on the grounds of absolute acquittal. I am grateful to Vladimir Evtushenkov, co-owner of AFK Sistema, and to German Gref, Chairman of Sberbank, who took part in the process of my return. Since Sberbank was the main creditor of Russneft, Gref's opinion was crucial, and I am grateful for his support of this project.

Q: How did they help you return?

I met with Evtushenkov in London at the end of 2009, when all the tax demands (*pretenzii*) had been withdrawn. The court cases were all over in 2009 but Evtushenkov did not then even know that I would be getting Russneft back. He simply came for advice on how best to manage [his own oil company] Bashneft. The conversation drifted to my return and the best way of conveying to the officials that I had been sentenced unjustly. Evtushenkov has helped selflessly and played not the last part in delivering the truth to those in high office. He did not have a personal interest, yet he helped to clear my name and asked nothing for it.

Q: So what about Russneft shares?

Had he made his help conditional on receiving shares in Russneft, I would have not considered it. People cannot talk to me from a position of force or issue ultimatums. But I am flexible, people can negotiate with me, on market and non-market conditions. Not use pressure, though. I offered the Russneft shares myself. Since they carry $7 billion worth of debt I offered him 49 per cent of the shares for free. He turned that down and paid $100 million.

Q: How have you managed to return when other Russian business-men who are hiding from Russian courts in London have not had the same success? What is the explanation?

It's fate. It was on the cards. I played and was lucky. I think that all who left, including myself, have themselves to blame. I had to 'ori-ent' myself correctly and show good timing, but I made mistakes, I didn't understand the situation and didn't take the right course of action. I tried, but clearly I was not clever or persistent enough.

I was rather guilty of pride and independence, while aggressively acquiring assets. What I have achieved in Russia made many envious.

. . . It was a sistema slander (*sistemnyi nagovor*) that built up over years. On the one hand, it was caused by the rapid development of the company, the growth in its resources and the aggressive acquisition of new assets; and, on the other, there were my ethnic origins, religion and a success achieved without any administrative resource. All of this took place against the background of the latent war in the Caucasus and the complex situation in Chechnya and Ingushetia.

Q: It is said that Putin was given a list of oil companies at a meeting of Russia's Security Council in 2005 in which Russneft led the field in the growth of its resources. Putin was outraged, it was rumoured, especially that Russneft had purchased some of the Yukos assets

I don't believe that myself. If they had not wanted it, they wouldn't have allowed that purchase to be made. I do not think my person is of interest to Putin. We belong to different weight categories.

Q: Perhaps your return is linked to the complex situation in the Caucasus? At a meeting in Makhachkala on 1 April Medvedev suggested that businessmen of Caucasian origins 'open their wallets and spend something on financing their own republics'.

There is no need to look for a Caucasian 'connection' in my return – only court decisions and the goodwill and fairness of the President and the Prime Minister. If the President thinks I need to open my wallet, I will be informed about it, but until now nobody has discussed it with me. No representatives from my region, as far as I know, took part in the process of my return. I used to spend $50 million of my personal income on charities in Russia, including charities in the North Caucasus. I invested tens of millions of dollars in Chechnya and have never regretted it. After the tragedy, we ought to help [the] Chechen people . . .

I knew that I would return sooner or later. All tax demands against me have now been annulled by decision of the Supreme Arbitration Court. There are no longer charges of unlawful enterprise. The law enforcement agencies have acted lawfully. I am grateful to Dmitri Medvedev and Vladimir Putin for looking into the situation and seeing that justice was done. Without them, the question of my return would never have been solved. I fully acknowledge this. It was approved (*soglasovano*) and my thanks go to them. I don't want this to look like flattery but I will be grateful to them for the rest of my life.

Q: Are you worried about the possibility of new charges? It is for good reason that we say in Russia: 'Show me the man, and I'll show you the article [in the Criminal Code] to fix him.'

I am no longer scared of anything. Three times I lost everything and three times I started again. This will be the fourth. I trust the President and the Prime Minister. Russia is not only my place of birth, it is my life. I have lived here for fifty years and will live here another hundred. Russian is my main language. I don't want to shout about patriotism but Russia does mean something to me. I'm happy to be back. I went to the cemetery where my son, my brother and my parents are now. I could not do this for three years. That was one reason I returned. I still blame myself for not taking my youngest son to London. I left him behind so that he could see with his own eyes the idiotic actions taken by Russian judges and officials. He was called in for questioning by the Investigative Committee. I assumed it would be useful for him. He would observe and draw conclusions about the country he is going to work and live in. He should be prepared. [Gutseriev's son Chingiskhan was subsequently killed in a car accident.]

Q: You explained the sale of Russneft in terms of the unprecedented pressure on yourself and your family. How did it happen?

Seventy criminal investigations were opened and there were constant raids on the homes of Russneft top managers.

Q: Why did 'Sistema' [Evtushenkov] become a shareholder of Russneft? So that you'd be tied up more securely? Or does Evtushenkov serve as an 'intermediary' for a high official, through whom the question of your return has been solved?

He doesn't 'mediate' for anybody (*ne frontiruet*). I repeat: I offered Evtushenkov a stake in Russneft on condition that I keep operational control. He is a strong, influential and clever partner, and I will also profit from a merger with Bashneft. The question of 'intermediaries' came up in a different context. I suggested to Evtushenkov that we register Russneft shares offshore, so that the transaction went ahead faster. However, to avoid rumours and insinuations, he said, we must do this through 'Sistema', a publicly listed company, where 60 per cent is owned by Evtushenkov and the rest by foreign investors. The transaction took four months to complete but now nobody can say that Evtushenkov was buying shares for somebody else.

Source: Reznik (2010).

The boundaries of *sistema* are tested when they are crossed. It has been suggested above that knowing the limits of *sistema* is the mastery of its unwritten rules. It is when people, knowingly or unknowingly, violate those rules that *sistema* turns against them. There are also instances when *sistema*'s defectors are admitted back into the ranks. Why and how it happens, and on what conditions, is context-bound. Gutseriev's story seems to suggest the following features of Putin's *sistema*. First, it is legalistic. The use of law as an arsenal, as ammunition for the *sistema* raiding of businesses is destructive for the business environment. Second, it is patriotic. In his 'manual control' style of leadership, Putin limits the rights of *sistema* inmates: overt displays of personal wealth are possible for 'our guys' (*svoi*) but moving that wealth abroad and breaking ties with *sistema* can lead to punishment and victims may be pursued through the international courts. Third, it is not just about business, it is personal. Personal loyalty rather than generalised loyalty should be displayed. Above all, Gutseriev's story confirms the effectiveness of the informal ways of conflict resolution within power networks and points to the issues of informal governance and leadership, to be considered in Chapter 7.

7 | *From dealership to leadership:* sistema *and informal governance*

Informal leadership

Research into how leaders rule and manage Russia is vast, but evidence of the informal ways of getting things done at the leadership level is fairly scarce. It is not that power networks, unwritten rules, double standards, multiple moralities and forms of self-deception, played out in the field of informal politics, are not applicable to the leadership level, but they are rather difficult to research. In this chapter, I explore the ways in which reliance on power networks and instruments of informal governance affects leadership style. In order to exercise leadership, the official has to become an experienced broker of *sistema*, to stay in control of power networks, monitor their dynamics and use the instruments of informal governance. Leadership implies a combination of methods applicable in official hierarchical contexts and those applicable to unofficial power networks, which often seamlessly transform into each other. The literature on informal governance is somewhat limited, whereas leadership theories tend to examine practices of informal management under the rubric of interpersonal skills, rather than associate them with the nature of the organisation.[1]

Similar to the daily use of networks for getting things done, the use of power networks in government jobs is taken for granted and often misrecognised. (Putin's use of power networks and reliance on informal governance is part of folklore.) The purpose of this chapter is to make informal governance an explicit part of the leadership story, to articulate and account for the instruments of informal management, so that they can be reflected upon by those who use them and those

---

[1] The *Novaya gazeta* website has a rubric on *Informal Leaders of Russia*, run by Alexander Donskoi, the former mayor of Arkhangelsk, where 'informal leadership' is defined widely as embracing spiritual leadership, reputational leadership, etc.

to whom they are applied. I argue that issues of informal governance deserve more systematic and in-depth analysis.

Leaders as patrons and patrons as leaders

In his contribution to the *Leading Russia* volume, Robert Service observes that studies of leadership in the USSR have traditionally interwoven questions of leadership with questions about its periodisation, its relationship with *nomenklatura* and the nature of the Soviet order (Service 2005). In his view, most writers have started from the leadership question but drifted to the others. Leadership was associated with the immense personal power of the Soviet general secretaries, each of whom had the automatic obedience of the party, government and the state, what became known as the 'totalitarian model of governance'. Even though there is now an overall consensus on the limitations of the latter, other existing models of the Soviet governance – the 'revisionist model' and the 'mono-organisational society' – do not offer a conception of leadership that provides an adequate alternative. Service explains the difficulty of defining the system by the 'schizoid nature of the USSR', stemming from the ambivalence of its central control, clientelist politics, widespread informal practices, misinformation going upwards and downwards, and popular cynicism (Service 2005: 71).[2]

Interest in informal power predominates in the Kremlinology of all times: the strength of ties is assessed through photographs, seating plans and frequency of meetings, with the purpose of determining those belonging to the inner circle.[3] Edward Keenan relies on proximity to the body of the tsar as the indicator of Muscovite power (Keenan 1986). Geoffrey Hosking emphasises the role of personal power networks, defined as hierarchical relationship between patrons and clients, and views them as the main pillars of governance during both tsarist

---

[2] The famous anecdote on the six paradoxes of socialism highlights the widespread informal practices serving to bridge the schizophrenic paradoxes of *sistema*. In this sense, these informal practices are not a problem but a solution (Ledeneva 2006, Ledeneva 2011a).

[3] The latest list of Putin's meetings, showing the frequency of his meetings with corporate leaders, appears in *The Moscow Times*, July 2011. Formal appointments, as his press officer Peskov notes, are only part of the story. There are also informal meetings.

and Soviet Russia. He identifies the foundations of the patron–client relationships in imperial Russia, such as kinship, geographical location and institutional position, which drew in those who had worked together in the same office, especially if it had a specialist function, such as the State Chancery or the Ministries of Justice or Finance (Hosking 2004).[4]

Hosking argues that the Russian political system cannot be characterised as purely autocratic at all times: if one sticks with the traditional view of the Russian state as simply authoritarian, in both its tsarist and Soviet forms, then one will find it difficult to understand a great deal about Russian history. If, on the other hand, one looks upon the Russian political system, under tsarist rule and the Soviet *nomenklatura*, as being a statised network of personal power, with marked elements of patronage and clientelism, then the dominant features of the present-day Russian state and its political economy can be more readily understood. Once the network dimension is integrated into the historical analysis (Mann 1992; see also Easter 1999; Gorlizki 2010; Khlevnyuk 2009; Mitrokhin 2008, 2011), the power becomes associated with networks as well as individual leaders.

Political scientists Thomas Christiansen and Simona Piattoni depersonalise the concept of clientelism and its double-faced nature – practically expedient but normatively suspect. Clientelism is often used to denote all long-term, mutually convenient (although not fully legitimate) deals that restrict competition within closed circles. These deals are not fully legitimate precisely because they tend to limit the selection of partners to pre-established groups of 'friends', who may have a common interest in exploiting some available pool of public resources and keeping 'outsiders' out. But they may also be explained by the simple convenience of not having to re-negotiate the terms of long-term relationships based on mutual knowledge and trust (quoted from Verdier 1995 in Christiansen and Piattoni, 2003).

In other words, clientelism is premised on very similar assumptions as those that sustain the networks through which informal governance typically works, including that within the European Union and elsewhere (Christiansen and Neuhold 2012). Patron–client relationships offer modest but definite benefits to the clients but they also carry

---

[4] G. Hosking, 'Patronage and the Russian state', *The Slavonic and East European Review*, 78 (2), 2000: 301–20.

potential dangers. Christiansen and Piattoni (2003) draw attention to the lack of enforceable and sanctionable procedures, which generates corruption and nepotism, on the one hand, and the necessity for formal hierarchies to undermine the networks' credibility and legitimacy in order to sustain and boost their power, on the other. This potentially damaging symbiosis of hierarchies and power networks highlights the question of legitimacy of informal governance, and the dilemma between such legitimacy and the efficiency of informal governance. Power networks tend to create effective yet illegitimate shortcuts that undermine the efficiency and legitimacy of formal institutional channels. Huskey points to patronage as a key instrument of Putin's political leadership, using the United Russia Party (and Just Russia) that supports his administration and offers a pool of personnel to be tapped to occupy key posts in the government (Huskey 2005: 63). My conception of *sistema* takes this point further, integrates the ambivalence of networks and practices into the governance model and focuses on the implications that they have for the leadership.

Putin's leadership: manual control and personal loyalty

Putin's leadership style is commonly associated with manual control and personal loyalty. The so-called 'manual control', also known as 'micro-management' and 'personalised governance', discussed in Chapter 3, was reflected upon by Prime Minister Putin in his 2010 live Q&A session on national television.[5] Answering a question on whether he was not afraid of micro-managing Russia, Putin said:

It is impossible to govern a country like Russia effectively in the micro-management mode. I can tell you that it is impossible to govern any country in the micro-management mode, a small Luxembourg or any other country,

---

[5] He was speaking to journalists after his annual phone-in on 16 December 2010, as shown on the state-owned Russian news channel *Rossiya 24*. Apparently the reading of the sentence in Khodorkovsky's second trial had been postponed so as not to divert the attention of the global media from Putin's answers, according to Natalia Vasil´eva, a press aide of Judge Victor Danilkin. In her interview to the TV channel *Dozhd´* on 14 February 2011, Vasil´eva has given an insider account of the end of Khodorkovsky's second trial and revealed that the final sections of the sentence were delivered from the Moscow City Court after the reading of the sentence had started. www.gazeta.ru/politics/2011/02/14_a_3524202.shtml.

not only an independent country but also any region. A system is required. But where the system does not work, one cannot be sitting back with one's arms folded or picking one's nose and say: well, the system is not working, therefore, we are sorry. Personal involvement is needed here. And one should not be afraid of responsibility.[6]

This statement is an example of Putin's rhetoric – there should be an effective system of governance in Russia as in any other country – but it is also an illustration of Putin's leadership style. Putin comes across as a hands-on leader, not afraid of personal involvement where needed and of taking responsibility for it. The scale of his personal involvement, his reliance on power networks and his choice of management instruments shape his actual leadership style and define the room left for the development of institutions.[7]

In their portrayal of Putin as a 'CEO of Russia Inc.', Manfred Kets de Vries and Stanislav Shekshnia use an eight-role model of an effective CEO to assess his performance. The authors state that since a leader's style is strongly influenced by his or her 'inner theatre', 'the unique life-script that each person enacts in response to deep motivational needs and in correspondence to the experience of interacting with the outer world', Putin's ineffectiveness is rooted in his personality and his earlier life experiences. They argue that Putin demonstrates a combination of controlling and paranoid dispositions, which have some productive elements: 'the first conducive to monitoring internal operations, the second to scanning the external environment' (Kets de Vries and Shekshnia 2008). However, too much control and too little trust at the very top quickly becomes highly dysfunctional, creating toxic environment and stalling development. One of my respondents also observes that Putin labels people as 'insiders' and 'outsiders' (*svoi* and *chuzhie*) rather harshly. It takes him a long time to consider someone a '*svoi*':

Putin takes information from *svoi* only. He seems unable to trust people and the delivery of information and signals-gathering occurs through *siloviki* but, make no mistake, they assemble it from all over the place (*po shirokomu frontu*).

---

[6] BBC Monitoring, 'Russian leadership needs to step in personally where system fails' – Putin, *Rossiya 24*, 16 December 2010.
[7] See Medvedev's address at the St Petersburg International Economic Forum on what can – and, more importantly, cannot – be done. *RT.com*, 20 June 2011, 11:18.

Kets de Vries and Shekshnia argue that for the first six years of Putin's Presidency, in spite of a favourable economic and political environment, his performance as a head of state had been modest both domestically and internationally (Kets de Vries and Shekshnia 2008). If one looks at their findings from the network perspective, Putin's high scores as 'communicator', 'processor', 'transactor' and 'builder' can be interpreted as his ability to ride the *sistema* forces, whereas his scores associated with *sistema* change – 'strategist', 'innovator', 'coach' and 'change catalyst' have not been so successful. His performance therefore may reflect not only his 'inner theatre' but also the power of *sistema*. Putin's skills in 'monitoring internal operations and scanning the external environment' result in the effectiveness of his hands-on management in the *sistema* context and in the real power it generates:

Putin has been different. He keeps changing every 2–3 years. But his method has remained the same – 'manual steering' (*ruchnoe razrulivanie*). He engages in conflict resolution and makes sure that his decisions are accepted. In contrast to Medvedev, who would not make a call, Putin would call and say, 'Do it like this'. Inevitably, issues end up on his desk, especially sensitive issues, especially those involving key players. This is why he remains at the steering wheel (*rulit do sikh por*). Now that he cares less and less, he still makes a call and says, 'can't do without me, eh?' (*opyat' bez menya ne spravilis'?*). Issues can be of a trivial nature – funding for a football team, support for a chess association, or telling off oligarchs – nothing is decided without him.

Most respondents in executive positions refer to constant monitoring of *sistema* as an absolute necessity. Constant involvement, a hands-on approach and mastery of conflict resolution are the foundations of informal governance and are considered to be an indication of real power. Sociologists associate the latter with informal status resulting from the centrality in the communication network that has frequently been the focus of studies of power (Blau 1963; Blau and Alba 1982). In colloquial terms, informal status in Russia is associated with an idiom meaning 'to solve problems' (*reshat' voprosy*), implying the effective use of informal networks and administrative resources.

From a theoretical perspective, the methods of informal governance can qualify as performance management instruments and fall under theories emphasising leaders' roles or functions (Shekshnia 2010; House and Aditya 1997). The existing lists of leaders' functions –

defining a vision, introducing organisational norms, setting goals, creating organisational instruments and mobilising resources – derive from Weber's analysis of power but none of them specifically includes instruments of informal governance.[8]

It is tempting to think about informal power, status and influence as a pyramid, by analogy with formal power, because the power networks involved in informal governance are also vertically integrated, somewhat hierarchical and can be similarly rigid and brutal – 'like a wolves' pack', in the expression of one respondent. Yet they surface in more subtle ways and involve constant and mutual monitoring by key players, including highly personalised checks and balances. According to a well-informed respondent, the monitoring function of *smotryashchie* (the watchers) is central for informal governance and should not be associated with some stereotypical *siloviki* planted everywhere to watch over businesses or projects. The checks and balances of *smotryashchie* emerge from Putin's networks' watching over one another and from their informal reporting:

In reality, *smotryashchie* is not a single eye. It's a complex system. Where there is some money, there should be control. Putin controls manually. He does not trust anybody. There are checks and balances and there are trusted watchdogs. There is Rottenberg. There is Akimov. There are [the] Koval'chuks. There is Timchenko, who also starts steering (*rulit´*).[9] All these people have access to Putin through a private room in his office. Each of them has Putin's ear and in the end he [Putin] gets a more or less adequate picture. He divides and rules. In each constituency, there are those associated with Berl Lazar and there are those associated with Adolf Shaevich.[10]

---

[8] Weber defined *domination* (authority) as the chance of commands being obeyed by a group of people and focused on legitimate authority, recognised by both the ruler and the ruled. *Rational–legal authority* depends for its legitimacy on the formal rules and established laws of the state, usually codified and complex. *Traditional authority* derives from long-established customs, habits and social structures. *Charismatic authority* is based on the personal charisma of a leader, originating in a higher power or inspiration, superior to the nature of traditional and rational–legal authority.

[9] R. Shleinov, 'Gazprom v okruzhenii priyatelei i rodstvennikov prem´er-ministra Rossii', *Novaya Gazeta*, 23 December 2009. See also Mokrousova (2011).

[10] Interviews with Russia's rabbi, Adolf Shaevich, *Novaya gazeta*, 5 July 2010, www.novayagazeta.ru/data/2010/071/25.html. The Federation of Jewish communities (Lazar) is different from the Congress of Jewish religious communities and organisations (Shaevich).

He also uses non-*sistema* sources that we know nothing about. It is like the operative work of reading dossiers, morning FSB reports (*utrennya spravka FSB*), general country reports (*obschaya spravka po strane*), [and] memos (*dokladnye zapiski*) that come from almost everywhere. It used to be Sechin who did the reading, now it must be somebody else's job. The operative work, however, continues as normal.

Informal networks are engaged in performing functions as outlined above, but this is not done explicitly. Informal aspects of leadership also seem to be omitted in theories emphasising the personal attributes of leaders – a certain quality of an individual personality by virtue of which he is set apart from ordinary men. In the context of Russian (s)elections and *blat* appointments (see Chapter 3), leadership qualities do not seem to matter at the point of recruitment – yet another testimony to the network-based governance model. When asked about leadership qualities in governing structures, an insider says:

Leadership qualities do not play a role as such. There are such entities (*edinitsy*), sometimes of weak character, who become leaders because they have a patron high up to place them in those positions, and then a team (*komanda*) is created to go under them. Not personally for them, but for a certain ministerial position or function (*pod zadazhu*). If we don't look at the very top, there are teams with a leader and teams without. If we look at the very top, well . . . [sighs, presumably about Medvedev].

The respondent slips off the subject. I do not pursue it either since personalities are not that important. The role of contacts surfaces clearly enough in the quantitative research. The data of the all-Russian national survey indicate that only 18 per cent consider it inappropriate to use *blat* networks for career purposes. 25 per cent believe that it is impossible to make a career without connections. 54 per cent acknowledge having used connections for their own careers because they have no alternative. The perception of the importance of connections for finding a good job is even higher (68 per cent).[11] The importance of connections for obtaining a leadership position must be higher still.

Although people in executive jobs are meant to be compliant, their personal qualities can make some difference. The same insider

---

[11] 'Opros: 25 protsentov rossiyan schitaet, chto bez blata kar´eru ne sdelaesh´´', *NEWSru.com*, 17 April 2011, 11:38. The VTsIOM survey took place on 12–13 March 2011, in forty-six regions of Russia. The poll was conducted online by a headhunting company among 3,163 respondents, www.newsru. com/russia/17apr201/karierra_print.html.

respondent links the scale of kickback practices with the personalities of leaders in particular departments:

Generally, creative officials can turn any position to their advantage, but much depends on the leadership (*lyudei naverkhu*). In some places bosses cover up and receive kickbacks, in other places not. In [the] Ministry of Economic Development, for example, there are departments where they have it, and there are departments where they don't, because [the] people in charge don't do it and try to [stamp] it out around them (*vyzhigat´ eto*).

Differences between leaders produce variations in recruitment practices. It is not impossible for a leader appointed by a patron to recruit his or her team on merit. It depends on the personal and professional qualities of the patron appointee. The level of appointment is also crucial in this respect. If *blat* networks, referred to in the national survey, are likely to be perceived as fairly common and semi-open (one can make contacts, if one doesn't have them), the patron–client networks referred to by the respondent above presume 'closed' opportunities for *svoi* people and imply long-term affiliation and loyalty.

In itself, loyalty would not be a problem, it is celebrated in a step-by-step practical management guide *Loyalty Rules!* by Frederick Reichheld. He distinguishes the six principles of loyalty leadership in business: play win/win (profiting at your partners' expense is a shortcut to a dead end); be picky (membership is a privilege); keep it simple (complexity is the enemy of speed and flexibility); reward the right results (worthy partners deserve worthy goals); listen hard, talk straight (long-term relationships require honest, two-way communication and learning); preach what you practice (actions often speak louder than words, but together they are unbeatable) (Reichheld 2001: 17; see also McGregor 2010). Putin's leadership, however, is based not on loyalty rules as outlined above, but on personal loyalty to Putin. Let me illustrate this point with reference to the folklore relating to Putin's leadership style, in itself a testimony of his popularity and ability to speak people's language.

Colloquially, Putin's leadership style is known as *patsanstvo* (lads, mates or buddies) associated with *patsanskie* rules – an informal code of honour and fairness, otherwise known as *poniatia*. The unofficial code of norms implies double standards applicable to insiders of the criminal underworld (*blatnye*) and to outsiders. *Patsany*, or *konkretnye patsany* are known for their slang, fair notions, brotherhood and laddishness (Solov´ev and Zlobin 2010).[12] The romanticised notion of *patsanstvo* refers to the post-siege code of honour in post-war Leningrad and strives for fairness.[13] Contemporary connotations also include symbols of cool – 'boys with toys'. A former banker, now a Londoner, observes, 'we've been laughed at for our obsession with appearances and material things' (*ponty*) and describes a recent encounter with *siloviki*, talking in quick slang that translates approximately as follows:

Of course, we have problems with *siloviki*, but we solve them. I help them, they help me. They come over. Each in his own plane. Each with a motorcade, three cars or more. Only Sasha drives himself, he loves it apparently. Last time he drove [a] Volkswagen Golf. 'The best car on rent at the airport', he said apologetically, 'but . . . you know it made 220 on diesel'. . . Sergei wouldn't have it. A Rolls Royce was driven from Zurich to meet him in London. Well, you know who is who.

Loyalty, trust and fairness among *patsany* should not be over-stated. On the basis of her archival research of Leningrad circles Catriona Kelly warns of the multiple informal codes, coexistent with a clear-cut division into 'us' and 'them,' '*svoi*' and '*chuzhie*'.[14] For instance, she cites memoirs about the film director Ilya Averbakh, who in his mid twenties already moved in five or six different circles at once:

He already had a set group of friends that was divided into several different classes. These included (a) former school mates, (b) fellow students from medical school, (c) card-players (he was addicted to games such as preference and, later on, bridge), (d) people he played sports with (for instance, volleyball and football out on the beach at Solnechnoe), (e) companions in activities of a rather less innocent kind to do with what one might politely call searching for female company, and (f) colleagues in film-making.[15]

Kelly suggests that trust operates at different levels within these different networks and makes an important observation resonating with the core argument in this book – *sistema*'s ambivalence:

---

[12] For an illustration of slang, see the chronology of Putin's vertical of power and his memorable phrases, in 'Putin u vlasti 1999–2009', *Trud*, 10 August 2009: 6.

[13] See, for example, www.newsland.ru/news/detail/id/683410/.

[14] Kelly (2012). See also L. Lur´e, 'Kak Nevskii prospekt pobedil ploshchad´ Proletarskoi Diktatury', *Zvezda*, 8, 1998: 210–13.

[15] M. Petrov, 'Fenomen Averbakha', *Zvezda* 1, 2006, http://magazines.russ. ru/zvezda/2006/1/pe13.html.

If there seems to have been more space for trust within [the] official Soviet culture than is sometimes acknowledged, one should perhaps, conversely, not overstate the extent to which social trust was safely enshrined in informal networks.[16]

As emphasised by many respondents in this study, for Putin the line between *svoi* and *chuzie* seems clear, whereas *svoi* are perceived to include a variety of people. As *svoi*, childhood friends-turned-tycoons, referred to as brothers (*bratki*) and entrepreneurs (*delovye*), are provided with business opportunities, or grazing grounds (*polyany*), and permitted what others are not. As one respondent phrased it: 'Certain businesses are tied to Putin himself (*podvyazannye pod Putina*), to his projects. There is a brothers' system: brothers this and brothers that, [the] brothers Rottenberg and [the] brothers Koval´chuk.'

The notions prescribe that brothers share their proceeds fairly (*delyatsya po-bratski*), including for their patron. Apart from *patsany* and *bratki*, one hears about *svoi* people performing personal services as a masseur or a trainer; and people engaged in financial services as *frontirovanie*; in informational services as *translyatory*, translating signals to and from Putin; and in services as *smotryashchie*, exercising informal 'checks and balances' as discussed above. While for my respondents it is the personalities behind these functions that are most important, I found it most striking that these functions, effectively the functions of informal governance, are so well defined and named colloquially.

Curiously, the folklore on informal governance fits with the cultural theory and four types of grid/group classification suggested by anthropologist Mary Douglas, and the affiliated outlooks characteristic of each combination. During the 1970s, Mary Douglas developed a two-dimensional framework for cultural comparisons: (a) grid or constraint by rules, and (b) group or incorporation into a bounded social unit. Formal positions are framed by the 'grid' and its prescriptions of autonomy, insulation, reciprocity and competition. Informal positions are defined by the 'group' and its characteristics – frequency, mutuality, scope and boundary (Douglas 1970: 54–68; Caulkins 1999). A 'strong group' exhibits a high degree of collective control, whereas a 'weak group' exhibits individual self-sufficiency. A 'strong grid' displays conspicuous and durable forms of stratification in rules, roles and

---

[16] Kelly (2012: 16).

♥	♣
Patsany	*Smotryashchie*
(setting up 'patsanskie rules' and codes)	*(translating signals and controlling*
Weak grid, strong group	*formal and informal hierarchies)*
	Strong grid, strong group
(Egalitarianism)	**(Hierarchy)**
♠	♦
Bratki, delovye	*Shestyorki*
(sponsoring, fronting, sharing)	*(complying, marching to the tune)*
Weak grid, weak group	**Strong grid, weak group**
(Individualism)	**(Fatalism)**

Figure 7.1 Putin's power networks expressed in slang

authority, whereas a 'weak grid' reflects a more egalitarian outlook. Just as there are universal features in the workings of bureaucracies around the world, informal patterns are also fairly universal for the leadership. Yet the combinations of the formal and the informal and their symbiosis differ significantly across societies, cultures and stages of modernity.

Each square in Figure 7.1 is also marked by a symbol of an ideal type of power network discussed in Chapter 2: heart, for the 'inner circle'; spade, for 'useful friends'; club, for 'core contacts'; and diamond, for 'mediated contacts'.[17]

Some core contacts, placed in formal hierarchies to implement policies and to control resources, are perceived to be players in the context of informal control and governance as well. Such conclusions normally derive from the pre-existing personal relationships of the leader:

[17] Note the card tags on the *sistema* charts. The symbols signify: ♥, trust and personal ties; ♠, use of personal relationships; ♣, burden of carrying out policies; ♦, compliance at the peripheries of networks. I am grateful to my graduate student Kiril Tasev who came up with the idea and helped with the charts.

All governmental programmes, like [the] Gazprom tower construction or Rosatom [state corporation for nuclear energy], are tagged to a particular physical person, responsible for the investment of huge state funds. For example, Alexei Miller is known to be a watchdog for Gazprom.

Although informal governance might present a solution to the problems of overlapping hierarchies or over-sized organisations, the emerging gap between the formal priorities and the priorities of various power networks creates problems, often associated with clashes of hidden interests, ambivalence and conflict. *Sistema* wisdom has it: 'Be ready to accept that you might never understand what had brought you down.' One respondent describes the obscure constraints that his Ministry faced while implementing state policies towards Gazprom:

Take the restructuring of natural monopolies: railways, oil and gas. That has been a serious and painful reform. Similar attempts have been made in all three sectors. Yet the outcome of these efforts made it crystal clear: there were monopolies that we could restructure and monopolies that we could not. Gazprom was a sinecure, and no equal treatment of monopolies was possible. Touch gas and your hands will be slapped every time. Meetings get cancelled at a short notice, Putin attends unexpectedly and diverts the agenda, all kinds of stuff happens.

Under the circumstances, one has to adjust to the ambivalence of *sistema*'s goals – the 'doubledeed' in their implementation and the gap between the facade and backstage discourses in their representation. A corporate manager told me a joke about a theatre dog and a famous opera singer invited to perform in a play:

A theatre dog, a regular at rehearsals, usually sleeps peacefully in the stalls. Every time the rehearsal ends, the dog wakes up and goes to exit to meet her master, an actor. It worked until Shalyapin was given a part. As soon as Shalyapin started acting, the dog woke up and walked out . . .

The point of the story was that Shalyapin's voice was real, not like those used on stage. The joke was meant to illustrate the gap between backstage normality and the facade culture of compliance that prescribes theatrical performance. Another respondent put it differently: 'I know state officials are normal people but in formal contexts they start behaving like aliens', and these contexts include not only the corridors of power but also the corporate contexts controlled by the state. It goes without saying that in the public sector, courts and the media, the 'nuts

and bolts' of *sistema*, have to display compliance – in the jargon, to
become a *shestyorka* (low-level contact) – to an even greater degree.

Managing power networks

Although one should not attach too much significance to the colloquial idioms in Figure 7.1, they are useful for starting the discussion of the ideal types of instruments of informal governance. The
four types of instruments of informal governance suggested below, if
only loosely, associate with the ideal types of power networks. The
leader's inner circle provides support for agenda setting, vision, or
programme. The leader's core contacts provide structure and organisation to ensure public policy implementation and mobilisation of
cadres. Useful friends help mobilise and control resources and support
important projects. Mediated contacts serve to communicate policies,
to create a buffer with the public and to ensure legitimacy and stability.

It is not the purpose of this chapter to compile an exhaustive list
of the instruments used to manage various power networks. Rather,
I focus on the instruments that came out prominently in interviews
and are relevant for an understanding of the implications of informal
governance. Let me start with an example.

The majority of the instruments of informal governance work
through informal communication. In such contexts, officials prefer
not to put their ideas in writing – rather, they make and receive telephone calls, or even set up meetings. Similarly signals and orientations
are preferable to direct requests. Needless to say, it is unusual to see
informal leverage exercised on Putin's behalf on record. I am therefore
persuaded to include parts of the Final Judgment of the Honourable
Judge Sir Anthony Colman in the pre-trial case *Boris Abramovich Berezovsky* v. *Roman Arkadievich Abramovich*, heard in July and November 2009. It registers the types of informal pressure that are claimed to
have been used on behalf of Russia's President. Berezovsky's account
of events is inevitably biased, as he is a political exile and a bitter
critic of Putin's regime. Moreover, Berezovsky's claims are completely
inconsistent with Abramovich's story. Yet both litigants provide an
extraordinary record of the instruments of informal governance in the
context of the 1990s power consolidation, media, natural resources,
transfer of assets and exit from *sistema*. The scale of issues, solved
informally, makes them hard to ignore – this commercial case has

made it to the top ten biggest commercial cases in the UK (estimated at £ 3.8 billion in damages).

Not only is the case big. Berezovsky's barrister conceded that it is 'incredibly complex': many of the crucial agreements had been made verbally – the preferred method, he said, for blackmailers. Another layer of difficulty stems from the fact that several of the protagonists are dead. Badri Patarkatishvili died of a heart attack in 2008, prompting a bitter legal battle between his relatives and Berezovsky. The British lawyer, Stephen Smith, who took notes of a crucial business meeting in the Georgian capital Tbilisi, died in a mysterious helicopter crash in 2004. The barrister said: 'The case is rather lacking in contemporaneous documents. But some documents stand out like a beacon.'

Without going into the details of this complicated case involving the ownership of the ORT manufacturing company, the Sibneft oil company and the RUSAL aluminium company, I reproduce parts of the factual background presented by Boris Berezovsky (hereafter BB) for the pre-trial and contested by the defence of Roman Abramovich (hereafter RA). The arsenal of instruments used for political and business purposes included oral commands, verbal trust arrangements, informal agreements, informal affiliations, informal agendas and state capture, the use of go-betweens, manipulation of law enforcement institutions in order to relieve owners of their assets, emotional blackmail, threats and torts. The account of events is much abridged (I quote paras. 9–15 and 29–33 from the 174 paragraphs of the judgment). The points on the instruments of informal governance are more or less self-explanatory but I put references to specific forms of informal leverage in *italics* (see Box 7.1).

Just as in the pre-trial, in the course of the 2011 High Court trial, dubbed the 'battle of the oligarchs', presided over by the Honorable Mrs Justice Gloster, RA denies the allegations and denies that BB is entitled to damages. RA wins the case, yet his testimony is also full of examples of informal instruments of influence within *sistema*. RA's inch-thick witness statement bears testament to the amount of money that changed hands in post-Communist Russia. Most astonishing are the payments to BB, once associated with Yeltsin's inner circle, or 'family', and his alleged cohort Arkady Patarkatsishvili, who had links to Chechen gangsters. The payments, RA claims, were made for 'protection' (*krysha*) and political influence during Yeltsin's rule. He says

---

Box 7.1 *Boris Abramovich Berezovsky* v. *Roman Arkadievich Abramovich*, The High Court of Justice, July and November 2009, extract from the judgment

ORT

9 On 12 August 2000 the Russian submarine KURSK was tragi-
cally lost in the Barents Sea and all the crew perished. Channel
One was highly critical of the government's handling of the disaster. At a meeting in Moscow with one Alexander Voloshin,
Chief of the PA, which took place later in August 2000, BB
was informed that President Putin wished to take control of the
management of ORT and that BB should therefore surrender
or procure the surrender of ORT-KB's and LogoVaz's share-
holdings to the state or to an acceptable body and if he failed
to do so, he 'would end up like Vladimir Gusinsky'. The latter, who controlled a private television network (NTV), had
on 13 June 2000 been *arrested and imprisoned, having been
charged with fraud. Three days later he was released and the
charges were dropped upon his signing an agreement to sell* his
shareholding in the company controlling NTV against a promise
by the Minister for Press, Television, Radio Broadcasting and
Media Communication that the charges would be dropped. In
the ECtHR in *Gusinsky* v. *Russia*, Application 70276/01, this
conduct of the Russian Government was subsequently not surprisingly condemned as a serious violation of Articles 5 and 18
of the European Convention on Human Rights.

10 In the course of that meeting with Mr Voloshin, BB asked to
meet President Putin. This meeting took place on the following
day. *President Putin repeated the demand for the transfer of the
shares, confirmed that he wished to manage ORT personally
and confirmed that BB would be imprisoned if he did not agree.*

11 Shortly after this meeting, Arkadii Patarkatsishvili[18] (hereafter
AP) was required to meet President Putin, by whom he was told

---

[18] Arkadii 'Badri' Patarkatsishvili died in February 2008 of heart failure in his
mansion in London. Mr Patarkatsishvili, protected by 120 bodyguards, had
been saying that he feared he would be assassinated in London by the Georgian
authorities. In December 2007, he said he had been the target of at least two
assassination attempts in Britain. The Georgian authorities had accused him of

that the President wished BB and AP to 'clear out' of ORT and that *he must negotiate to sell the shares*. A price was subsequently offered to AP but BB refused to sell and in September 2000 he made a public announcement that in order to preserve the independence of ORT from the government, he would put the shares into a trust. His relations with the President got worse and on 30 October 2000 he left Russia for France. In the event, the trust was not created.

12 On 7 December 2000 one Nicolai Glushkov, a close personal friend and business associate of BB and AP, was arrested. From 1996 to 1998 he had been First Deputy Director General of Aeroflot. He subsequently helped BB and AP to set up Logo-VAZ, as part owner of ORT, and became its first financial manager. He was not in good health but was imprisoned in the harsh environment of Lefortovo Prison operated by the FSB. He has, it is alleged, consistently denied the charges regarding his administration of Aeroflot.

13 In December 2000, according to BB, there took place a meeting at BB's home in Cap d'Antibes, France, between BB, AP and RA. These three had an existing business relationship relating to the oil and gas company called Sibneft... In the course of that meeting RA stated that he had come on the orders of the President and Mr Voloshin, that BB and AP had to sell their interests in ORT immediately, and if they did so, *Mr Glushkov would be released from prison and they would be paid $175 million but, if they refused to do so, Glushkov would remain in prison for a very long time and the President would seize their interests in ORT*. BB says that he and AP had no alternative but to sell their interests for that price, which represented a substantial under-value. That is what they did, but Mr Glushkov was not released.

14 I interpose that RA denies that any such conversation took place. He says that some time before 25 December 2000 at a venue which he cannot remember he met with BB and AP and was

plotting a coup, see D. Kennedy and A. Fresco, 'Badri Patarkatsishvili: exiled oligarch who lived in the shadow of death', *The Times*, 14 February 2008, Obituaries, www.timesonline.co.uk/tol/news/uk/crime/article3365806.ece. (Accessed May 2011.)

told by BB that he wanted to sell his interests in ORT and that BB invited RA to purchase them for a price of $150 million which RA assumed also to cover AP's interests. RA says that he eventually agreed to pay them $175 million – an amount in excess of the true value of those interests – and that the interests of BB and AP were sold to companies controlled by RA. *It is denied by RA that the Russian state was operating through him in persuading BB and AP to dispose of their interests in ORT.* (*Boris Abramovich Berezovsky* v. *Roman Arkadyevich Abramovich*: 3–4)

Sibneft

15 Meanwhile, in the period from about August 2000 to early 2001, in the course of a number of meetings between AP and RA, the latter stated that it was known by the Kremlin that BB and AP had interests in Sibneft and that there was mounting pressure from the Government such that those interests could be expropriated. AP understood that the implication of such remarks was that if they did not agree to dispose of their interests in Sibneft both he (who did not leave Russia until March 2001) and BB, who had already fled the country, would face serious consequences and he so informed BB.

     . . .

29 Following the meetings between AP and RA from August 2000 to early 2001 referred to in para. 15 above, BB and AP decided that they were in principle willing to sell their 'interests' in Sibneft to RA and that they should meet with him in order to negotiate the terms of the sale. That decision was, according to BB's evidence, strongly influenced by BB's fear, induced by what RA had told AP, that, if they refused to sell, *RA would procure President Putin's intervention and the consequent expropriation of their interests.*

30 A meeting with RA was set up at Munich Airport in early May 2001 between AP and RA. In the course of that meeting *AP returned to the issue of the release from prison of Mr Glushkov. RA said that if AP and BB were to sell their interests in Sibneft to him, Mr Glushkov would now be released.*

31 AP named a price of $2.5 billion for those interests, which he said was significantly less than they were worth, but RA refused to pay more than $1.3 billion. AP also requested payment of their due proportions of all the amounts which Sibneft had paid out since December 2000 and which would be paid out up to completion of the full payment of the purchase price, but RA turned this down.

32 BB and AP discussed RA's offer. BB concluded that, as he put it in his witness statement, even although the price grossly under-valued Sibneft, they 'had no real choice in the matter' because there was a prospect that if they agreed, Mr Glushkov would be released and that *if they refused RA's relationship with President Putin was such that RA would be in a position to bring about seizure by the Government of their interests in Sibneft which would be unchallengeable in the Russian courts.*

Krysha: Political assistance and protection were estimated at a $1.3bn exit fee

33 The case advanced by RA is completely inconsistent with BB's account. He says that at a meeting at St Moritz Airport, not Munich Airport, in January or February 2001, prior to the Munich Airport meeting, AP *requested him to pay $1.3 billion to BB in recognition of the political assistance and protection BB had provided in respect of the creation of Sibneft* and taking account of the fact that BB and AP would no longer be receiving any financial benefit from the funding of ORT by RA, having no further interest in ORT. *RA says that he agreed to make this payment on the basis that it would be the final request for payment by BB and that AP and BB would cease to associate themselves with him and his business interests publicly,* including Sibneft. Above all, however, RA denies that BB and RA ever owned legally or beneficially, directly or indirectly, or controlled any interests in any part of the issued share capital of Sibneft. Therefore they had no interest in selling to RA. The meeting at Munich Airport was thus merely to agree the mechanics for the payment of the $1.3 million.

that BB was paid millions of pounds for his services as a 'political godfather' but was not a business partner. He said matter-of-factly:

'The government of the time was dominated by old-style ministers from the Soviet era. Having someone who could have a voice in that inner circle was vital if one wanted to build a business that required government support.' He said that the original demand by the pair, in 1995, was for £20 million a year. And he claimed that each year a new, larger, figure was agreed, until the demands ended up 'out of all proportion'. By 2000 they were demanding $160 million for protection and a mystery additional amount of $305 million. Abramovich added: 'By the end of December 2000 I had paid Mr Berezovsky approximately $490 million.' He claims things came to a head in a dramatic meeting between the trio at the French ski resort of Courchevel in January 2001. He says he agreed to pay the pair $1.3 billion – ensuring that they were both 'set up for life'. RA added: 'As far as I was concerned, by agreeing to make a single last huge payment, I was "buying myself my freedom".'[19]

Regardless of Roman Abramovich's victory in this case, it is clear that 'the political assistance and protection BB had provided', or was capable of providing, had turned out to be costly for former associates, both finding themselves on the receiving end of political pressure to some extent. Both stories would seem trivial – there is nothing new about use of contacts and payments for getting things done – had it not been for their scale, the status of those implicated and the state interests involved. One does not commonly associate the leadership with instruments of informal governance. Yet, in theory at least, the links between a leader and his power networks, between the leadership style and the methods of informal governance, are worth exploring. Leadership can benefit from the use of informal governance in order to manage power networks, but can also be undermined and threatened by them. As illustrated by this legal case, in Putin's Russia informal governance was essential to serve the key operational needs of *sistema*: to re-allocate resources and to control the financial flow; to implement policies and to ensure the manageability of formal institutions; to maintain stability and to initiate change.[20]

---

[19] 'The dangerous world of Roman Abramovich and Russia's oligarchs', *The Mirror*, 5 November 2011, www.mirror.co.uk/news/top-stories/2011/11/05/.

[20] Managing power networks, like any group or corporation, involves facing four types of structural problems: integration, adaptation, goal attainment and pattern maintenance. The ways in which these problems are solved determines the nature of power networks.

Methods of informal governance

To present the key types of instruments of informal governance articulated by my respondents, as well as litigants in the London court cases, I integrate the functions and the ideal types of power networks (illustrated in Figures 2.1, 2.2 and 7.1) with the ideal types of leadership tasks, and follow up with a description of the instruments of informal governance that can be used for performing them: informal incentives, informal affiliations, informal agendas and informal signals (Figure 7.2).

♥	♣
Network type: 'inner circle'	*Network type*: 'core contacts'
Functions: back-up/free-riding	*Functions*: safety net/lock-in effect
Leadership task: agenda-setting	*Leadership task*: policy implementation
♠	♦
Network type: 'useful friends'	*Network type*: 'mediated contacts'
Functions: survival kit/limited rights	*Functions*: buffer effect/path dependence
Leadership task: resources control	*Leadership task*: stability and succession

Figure 7.2 Types, functions of power networks and associated leadership tasks

Informal incentives

The inner circle is associated with those participating in decision-making and filtering information; they are particularly attuned to positive and negative incentives applied informally. The members of Putin's inner circle are perceived to be generously rewarded in a material sense, but the channels can be informal:

There are '*svoi*' in the top layer of state officials. Naturally, they do not take any kickbacks or have anything to do with business – they are rewarded through insider channels. It is fair to make it up to them to a decent level, a few millions a year. These salaries–bonuses come from '*svoi*' funds, some unofficial coffers (*iz chyornyx kass*), perhaps those collected from businesses or from the political funds. It is important that people like this do not feel themselves relatively deprived (*obdelyonnymi*). Because, you know, there are officials who make serious money in [the] private sector, and this is also somehow allowed. Everybody knows vice premiers who own metallurgical complexes (*v osobo krupnykh razmerakh*), and vice premiers who fly in their own jets, there are ministers who fly in their own jets and there are heads of various ministerial departments who fly in their own jets. And somehow it's okay. There are certain agreements, and *sistema* stays rather open-minded about all this.[21]

According to BB's version of events, his former partner-turned-opponent RA was lavishly rewarded by *sistema* – the state-controlled Gazprom bought his Sibneft company for $13 billion and he was first elected and later re-elected a governor of Chukotka.

Positive incentives are not unrelated to negative ones. One hears about certain dependencies, vulnerabilities and 'informal hooks' kept for the insiders of power networks, thus enhancing their participation, collective responsibility (*krugovaya poruka*) and compliance. For example, if necessary, federal leaders can resort to the use of informal leverage to increase the manageability of regional leaders (their core contacts), to control their policies and to make them support important initiatives.[22] An informal mobilisation of resources can also be effective. 'I do not rule out that Mr Abramovich may take part in one of these projects', Putin said in televised comments. 'Let him open his wallet a little. It's no big deal – he won't feel a pinch. He has plenty of money.'[23]

In my conversation with one of the respondents about the management of resources for informal governance, otherwise known as black coffers (*chyornaya kassa*), I asked a Borat-type question 'isn't this corrupt?' and heard yet another story about the blurred boundaries between the public and the private in Russia:

I would not call such party funding corrupt. This money is not going into private pockets, they are used for stabilising the situation (*na uderzhanie*

[21] E. Ivanova, 'Pochemu chinovniki ne letayut kak lyudi?', *Novaya gazeta*, 24 April 2011.
[22] For example, the Chelsea football club owner is expected to invest heavily and take a key role when Russia hosts the 2018 World Cup, see Parfitt (2012: 5).
[23] Parfitt (2012).

situatsii)... Well, naturally it ends up in some people's pockets as well. Generally, such 'political' funds cover up for [a] corrupt financial flow, because these funds, set up on [a] semi-official basis by that department, are non-transparent. None of the donors in Gazprom, Rosneft, or Transneft, who do their homework and [in] bring their millions..., actually know where it all goes, who has got what and what for, this is not their question.

Some of the rewards for the contribution of members of the inner circle are non-material. According to a number of respondents, the insiders appreciate the trust extended to them and respond with cooperation, loyalty and drive. One of the most special rewards is the sense of belonging. I asked one former Kremlin staffer to assess his own proximity to the Kremlin leadership on the scale from 1 to 10 after his departure, with 10 being as close as he was in his formal position. His answer highlights both the non-material incentives and the pressure to pursue material benefits:

Luckily, he said, my position is not available. If it were, it would create a difficult dilemma: the most interesting job in the world (like others in the Kremlin, I am a bit of an addict) v. making money for my family and having a family life. How would I rate my current proximity... well, one friend of mine has just become a president, another one has just become the first vice-PM.

The first half of the answer reveals the existing tensions between public role and private life, the second half that between formal appointment and informal relationships. Whereas formal power is associated with a position in a formal hierarchy and 'vertical' proximity to a boss, the informal power is associated with personal relationships and 'horizontal' proximity to a boss in a social network. Patterns of informal affiliation both support and subvert the workings of formal hierarchies. As an instrument of informal governance, however, informal affiliations are associated with access to the administrative resource.

Informal affiliations

State intervention in business is evidently a reflection of Putin's 'hands-on' leadership style. 'One has to see this through the prism of Putin's attitude to business', ventures a business lobbyist, 'He doesn't like it'.[24] In theory, businessmen determine their own goals, implement their own business decisions and resolve their own problems. If they make a profit, it is also their own. In Putin's *sistema*, property rights remain weak and delegation, associated with a democratic leadership style, is rare. However, informal alliances between state officials and businessmen, between the leaders and their 'useful friends' are perceived to be mutually beneficial. I call them 'informal affiliations', borrowing from Daniel Goleman's definition of affiliative leadership style as one which connects people, focuses on them rather than on a task and creates a favourable environment for productive behaviour of the followers rather than impacting on them directly (Goleman 2000):

> Putin thinks [that] businessmen are opportunists who let down anybody for money (*vsekh kinut*), and he has a point, at least in relation to some people. Top businesses have all adjusted and do not go into politics. The likes of Kerimov or Friedman have deeper agreements than others, but overall all businesses are tied up in power networks one way or another (*ser´yoznye zavyazki s vlast´yu*) and they pay their dues, complete their home assignments [contribute cash to designated funds – AL] and finance pet projects. This makes them feel confident. When their interests cross with some of Putin's insiders, well, then they have a serious problem, because as a rule VVP [Putin] believes his people's version of events. So they solve such problems by losing part of their businesses, or the whole business. There are some recent examples.[25] Besides, our top thirty businessmen are not that simple and have teeth, so they find their ways with the VVP inner circle. So we now see spectacular binary partnerships: one takes up the responsibility for the political resource, the other takes up the rest.

By 'deeper agreements' the respondent must have meant the practice of cover-up (*frontirovanie*) or home assignments (*domashnie zadaniia*) based on informal affiliations between businessmen and state officials. Some examples of such practices are referred to in the Forbes' investigation of Suleiman Kerimov, allegedly assembling assets into the Presidential 'pension fund'.[26]

---

[24] The opposite view can be found in Belkovskii and Golyshev (2006).

[25] See the story of Dmitri Rybolovlev in O. Mordyushenko, 'Suleiman Kerimov zhdyot vseobshchego udobreniia', *Kommersant*, 11 August 2010: 9.

[26] 'Opasnyi igrok: Kak Suleiman Kerimov perezhil dve katastrofy, edva ne stoyavshie emu zhizni i sostoyaniia', *The Forbes Magazine*, 7 February 2012 09:41, www.forbes.ru/sobytiya/lyudi/79051-opasnyi-igrok-kak-suleiman-kerimov-perezhil-dve-katastrofy-edva-ne-stoivshih-em.

The outcome of these partnerships is the lack of clear boundaries between the public and the private, privileged access to resources and limited property rights, stifled competition and uncontrolled flows of capital:

There is a problem with informal affiliations and informal flows of capital. The banks receive formal guarantees, but at the end of the day, everything is done on a handshake. You lose your job, you might lose it all. And let me tell you from observation, top jobs are not much fun. They get up in the morning and run like a squirrel on a treadmill . . . ambassadors, orphans, meetings, one after another, back to back, and there is no end to it. In the meantime, cash accumulates, it sits on [the] accounts of affiliated persons, nominal directors, remote relatives, various nephews and God knows who. This actually creates a problem: one wants to be able to spend some of it and have a life at the end of the tunnel, at the same time it's hard to get out of *sistema* and secure control of informal income. Besides, the same people – informal affiliates – cannot afford [to let] Putin out, because their own fortunes are not fully legitimate either.

Another respondent spoke about the same effect:

One cannot succeed Putin today. He is the leader of the party. They have captured the Duma, it is totally docile. They change the Constitution as they wish. They have the judiciary in their pocket just in case some people out there become interested in politics.

These views project an image of Putin's strength that makes him a guarantor and thus a hostage of *sistema*'s stability. Elites have no option but to engage in political games if they are to sustain their positions in power networks; the population at large remains politically passive and cynical. Party politics and competitiveness are replaced by hidden conflicts that tend to result in the monopolisation of access to the leadership – the 'person of the tsar' – thus making the 'tsar' and his power networks 'prisoners of *sistema*'. In a comment to the *Vedomosti* newspaper, Sergei Petrov, a Duma deputy from the Just Russia party and founder of the ROLF group of automotive businesses, draws parallels between Putin's and Brezhnev's situations:

Vladimir Putin is hostage to the political dead-end he himself [has] created. It is very similar to the trap that former Soviet leader Leonid Brezhnev set for himself and the country. If we assume, for one second, that Putin does want to radically modernise and liberalise his autocratic system – or even retire if he so desired – he would not be allowed to do so by the elite who surround him. This is the elite who believe the government to be their personal property. After betraying his role as a guarantor of the Constitution, Putin has effectively become a guarantor of corruption – he guarantees the financial well-being of millions of bureaucrats, government employees and well-connected businesspeople.[27]

The ambivalence arising from officials functioning, simultaneously, in their public-serving, network-serving and self-serving capacities (though not necessarily in that order), and who operate without clearly defined boundaries, constitutes a leverage but also an obstacle to Russia's modernisation.[28] The modernisation agenda may refer, variously, to the issues stemming from the public–private crossover and corruption, the tensions existing between the public positions held by state officials and their private interests, and the blurred boundaries between the relationship and the uses of that relationship. Even then, the implications of the informal governance required to manage power networks in the Russian model are neither discussed nor targeted directly. It would amount to social modernisation if the use of personal networks and the impersonal use of institutions were more balanced, if boundaries between the public and the private were better respected and if the gap between the facade and inner workings of institutions were reduced.

Informal agendas

Politicians of all times pursue hidden agendas in addition to declared visions and goals; however, within *sistema* they not only become factors of a permanent nature, but serve as important management instruments. When the government took control of both NTV and ORT many commentators stated that the goal was to ensure state control over the mass-media. Yet it was suggested to me that 'there was a more important agenda behind these cases – "to clean the house", to eliminate a key king-maker of Yeltsin's times – Berezovsky – from *sistema*. I am pretty sure nobody stated it as a goal, but insiders knew how to read the signals.'

---

[27] S. Petrov, 'Can Russia survive through 2020?', *The Moscow Times*, 5 August 2011: 8.
[28] A lack of boundaries, whereby the leader sacrifices his personal life for service to the people, is similarly dangerous.

Respondents who suggested that top-down and bottom-up signals are very important in Putin's management have also noted an increasingly structured framing of informal agendas, 'by the book' tendency, especially in comparison with Yeltsin's times. When asked to clarify his point about informal agendas and structured signals, a participant observer explained:

They are lawyers, you know, they have respect for the law. Now everything is decided by subtle instructions, by creating certain legal constraints, and signals are channelled through encoded directives. Not even through directives – through orientations (*ustanovki*). Where they cannot bend the law, they don't. There is a conventional system of channelling signals instead. Everyone comes to a meeting (*soveshchanie*), they make up an agenda, decide something, these decisions prompt directives, which in their peculiar ways reach out, get contested, come back, then go out again, then someone takes a note of something, bam-bam, and there appears a legislative initiative, a draft [goes] off to [the] Duma, etc.

Another respondent, a former government official, however, emphasised that informal agendas are pervasive in the daily workings of the government. One has to constantly monitor decisions with a view to the informal agendas behind them:

Deputies of [the] Prime Minister, the drivers of executive power, have to make experts to look into particular decisions with a view to their corrupt implications. Each decision is an arena for trade-offs (*rastorgovka*), with its specific details reflecting the outcome of [a] trade-off between [the] interests involved in this legislation. There are errors of two types: to block a good decision and to approve a bad decision. On a plus side, *sistema*'s filters are such that where good decisions are blocked the bad ones are not allowed through either, at least in theory. In practice, there are no checks and balances, institutionalised or personalised opposition to our main decision-makers on the inside. There are also issues with competence, lack of focus, un-professionalism of managers. It is a common viewpoint that almost everyone can teach children and manage people. Such [a] mentality is widespread among government managers. Some believe it for real, some are mimicking, and some demonstrate such an approach publicly.

The culture of personal loyalty and patronage-based appointments – the *svoi* managerial culture – accounts for some instances of incompetence, which in turn reinforce the potential of informal governance. This is not to say that one should under-estimate the importance of formal channels. The latter featured prominently when I asked my respondent to clarify the paradox between the state being the victim of abuse by its agents (*terpilo*) and the state acting like a predator itself (*naezdy, bespredel*), borrowing both expressions from his earlier remarks:

Let us look at the economy as a field of state budget cash flows available for grabs. *Svoi* people are appointed to control financial flows (*ponyatnye luidi rasstavlyayutsya na ponyatnye potoki*). As a rule, these people are professional, capable of organising the technical side in an adequate way. This is on one level, formally. On another level, there are people who devise and push through certain financial schemes, chains of financial operations, just as I used to sign off VAT schemes. Of course such schemes are covered up by layers and layers of formal procedures: tenders, commissions, committees. When a scheme is constructed, it is dissociated from every particular institution. One has ordered non-existent services, another one has paid for them, yet another one has executed them, and the responsibility is dissolved in the process.

In other words, the state can be abused informally because it is seen as formally controlled, but the formal control is applied selectively: there is room for discretion, for deciding where to look and where not to look. There is no informality if you do not look for it. But if you look for it, you go against *sistema*. Besides, law enforcement organs and the Audit chamber are full of *svoi* people that ensure that the state can turn into a predator at times.

I am also told that informal agendas are 'bad for the soul':

Everyone thinks: who is playing what, for whom and what for? Manipulative, double-bottom, black box schemes are on everybody's mind. People become cynics and have to search for [their] soul elsewhere: in religion, in the occult, in hedonism . . . I hear the former Prime Minister Kasianov has gone on record in a witness statement in a London court, saying that he believes in reincarnation and is now compensating (*otrabatyvaet*) for the damage he had done to the people.

When I suggest that cynicism is instrumental for the authorities, my respondent reminds me of my own thesis of the ambivalence of *sistema* by saying:

Cynicism might be handy in the sense that people love money and power so much that they play by the rules as suggested and commonly display the attitude 'I don't know the word "no" [to the authorities]' (*slova 'net' ne znayu*). In a way, *sistema* is still capable of buying itself out of the real effort of doing something about the formal institutions. However, when a real change is needed, cynicism will block real reform. We are all used to saying 'no' to the question: 'Do I need this?' (*a mne eto nado?*), and to claim that the change is impossible. The problem is: nobody even tries to change the system. It has grown convenient to all. The non-*sistema* people (*nesistemnye*) blame the leaders or comfort their souls in alternative ways.

Informal signals

Vertushka communications and forms of non-transparent control of the media and courts, discussed in Chapters 4, 5 and 6, are illustrations of the workings of informal commands and signals. One respondent linked this particular mode of governance to the parasitism of the population and the impotence of civil society in Russia:

In Soviet times, and generally in *sistema* since 300 years ago, all reforms since Peter the Great [have been] conducted on the basis of deep distrust between 5 per cent and 95 per cent of [the] population. Those 95 per cent are somewhat inadequate people who do not take responsibility for their own lives and well-being. They push away this responsibility to whoever, to Putin, for example, so that he pays their electricity and heating bills. [The] reforms of the 1990s are misunderstood. Crowds love Putin. He is reliable. He is permissive of their undeveloped skills, laziness relative to other nations, and long holidays, while oil money covers up for it. It is impossible for people to understand that they are parasitic. The elites are satisfied with such [a] state of affairs, but worry about future stability. Parasitism has come into contradiction with modernity. *Sistema* faces both external pressures such as the Olympics and competition on the international arena, and internal threats such as the budget deficit, low revenues and elites' frustration with Putin. This is the puzzle.

It is common to blame the population for not responding to any other leadership style than a 'strong hand'. One hears repetition of the 'each nation deserves its leader' dictum rather often in interviews with Russian elites: a parasitic population deserves 'virtual' party politics, a crooked population deserves corrupt courts; a passive population deserves the 'remotely controlled' television and soap operas they are getting. 'This is not just informal governance', sighs an expert to whom I explained my interest in informal politics, 'this is centralised informal governance'. He talks about the department of domestic politics of the Kremlin Administration, then led by Vladislav Surkov:

All [political – AL] parties receive money in a centralised way these days. It is impossible to secure party funding outside *sistema*. Even Communists must drag their supporters to somebody like Chesnakov, not the level of Surkov, so that they submit funds into a common fund (*obschii kotyol*), so that the Communists would get centralised support. This makes it very easy to control party leaders and direct party politics.

In Putin's Russia, leadership instruments are oriented upon compliance. It has been said that not only do people prefer the comfort of receiving commands, where it frees them from responsibility – they are keen to seek them, to read signals and display compliance before the command is even given. Patterns of personality cult, information control and manipulating succession are power aspects of all times and people (Shekshnia and Kets de Vries 2008). The role of informal governance is legitimised by the inefficiency of formal institutions, but its impact is detrimental for institutions: their shortcut effectiveness preserves the facade nature of formal institutions and undermines formal order and hierarchy, as well as accounting for the *de facto* lack of separation of powers in Russia.

A former *sistema* insider explains the symbiotic nature of formal procedures and informal ways of circumventing them in *sistema*:

Formal procedures are kept complex and over-regulated so that one uses informal channels. Moreover, the system seems to sustain defects in formal rules at a level that would continue to feed those in positions to make decisions. It is not even a choice for a bureaucrat but a prescription. The key feature of this system is that an individual has no option but to develop a reflex of compliance. It is very tricky even to make a complaint about the system – it backfires, whistle-blowing is even more dangerous.

The punitive bias of *sistema*'s law enforcement, and its link with formal criteria of performance of state officials and incentives, reinforces the need for informal governance-bridging individuals and institutions (Paneyakh 2011), while its reliance on the subtlety of informal signals ensures its reproduction.

The continuity of *sistema* is predicated upon institutionalisation, misrecognition and compliance with informal signals, thus keeping the workings of *sistema* non-transparent and non-articulated.[29] Why would insiders favour the *status quo*? The following quotation suggests a few leads. For purposes of anonymity, I have removed the names in it, but it is still indicative of the inner circle's private concerns, choices and attitudes:

One time, I remember, I gave them a fright. Something they were discussing, something they were having problems with, led the talk to their enemies and whether they would or would not resort to physical violence . . . Would Khodorkovsky [take] revenge? They wondered whether they were under threat. 'Well, if you were to touch my relatives', I told them, 'I would send your Kremlin to hell at the first opportunity'. They looked startled [laughs]. I said, 'Honestly, I would not have waited like Khodorkovsky – you all would go up in flames at once. Everything would go straight to the devil. Look, I'm a man and I have to defend my family. I would not wait to see how you maltreat them (*izdevaetes´*). In fact, you are lucky that his people turned out to be kind of decent.' God forbid, if some *silovik* sent my relatives to prison – I would just kill the guy; I wouldn't give it more than five minutes' thought and would take my revenge in the crudest way [angry]. Would I rely on the judicial system when that system is in his pocket? What options do I have? I don't have any options. And neither do these *siloviki* – they have to cling to their positions. Otherwise it's scary out there.[30]

The respondent has made an effort to distance himself from *sistema*, it would seem, especially in his repeated distinction between 'I' and 'them'. Yet his statement also represents a threat; a strong and clear signal sent by one powerful member of *sistema* to the others. He is warning them of the disproportionate collateral damage that

---

[29] The film, *The Shawshank Redemption* (1994), demonstrates the 'institutionalising' effect prisons have on people; see also Vasilii Shukshin's film *Snowball Cherry Red (Kalina krasnaia)*, 1973). The 'institutionalisation' effect in oppressive institutions has been well researched in the context of mental health in *Asylums* (Goffman 1961).

[30] Khodorkovsky also noted that the case against him was driven by political and corrupt motives: 'It is caused by the fear of my opponents that I might come out of prison. The political motivation is twofold: I am banned from supporting the opposition and I am deprived of property rights in the largest and best Russian oil company.' Cited in Z. Svetova, 'Report on the second trial of Khodorkovsky', *The New Times*, 12 April 2010: 26. See also Sakwa (2009) and Sixsmith (2010). The absurdity of the second *Yukos* trial provoked a range of signalling artefacts: mittens sewn in prison, the pocket-sized 'Fear-2010' calendars, the spoof 'Mishka in the North' chocolates and the comic-strip book *Trial (Protsess)*: 25.

might occur should something happen to his family. Even more striking, perhaps, is the taken-for-granted admission of the in-the-pocket
nature of the judicial system and its incapacity to protect individuals,
even the most senior, should *sistema* turn against them. Although this
rather dispirited and emotional threat to send 'everything... to the
devil' is unlikely to be acted upon, it reveals the emotional state of a
sistema insider: the fear for one's safety and the jungle-like sense of
self-reliance, together with a complete distrust of the judicial system
and the insecurity this entails. Such feelings might be the source of
sistema's domination, but they are also the source of *sistema*'s vulnerability: the frustration of insiders results in the 'exit strategy' of
national elites, legal nihilism and individual and collective revolts. *Sistema* seems to transform its long-serving insiders in similar ways: they
are becoming chronically dependent on *sistema* but also bitter about
it, if not quite biting the hand that feeds them. The ambivalence of
sistema makes double standards and cynicism a survival strategy. By
expressing boldness while being insecure; enjoying impunity while living in fear; and exercising arbitrariness (*proizvol*) while being subject to rigid subordination, *sistema* insiders help themselves but also
help to reproduce the cage of the double standards in which they
live.

Measuring informal governance

I argue that the use of informal instruments – or, rather, the scale of
their use – is what determines the distinctiveness of Russia's power
networks. In societies with more developed institutions than Russia –
say, in France or Italy – the use of power networks is less of a necessity, on the one hand, and more guarded by 'checks and balances',
on the other. The power networks seem to be also in place but their
scale, significance and effectiveness are different because the workings
of power networks are restricted by institutions. In societies where formal institutions do not work to their full potential and where people
rely on informal ways of getting things done, the leadership is bound
to rely on the use of informal instruments as well. Leaders can only
be leaders once they master and control informal networks. The manageability of informal networks is often achieved with informal means
and instruments: by steering appointments towards the loyal people,
by regulating access to resources, by ensuring that resources are in the

'right' hands and their property rights are to some extent reversible, and by controlling the periphery ensuing their submissiveness.

The reverse side of the use of informal means and instruments is that the leader finds himself bound by informal and reciprocal ties. These bonds can function, as with Putin's appointments, to enhance the power *vertikal´* but also undermine that *vertikal´* through the very channels that helped create it. They help the leadership to survive and to be financially sustainable, but they also keep the leader hostage to his useful friends, allies and sponsors. They help ensure that any mediated contacts are supportive of the leadership and play a buffer role between the authorities and society, but they also demonstrate the path dependency in the governance mode, not conducive to the development of institutions. To date, there is no way of measuring informal governance, or monitoring its standard operating procedures. In this context, the modernisation of institutions in Russia, as well as the creation of institutional avenues for checks and balances, is essential. But they can only occur with the concurrent modernisation of power networks and leaders' self-monitoring and self-restraint in the use of instruments of informal governance.

Conclusion

Memories of *sistema*

There is an insightful commentary on *sistema* in Joseph Brodsky's memoirs.

If one had brains, one would certainly try to outsmart the system by devising all kinds of detours, arranging shady deals with one's superiors, piling up lies and pulling the strings of one's [semi-nepotistic] connections. This would become a full-time job. Yet one was constantly aware that the web one had woven was a web of lies, and in spite of the degree of success or your sense of humour, you'd despise yourself. That is the ultimate triumph of the system: whether you beat it or join it, you feel equally guilty. The national belief is – as the proverb has it – that there is no Evil without a grain of Good in it and presumably vice versa. Ambivalence, I think, is the chief characteristic of my nation. (Brodsky 1986)

In one of my interviews, a respondent recalled his first experience of the Soviet *sistema*:

It actually happened rather early. I was about 12 and went to a sports camp, as one did back then. My friends were fishing near the camp and wanted to cook fish soup on the fire, so I went to the kitchen to ask for a saucepan and a couple of potatoes. I knew a girl in the kitchen and she gave me a saucepan and told me to pick up some potatoes from the cellar. As I was coming out of the cellar with four potatoes in the saucepan, I bumped into the Director of the camp. He decided I was a potato thief at once. Everyone was scared of him and I guess the kitchen girl denied her involvement. I was grounded to 'think about my behaviour' but remained fairly confident that I had done nothing wrong. By the evening of that day a man passed by, flipped his ID and introduced himself as a security officer. He threatened to lock me away as a young offender if I didn't confess to the wrongdoing (*popugal*). I cried through the night and into the next day. Others were instructed not to talk to me, until one morning an elderly trainer came over and spoke to me like a good cop. He said he understood I didn't mean it and I didn't do it, he said the man who threatened me was only some friend of the director; and he said it would be easier for everyone if I simply apologised – then everything would be back to normal. He looked old, wise and trustworthy, and I couldn't bear my isolation any longer, so I gave in. My memory blocked how exactly the apology went, but I felt shame, fear and disgust every time I saw the Director in subsequent years. This was what *sistema* did to 'initiate' people – it made them lie: to accept responsibility for what one didn't do and vice versa; to compromise oneself by wrongdoing or by admitting wrongdoing in order not to get others into trouble, to apologise for what one didn't do in order to be allowed to break free and enjoy life. Yet one never breaks free from *sistema*.

This respondent said the story haunted him for years and he often wondered if he was an accidental target or was spotted as a non-*sistema* type (*nesistemnyi*). It was strange, he recalled, that his parents were not informed of the incident. He also claimed that ever since that incident he knew intuitively the logic and the constraints of *sistema* without feeling the need to or being able to articulate them. I wondered whether the majority of people could identify their first experience of *sistema*, or whether the majority fitted in rather smoothly, without testing its boundaries. Like many others, my respondent learned the rules of the game through violation of some written rules or informal norms, or through inability to fit in. In this book I relied on my informants' perceptions of *sistema*, both Soviet and post-Soviet, and construed an ethnography of *sistema* on the basis of in-depth interviews.

Written evidence on *sistema* constraints

Increasingly, the 'open secrets' of *sistema* transpire in legal documents, substantiating individual perceptions of respondents in this study. Thus one court ruling, discussed earlier, sums up the pressures on the claimants' witnesses:

First, most of the central witnesses of fact were willing to give dishonest and untruthful evidence. In the case of those of the claimants' witnesses who live in Russia, and particularly those who are employed by the Sovcomflot group or NSC group, I recognise the force of the defendants' submission that they are likely to have felt great pressure to support the claimants' case, and I am driven to conclude that sometimes untruthful allegations were made or supported by generally honest witnesses called by the claimants . . . Secondly, the claimants' witness statements were shown in cross-examination to be distinctly unreliable . . . Thirdly, witnesses manufactured an account of events, or supported a manufactured account of events, that was designed to build a fiction consistent with the documents, and the documents, as I conclude, inspired a false account rather than corroborate[d] a true one. (Mr Justice Andrew Smith, paras. 36–39)[1]

The strains and pressures of *sistema* are shouldered by individuals, most notably by those in positions of responsibility, but where do these pressures come from? Evidence presented by witnesses in legal cases point to both formal and informal constraints. Formal constraints are defined by the official duties within Russia's *vertikal´* of power and are enforced by its centralised hierarchies.[2] For example, ministers taking the witness stand would refer to their duty to remain impartial and refrain from lobbying on behalf of businesses that they might be affiliated with informally or where they, until recently, were on the board of directors. Informal constraints originate in power networks, whereby one gets involved in initiating, channelling, or receiving various signals of informal governance, thus to some extent undermining the *vertikal´* and diverting official policies. These networks are maintained by carefully recruited and compromised insiders, mechanisms of collective vigilance and mutual control, 'material hooks' and other forms of stimuli, subtle signals and undeclared affiliations.

The formal and informal constraints may clash or reinforce each other in theory, but in practice they form a symbiotic relationship – a co-dependence between official policies and unofficial influences, between overlapping formal hierarchies and intertwined informal networks. The outcome is perceived as unpredictable: an anonymous force that rejects personal integrity and independence but instead favours personal loyalty and compliance. Loyalty is essential because it helps to avoid responsibility and punishment. The wrongdoings of loyal insiders tend to be overlooked. In other words, in order to accommodate the ambivalent nature of *sistema* constraints, one has to go with the flow. In our example, ministers wear a variety of hats and testify

---

[1] The High Court of Justice, Queen's Bench division, Commercial Court, dated 10 December 2010, Neutral Citation Number: [2010] EWHC 3199 (Comm).

[2] Putin became known for creating parallel bodies with overlapping responsibilities that complicated the hierarchical structure.

accordingly, thus carrying the burden of *sistema* that puts them into positions of conflict of interest. The power of *sistema* rests on practices associated with the navigation of formal rules and the flexibility of their enforcement – the doubledeed – and the ambivalent norms and multiple moralities – the doublethink – as exercised by its loyal brokers.

Blat and *sistema*

This book was originally planned as a sequel to *Russia's Economy of Favours* (Ledeneva 1998) and in some ways the story of power networks in *sistema* is indeed complementary to the story of *blat* networks at the grassroots. One important distinction has to be emphasised. If an 'economy of favours' had to some extent an equalising effect on the chances of accessing resources for networked individuals and thus reduced the privilege gap between insiders and outsiders, the trickle-down effect of the present-day 'economy of kickbacks' is the reverse – it undermines competition and rewards insiders through network-based allocation and mobilisation. If *blat* networks tend to operate on the basis of reciprocal obligation and are perceived as 'mutual help', power networks tend to operate on the basis of a hierarchical, patron–client logic and are presented as part and parcel, if not a bare necessity, of 'manual control'. This difference also stems from the political and economic frameworks in which networks operate. As the Soviet system was not economically viable due to its rigid ideological constraints, the economy of shortage and the limited role of money, *blat* networks served individuals as the 'weapon of the weak' in oppressive conditions, and to some extent served the economic needs of the central distribution system. In Putin's Russia, power networks operate without those constraints and extract multiple benefits from the post-Soviet reforms, while effectively undermining the key principles of market competition – equality of economic subjects and security of property rights – and the key principles of the rule of law – equality before the law. There is an important similarity between *blat* and power networks, too. In order to modernise Russia, people at all levels have to modernise their own attitudes to '*svoi*', to stop using personal networks for getting things done, and to stop cutting corners and bending the rules.

Specifics of Putin's *sistema*

Putin's *sistema* functions with some elements from the 'administrative-command' system of Brezhnev's socialism. Administrative-command methods remain effective for mobilising new elites and allocating resources, adjusted to present-day objectives and priorities. But there are also significant differences: the party ideology has given place to market interests, state property to privatised assets, informal exchange of favours to monetised kickbacks, planning to the constraints of global finance, local-bound infrastructure to hi-tech technologies and overtly command methods to more subtle informal signals.

The key difference of Putin's *sistema* is its orientation on wealth. Due to the monetisation of the economy, the power networks that used to be aimed at obtaining privileges have become oriented towards monetary income and capital. In the Soviet economy, favours of access to resources had to be routinely exchanged as the resources themselves were not alienable. Power networks rewarded their members with exclusivity – privileges of access to resources but not resources *per se*. During Russia's transition to a capitalist economy, the assets themselves were granted, privatised, sold to foreign investors and taken out of the country.

Putin's Russia has seen an increase in economic growth but also an increase in the scale of the economy of kickbacks, widespread practices of informal deals over the budget funds and informal capital flows. Stanislav Belkovskii coined the term of the 'economy of r–o–z', referring to three common forms of corruption: splitting profits, paying kickbacks and operating by bribes (*raspil, otkat* and *zanos*). He quoted corresponding percentages on deals with informal income and emphasised the quantitative specifics of present-day *sistema*: from the 25 per cent splits, 10 per cent kickbacks and 2 per cent bribes in the 1990s to the 60 per cent splits, 30 per cent kickbacks and 10 per cent bribes in 2010.[3] Informal income has become a 'drug for thousands of thousands of bureaucrats and businessmen and their dependents', he says: '[p]ractically all elites are addicted to the injections of informal income.'[4] Where access to resources is granted and controlled through appointments, the appointments themselves can be traded. 'Many state

[3] 'Otkat, raspil, zanos', *The Forbes Magazine*, www.forbes.ru/svoi-biznes/predprinimateli/58657-otkat-raspil-zanos.
[4] *Ibid.*

officials understand that they should fight this addiction, but cannot resist another dose.'[5] Vladimir Solov'ev points to the imperial roots and all-pervasive nature of corrupt practices in Russia's history, thus playing down the specifics of Putin's *sistema* (Solov'ev 2012).

Sistema's ambivalence

In my view, *sistema* should not be associated simply with corruption and dysfunctionality. *Sistema* benefits from corruption, but also restricts it with its inner channels of checks and balances. It sustains informal control over assets and appointees and reserves informal leverage for re-negotiating property rights and positions. The vulnerability of individuals, the flexibility of rules and the ambivalence of constraints are at the core of the functioning of *sistema*. *Sistema* is complex, anonymous, unpredictable and seemingly irrational, but it serves to glue society together, to distribute resources and to mobilise people; it contributes to both stability and change; and it ensures its own reproduction. Present-day *sistema* incites people to work, offers effective stimuli and adequate motivation, but does so in an ambivalent and even paradoxical way. Its incentives prioritise short-term profit at the expense of long-term sustainability, loyalty at the expense of professionalism, safety and collective responsibility at the expense of leadership, and innovative circumvention of *sistema* constraints at the expense of productive innovation. Self-made businessmen often comment on their success being achieved against the odds and despite the forces of *sistema*, whereas *sistema* businessmen prefer to avoid the subject of building close links with influential politicians, or deny the links altogether. Power networks enable the leaders to receive support and to trust others (inner circle), to access resources (useful friends), to mobilise cadres for solving problems (core contacts) and to reduce risks and uncertainty (mediated contacts). As argued in Chapter 2, none of these functions are without strings attached.

Sistema works

It is tempting to assume that there are obvious reform measures that Russia could undertake to replace *sistema* with a market economy and the rule of law. It would be a mistake, however, to associate *sistema*

[5] *Ibid.*

with a failed state. It would be too simplistic to claim that Putin's micro-management does not work. Quite the opposite: it is amazing how much does get done in Russia despite the infrastructural problems and institutional inefficiencies, and the explanation lies in the effectiveness of networks and relationships. *Sistema*'s output is impressive because it is capable of mobilising people, of recruiting youth and of creating opportunities. When it comes to individual recruitment, offers that came from the authorities are difficult to resist and hard to refuse. Moreover, such offers are met with enthusiasm and selflessness. Businessmen rationalise their participation by future gains for business and for themselves through *sistema*'s promise of scale and potential, and often disregard *sistema*'s downsides. If successful, their businesses will be used by *sistema* or appropriated through *sistema* raiding; if unsuccessful, a new generation of businessmen will be mobilised. Just as people exploit *sistema*'s shortcomings, *sistema* exploits people's shortcomings. Breaking out of this reproductive circle can be assisted by honesty and integrity at individual level, the idea of common good recognised by all, equality before the law, security of property rights – which thus far have been kept unstable in order to keep asset holders in control – and accountability of the leadership's informal governance. These points constituted a basis for consensus among the peaceful protestors in Russia after the parliamentary elections of December 2011 and inform our thinking about the future of *sistema*, even if the actual critique of it at the time was somewhat personalised.[6] The protests themselves have generated political changes that fit in with other significant challenges to *sistema*.

Factors of change: financial integration, technological modernisation, legal globalisation

The financial integration of Russia into the global community created possibilities of moving wealth and capital from Russia, which were especially visible when associated with individual exits from *sistema*. According to a 2011 national opinion poll, 65 per cent of Russians are convinced that state officials have bank accounts abroad and another

---

[6] Journalist Artemii Troitskii called for Putin to disclose how much money he had, and to let everyone see his wife. The blogger Alexei Naval'nyi referred to the leadership as 'botox boys'. Those who spoke about the future did not suggest any particular projects, but called for an honest Russia (Boris Akunin), and for the increase of people's influence on politics (Ksenia Sobchak).

26 per cent consider it likely, thus making 91 per cent of affirmative responses as opposed to over 2 per cent of those who think that state officials do not have bank accounts abroad. 6 per cent did not answer.[7] How can people be so sure? Such perceptions are backed up by their experience of the monetisation of Russia's economy of favours and its replacement by practices of kickbacks, as detailed in Chapter 3.

Another factor essential for the opening up and consequent transformation of *sistema* is associated with the globalisation of technology and infrastructure. Advances in mobile communication technology, the rise of Internet access and Russia's openness and exposure to a global infrastructure are not only changing the behaviour of the elites but also bringing about some unintended consequences. The culture of privileges for *sistema* insiders is transforming under such a global influence, and there are also transformations in the public understanding of the common good and infrastructural equality, as depicted in Chapter 4.[8]

The third challenge to *sistema* is the loss of sovereignty in legal affairs. The analysis of legal materials and appeals to international courts reveals signs of legal globalisation (for those who can afford it) and a relative weakness of *sistema* outside Russia, as shown in Chapter 5. Given the large number of cases initiated by Russian citizens against the Russian Federation, experts refer to the ECtHR as the 'Supreme Court of Russia'. Yet international courts are also used by the government for the purposes of asset recovery from *sistema* fugitives, as demonstrated in Chapter 6. British commercial courts are argued to be the centre of international commercial litigation due to the expertise of judges and, unlike the US courts, the lack of a jury. The services of commercial courts constitute one of the largest British exports: in over 80 per cent of cases at least one litigant is foreign; in about 50 per cent of cases both are foreign.[9] Russian cases are particularly large-scale and high-profile.

[7] Levada Centre, *Obshchestvennoe mnenie: ezhegodnik* (*Russian Public Opinion: Annual Report, 2011*) (Moscow: Levada Centre Publishing 2011). Question: 'Do state officials have bank accounts abroad?', Table 8.11.5: 127.

[8] Levada Centre, *Obshchestvennoe mnenie: ezhegodnik*. In response to the Question: 'Do you use the Internet apart from e-mail', 53 per cent said they never used the Internet (down from 95 per cent in 2001), Table 21.37: 266.

[9] These 2004–5 percentages have not altered much over recent years. It indicates that the Commercial Court remains predominantly an international court. Judiciary of England and Wales, *Report of the Commercial Court and the Admiralty Court*, 2004–5: 4–5, www.judiciary.gov.uk/Resources/ICO/Documents/Reports/annual report_comm.admiralty_ct.0405.pdf.

None of these developments by itself can be sufficient for the transformation of *sistema*. It is so complex that its change must be an outcome of multiple factors, including the transformation of the leadership, as argued in Chapter 7.

The future of Putin's *sistema*: the modernisation trap of informality

Sistema cannot simply be 'reformed' in the traditional sense of the word. First, challenging *sistema* could get the reformers expelled from their formal positions, from informal networks, or even from the country. Second, if *sistema* unravelled, the consequences would be hard to manage, as it is also the glue that keeps Russia's economy and society together. Third, it requires an enlightened leadership, capable of self-restriction, fighting *sistema*'s destructive forces while preserving its capacity for innovation, replacing informal tools with effective alternatives. Russia cannot modernise to its full potential unless the issues of informal governance are spelled out and tackled. In the short run, tools of informal governance can help leaders to pursue their policy objectives. Such tools can help them to exert control over the media, bureaucracy and judiciary as well as parts of the economy for the purposes of stability. For example, companies in Russia know that the political leadership expects them to show 'corporate responsibility' through supporting political, social, youth, environmental and charity programmes. The leadership also uses informal leverage and networks to promote its modernisation agenda. So companies feel compelled, if not privileged, to sign up to Kremlin-sponsored projects such as the Skolkovo Innovation City, even if they do not believe in their viability. In the long run, however, the informal tactics for mobilising elites and allocating resources to insider networks undermine the fundamental principles of the rule of law, the separation of powers and the security of property rights. Ultimately, they reduce Russia's chances of achieving the strategic goals of modernisation. I call this the 'modernisation trap of informality': one cannot use the potential of informal networks without triggering their negative long-term consequences. Informal networks enable Russia to complete modernisation projects, but in the process they create vested interests and lock politicians, bureaucrats and businessmen into informal bargains and pledges of loyalty that subsequently impede change and modernisation. Unless Russia's leaders address this governance paradox, there is no obvious way of tackling the change of *sistema* without weakening the social cohesion of Russian society.

The paradox of informal power

Leaders rely on informal networks for getting things done, but are also limited, if not imprisoned, by them. They can apply sanctions to particular members and weaken some specific networks but leaders cannot radically modify their own dependence on informal governance. Reliance on networks *per se* should not be viewed as defective as it is effective in enabling the leadership and society to function at all. The effectiveness of the leadership can only be achieved in synergy with *sistema* – the leader's power is not strictly speaking personal, it is ingrained in power networks that the leader can mobilise. The more leaders try to change *sistema*, the more they have to rely on the informal means of execution of power and decision-making outside of formal procedures. The more they rely on them, the more they get entangled and eventually tied up with *sistema*'s power networks. The more reliant on institutions, and thus less interventionist, leaders are, the less credit they receive for their leadership. It is almost as if informal leadership is the key characteristic of leadership in Russia, unachievable without instruments of informal governance. Modernisation in Russia cannot succeed as long as this system of informal power and network-based governance remains untouched. I argue that the modernisation of *sistema* should start with the modernisation of the networks it relies on. Russian leaders keep talking about changing Russia top-down, without ever addressing the informal rules and constraints that govern their own behaviour and that of the political, bureaucratic and business elites. Modernising leaders' own networks by gradually reducing their use, or even by being aware of their use, has the potential to change *sistema* from within. Channels of recruitment have to accommodate those with loyalty to Russia, but not necessarily to its leadership. Exposure to global education and professional training can lead to the modernisation of loyalty patterns within hierarchies and the modernisation of relationships within horizontal networks.

Reflexive modernisation

The starting point is a reflexive awareness of one's own leadership style, recognition of the degree of reliance on informal governance, the ability to distinguish between personalised and corporate loyalty and the will to recognise a boundary between friendship and the use of friendship. The motivation for the leadership to change may arise from both internal and external sources. The December 2011 peaceful protests certainly demonstrated the need for reflection from leaders, their followers and protestors alike and created a significant shift in policies. A number of events before, during and after the 2011 parliamentary elections contributed to the protests. The announcement in September 2011 regarding the decision by the Putin–Medvedev tandem that Putin would run for President, and Medvedev would be Putin's choice for Prime Minister, triggered a reflexive change in the middle class. The arrogance of the job swap announcement motivated many successful, self-respecting and apolitical people to vote for the first time. Crude manipulation of the election outcome, rather than the use of the more sophisticated political technologies applied in previous elections, became another factor in the protests. Even among his supporters, Putin's return as President came to be perceived as pursuing personal ambition, rather than any *sistema* necessity. Internet-based forums have turned into hubs of reflexivity, and social networking sites have turned out to be more effective for channelling protest moods than oppositional activism.[10] The December 2011 protests have initiated a wave of 'reflexive modernisation' – a self-instigated change in people's attitudes to politics and voting behaviour. Although the spectrum of attitudes includes everything from 'we have to lead the country'[11] to

[10] Sources on the Internet include ConScore, 'Russia Has Most Engaged Social Networking Audience Worldwide', *Comscore online*, October 2010, www.comscore.com; E. Morozova and I. Miroshnichenko, '*Setevye soobshchestva v usloviyakh chrezvychainykh situatsii: Novye vozmozhnosti dlya grazhdan i dlya vlasti*', www.polistudies.ru/fulltext/2011/1/10.pdf; J. Kelly *et al.*, *Mapping Russian Twitter*, Research Publication No.2012-3, The Berkman Centre for Internet and Society at Harvard University, http://ssrn.com/abstract=2028158 (2012); M. Lonkila, 'The Role of Social Media in the Moscow Opposition Demonstration in December 2011', Briefing Paper 98, The Finish Institute of International Affairs (2012).

[11] 'Russian paratroopers' unlikely protest song hits a chord with anti-Putin protesters', Associated Press, Updated: Sunday, 5 February, 2:28, www.youtube.com/watch?v=dCrjfQjB5GU.

'we have to leave the country',[12] with the February 2012 addition of 'we have a lot to lose' slogan in support of Putin in the Presidential elections, the ultimate source of all these demonstrations – pro or contra – is Putin's *sistema*. The outcome of the 2012 Presidential elections demonstrates that personal loyalty and compliance within power networks continue to be more important than loyalty to universal values. It also indicates that the protest movement is personalised as well. It propagates an elimination or replacement of Putin's networks, rather than rejecting the network-based system of governance altogether. The protests are pitched more against Putin than for the general principle of leadership changeover. Standing up for universal principles does not make a viable position in Russia, where 'beating the system' and 'privileged access' remain both a national sport and a survival strategy.

It is essential, however, not to over-state the personalisation of *sistema* in the sense that Putin's *sistema*, which he shaped by mobilising his personal networks, is not really controlled by him. Like everyone else, leaders are 'locked' into their networks while relying on them to perform their public functions and satisfy their private needs. Conversely, not relying on networks might also limit, if not undermine, the leadership capacity – they have to operate within the culturally acceptable codes and discourses, otherwise they lose their base. Thus, the main implication of the ambivalence of *sistema* is that its leader is also its hostage.

[12] A group of multi-millionaire Russian businessmen who fled from Moscow for fear of their lives say that they will use Britain as a base from which to expose the corruption at the heart of the Kremlin. They claim to have identified fifty bureaucrats in the government of Vladmir Putin who have plundered hundreds of millions of pounds from the state and hidden it abroad. D. Leppard, 'London exiles to name "corrupt" Kremlin aides', *Sunday Times*, 29 January 2012: 1, 8.

Appendix 1
Survey questions

The Levada Centre Omnibus Survey: 21–27 December 2007

Sampling was based on a multi-stage stratification scheme. Firstly, from seven federal regions (North-Western, Central, Southern, Povolzhskii, Uralskii, Siberian and Far Eastern), 128 primary sampling units (PSU) were selected: 88 urban settlements and 40 rural districts in 46 subjects of the Russian Federation. Secondly, secondary sampling units (SSU) were randomly selected within each PSU. Thirdly, households from each SSU were randomly selected. And finally, with the help of the 2002 National Census data, one respondent was selected within each household, taking into account sex, age and education. Of the 4,398 households visited, the interviewers had contacts with 2,912 people and completed 1,603 interviews. After the regional offices supervisors had conducted quality controls on the work of the interviewers, 2 interviews were rejected. Therefore 1,601 interviews entered the sample. Further details of sampling can be found at www.levada.ru.

Survey on *blat*

1 *In the past seven years, did you or someone you know encounter any of the following informal practices?*

> Gave money/bribe to solve problems
> Received money/bribe for helping with a problem
> Gave gifts to solve problems
> Received gifts from an interested party
> Used your *blat* connections
> Asked a public servant you know or a friend of a friend for help
> Used your official position or influence to solve your own problems or at somebody else's request
> Asked for a public servant's help through personal channels

Used your personal connection with the power structures
Helped someone because you work or know someone in the power structures
Received your salary in black cash (*chyornym nalom*)
Paid salaries in black cash (*chyornym nalom*)
Used information obtained from acquaintances for profit-making
Passed valuable information to acquaintances

Other

Nobody I know has encountered any of the above-mentioned informal practices

2 *How do you define* blat? *(Multiple choices possible)*

'*Po blatu*' means 'by acquaintance' or 'through connections'
Blat is best expressed by the saying 'don't have 100 roubles, but have 100 friends'
Exchange of favours: 'I scratch your back, you scratch mine'
The word *blatnoi* means criminal
The term *blat* is out of use, nowadays it all is about money
Blat is still necessary to give a bribe
Today *blat* means problem-solving in difficult situations
Today *blat* means access to administrative resources
Blat is the circumvention of formal rules and procedures

Other

Difficult to answer

3 *In your opinion, how widespread is* blat *in your city or region now?*

Widespread
Rather widespread
Not very widespread
Practically absent

Other

Difficult to answer

4 *What did you or your family use your contacts for in the last seven years? (Multiple choices possible)*

For daily needs
Foodstuffs
Consumer goods
Everyday services
Hobbies
All these services at better quality or better price

For regular problems
Help with travel tickets and business trips
Help with organising tours and holidays
Help with tickets for events, theatre, concerts
Help with registration of a vehicle and MOT
Solving problems with the traffic police
Repairs of housing, garages, dachas
All these services at better quality or better price

For lifecycle problems
Obtaining housing
Place in kindergarten and primary school
Place in secondary and higher education
Problems with army conscription
Finding a job
Legal services and courts
Other legal and solicitor services
Better medical services
Arranging a hospital bed
Arranging a surgery
Arranging a funeral
All these services at better quality or better price

To solve business-related problems
Launching and registration of a business
Access to resources to run a business (land for development,
    premises, property rights registration)
Business security
Help with financing business, banking
Solving problems with tax inspectors and other control organs
All these services at better quality or better price
Other
Never happened
Difficult to answer

5 *In the past seven years, did you personally have to 'informally' help other people or companies?*

Frequently
Rather frequently
Sometimes
Never

Surveys on telephone justice (*telefonnoe pravo*)

Two surveys were conducted in 2007 and 2010, with the aim of monitoring changes in popular perceptions of 'telephone justice' and of the independence of the judiciary. The 2010 nationwide survey was conducted jointly by the author, the Levada Research Centre and the EU-Russia Centre. The questions of the 2010 Survey repeat those asked in 2007. More than one answer is possible, unless stated otherwise.

1 *Have you had any personal experience of the judicial system in the past seven years (as a litigant, plaintiff or defendant, a suspect, a witness or a jury member, etc.)? Choose one answer.*

Yes, personally
Yes, through relatives or friends
Yes, through acquaintances, colleagues or neighbours
Yes, through other sources
No, never

2 In your opinion, what is 'telephone justice'?

Court decisions are taken on command 'from above'
Pressure on judges/procurators by state officials (*chinovniki*)
Court decisions are taken on orders (*po zakazu*)
Cases are opened and closed on orders (*po zakazu*)
Selective law enforcement: court decisions are influenced by the status of the litigant
Selective law enforcement: opening/closing cases is influenced by the status of the opponent
Right of the detained to telephone
Legislation in the area of telephone communications, tariffs, etc.
Basmannoe justice: the way the Khodorkovsky case was heard, judged, conducted

Pressure on judges/procurators by security services (*spetssluzhby*)
Pressure on judges/procurators by criminal groups
Pressure of procurators on judges

3 *Do you think that the Russian judicial system has been used for unlawful purposes in the last seven years?*

Yes, show trials are conducted to demonstrate to the society the attitude of the authority to certain actions or phenomena

Yes, the judicial system is used for political ends, in order to pursue and to get rid of political opponents

Yes, the judicial system is used in order to settle personal conflicts and for revenge

Yes, the judicial system is used to undermine business competitors, to ruin their reputation or to capture their business

Yes, in other ways

It might be used, but little is known about it

Even if it is used, it serves the right purposes

No, the judicial system in Russia is not used for any unlawful purposes

4 *In your opinion, what, aside from the law, exerts the strongest influence on the work of Russian courts and judges?*

Personal profit, money, bribes
Personal requests, favours and promises
Direct or indirect lobbying
Informal orders from local authorities
An atmosphere in which the judge understands what the 'party line' is
Disciplinary measures and other forms of persecution
Threats to life and family safety
Other

5 *What, aside from the law, guides the activities of Russian procurators and what influences their actions?*

State and public interest
Nothing but the law
Professional ethics
Personal interest

Material gains
Directives from above
Personal ambition
Telephone calls from the Kremlin
Status of the litigant
Pressure from criminal groups
Pressure from security services (*siloviki*)
Political cause

6 *Telephone justice existed in the Soviet system. Why do you think it is still part of the judicial system after all the reforms?*

It is a legacy from the Soviet past
Where there is technical possibility of doing so (*vertushka*), it is used
Because of defects of the legislation on the powers of the judiciary
Because of the insufficient attention to the education of judges
Because of the insufficient financial independence of judges
Because of the insufficient morality of judges
Because judges are corrupted
Because of the dependency of judges on the court chairmen

7 *In what way are court decisions in your locality most often made? Choose one answer.*

All, or practically all, court decisions are made by law
There are judges who take bribes and are subject to pressure from above, but they are few
Judges, as a rule, take bribes and are subject to pressure from above, but there are also principled judges
Even principled judges react to pressure from above in certain cases
Practically all court decisions are taken for a bribe or under pressure from above
Do not agree with any of these

8 *Why do you think only judges who fell out of the judicial system talk about telephone justice?*

They are no longer afraid
They can talk because they do not depend on *sistema* any more

They try to change a system that cannot be changed from the
    inside
They want to draw attention to this sensitive subject
They want to discredit their colleagues
They want to take revenge for their dismissal
One can see better from the outside
Other

9 *If you were to have a case considered before a court, and, in your
opinion, it was unfair, which of the following would you most likely
do next?*

I will not appeal because it is useless
I do not have enough money to appeal to anybody
I do not have anybody to appeal to
I would consult a lawyer, to file an appeal
I would consult a lawyer, to file a complaint about the carrying
    out of the trial or the judge's decision, to the higher authorities
I would consult an independent human rights organisation
I will find somebody to turn to
I will think about it when it happens

The results of these surveys are discussed in (Ledeneva 2008a, 2009,
2011b).

Appendix 2
Interview questions

1 *On the workings of informal power and* sistema

I am interested in everything related to informal relationships within power elites and informal power. How would you define informal power?

How does it relate to formal power?

How can one recognise the existence of informal power? What are its signalling factors?

What did you know about informal power relationships before you took up your current position?

How does informal power work: vertically or horizontally?

Is it possible to escape templates and analogies with formal power when thinking about informal power?

What are the sticks and the carrots of informal power? What constitutes its pressure?

What are the indicators of informal power? Is it possible to measure it? How?

Why do people comply with informal requests that often come as oral commands?

Why are people pressed to play by rules that deviate from the law?

Why is it not possible just to live by the law?

What is *sistema* (the system)? How would you define it? Do your remember your first encounter with *sistema*?

Is it possible to get out of the system? What kinds of problems arise? Why?

Cynicism and lawlessness lead to the strengthening of authorities. Is dictatorship inevitable?

What is your first memory of *sistema*? Was it personal? What would explain your situation?

Kinship, access to powerful patron, network, loyalty to the boss – who needs this? The patron, the client, the intermediary? The system?

2 *Questions on informal power and clans*

Does it make sense to talk about 'clan politics'?

Why can members of one 'clan' be seen in a different 'clan'?

What does this tell us about the openness and closeness of power networks?

In which sense are they open? (describe specifics of recruitment, 'parachuted' appointments)

In which sense are they closed? What is the role of birthday celebrations in *sistema*? Do you always see the same people at all birthday parties? How would you define the difference in the circle of those invited?

What is a '*korporativnyi chelovek*' (corporate person) in your view? Is it an insider of a certain network or clan, or simply the one who knows how to behave (to go on under certain circumstances) and displays mastery of unwritten rules of the system?

Would you say that 'corporate people' tend to be more successful with their careers?

Do you know of any 'non-corporate man' who has been appointed or promoted?

3 *Questions on power networks*

Do you think informal networks of people at the top are different from informal networks of people at the bottom?

In which sense are they the same?

In which sense are they different? Size and frequency of contacts? Structure and composition (relatives, friends, compatriots, colleagues, acquaintances, other)?

What can you tell me about the history of formation of power networks?

What are their functions? What are they used for?

What kinds of resources are used within these networks by people in power? Is involvement in these networks rational/conscious or reflexive/unconscious?

In your opinion, do people in power make a distinction between friendship and the use of friendship (these used to be blurred under socialism)?

Is there a boundary between networks and the use of networks?

Is reciprocity within power networks different from that within the informal networks at the grassroots?

Which forms of networking are possible in contemporary Russia? Are they different from networking abroad? How?

4 *Questions about trust*

In the 1990s doing business with friends was associated with losing both the friend and the business. How would you characterise the trend today (in your industry, sector, department)?

Trust in friends is an important element of informal power, how does it work? Is it always pre-existing at the time of need?

Is it possible to create trust in a short span of time? How? What is the role of information, intelligence, *kompromat* and recommendations in building trust?

Whose recommendations would work for you? On which basis? Is your preference related to the potential use of informal pressure?

What kind of obligation is imposed on the person who is 'recommended'? Are there forms of trust, loyalty, mutual support that become part of the package?

How are obligations, loyalty, or gratitude expressed?

Imagine, somebody has recommended you for a senior role, would it possible to 'pay off' the indebtedness and free yourself from any further obligations? Would you be allowed to 'pay off'? Or would you be put in a position of 'no return' (i.e. irreversible debt)?

How 'bound' does the system make its insiders? Could you give some estimates of 'indebtedness'?

5 *Questions about telephone justice* (telefonnoe pravo)

What is *telefonnoe pravo*? How would you define it if you had to explain its meaning to a foreign audience?

Who coined the term? Who uses the term today?

When did you first hear the term? What other terms would you associate with it?

When is *telefonnoe pravo* used? In which contexts does it appear most often?

Where (territory, sector, context) is it more widespread?

How geographically widespread do you think *telefonnoe pravo* is? Is the system different depending on the administrative level it occurs at (federal, regional, local)?

What is the difference between *telefonnoe pravo* in the Soviet system and now?

Why does *telefonnoe pravo* exist today? How is it possible that it continues to exist regardless of all the reforms?

How does this mysterious 'telephone call from the Kremlin' work? Is it necessarily personal? Have you ever received any such call?

Who calls whom? How long is the call? What is it about? What kind of language is used? Can you give any examples?

Why does one have to call around to check before showing up at the prosecutor's office?

What is *telefonnoe pravo* used for?

Who benefits from *telefonnoe pravo*? In which way?

Who suffers from *telefonnoe pravo*? In which way?

Who are the 'enemies' and who are the 'allies' in the *telefonnoe pravo* system?

What, in your view, are the implications of *telefonnoe pravo* for the political regime? For the economy? For the society?

Are there differences between how you used to see the system when you were an insider and how you see it now as an outsider?

What do people do if *telefonnoe pravo* is used against them, or their case is considered in the court unjustly because of it?

Can one defend oneself with *kompromat* (for example, a tax lawyer releasing material on tax schemes)?

Why do you think only judges who have fallen out of the judicial system talk about telephone justice?

How do people, professional communities, social groups, law enforcement officials treat the whistleblowers?

6 *Questions about the Three Whales* (Tri Kita) *case*

Can the case be defined as the 'criminal case of Putin's Russia'?

Why couldn't the opponents find an agreement?

What was the outcome of the arbitration case? What was the position of the tax inspection (*nalogovaya*)?

How would you comment on Chairwoman Egorova's statement that 'Fighting the system is like tilting at windmills'.

Where does Court Chairman Egorova fit into *sistema*?

Many say that she is not acting independently. Is that so?

Did you have personal connections in the judiciary?

Are the Arbitration Courts freer from telephone justice?

7 *Questions on* vertushka

Can you explain how *vertushka* worked? May I see the phonebook?

Do you remember anything about the budget or the payment for *vertushka* in the 1990s? Do you have any personal memory of the installation? Examples? Jokes?

Are there any rituals around becoming part of the circle and a line in the *vertushka* phonebook? Is there a sort of initiation ceremony? And what happens when somebody is taken out of the phonebook?

Are there any signals that indicate eminent connection or disconnection?

How can one become part of or exit the *vertushka* system?

Do you remember anything about the role of individuals (Viktor Ivanov as head of the commission for *vertushka*'s lists or General Matyukhin)?

Did *siloviki* control *vertushka*?

Could newly emerging business sectors receive access to *vertushka*? How? To what extent?

What is it important for a new user to know? Do new users learn through their mistakes?

Many are at the receiving end but nobody calls the other way round. Do you have any examples of this?

Only the owner must answer. Was this maintained? Who answers the phone now?

Communications are secret and safe. To what extent was it technically feasible to protect communications? Was there a special department that takes care of this? People anyway say that communication is never completely safe, why?

Are there exceptions to the rules? Who is not afraid? Why?

Do you know any stories about *vertushka* (gossip, legends, anecdotes, jokes)?

You must have had *vertushka* in your office. What were the advantages and disadvantages of it? What about its costs? What did it tell about your status? What was it used for in your experience?

What has changed with the arrival of Putin?

What are the implications of the commercialisation of *vertushka*? Has the use of technology changed things?

What was more important for the change of the status of *vertushka*: Reiman's management style or technological change?

What do we learn about the *vertushka* hierarchy now it is being dismantled during the 2000s?

Does Medvedev use *vertushka*?

What does *vertushka* symbolise today? Is it still important and do people still aspire to have it? Is it possible to pay for it commercially? How much?

8 *Questions on* Vertu

Questions to owners according to the 'biography of a thing' logic

Conception: when did you first hear about Vertu? From whom? Who already had one? Why did you decide to have one? Who set up an example?

Birth: How did you get it, where, when, on whose recommendation/introduction/advice, who went with you, how much and how did you pay?

Gender: are there men's and women's models? How do they differ? Which one(s) did you have?

Growth: Did you like it straight away? How did it feel?

Adolescence: Do you remember the first call to your *vertushka*/your Vertu? And the first call you received from Putin?

Have there been any changes since you've acquired the phone? Did people treat you in a special way? Did you feel different?

Education: What did you learn in association with Vertu? Types, models, prices, fake/authenticity, any special skills? How to organise protection? How not to lose the phone? Insurance? Change in personal behaviour and care for the phone?

Career: Does the phone help with business, work, people, institutions? What powers does the phone have?

Making it: [question not to ask but to sense] Do the owners feel they belong to a narrow circle of owners? How narrow? Are they a priori *svoi lyudi*? Signals?

Reproduction:

Gifts and exchanges: Instances when the phone was given as a gift to family, friends and useful people.

Contacts: Did new contacts emerge from Vertu ownership? Would you help an owner of a Vertu?

Introductions: Introducing other people to Vertu.

Accidents: Stories of the phone being lost or found, noticed by others or not noticed on purpose (jealousy), calls received at the wrong moment or right moment, which moment is which?

Illnesses: Did it ever break? What happened? Had it to be taken for emergency repair? What are services like for Vertu?

Death: Why did you give up your first Vertu? Where is that phone? What happened to it? Process of recycling, if any, depending on metal, stone, material?

Artefacts: Fond memories? Photographs? Other visuals, cartoons, pictures?

Discourse: Do you know any stories about Vertu, gossip, legends, social myths, or anecdotes?

Questions to experts:

What do you know about the mobile phone market in Russia? What is the number of mobile phones sold in Moscow in the last year? What are market trends over the last ten years (both for Vertu and for other phones)? Has there been a decline in mobile phone sales since the beginning of the 2008 economic crisis?

What do you think the regional distribution of Vertu users is? How would you rate the Russian regions depending on Vertu distribution? Any information on Vertu sales in the regions, in Moscow and in St Petersburg?

What do you know about Vertu mobiles' price range (are there differences between real prices and prices quoted on compromat.ru)? And what about discounts, special sales at the local level, payment methods, types of contracts and tariffs?

DoVertu mobiles guarantee communication security? Are the mobiles protected by some sort of insurance plan?

Are there any specific topics discussed on *vertushka* as opposed to a mobile phone? Is there any difference?

Has the shift of officials to mobile phones entailed any change in the level of formality of communications? Did conversations become more informal?

Are the mobile phones linked to the switchboard, where the call is transferred from the office number to a mobile number?

Mobile phone contacts v. phonebooks? How does having a mobile
phone number differ from being able to place a call? How many
mobile numbers do 'lonely people at the top' have in their mobiles'
contacts?

Appendix 3
List of interviews

Respondents in this project will remain anonymous. Interviews were conducted between 2007 and 2011, in London, Paris, Moscow and St Petersburg, in total 42 interviews. In personal interviews I avoided interviewing the 'usual suspects' – the vocal critics of *sistema* – and those whose positions in *sistema* make them too vulnerable. Published interviews and materials have also informed this study. The list below illustrates the most interesting materials:

Chronology of Putin's vertical of power and his memorable phrases, in 'Putin u Vlasti 1999–2009', *Trud*, 10 August 2009: 6.

Head of FSKN, Russian anti-narcotic service, Viktor Cherkesov, in V. Cherkesov, 'Nel´zia dopustit´, chtoby voiny prevratilis' v torgovtsev', *Kommersant Daily*, 9 October 2007: 1.

Owner of Russneft, Mikhail Gutseriev, 'Ya reshil uiti', *Vedomosti*, 30 July 2007.

Owner of Russneft, Mikhail Gutseriev, in Reznik (2010). 'Ya nikogda ne torgoval Rossiei', *Vedomosti*, 19 May 2010.

Kremlin Property Chief, Vladimir Kozhin, in Korobov and Kashin (2011: 1), http://dlib.eastview.com/browse/doc/24625234.

First deputy chairman of the Federation Council's committee on economic policy, entrepreneurship and property Vladimir Gusev, in Yudina (2008: 2).

Chairman of the Special Information Service group, Sergei Minaev, in M. Zhogleva, 'Okhotniki na reiderov', *Birzha*, 13, 7 April 2008.

Head of Interpol-Russia, Timur Lakhonin, in M. Stepenin, 'Timur Lakhonin: k Berezovskomu prisoedinilis´ Gutseriev i Chichvarkin', *Trud*, 30 January 2009: 8.

Former owner of Evroset´, Evgenii Chichvarkin, in V. Sokolov, 'Prosto Chichvarkin', *Kommersant UK* 2010: 16.

Owner of Metalloinvest, Alisher Usmanov, in R. Iambaeva and A. Balashova, 'Rech´ idet o soiuze mezhdu mnoyu personal´no i Olegom Deripaskoi', *Kommersant. Daily*, 19 April 2011: 1.

Commentaries on Gennady Timchenko, in Reznik (2010: 4).

Chairwoman of the Moscow Federal Arbitration Court Lyudmila Maikova, in L. Maikova, 'Interv´iu predsedatelia Federal´nogo Arbitrazhnogo Suda Moskovskogo okruga Liudmily Nikolaevny Maikovoi Parlamentskoi gazete', *Parlamentskaia Gazeta*, 21 September 2005, www.fasmo.arbitr.ru/news/msg.asp?id_msg=56.

First Deputy Head of the MVD Investigative Committee Anton Zaritovskii, 'Pervyi zamestitel´ nachal´nika Sledstvennogo komiteta pri MVD Evgenii Timlev: Dela v 200–300 tomov – dlia nas normal'noe yavlenie', *Izvestiia*, 25 January 2008: 13.

Former Head of the Bank Moskva Andrei Borodin, on Kerimov's link to the special representative of President Medvedev, Igor Yusufov. Interviewed by I. Reznik and T. Voronova, 'U Yusufova byl mandate ot Medvedeva', *Vedomosti*, 21 November 2011: 6.

Privatised ATS-2, General Director of OAO ASVT, Anastasiya Ositis, interviewed by V. Kodachigov, 'Konsolidatsiya konkurentov dlya nas nichego ne menyaet', *Kommersant Daily*, 26 October 2005: 20. See also A. Boreiko, '"Sistema" ne dayot razvoda', *Vedomosti*, 4 July 2005.

Chairman of the Board of Directors of AFK 'Sistema', Vladimir Evtushenkov, Editorial, 'Deistvuyushchie litsa', *Vedomosti*, 10 June 2004: 1. 'Evtushenkov: ruku Borodinu ne podam, vremia Chichvarkina proshlo', in conversation with Marina Zateichuk, *TV-Dozhd´*, 21 March 2012, http://slon.ru/economics/evtushenkov_ruku_borodinu_ne_podam_vremya_chichvarki_na_proshlo-766095.xhtml.

Glossary

administrativnaya renta – literally, administrative rent, entitlement to a cash flow that comes with a position; restrictions on access, so that the rent is charged by an official for lifting these restrictions.

administrativnyi resurs – literally, administrative resource, widely used to denote access to political influence and forms of administrative mobilisation for political, financial, business, or media advantage.

bespredel – literally, 'limitlessness', designates behaviour that disregards not only formal rules but also informal norms and *poniatia (q.v.)*.

blat – a colloquial way of referring to the use of personal networks for obtaining goods and services in short supply, or for circumventing formal procedures.

blatnoi – an adjective to denote someone who used *blat (q.v.)* with the original meaning of someone from the criminal underworld.

boyarstvo, novoe boyarstvo – literally, the aristocracy surrounding Russian tsars, the new Russian elite.

byvshikh ne byvaet – literally, 'there are no ex-security officers', 'once an officer, always an officer', sayings referring to the skills and loyalty developed in the security service.

chekist(y) – from ChK, the original name of the security forces, subsequently KGB and FSB.

chernaya kassa – literally, 'black box', refers to the accumulation of 'black cash' that does not appear in the accounts.

chinovniki – bureaucrats, state officials.

chuzhie – *see svoi.*

civilik(i) – mates of Dmitri Medvedev – graduates of the faculty of civil law at St Petersburg State University.

delit´sya, ne delit´sya – sharing informal income, not sharing informal income (*moi nogi ne odnogo volka kormyat, a tseluyu stayu*: my feet feed not just one wolf, but a whole pack).

ekonomika otkata – literally, economy of kickbacks, widespread informal sharing of funds, informal capital flow, associated with *raspil (q.v.)* and *zanos (q.v.)*.

ekonomika r–o–z – widespread practices of *raspil, otkat* and *zanos (qqv)* based on expected percentages of informal income (25 per cent–10 per cent–2 per cent in the 1990s; 60 per cent–30 per cent–10 per cent in 2010) (Belkovskii and Golyshev 2006); r–o–z has become a 'drug' for thousands of bureaucrats and businessmen and their dependents. Practically all 'elites' are addicted to injections of informal income. Many of them understand that they should fight this addiction, but cannot resist another dose.

evroremont – renovation with imported, preferably Italian, materials and furnishings from Europe.

frontirovat´/frontirovanie – to do fronting, to serve as a front person, company or charity serving the real owner and preserving the privacy of high officials; also to represent an official who *de facto* allows *sistema* exiles a re-entry.

gosorgany – state organs, branches of the state hierarchy.

izderzhki – the costs of a transaction.

kolkhoz or sovkhoz – collectively-owned or state-owned farms.

kompromat – compromising materials, blackmail files.

korporativnyi chelovek – a loyal and compliant employer, who has been tried and tested in the past.

koshmarit´ business – literally, to induce businesses' nightmares, to give businesses a hard time, which benefits state control officials; also associated with extortionate practices (*otzhimat´ business*).

kremlyovka – exclusive range of privileges, such as special canteens, dachas, access to shops and tailoring, including *vertushka*.

krugovaya poruka – a pattern of joint/collective responsibility that results in excessive influence, co-dependence and control over individuals.

krysha – political and criminal protection in exchange for payments or financial support provided by businessmen.

kumovstvo – nepotism, ties between people related to each other in some way, not necessarily by close family ties.

kuratory – *see smotryashchie*.

lichnoe poruchitel´stvo – literally, 'personal vouching', a recommendation that guarantees the personal loyalty of an appointee and/or implicates the guarantor.

lobbying – providing expertise and funding for pushing or influencing the legislative process.

loyal´nost´ – mainly understood as personal loyalty rather than loyalty to principles.

migalki – the lights and sirens that provide privileged access and rights of passage on the roads.

na kryuke, v kompromisse – 'hanging on a hook' or 'being compromised'; refers to a leverage against an employee in order to ensure that s/he is compliant with the unwritten rules and is loyal in daily operations, as well as having a stake in reproducing *sistema*.

nesistemnye biznesmeny – literally, businessmen not integrated into *sistema*, not part of the economy of r–o–z or connected to those in the power vertical or power networks in any way.

nomenklatura – party elite, formed on the basis of appointments and promotions of state officials being vetted, cleared, recommended and confirmed by Party committees at every level.

oblast´ – administrative region.

oborotni v pogonakh – 'werewolves in epaulets' or 'werewolves in uniform', engaged in 'moonlighting', crossing the boundary between their public duties and their private (or affiliated) businesses. By day the 'werewolves' perform their public duties; by night they engage in self-serving *reiderstvo* and extortion, empowered by access to both formal hierarchies and informal networks.

obvinitel´nyi uklon – punitive bias, judges' propensity to side with the prosecution.

obyski, vyemki, proslushka – raids of offices, withdrawal of documents, bugging equipment – standard measures to pressurise businesses.

odnoklassniki – classmates, one of the most popular social networks in Russia, analogous to the original idea of facebook.com – odnoklassniki.ru – now similar to vkontakte.ru, analogous to linkedin.com.

okhotnik(i) – hunter(s).

otkat(y) – kickbacks, informal payments (monetary and non-monetary) that help ensure that formal transactions are completed.

otkaznye pis´ma – signing off property while being detained, in prison or under other forms of pressure.

'Ozero' – dacha co-operative near St Petersburg, set up by Putin and his mates.

parashyutisty – literally 'parachuters', appointments of people with political or corporate connections from above, over the heads of their formal bosses, overruling the formal hierarchy; cf. *kreatura*, a politically motivated 'creation' or appointment of someone not heard of before, associated with Putin's era.

patsanstvo – literally, a code of friendship among lads; also a colloquial reference to Putin's leadership style.

pilit´, popilit´ byudzhet – split between different groups, stakeholders, *see also raspil*.

piterskie (chekisty, yuristy, svyazisty, fiziki) – appointees from St Petersburg (security officers, lawyers, telecom specialist, physicists).

polyana – grazing ground or playground for nourishing authorised businesses, reserved for exclusive use.

pomoshchnik – literally, helper and advisor; in *sistema* contexts, 'advising' means power brokerage, blocking information to whoever you advise and blocking access to the body for other advisors.

ponty – maintaining an appearance that symbolises certain status.

ponyatiya – literally, 'notions', originally the unofficial code of honour of the criminal underworld; in the post-Communist world it designates an informal code of behaviour in business, politics and related domains.

po ponyatiyam – following unwritten rules or informal codes of various circles, including the '*patsanskii* code' (code of brotherhood laddishness and friendship) of the leadership.

po znakomstvu – by acquaintance, by *blat*.

poruchitel´stvo, vziat´ na poruki – to vouch for somebody, to recommend them for an appointment, to guarantee or take responsibility for somebody's future behaviour.

prisosalis´ k kormushke i zhivut – leeches who stay close to the feeding place and live off it.

pritirki – (originally from criminal jargon *tyorki*) tough negotiations in circumstances of conflicting interests, learning to co-exist through a rough contact.

proizvol – arbitrariness, ability to violate both formal rules and informal codes.

proslushka – literally, 'dubbing', an eavesdropping service or bugging equipment for obtaining information/*kompromat*/other forms of intelligence.

raider, raiders' attack – professional attacker or attack on another's assets with the use of illegal methods.

rasklad – constellation of interests and positions.

raspil, po raspilu – refers to a range of practices such as fraud and theft of taxpayers' money through the state purchase of hugely over-priced goods and services; schemes used by commercial, banking and investment companies based on trading at negotiated rather than market prices, *see also pilit´, ekonomika r–o–z* and http://bondraspil.ru/Home/raspil.

rastorgovka – bargaining and trade-offs.

rasstanovka sil – balance of interests and influences.

razrulivanie – steering a way out of a troublesome situation, refereeing conflicts, conflict resolution.

razvodka – a set up, a trap.

reshat´ voprosy – to solve problems, to get things done, to be effective in dealing with (in) problematic situations.

rokirovka – a swap of jobs, say between the President and Prime Minister, or between the heads of Ministries, General Prosecutor and Minister of Justice.

sarafannoe radio – Chinese whispers, a 'broken radio' translating news in a distorted form.

sem´ya – literally, family, the term referring to Yeltsin's inner circle in the 1990s, but also has the general connotation of Mafia families, family-based governance.

setevoi/nesetevoi – literally a networked, non-networked person; distinguishes those with personal networks and informal channels of circumventing formal procedures from those who do not have them.

siloviki – officers or former employees of the army, security services, police and others, sometimes used interchangeably with *chekisty* and *piterskie chekisty (qqv)*.

silovye struktury – security services, the military, other 'uniformed' ministries.

sistema –

(1) from Greek, 'sustema', creation (*sozdanie*), constitution (*sostavlenie*), order or structure of correlated and co-ordinated parts, working in a synchronised way;

(2) in political contexts, a political system or system of governance;

(3) in the vernacular, a euphemism for the informal corporate code followed in organisations;

(4) in hippy jargon, self-definition of the hippy movement in the USSR and, more widely, dependence on the systematic intake of heroin, drugs, living from dose to dose;

(5) in corporate contexts, the '*Sistema*' corporation headed by Evtushenkov;

(6) in this book, the system of governance with its peculiar formal rules and informal norms, combined in a way that is non-transparent for outsiders but recognised by insiders of the public administration in Russia. In the context of Putin's rule, a co-dependence of parasitic power elites and parasitic masses; an implicit social contract between the rent-seeking elites conniving at enriching themselves at the expense of public resources or raiding while not reforming/diversifying the economy, and the compliant masses, living at the expense of the trickle-down income from the oil-dependent economy, producing little but engaged in entrepreneurial scheming.

sistemnyi nagovor – a set up by anonymous forces associated with the establishment.

sistemnyi/nesistemnyi – a person integrated into the formal hierarchy of *sistema*, associated with the establishment or knowing the rules of the game, distinguished from those who are not integrated, do not belong or simply display an unruly, non-compliant behaviour – the same use as *v sisteme/ne v sisteme*, belonging or not belonging to *sistema*.

sistemnoe reiderstvo – use of formal or informal affiliations with the state for taking over assets, businesses, or zones of influence.

sluzhebnaya renta – *see administrativnaya renta*, the use of an official position for generating personal income (*sluzhebnoe polozhenie*).

smotryashchie – one entrusted to represent the interests of key stakeholders, sometimes also called a curator (*kuratory*), a person in charge of informal oversight, a much-feared person.

spravedlivost´ – justice and fairness, often opposed to law and legality.

state capture – control of the legislative process by business.

strelka – meeting set up by the claiming party in order to signal status and achieve informal settlement, also *razborka*.

svoi, svoi lyudi – people of the circle, tried and tested, entitled to be trusted, helped and receive benefits from each other; opposed to *chuzhie*, excluded from the circle, also *nash/ne nash*.

telefonnoe pravo – political influence or pressure on the judiciary.

tenevye skhemy – literally, 'shadow schemes', referring to schemes that involve hidden operations and do not appear in the books.

terpilo – in criminal contexts, a person who does not fight back when repeatedly offended against; in contemporary contexts, a person who is convicted without a crime, a pre-determined convict in a commercial or criminal case.

vertikal´ (vlasti) – literally, power vertical; refers to the hierarchy of power based on compliance with orders from above.

vertet´sya – spin around in order to get things done, resourceful dealing.

vertushka – (from *vertet´*, to dial, to rotate) slang for the Kremlin's secure telephone network, occasionally referred to as *kremlyovka (q.v.)*, a generic term for the Kremlin's privileges, also used to refer to helicopters.

vlast´, vo vlasti – power, authority, a place in the hierarchy or vertical of power, working for executive branches of power.

vyskochki – people who stick out or behave above their rank.

vyzov na kovyor – literally, 'going to the mattresses' for 'telling off' or 'show beating' *(pokazatel´naya porka)*. A specific feature of the present-day 'show-beating' is that it can be followed up by an informal 'making-up', thus enacting the double standards.

zakazchiki – those who are the driving force behind raiding.

zakaznoe delo – case, court decision, publication – pre-ordered, pre-paid, unlawful legal cases, instigated to get an advantage in a political, financial or business conflict; commissioned criminal prosecutions with the purpose of neutralising individuals.

zakhvat i peredel sobstvennosti – capture and redistribution of property.

zakonnost´ – legality, often opposed to justice *(spravedlivost´)*.

zanos, zanesti naverkh – to bribe or to pay regular tribute among the tried and tested, linked to systematic kickbacks payments *(otkat* and *raspil (qqv))*.

zasvetit´sya – to be noticed in an unusual context (company, place or doing something).

zavolokichennye dela – backlog cases, cases that are deliberately not considered.

Bibliography

Aidis, R. and Adachi, Y. 2007. 'Firm entry and survival barriers', *Economic Systems* 31: 391–411

Aidis, R., Estrin, S. and Mickiewicz, T. 2008. 'Institutions and entrepreneurship development in Russia: a comparative perspective', *Journal of Business Venturing* 23: 656–72

Alatas, S. H. 1990. *Corruption, Its Nature, Causes and Functions*. Aldershot: Avebury

Allina-Pisano, J. 2007. *The Post-Soviet Potemkin Village*. Cambridge University Press

Applebaum, A. 2003. *Gulag: A History*. New York: Doubleday

Astakhov, P. 2007a. *Reider*. Moscow: Eksmo

2007b. *Mer*. Moscow: Eksmo

2008. *Shpion*. Moscow: Eksmo

Baker, W. 1993. 'Illicit networks', *American Sociological Review* 58: 837–60

2000. *Achieving Success Through Social Capital*. San Francisco, CA: Jossey-Bass

Barnard, C. 1938. *The Functions of the Executive*. Cambridge, MA: Harvard University Press

Barsukova, S. 2009. *Neformal'naya ekonomika: kurs lektsii*. Moscow: Higher School of Economics

Bass, B. M. 1990. *Bass & Stogdill's Handbook of Leadership: Theory, Research, and Managerial Applications*. London: Collier Macmillan

Baturin, Y. M. *et al.* 2001. *Épokha Yel'tsina: ocherki politicheskoi istorii*. Moscow: Vagrius

Beck, U. 2005. *Power in the Global Age: A New Global Political Economy*. Cambridge: Polity

BEEPS 1999, 2002, 2005, 2009. *Business Environment and Enterprise Performance Survey*, http://data.worldbank.org/data-catalog/BEEPS

Belin, L. 2004. 'Politics and the mass media under Putin', in C. Ross (ed.), *Russian Politics Under Putin*. Manchester: Manchester University Press: 133–51

Belkovskii, S. and Golyshev, V. 2006. *Biznes Vladimira Putina*. Ekaterinburg: Ultra. Kul´tura

Belton, C. 2011. 'Russian police quiz Lebedev in graft probe: Kremlin critic hits at "bandit raids"', *Financial Times*, 19–20 February: 3

Bennis, W. G. 1959. 'Leadership theory and administrative behavior: the problem of authority', *Administrative Science Quarterly* 4: 259–301

Berenson, M. P. 2008. 'Rationalizing or empowering bureaucrats? Tax administration reform in Poland and Russia', *Journal of Communist Studies and Transition Politics* 24 (1): 135–55

Berliner, J. S. 1957. *Factory and Manager in the USSR*. Cambridge, MA: Harvard University Press

Bernstein, J. 2007. 'Vladimir Milov: Putin trapped in a foros of his own making', *Eurasia Daily Monitor*, 205 (4).

Beumers, B., Hutchings, S. C. and Rulyova, N. 2009. *The Post-Soviet Russian Media: Conflicting Signals*. Oxford: Routledge Taylor & Francis

Blau, J. and Alba, R. 1982. 'Empowering nets of participation', *Administrative Science Quarterly* 27: 363–79

Blau, P. M. 1963. *The Dynamics of Bureaucracy: A Study of Interpersonal Relations in Two Government Agencies*, rev. 2nd edn. University of Chicago Press

Blundo, G. and Le Meur, P. Y. (eds.) 2009. *The Governance of Daily Life in Africa: Ethnographic Explorations of Public and Collective Services*. Leiden: Brill Academic Publishers

Blundo, G. and de Sardan, J.-P.-O. (eds.) 2006. *Everyday Corruption and the State: Citizens and Public Officials in Africa*. London: Zed Books

Bourdieu, P. 1986. 'The forms of capital', in J. G. Richardson (ed.), *Handbook of Theory and Research for the Sociology of Education*. New York: Greenwood Press: 241–58

1990. *The Logic of Practice*. Cambridge: Polity

Bourdieu, P. and Wacquant, L. 1992. *An Introduction to Reflexive Sociology*. University of Chicago Press

Brandenberger, D. 2009. *Political Humour Under Stalin*. Bloomington, IN: Slavica

Brodel´, F. 2007. *Material´naia tsivilizatsiia, ekonomika I kapitalizm, XV–XVIII*. Moscow: Ves´Mir

Brodsky, J. 1986. *Less Than One: Selected Essays*. Penguin: 9–10

Brown, A. 2005. 'Conclusion: the past, present and future of post-Communist political culture studies', in S. Whitefield (ed.), *Political Culture and Post-Communism*. New York: Palgrave Macmillan: 180–202

Brown, A. and Shevtsova, L. (eds.) 2001. *Gorbachev, Yeltsin, Putin: Political Leadership in Transition*. Washington, DC: Carnegie Endowment

Browne, J. 2010. *Beyond Business*. London: Weidenfeld & Nicholson

Brusnitsyn, N. A. 2000. *Kto podslushivaet prezidentov: ot Stalina do Yeltsina*. Moscow: Vita Press

Brym, R. J. and Gimpelson, V. 2004. 'The size, composition and dynamics of the Russian state bureaucracy in the 1990s', *Slavic Review* 63 (1): 90–1

Buchanan, M. 2002. *Nexus: The Groundbreaking Science of Networks*. New York: W. W. Norton

Buchli, V. (ed.) 2002. *The Material Culture Reader*. Oxford: Berg

Burger, E. S. and Holland, M. 2008. 'Law as politics: the Russian procuracy and its Investigative Committee', New York University Public Law and Legal Theory Working Papers, No. 108

Burt, R. S. 1992a. *Structural Holes: The Social Structure of Competition*. Cambridge, MA: Harvard University Press

1992b. 'The social structure of competition', in N. Nohria and E. Eccles (eds.), *Networks and Organizations, Structure, Form and Action*. Boston, MA: Harvard Business School Press

1997. 'The contingent value of social capital', *Administrative Science Quarterly* 42: 339–65

Bykov, D. 2008. *Spisannye*. Moscow: Proza i K

Caldwell, M. L. 2004. *Not by Bread Alone: Social Support in the New Russia*. Berkeley and Los Angeles, CA: University of California Press

Castells, M. 2000. *The Rise of the Network Society*. Oxford: Wiley–Blackwell

2009. *Communication Power*. Oxford University Press

Caulkins, D. D. 1999. 'Is Mary Douglas's grid/group analysis useful for cross-cultural research?' *Cross-Cultural Research*, 33 (1): 108–28

Chernomyrdin, V. 2011. *Tak govoril Chernomyrdin: 77 luchshikh vyskazyvanii*. Moscow: Eksmo

Chesnokova, T. and Cherkesova, N. 2007. *Russia-Delete? 2030 god: Global'naya Skhvatka tsivilizatsii*. Moscow: Yauza, Eksmo

Christiansen, T. and Neuhold, C. 2012. *International Handbook on Informal Governance*. Cheltenham: Edward Elgar

Christiansen, T. and Piattoni, S. 2003. *Informal Governance in the European Union*. Cheltenham: Edward Elgar

Cohen, D. and Prusak, L. 2001. *In Good Company: How Social Capital Makes Organizations Work*. Cambridge, MA: Harvard Business School Press

Coleman, J. S. 1988. 'Social capital in the creation of human capital', *American Journal of Sociology* 94: 95–120

1990. *Foundations of Social Theory*. Cambridge, MA: Harvard University Press

1993. 'The rational reconstruction of society', *American Sociological Review* 58: 1–15

Coles, N. 2001. 'It's not what you know – it's who you know that counts', *British Journal of Criminology* 41: 580–94

Collins, K. 2006. *Clan Politics and Regime Transition in Central Asia.* Cambridge University Press

Colton, T. J. 2007. *Yeltsin: A Life.* New York: Basic Books

Condee, N. 2009. *The Imperial Trace.* Oxford University Press

D'Agostino, A. 1988. *Soviet Succession Struggles: Kremlinology and the Russian Question From Lenin to Gorbachev.* London: Allen & Unwin

Darden, K. A. 2001. 'Blackmail as a tool of state domination: Ukraine under Kuchma', *East European Constitutional Review* 10 (2/3): 67–71

Davydova, M. 2006. '*Vzyatki i otkaty*', *Kompaniya*, 30 January, http://compromat.ru/main/top50/vzyatki.htm

Deliagin, M. and Sheyanov, V. 2009. *Mir naiznanku: chem zakonchitsya ekonomicheskii krizis dlia Rossii.* Moscow: Kommersant, Eksmo

De Sardan, J.-P.-O. 2011. 'The eight modes of governance in West Africa', *IDS Bulletin* 42 (2): 22–31

De Sardan, J.-P. O., Blundo, G. and Cox, S. 2006. *Everyday Corruption and the State: Citizen and Public Official in Africa.* London: Zed Books

De Soto, H. 2002. *The Other Path: The Economic Answer to Terrorism.* New York: Basic Books

Dolgopyatova, T., Iwasaki, I. and Yakovlev, A. 2009. *Organisation and Development of Russian Business: A Firm level Analysis.* London: Palgrave Macmillan

Douglas, M. 1970. *Natural Symbols: Explorations in Cosmology.* London and New York: Barrie & Rockliff

Drobizheva, L. M. 1996. *Govoirit elita respublik Rossiiskoi Federatsii: 110 interview Leokardii Drobizhevoi.* Moscow: Izd-e Valeriya Belousova

Dryzhenko, A. 1997. 'Toska po vyzovam na kover', *Izvestiia (Rossiia)* 226, 28 November

Dufy, C. and Weber, F. *L'ethnographie économique.* Paris: La Decouverte

Dymarskii, V. 2008. '*Est´ zhenshchiny v russkikh sudakh*', *Rossiiskaia Gazeta*, 3 July

Easter, G. M. 1999. *Reconstructing the State: Personal Networks and Elite Identity in Soviet Russia.* Cambridge University Press

The Economist 2008. 'Following the Russian standard', 388 (8595): 23

Elder, M. 2008. 'Medvedev to tackle corruption, red tape', *The St Petersburg Times*, 19 February

  2009.'Russian president Dmitry Medvedev poised to replace officials loyal to Vladimir Putin', *Telegraph news*, 14 March

Ericson, R. E. 1991. 'The classical Soviet-type Economy: nature of the system, and implications for reform', *Journal of Economic Perspectives* 5 (4): 11–27

Ermakov, D. 2008. 'Reidery prorvali oboronku', *Moskovskii komsomolets*, 11 April: 2

Fainsod, M. 1963. *How Russia is Ruled*. Cambridge, MA: Harvard University Press

Fedorov, V. and Tsuladze, A. 2003. *Epokha Putina: tainy i zagadki 'kremlyovskogo dvora'*. Moscow: Eksmo

Firestone, T. 2008. 'Criminal corporate raiding in Russia', *International Law* 42: 1207–29

2010. 'Armed injustice: abuse of the law and complex crime in post-Soviet Russia', *Denver Journal of International Law and Policy* 38 (4): 555–80

Fitzpatrick, S. 2000a. '*Blat* in Stalin's time', in S. Lovell, A. Ledeneva and A. Rogachevskii (eds.), *Bribery and Blat in Russia: Negotiating Reciprocity from the Middle Ages to the 1990s*. Basingstoke: Macmillan: 166–82

2000b. *Everyday Stalinism: Ordinary Life in Extraordinary Times. Soviet Russia in the 1930s*. New York: Oxford University Press

Fitzpatrick, S. and Gellately, R. (eds.) 1997. *Accusatory Practices: Denunciation in Modern European History, 1789–1989*. London: University of Chicago Press

Foley, M. W. and Edwards, B. 1996. 'The paradox of civil society', *Journal of Democracy* 7 (3): 8–52

1997. 'Escape from politics? Social theory and the social capital debate', *American Behavioral Scientist* 40 (6): 550–61

Fontaine, L. and Weber, F. (eds.) 2011. *Les paradoxes de l'économie informelle*. Paris: Karthala

Fossato, F. and Lloyd, J. with Verkhovsky, A. 2008. *The Web that Failed: How Opposition Politics and Independent Initiatives Are Failing on the Internet in Russia*. Oxford: Reuters Institute for the Study of Journalism

Foucault, M. 1979. 'Power, truth, strategy', in M. Morris and P. Patton (eds.), *Michel Foucault: Power, Truth, Strategy*. Sydney: Feral Publications: 78–9

Frye, T. 2011 *Building States and Markets After Communism: The Perils of Polarized Democracy*. New York: Cambridge University Press

Fukuyama, F. 1995. 'Social capital and the global economy', *Foreign Affairs* 74: 89–103

Gaman-Golutvina, O. 2006. *Politicheskie elity Rossii: vechi istoricheskoi evolyutsii*. Moscow: Rosspen

Gambetta, D. 1993. *The Sicilian Mafia: The Business of Private Protection*. Cambridge, MA: Harvard University Press

2009. *Codes of the Underworld: How Criminals Communicate*. Princeton University Press

Garton Ash, T. (ed.) 2009. *On Liberty: The Dahrendorf Questions*. Oxford: Medical Informatics Unit, MDCLS, Oxford University

Gehlbach, S. 2010. 'Reflections on Putin and the media', *Post-Soviet Affairs* 26: 77–87

Gel'man, V. 2007. *Tretii elektoral'nyi tsikl v Rossii, 2003–2004 gody*. St Petersburg: Evropeiskii Universitet

2012. 'Subversive institutions and informal governance in contemporary Russia', in T. Christiansen and C. Neuhold, *International Handbook on Informal Governance*. Cheltenham: Edward Elgar, 135–53

Genis, A. 2002. *Raz! Dva! Tri!* Moscow: Podkova-Eksmo

Gessen, M. 2012. *The Man Without a Face: The Unlikely Rise of Vladimir Putin*. London: Granta Books

Getty, J. A. 1986. *Origins of the Great Purge: The Soviet Communist Party Reconsidered, 1933–1938*. New York: Cambridge University Press

Giddens, A. 1999. *Runaway World*. London: Profile Books

Gilinskii, Y. 2009. *Globalizatsiya, deviantnost', sotsial'nyi kontrol'*. St Petersburg: DEAN

Gill, G. 1990. *The Origins of the Stalinist Political System*. New York: Cambridge University Press

Global Corruption Report 2007. *Corruption in Judicial Systems*. Transparency International with Cambridge University Press

Goffman, E. 1961. *Asylums: Essays on The Social Situation of Mental Patients and Other Inmates*. New York: Anchor Books

1971. *The Presentation of Self in Everyday Life*. Harmondsworth: Penguin

Goleman, D. 2000. 'Leadership that gets results', *Harvard Business Review* March–April: 78–90

Gorbachev, M. 2010. 'Perestroika, 25 years later', *International Herald Tribune*, March 13–14

Gorbuz, A. K., Krasnov, M. A., Mishina, E. A. and Satarov, G. A. 2010. *Transformatsiya Rossiiskoi sudebnoi vlasti, opyt kompleksnogo analiza*. Moscow: Fond INDEM; St Petersburg: Norma

Gorlizki, Y. 1997. 'Political reform and local party interventions under Khrushchev', in P. Solomon (ed.), *Reforming Justice in Russia, 1864–1996*. Armonk, NY: M. E. Sharpe: 256–81

2010. 'Too much trust: regional party leaders and local political networks under Brezhnev', *Slavic Review* 69 (3): 676–700

Grabher, G. 1993. 'The weakness of strong ties: the lock-in of regional development in the Ruhr area', in G. Grabher (ed.), *The Embedded Firm, on the Socioeconomics of Industrial Networks*. London: Routledge: 255–77

Graen, G. B. and Uhl-Bien, M. 1995. 'Relationship-based approach to leadership: development of the leader–member exchange (LMX) theory of leadership over 25 years. Applying a multi-level multi-domain perspective', *Leadership Quarterly* 6 (2): 219–47

Granovetter, M. 1973. 'The strength of weak ties', *American Journal of Sociology* 78: 1360–80

1985. 'Economic action and social structure: the problem of embeddedness', *American Journal of Sociology* 91: 481–510

Grant, B. 1995. *In the Soviet House of Culture*. Princeton University Press

Granville, C., Hanson, P. and Ledeneva, A. 2012. 'Why is Russian modernisation so difficult?', in K. Barysch (ed.), *Three Views on Modernisation and the Rule of Law in Russia*. London: Centre for European Reform: 5–16

Gudkov, L. 2004. *Negativnaya identichnost': stat'i 1997–2002 godov*. Moscow: Novoe Literaturnoe Obozrenie

Gudkov, L., Dubin, B. and Levada, Y. 2007. *Problema elity v segodniashnei Rossii*. Moscow: Fond Liberal'naya Missiia

Gudkov, L., Dubin, B. and Zorkaya, N. 2008. '*Srednii klass' as if: mneniia i natroeniia vysokodokhodnoi molodyozhi v Rossii*', *Vestnik Obshchestvennogo Mneniia/The Russian Public Opinion Herald* 3 (95): 27–41

Gutterman, S. 2008. 'Judge talks of bribes, pressure in Russian system', *The Associated Press*, May 29

Habermas, J. 2003. *The Future of Human Nature*. Cambridge: Polity

Hainsworth, R. and Thomson, W. 2001. 'The taxation of Russian banks', Centre for East European Strudies Working Paper 30

Hanson, P. 2009. 'The resistible rise of state control in the Russian oil industry', *Eurasian Geography and Economics* 50 (1): 14–28

2011. 'Networks, Cronies and Business Plans: Business–State Relations in Russia', in V. Kononenko and A. Moshes (eds.), *Russia . . .* Macmillan

Harding, L. 2008. 'Raiders of the Russian billions', *The Guardian*, 24 June

2009. 'Russian billionaire drops libel case' *guardian.co.uk*, 30 July, www.guardian.co.uk/world/2009/jul/30/russian-billionaire-timchenko-libel-economist

Harrison, M. 2005. 'Economic information in the life and death of the Soviet command system', in S. Pons and R. Federico, *Reinterpreting the End of the Cold War: Issues, Interpretations, Periodisations*. London: Frank Cass: 93–115

Heidenheimer, A. 1970. *Political Corruption: Readings in Comparative Analysis*. New Brunswick, NJ: Transaction Books

Heinzen, J. 2007. 'The art of the bribe: corruption and everyday practice in the late Stalinist USSR', *Slavic Review* 66 (1): 389–12

Held, D., McGrew, A., Goldblatt, D. and Perraton, J. 1999. *Global Transformations: Politics, Economics and Culture*. Cambridge: Polity

Hellman, J. S., Jones, G., Kaufmann, D. and Schankerman, M. 2003. 'Measuring governance, corruption, and state capture', World Bank: Policy Research Working Paper Series, No. 2312, www.wds.worldbank.org

Helmke, G. and Levitsky, S. 2004. 'Informal institutions and comparative politics: a research agenda', *Perspectives of Politics* 2 (4): 725–40

Hendley, K. 2007. 'Are Russian judges Still Soviet?', *Post-Soviet Affairs* 23 (3): 240–74

    2009. '"Telephone law" and the "rule of law": the Russian case', *Hague Journal on the Rule of Law* 1 (2): 241–62

Hertog, S. 2010. 'The sociology of the Gulf rentier systems: societies of intermediaries', *Comparative Studies in Society and History* 52 (2): 282–318

Hollingsworth, M. and Langsley, S. 2009. *Londongrad: From Russia with Cash. The Inside Story of Oligarchs*. London: Fourth Estate

Hosking, G. 2004. 'Forms of social solidarity in Russia and the Soviet Union', in I. Markova (ed.), *Trust and Democratic Transition in Post-Communist Europe (Proceedings of the British Academy)*. Oxford University Press: 47–62

House, R. J. and Aditya, R. N. 1997. 'The social scientific study of leadership: quo vadis?', *Journal of Management* 23 (3): 409–73

Humphrey, C. 2000. 'Dirty business, "normal life", and the dream of law', in A. Ledeneva and M. Kurkchiyan (eds.), *Economic Crime in Russia*. London: Kluwer Law International: 177–90

    2002 *The Unmaking of Soviet Life: Everyday Economies after Socialism*. Ithaca, NY and London : Cornell University Press

Huskey, E. 1992. 'The administration of justice: courts, procuracy, and the Ministry of Justice', in E. Huskey (ed.), *Executive Power and Soviet Politics: The Rise and the Decline of the Soviet State*. Armonk, NY: M. E. Sharpe: 221–46

    2004. 'From Higher Party Schools to Academies of State Service: the marketization of bureaucratic training in Russia', *Slavic Review* 63 (2): 325–48

    2005. 'Putin as patron: cadres policy in the Russian transition', in A. Pravda (ed.), *Leading Russia: Putin in Perspective*. Oxford University Press: 161–78

Hutchings, S. C. and Rulyova, N. 2009. *Television and Culture in Putin's Russia: Remote Control*. Oxford: Routledge Taylor & Francis

Inglehart, R. and Baker, W. 2000. 'Modernization, cultural change and the persistence of traditional values', *American Sociological Review* 65: 19–51

Iusupova, D. 2007. 'Novyi srednii', *Vedomosti*, 2 February

Johnston, M. 1986. 'The political consequences of corruption: a reassessment', *Comparative Politics*, 18 (4): 459–77

2005. *Syndromes of Corruption: Wealth, Power, and Democracy*. Cambridge University Press

Kabakov, A. 2010. *Russkie ne pridut*. Moscow: AST

Kaminskaya, D. 2009. *Zapiski advokata*. Moscow: Novoe izdatel'stvo

Karklins, R. 2005. *The System Made Me Do It: Corruption in Post-Communist Societies*. Ithaca, NY: M. E. Sharpe

Karpov, A. and Salakhitdinova, M. 2007. 'Eti braki zakhlyuchayutsia na politicheskikh nebesakh', *Trud* 670, 20 September

Kaufmann, D. 1997. 'Corruption: the facts,' *Foreign Policy*, 107: 114–31

Kaufmann, D. and Vicente, P. C. 2005. 'Legal corruption', *Social Science Research Network*, 24 November, http://ssrn.com/abstract=829844

Kelly, C. 2012. 'Trusting your friends? The multiple meanings of *doverie* in late Soviet Leningrad', paper presented at the Trust/Distrust Conference at SSEES/UCL, 17–18 February 2012.

Keenan, E. 1986. 'Muscovite political folkways', *The Russian Review* 45: 115–81

Kets de Vries, M. F. R., Florent-Treacy, E., Korotov, K. and Shekshnia, S. 2004. 'The anarchist within' and 'An East–West dialogue', in M. F. R. Kets de Vries, E. Florent-Treacy, K. Korotov and S. Shekshnia, *The New Russian Business Leaders*. Cheltenham: Edward Elgar: 3–42, 43–81

Kets De Vries, M. F. R. and Shekshnia, S. 2008. 'Vladimir Putin, CEO of Russia, Inc.: the legacy and the future', *Organizational Dynamics* 37 (3): 236–53

Khakamada, I. 2006. *Sex v bol'shoi politike*. Moscow: Novaya Gazeta, Knizhnyi klub 36.6

Khinshtein, A. 2000. 'Politics and economy: loyal *Vertushki*', *Moskovskii komsomolets*, 1 December

Khinshtein, A. 2007. *Berezovskii and Abramovich: oligarkhi s bol'shoi dorogi*. Moscow: Olma Media Grupp

Khlevnyuk, O. V. 2009. *Master of the House: Stalin and His Inner Circle*. Newhaven, CT: Yale University Press

Klyuchevskii, V. O. 1987. *Kurs russkoi istorii. Sochineniia v 9 tomakh*, Vol. 2. Moscow: Mysl'

Knack, S. 2006. 'Measuring corruption in Eastern Europe and Central Asia: a critique of cross-country Indicators', World Bank Policy Research Working Paper 3968, July, www.wds.worldbank.org/servlet/WDSContentServer/WDSP/IB/2006/07/13/000016406_20060713140304/Rendered/PDF/wps3968.pdf

Kolesnikov, A. 2005a. *Ya Putina videl*. Moscow: Eksmo

2005b. *Uvidet' Putina i umeret'*. Moscow: Eksmo
2008a. *Spichraitery*. Moscow: Khranitel'
2008b. *Radvoenie VVP: kak Putin Medvedeva vybral*. Moscow: Eksmo
Kolyshevskii, A. 2007a. *MZh*. Moscow: Eksmo
2007b. *Otkatchiki*. Moscow: Eksmo
2008. *Patriot*. Moscow: Eksmo
2009. *Vzyatki*. Moscow: Eksmo
Kommersant-Online 2008. 'Podpisano predstavlenie o lishenii polnomochii predsedatelya FAS', 20 May, www.kommersant.ru/online.aspx?date= 20080520
Konchalovsky, A. 2010. 'Russkaya mental'nost' i mirovoi tsivilizatsionnyi protsess', *Polis* 5: 38–47
Kononenko, V. and Moshes, A. (eds.) 2011. *Russia as a Network State: What Works in Russia When State Institutions Do Not?* Basingstoke: Palgrave Macmillan
Kopytoff, I. 1988. 'The cultural biography of things: commoditisation as process', in A. Appadurai, *The Social Life of Things: Commodities in Cultural Perspective*. Cambridge University Press
Kordonskii, S. 2000. *Rynki vlasti: administrativnye rynki SSSR i Rossii*. Moscow: OGI
2010. *Rossiya: pomestnaya federatsiya*. Moscow: Evropa
Korobov, P. and Kashin, O. 2011. (Interview with Kremlin Property Chief, Vladimir Kozhin) 'Vot chego-chego, a kontrolyorov u nas khvataet', *Kommersant. Daily*, No. 69, 20 April: 1, http://dlib.eastview.com/browse/doc/24625234
Korzhikhina, T. P. 1992. *Administrativno-komandnaya sistema upravleniia*. Moscow: RGGU
Kosals, L. 2007. 'Essay on clan capitalism in Russia', *Acta Oeconomica* 57 (1): 67–85
Kosyrev, M. and Abakumova, M. 2009. 'Za chto borolis': Rotenbergi', *Forbes*-Russia, November: 114
Kramer, A. E. 2010. 'Ikea fires 2 officials in Russia bribe case', *The New York Times*, February 16, www.nytimes.com/2010/02/16/business/global/16ikea.html
Krasil'nikova, T. 2010. 'Bez migalki, no na ZILe', *Trud*, 19 May
Krasnov, M. A., Talapina, E. V. and Tikhomirov, Y. A. 2004. *Analiz korruptsiogennosti zakonodatel'stva*. Moscow: Tsentr Strategicheskikh Razrabotok
Krastev, I. 2004. *Shifting Obsessions: Three Essays on the Politics of Anti-corruption*. Budapest: Central European University Press
Krastev, I., Leonard, M. and Wilson, A. 2009. *What Does Russia Think?* London: European Council on Foreign Relations

Kryshtanovskaya, O. 2005. *Anatomiia rossiiskoi elity*. Moscow: Zakharov
    2008. 'Best supporting actor in a lead role', *Transitions Online*,
    18 August, www.tol.org/client/article/19864-best-supporting-actor-
    in-a-lead-role.html
Kryshtanovskaya, O. and White, S. 2003. 'Putin's militocracy,' *Post-Soviet*
    Affairs 19 (4): 289–306
    2005. 'Inside the Putin court: a research note', *Europe-Asia Studies*
    57 (7): 1065–75
    2011. 'The formation of Russia's network directorate', in V. Kononenko
    and M. Arkady (eds.), *Russia as a Network State: What Works in Russia*
    When State Institutions Do Not? Basingstoke: Palgrave Macmillan: 19–
    38
Kulikov, V. 2005. 'Telefonnoe pravo podsudno', *Rossiiskaya Gazeta*,
    6 September, www.rg.ru/2005/09/06/telefonnoe-pravo.html
Lauth, H.-J. 2000. 'Informal institutions and democracy', *Democratization*
    7 (4): 21–50
Latour, B. 2005. *Reassembling the Social – An Introduction to Actor-*
    Network-Theory. Oxford: Oxford University Press
Latynina, Y. 2007. 'Bolshoi brat slyshit menia: Voina spetssluzhb eto nashe
    "razdelenie vlastei"', *Novaia Gazeta*, 11 October
    2008. 'Discarded like a worn-out pair of shoes', *The Moscow Times*,
    No. 3925, 18 June: 8
    2009. 'Swarm or the Antibaker: how modern Russia actually works',
    Third Way Liberal Discussion Forum, 26 March 2010, www.3rdway.
    org, Russian version in *Novaya gazeta*
Ledeneva, A. 1997. 'Informal sphere and *blat*: civil society or post-Soviet
    corporatism', *Pro i Contra* 9: 113–24
    1998. *Russia's Economy of Favours: Blat, Networking and Informal*
    Exchange. Cambridge University Press
    2001. *Unwritten Rules*. London: Centre for European Reform
    2004. 'The genealogy of *krugovaya poruka*: forced trust as a feature
    of Russian political culture', in I. Markova (ed.), *Trust and Demo-*
    cratic Transition in Post-Communist Europe. Proceedings of the British
    Academy. London: British Academy: 85–108
    2006. *How Russia Really Works: The Informal Practices That Shaped*
    Post-Soviet Politics and Business. Ithaca, NY: Cornell University Press
    2007. 'Informal networks in post-Communist economies', in T. Lahusen
    and P. H. Solomon (eds.), *What is Soviet Now? Identities, Legacies,*
    Memories. Münster: LIT Verlag: 57–77
    2008a. 'Telephone justice in Russia', *Post-Soviet Affairs* 24 (4): 324–50
    2008b. '*Blat* and *guanxi*: informal Practices in Russia and China', *Com-*
    parative Studies in Society and History 50 (1): 118–44

2009. 'From Russia with *blat*: can informal practices help modernize Russia?', *Social Research* 76 (1): 257–88

2011a. 'Open secrets and knowing smiles', *East European Politics and Society* 25 (4): 720–36

2011b. 'Telephone justice in Russia: an update', *EU-Russia Centre Newsletter* XVIII, Preface by Marie Mendras

Ledeneva, A. and Shekshnia, S. 2011. 'Doing business in Russian regions: informal practices and anti-corruption strategies', *IFRI Russia/NIS Centre*, Russie.Nei.Visions 58

Leksin, V., Leksin, I. and Chuchelina, N. 2006. *Kachestvo gosudarstvennogo i municipal'nogo upravleniia i administrativnaia reforma*. Moscow: Evroproekt

Lenin, V. 1923. 'Kak nam reorganizovat' RABKIN', *Sochineniia*, Isd-e 4, 33: 440–4

Levada Centre 2011. *Obshchestvennoe mnenie: ezhegodnik*. Moscow: Levada Centre Publishing

Lipman, M. and McFaul, M. 2005. 'Putin and the media', in D. R. Herspring (ed.), *Putin's Russia: Past Imperfect, Future Uncertain*. Plymouth: Rowman & Littlefield: 55–74

Lipman, M. and Petrov, N. (eds.) 2011. *Russia in 2020: Scenarios for the Future*. Washington, DC: Carnegie Endowment

Lipovetsky, M. 2011. *Charms of the Cynical Reason: The Trickster's Transformations in Soviet and Post-Soviet Culture*. Brighton, MA: Academic Studies Press

Lonkila, M. 2011. *Networks in the Russian Market Economy*. Basingstoke: Palgrave Macmillan

Loshak, A. 2010. 'Kafka's castle is collapsing', *openDemocracy*, 19 March, www.opendemocracy.org

Lovell, S. 2008. 'Power, personalism, and provisioning in Russian history', *Kritika: Explorations in Russian and Eurasian History* 9 (2): 373–88

Lovell, S., Rogachevskii, A. and Ledeneva, A. (eds.) 2000. *Bribery and Blat in Russia: Negotiating Reciprocity from the Early Modern Period to the 1990s*. Basingstoke: Palgrave Macmillan

Luzhkov, Y. 2008. *Russkie kharaktery*. Moscow: Moskovskie uchebniki i kartolitografiya

Maccaglia, F. and Matard-Bonicci, M. 2009. *Atlas des mafias*. Paris: Éditions Autrement

Macaulay, S. 1992. 'Non-contractual relations in business: a preliminary study', in M. Granovetta and R. Swedberg (eds.), *The Sociology of Economic Life*. Boulder, CO: Westview Press: 265–83

Malyi, M. 2002. 'Kak sdelat' Rossii normal'noi stranoi', www.matthew-maly.ru/book/cr-01.html

Mann, M. 1992. *The Sources of Social Power.* Cambridge University Press

Manning, N. and Parison, N. 2003. *International Public Administration Reform: Implications for Russian Federation.* New York: World Bank Publications

Mars, G. 1983. *Cheats at Work: An Anthropology of Workplace Crime.* London: George Allen & Unwin

Mazo, B. 2003. *Piterskie protiv Moskovskikh, li kto est' kto v okruzhenii V. V. Putina.* Moscow: Eksmo

McAndrew, D. 1999. 'The structural analysis of criminal networks', in D. Canter and L. Alison (eds.), *The Social Psychology of Crime.* Aldershot: Ashgate: 52–92

McGregor, R. 2010. *The Party: The Secret World of China's Communist Rulers.* London: Allen Lane

Medinskii, V. 2008. *O russkom vorovstve, osobom puti i dolgoterpenii.* Moscow: OLMA Media Grupp

2010. *O russkoi gryazi i vekovoi tekhnicheskoi otstalosti.* Moscow: OLMA Media Grupp

Mereu, F. 2007. 'Sechin's clan the loser in the week of surprises', *Moscow Times,* 17 December: 1

Messner, D. 1997. *The Network Society: Economic Development and International Competitiveness as Problems of Social Governance.* London: Frank Cass

Meyerson, E. M. 1994. 'Human capital, social capital and compensation: the relative contribution of social contacts to managers' incomes', *Acta sociologica* 37: 383–99

Midgley, D. and Hutchins, C. 2004. *Abramovich: The Billionaire From Nowhere.* London: HarperCollins

Miller, D. 2008. *Comfort of Things.* Cambridge: Polity

Miller, W., Grodeland, A. B. and Koshechkina, T. 2001. *A Culture of Corruption.* Budapest: Central European University

Mills, C. W. 1956. *The Power Elite.* Oxford University Press

Mironov, V. 2005. 'Kommentarii. Adminreforma: udvoenie apparata', *Vedomosti* 108, 16 June

Mishina, E. and Krasnov, M. (eds.) 2006. *Otkrytye Glaza Femidy.* Moscow: Fond Liberal'naia missiia

Mitrokhin, N. 2008. 'Regional clans and teams in the USSR and the Central Party Committee in 1965–1985', Paper presented at the ESRC Workshop on Regional Networks, Manchester, 17–18 September

2011. 'The rise of political clans in the era of Nikita Krushchev: the first phase 1953–1959', in M. Ilic and J. Smith (eds.), *Krushchev in the Kremlin: Policy and Government in the Soviet Union, 1953–1964.* Abingdon: Routledge: 26–40

Mokrousova, I. 2011. *Druz'ya Putina: novaya bisznes-elita Rossii*. Moscow: Eksmo

Monaghan, A. 2011. 'The Russian vertikal: the tandem, power and the elections', NATO Defence College: Russia and Eurasia Programme Paper REP, London: Chatham House

Morozov, E. 2011. *The Net Delusion: How Not to Liberate the World*. London: Allen Lane

Mukhin, A. 2005. *Nevskii-Lubyanka-Kreml': proekt-2008*. Moscow: Centre for Political Information

2006. *Oligarkhi: poslednyaya pereklichka*. Moscow: Algoritm

Myant, M. and Drahokoupil, J. 2011. *Transition Economies: Political Economy in Russia, Eastern Europe, and Central Asia*. Hoboken, NJ: John Wiley

Naishul', V. 1991. 'Vysshaya i poslednyaya stadiya sotsializma', in T. Notkina (ed.), *Postizhenie*. Moscow: Progress: 31–62

1993. 'Liberalism, customary rights and economic reforms', *Post-Communist Economies* 5 (1): 29–44

Nemtsov, B. and Milov, V. 2008. *Putin: Itogi: Nezavisimyi ekspertnyi doklad*. Moscow: Novaya Gazeta

Nesmachnaya, E. 2009. 'Ego velichestvo *blat*', *Pravda Severa*, 3 September

NEWSru.com 2008a. 'Medvedev vzyalsya za sudy: Reshenii "po zvonku" ili za den'gi byt' ne dolzhno', *NEWSru.com*, 20 May, http://www.newsru. com/russia/20may2008/medvedsud_print.html

2008b. 'U Ministerstva oborony RF ukrali 11 millionov rublei s pomoshch'yu fiktivnogo konkursa', *NEWSru.com*, 15 October

Nohria, N. and Khurana, R. 2010. 'Advancing leadership: theory and practice', in N. Nohria and R. Khurana (eds.), *Handbook of Leadership Theory and Practice*. Boston, MA: Harvard Business School Press: 3–25

Nonet, P. and Selznick, P. 1978. *Law and Society in Transition: Toward Responsive Law*. New Brunswick, NJ: Transaction Publishers

Nordstrom, C. 2004. *Shadows of War: Violence, Power, and International Profiteering in the Twenty-first Century*. Berkeley, CA and London: University of California Press

North, D. C. 1990. *Institutions, Institutional Change and Economic Performance*. Cambridge University Press

1991. 'Institutions', *Journal of Economic Perspectives* 5 (1): 97–112

Nove, A. 1977. *The Soviet Economic System*. London: Allen & Unwin

Oates, S. 2007. 'The neo-Soviet model of the media', *Europe-Asia Studies* 59 (8): 1279–97

Obolonskii, A. V. 1994. *Drama rossiiskoi politicheskoi istorii: sistema protiv lichnosti*. Moscow: Institut gosudarstva i prava

O'Donnell, G. 1996. 'Illusions about democracy', *Journal of Democracy* 7 (2): 34–51

OECD 2006. *Economic Survey of the Russian Federation*. Paris: OECD Publishing

Oleinik, A. N. 2003. *Organized Crime, Prison and Post-Soviet Society*. Aldershot: Ashgate.

2008a. 'Introduction: putting administrative reform in a broader context of power', *Journal of Communist Studies and Transition Politics* 24 (1): 1–16

2008b. 'Triangulyatsiya v kontent-analize: primer uglublennykh interv´yu s predstaviteliami rossiiskoi elity', *Vestnik Obshchestvennogo Mneniia/ The Russian Public Opinion Herald* 3 (95): 62–75

Olson, M. 1982. *The Rise and Decline of Nations*. New Haven, CT: Yale University Press

Pachenkov, O., Sokolova, M. and Chikadze, E. 2005. *Bespredel´naya sotsiologiia*. St Petersburg: CISR Unplugged

Padgett, J., Bonacich, P., Skvoretz, J. and Scott, J. 2000. *Social Network Analysis*. London: Sage

Paneyakh, E. 2011. 'Transaktsionnye effekty plotnogo regulirovaniya na stykakh organizatsii', *Politiya* 61 (2): 38–59

Panfilova, E. and Sheverdyaev, S. (eds.) 2005. *Rukovodstvo po prakticheskomu protivodeistviyu zloupotrebleniyu administrativnym resursom na vyborakh*. Moscow: De Novo and Transparency International – Russia

Panyushkin, V. 2006. *Mikhail Khodorkovsky: uznik tishiny*. Moscow: Sekret firmy

Panyushkin, V. and Zykar´, M. 2007. *Gazprom: novoe Russkoe oruzhie*. Moscow: Zakharov

Parfitt, T. 2012. 'Putin looks to Abramovich to pay for 2018 ', *The Observer*, 5 December: 5

Pastukhov, V. 2002. 'Law under administrative pressure in post-Soviet Russia', *East European Constitutional Review* 11 (3): 66–74

2010a. 'Mutnye instituty, Reforma MVD i krizis regulyuarnogo gosudarstva v Rossii', *polit.ru*, 10 Februrary, www.polit.ru/analytics/2010/ 02/10/smuta.html

2010b. 'Oshibka Prezidenta', *polit.ru*, 21 Februrary, www.polit.ru/ institutes/2010/02/21/mistake.html

2012. *Restavratsiya vmesto reformatsii*. Moscow: OGI

Parshikov, V. 2008. 'Professor nuzhnykh svyazei', http://compromat.ru/ page_27383.htm

Pavlenko, S. 2002. *Nauka oshibok. Stat´i i proekty 1994–2000*. Moscow: Modest Kolerov i tri kvadrata

Pelevin, V. 2000. *Chisla*. Moscow: Eksmo

2006. *Empire V.* Moscow: Eksmo

2008. *Proschal'nye pesni politicheskikh pigmeev pindostana.* Moscow: Eksmo

Perkmann, M. 1999. 'The two network societies', *Economy and Society* 28 (4): 615–28

Perle, R. 1992. *Hard Line*. New York: Random House

Pesman, D. 2000. *Russia and Soul: An Exploration.* Ithaca, NY: Cornell University Press

Petrov, N. 2011. 'The *nomenklatura* and the elite', in M. Lipman and N. Petrov (eds.), *Russia in 2020: Scenarios for the Future.* Washington, DC: Carnegie Endowment: 499–530

Pincon, M. and Pincon-Charlot, M. 2010. *Le President des Riches.* Paris: Parution

Platteau, J. P. 1994a. 'Behind the market stage, where real societies exist, Part I: The role of public and private order institutions', *Journal of Development Studies* 30 (3): 533–77

1994b. 'Behind the market stage, where real societies exist, Part II: The role of moral norms', *Journal of Development Studies* 30 (3): 753–817

Plattner, S. (ed.) 1989. *Economic Anthropology.* Stanford University Press

Polanyi, K. 1944. *The Great Transformation.* New York: Rinehart

1957. 'The economy as instituted process', in K. Polanyi and C. Arensberg (eds.), *Trade and Market in the Early Empires.* Glencoe, IL: Free Press

Portes, A. 1998. 'Social capital: its origins and applications in modern sociology', *Annual Review of Sociology* 24: 1–24

2000. 'Social capital: its origins and applications in modern sociology', in E. L. Lesser (ed.), *Knowledge and Social Capital: Foundations and Applications.* Woburn, MA: Butterworth–Heinemann

Portes, A. and Landolt, P. 1996. 'The downside of social capital', *The American Prospect* 26: 18–21

Portes, A. and Sensenbrenner, J. 1993. 'Embeddedness and immigration: notes on the social determinants of economic action', *American Journal of Sociology* 98 (6): 1320–50

Pravda, A. (ed.) 2005. *Leading Russia: Putin in Perspective.* Oxford University Press

Prendergast, J., Foley, B., Menne, V. and Issac, A. K. 2008. *Creatures of Habit? The Art of Behavioural Change.* London: Social Market Foundation

Prokhorov, A. 2002. *Russkaya model' upravleniia.* Moscow: ZAU 'Zhurnal Ekspert'

Promptova, O. and Chernov, A. 2004. 'Blat uzhe ne aktualen', *Vedomosti*, 3, 24 January

Prown, J. D. 1982. 'Mind in matter: an introduction to material culture theory and method', *Winterthur Portfolio*, 17 (1): 1–19

Pushkov, A. 2009. *Putinskie kacheli*. Moscow: Algoritm

Putnam, R. D. 1995. 'Bowling alone: America's declining social capital', *Journal of Democracy* 6 (1): 65–78

1996. 'The strange disappearance of civic America', *American Prospect* 24: 34–48

Putnam, R. D., Leonardi, R. and Nanetti, R. Y. (eds.) 1993. *Making Democracy Work: Civic Traditions in Modern Italy*. Princeton University Press

Reichheld, F. F. 2001. *Loyalty Rules!* Boston, MA: Harvard Business School Press

Reuters 2007. 'Corruption in Russia business worsens: survey', 28 October, www.reuters.com/article/topNews/idUSL1867863220071018

Reznik, I. 2010. 'Ya nikogda ne torgoval Rossiei', *Vedomosti*, 19 May

RIA Novosti 2007. 'Russian prosecutors confirm arrest of Deputy Finance Minister', 17 November, www.en.rian.ru

Richards, S. 2009. *Lost and Found in Russia*. London: I. B.Tauris

Ries, N. 1997. *Russian Talk: Culture and Conversation during Perestroika*. Ithaca, NY: Cornell University Press

Rifkin, J. 2001. *The Age of Access: The New Culture of Hypercapitalism, Where all of Life is a Paid-For Experience*. New York: Tarcher

Rigby, T. H. 1981. 'Early provincial cliques and the rise of Stalin', *Soviet Studies* 33 (1): 3–28

1986. 'Was Stalin a disloyal patron?', *Soviet Studies* 38 (3): 311–24

Rivkin-Fish, M. 2005. *Women's Health in Post-Soviet Russia: The Politics of Interventon*. Bloomington, IN: Indiana University Press

Rochlitz, M. 2011. '"Embedded autonomy": state involvement in corporate raiding and economic modernization in post-crisis Russia', 6th Changing Europe Summer School, Moscow, 1–7 August

Rogov, K. 2006. 'Vzglyad na kontrabandu. Slon i kit: kliuchi ot rossiiskoi politiki ne neft´ i gaz, a mebel', *Kommersant*, 12 December

Rose, R. 2000. 'Uses of social capital in Russia: modern, pre-modern and anti-modern', *Post-Soviet Affairs* 16 (1): 33–57

2001. 'Getting things done in an anti-modern society: social capital networks in Russia', in P. Dasgupta and I. Serageldin (eds.), *Social Capital: A Multifaceted Perspective*. Washington, DC: World Bank Publications: 147–71

2009. *Understanding Post-Communist Transformation: A Bottom-Up Approach*. Abingdon: Routledge

Rose, R. and Mishler, W. 2007. 'Explaining the gap between the experience and perception of corruption', *Studies in Public Policy*, No. 432. University of Aberdeen

Rose-Ackerman, S. 1999. *Corruption and Government: Causes, Consequences, and Reform.* Cambridge University Press

Rothstein, B. 2011. 'Preventing societies from self-destruction', in B. Rothstein, *The Quality of Government: The Political Economy of Corruption, Social Trust and Inequality in an International Comparative Perspective.* Chicago University Press: 207–25

Roxburgh, A. 2011. *The Strongman: Vladimir Putin and the Struggle for Russia.* London: I. B. Tauris

Rubanov, A. 2009a. *Sazhaite i vyrastet.* St Petersburg and Moscow: Limbus Press

2009b. *Gotov'sya k voine.* Moscow: Eksmo

Russia Today 2008. 'Russia starved of top professionals', *Russia Today* 24 July, www.russiatoday.ru/news/news/27999/video

Ryvkina, R. 2011. *Drama Peremen.* Moscow: Delo

Sakwa, R. 2008. *Power and Politics in Putin's Russia.* Moscow: Routledge

2009. *The Quality of Freedom: Khordokovsky, Putin, and the Yukos Affair.* Oxford University Press

2011. *The Crisis of Russian Democracy: The Dual State, Factionalism and the Medvedev Succession.* Cambridge: Cambridge University Press

Satarov, G. A. *et al.* 2005. 'Corruption process in Russia: level, structure, trends (INDEM diagnostics of corruption markets on the basis of the 2001 and 2005 ROMIR Monitoring surveys)', www.indem.ru/en/publicat/2005diag_engV.htm. (accessed at www.indem.ru/en/publicat/2005diag_engV.htm, April 2008)

Saviano, R. 2007. *Gomorrah: Italy's Other Mafia.* London: Macmillan

Schatz, E. 2005. *Modern Clan Politics and Beyond: The Power of 'Blood' in Kazakhstan.* Seattle, WA: University of Washington Press

Scheppele, K. L. 1988. *Legal Secrets: Equality and Efficiency in the Common Law.* University of Chicago Press

Schmidt, S. W. (ed.) 1977. *Friends, Followers and Factions: A Reader in Political Clientelism*, Berkeley, CA: University of California Press

Sergeeva, A. V. 2008. *Russkie: Stereotipy povedeniia, traditsii, mental'nost'.* Moscow: Flinta-Nauka

Service, R. 2005. In A. Pravda (ed.), *Leading Russia: Putin in Perspective.* Oxford University Press

Shapiro, S. P. 1987. 'The social control of impersonal trust', *American Journal of Sociology* 93 (3): 623–58

Sharafutdinova, G. 2011. *Political Consequences of Crony Capitalism.* University of Notre Dame Press

Shekshnia, S. 2003. *Kak eto skazat' po-russki.* Moscow: OOO Zhurnal upravleniya personalom

2010. *Kak effektivno upravlyat' svobodnymi lyud'mi.* Moscow: Alpina

Shekshnia, S. and Kets De Vries, M. F. R. 2008. 'Russia's succession paradox,' *Organisational Dynamics*, 37 (3): 266–76

Shenderovich, V. 2008. *Plavlennye syrki – 2*. St Petersburg: Amfora

Shevtsova, L. 2003. *Putin's Russia*. Washington, DC: Carnegie Endowment for International Peace

2007. *Russia: Lost in Transition. The Yeltsin and Putin Legacies*. Washington, DC: Carnegie Endowment foir International Peace

Shtykina, A. 2010. 'Grazhdane podderzhivayut bor´bu s migalkami', *Kommersant*, 30 April

Sik, E. and Wellman, B. 1999. 'Network capital in capitalist, Communist and post-Communist countries', in B. Wellman (ed.), *Networks in the Global Village*. Boulder, CO: Westview Press: 225–55

Sixsmith, M. 2010. *Putin's Oil: The Yukos Affair and the Struggle for Russia*. London: Continuum

Skocpol, T. 1996. 'Unraveling from above', *The American Prospect* 25: 20–5

Skoibeda, U. 2007. '"Tri Kita" finansirovali voinu Chechni protiv Rossii?', *Komsomol´skaia Pravda*, 29 January

Slater, W. and Wilson, A. (eds.) 2004. *The Legacy of the Soviet Union*. Basingstoke: Palgrave Macmillan

Sloterdijk, P. 1987. *Critique of Cynical Reason*. University of Minnesota Press

Smith, P. B., Torres, C., Leong, C.-H., Budwar, P., Achoui, M. and Lebedeva, N. 2011. 'Are indigenous approaches to achieving influence in business organizations distinctive? A comparative study of guanxi, wasta, jeitinho, svyazi and pulling strings', *The International Journal of Human Resource Management*, 23 (2): 333–48

Soldatov, A. and Borogan, I. 2011. *Novoe dvoryanstvo*. Moscow: United Press

Solomon, P., Jr. 1992. 'Soviet politicians and criminal prosecutions: the logic of intervention', in J. Millar (ed.), *Cracks in the Monolith*. Armonk, NY: M. E. Sharpe: 3–32

2008. 'Assessing the courts in Russia: parameters of progress under Putin', *Demokratizatsiya: The Journal of Post-Soviet Democratisation* 16 (1): 63–73

2010. 'Authoritarian legality and informal practices: judges, lawyers and the state in Russia and China', *Communist and Post-Communist Studies* 43 (4): 351–62

Solomon, P., Jr. and Foglesong, T. S. 2000. *Courts and Transition in Russia: The Challenge of Judicial Reform*. Boulder, CO: Westview Press

Solov´ev, V. 2008. *Putin: putevoditel´ dlya neravnodushnykh*. Moscow: Eksmo

2012. *Imperiya korruptsii: territoriya russkoi natsionalnoi igry*. Moscow: Eksmo

Solov'ev, V. and Zlobin, N. 2010. *Putin–Medvedev: chto dal'she?* Moscow: Eksmo

Solzhenitsin, A. 1973. *The Gulag Archipelago*. Paris: Éditions du Seuil

Sorokin, V. 2006. *Den' oprichnika*. Moscow: Zakharov

Stack, G. 2008. 'All the next President's men: Dmitry Medvedev's *civiliki*', *Russia Profile* 5 (2): 8–10

Stark, D. and Bruszt, L. 2001a. 'One way or multiple paths? For a comparative sociology of European capitalism', *American Journal of Sociology* 106 (4): 1129–37

  2001b. 'Postsocialist pathways: transforming politics and property in East Central Europe', *American Journal of Sociology* 106 (4): 7–8, 82–3

Steen, A. 2003. 'The network state', in A. Steen (ed.), *Political Elites in the New Russia: The Power Basis of Yeltsin's and Putin's Regime*. London: Routledge Curzon: 141–66

Stenning, A., Smith, A., Rochovská, A. and Świątek, D. 2010. *Domesticating Neo-Liberalism: Spaces of Economic Practice and Social Reproduction in Post-Socialist Cities*. Hoboken, NJ: Wiley–Blackwell

Skogoreva, A., Aleshkina, T., Tkachuk, S. and Terekhov, A. 2003. 'Porochashchaya svyaz'', *Novye Izvestiia*, 26 November

Swamy, A., Knack, S., Lee, Y. and Azfar, O. 2001. 'Gender and corruption', *Journal of Development Economics* 64: 25–55

Tanzi, V. 1998. 'Corruption around the world: causes, scope and cures', IMF Working Paper WP/98/63

Thaler, R. H. and Sunstein, C. R. 2008. *Nudge: Improving Decisions About Health, Wealth, and Happiness*. New Haven, CT: Yale University Press

The New Times 2011. 'Korporatsiya "Rossia": Putin s druz'yami podelili stranu', 31 October: 4–12

Thurbron, C. 2004. *Among the Russians*. London: Vintage Books

Tilley, C. 2002. 'Metaphor, materiality and interpretation', in V. Buchli (ed.), *The Material Culture Reader*. Oxford: Berg: 23–56

Tilly, C. 1998. *Durable Inequality*. Berkeley and Los Angeles. CA: University of California Press

  2005. *Trust and Rule*. Cambridge: Cambridge University Press

Tilley, C., Keane, W., Kuchler, S., Rowlands, M. and Spyer, P. 2006. *Handbook of Material Culture*. London: Sage

Timofeev, L. 1993. *Chyornyi rynok kak politicheskaya sistema*. Vilnius and Moscow: VIMO

Tolstykh, P. A. 2006. *Praktika lobbizma: v gosudarstvennoi dume federal'nogo sobraniia Rossiiskoi Federatsii*. Moscow: Kanon Reabilitatsiya

Tompson, W. 2007. 'From "clientelism" to a "client-centred orientation"? The challenge of public administration reform in Russia'; Paris: OECD, Economics Department Working Paper 536 ECO/WKP(2006)64; also available at London: Birkbeck e-Prints, http://eprints.bbk.ac.uk/archive/00000505

Tompson, W. in collaboration with Price, R. 2009. *The Political Economy of Reform*. Paris: OECD

Transparency International 2004. *Monitoring the Misuse of Administrative Resources during the Campaign of the December 2003 State Duma Elections*. Moscow: Transparency International – Russia

2007. *Global Corruption Report 2007: Corruption in Judicial Systems*. Cambridge: Transparency International with Cambridge University Press

Trochev, A. 2008. *Judging Russia: Constitutional Courts in Russian Politics, 1990–2006*. Cambridge University Press

UNDP. 2004. *Practice Code: Anti-corruption*, www.undp.org/governance/docs/AC_PN_English.pdf

Urban, M. 2010. *Cultures of Power in Post-Communist Russia: An Analysis of Elite Political Discourse*. Cambridge University Press

Uskova, O. 2010. 'Otkaty po goskontraktam v IT-sektore dostigli 75 protsentov', Prime-TASS, 19 April, www.vedomosti.ru/newsline/news/2010/04/19/996526

Uzzi, B. 1999. 'Embeddedness in the making of financial capital: how social relations and networks benefit firms seeking financing', *American Sociological Review* 64 (4): 481–505

Vaksberg, A. 1986. 'Kak slovo otzovyotsya', *Pravda*, 7 May: 12

Varese, F. 2001. *The Russian Mafia*. Oxford University Press

Vasilyeva, N. 2009. 'Ikea expansion in Russia stalled', *Daily Reporter*, 15 June, http://dailyreporter.com/blog/2009/06/15/ikea-expansion-in-russia-stalled/

Verdier, D. 1995. 'The politics of public aid to private industry: the role of policy networks', *Comparative Political Studies* 28 (1): 3–42

Viktorova, L. 2008. '7 *millionov evro – i ty gubernator'*, *Komsomol'skaya pravda*, 109, 26 July, http://dlib.eastview.com/sources/article.jsp?id=18669811

Veblen, T. 1962. *The Theory of the Leisure Class: The Challenging Analysis of Social Conduct that Ironically Probes Misused Wealth and Conspicuous Consumption*. New York: Vanguard

Volkov, V. 2002. *Violent Entrepreneurs*. Ithaca, NY: Cornell University Press

2004. 'The selective use of state capacity in the Russian economy: property disputes and enterprise takeovers, 1998–2002', in J. Kornai,

B. Rothstein and S. Rose-Ackerman (eds.), *Creating Social Trust in Post-Socialist Transition*. New York: Palgrave Macmillan

Volkov, V. *et al.* 2011. *Plokhie instituty*, Report of the Institute of Law Enforcement. St Petersburg: European University

Volkova, V. N. and Denisov, A. A. 2010. *Teoriya system i sistemnyi analiz*. Moscow: Yurait

Voslenski, M. 1991. '*A ballad about telephones*', *Nomenklatura* (Moscow: October 1991, originally published 1980), http://bookz.ru/authors/voslenskii-m/woslenskij/page-21-woslenskij.html

Vyzhutovich, V. 2006. 'Politika: vzyatki gladki', *Rossiiskaya Gazeta*, 140, 30 June

Waller, M. 2005. 'The presidency', in M. Waller, *Politics Today: Russian Politics Today*. Manchester University Press: 23–47

Wasserman, S. and Faust, K. 1992. *Social Network Analysis: Methods and Applications*. Cambridge University Press

Weber, M. 1968. *Economy and Society, Vol. 1*. New York: Bedminster

Wedel, J. R. 2001. *Collision and Collusion: The Strange Case of Western Aid to Eastern Europe 1989–1998*. New York: St Martin's Press

2003. 'Clans, cliques and captured states: rethinking transition in Central and Eastern Europe and the Former Soviet Union', *Journal of International Development* 15 (4): 427–40

2009. *Shadow Elite: How the World's New Power Brokers Undermine Democracy, Government, and the Free Market*. New York: Basic Books

Wellman, B. (ed.) 1999. *Networks in the Global Village*. Boulder, CO: Westview Press

Wellman, B. and Berkowitz, S. D. 1988. *Social Structures: A Network Approach*. Cambridge University Press

Wellman, B. and Wortley, S. 1990. 'Different strokes from different folks: community ties and social support', *American Journal of Sociology* 96: 558–88

White, H. 1992. *Identity and Control*. Princeton University Press

White, S. (ed.) 2008. *Media, Culture and Society in Putin's Russia*. Basingstoke: Palgrave Macmillan

Whitefield, S. (ed.) 2005. *Political Culture and Post-Communism*. St Antony's Series, London: Palgrave Macmillan

Wilkinson, R. and Pickett, K. 2009. *The Spirit Level: Why Equality Is Better For Everyone*. London: Penguin

Wilson, A. 2005. *Virtual Politics*. New Haven, CT: Yale University Press

Woolcock, M. 1998. 'Social capital and economic development: toward a theoretical synthesis and policy framework', *Theory and Society* 27: 151–208

Yakovlev, A. A. 2009. *Agents of Modernisation*. Moscow: Higher School of Economics

2012. 'Russia's protest movement and the lessons of history', *Russian Analytical Digest* 108: 6–10

Yakubovich, V. 2005. 'Weak ties, information and influence: how workers find jobs in a local Russian labor market', *American Sociological Review* 70: 408–21

Yakubovich, V. and Shekshnia, S. 2012. 'The emergence of the Russian mobile telecom market: local technical leadership and global investors in a shadow of the state', in J. Padgett and W. Powell (eds.), *Market Emergence and Transformation*. Princeton University Press

Yamshanov, B. 2006. 'Basmannoe pravosudie so sluzhebnogo khoda' (Interview with the Chairman of the Moscow City Court Olga Egorova), *Rossiiskaya Gazeta*, 24 March, www.rg.ru/2005/03/24/egorova-pravosudie.html

Yanov, A. L. 2007. *Rossiya i Evropa: zagadka Nikolaevskoi Rossii: 1825–1855*. Moscow: Novyi Khronograf

2008. *Rossiya i Evropa: Evropeiskoe stoletie Rossii: 1480–1560*. Moscow: Novyi Khronograf

Yasman, V. 2006. 'Russia: corruption scandal could shake Kremlin', *RFE/RL*, 26 September

Yudina, L. 2008. 'Protivoyadie ot reidera', *Tribuna* (13), 11 April: 12

Yurchak, A. 1997. 'The cynical reason of late socialism: power, pretense, and the *Anekdot*', *Public Culture* 9 (2): 161–88

2005. *Everything Was Forever, Until It Was No More: The Last Soviet Generation*. Princeton University Press

Zaleznik, A. 1966. *Human Dilemmas of Leadership*. New York: Harper-Collins

Zaslavskaya, T. 1990. *The Second Social Revolution*, Foreword by T. Shanin. London: I. B. Tauris

2007a. *Sotsial'naya ekonomika i ekonomicheskaya sotsiologiya*, 1. Moscow: Ekonomika

2007b. *Transformatsionnyi protsess v Rossii. Izbrannoe*, 2. Moscow: Ekonomika

Zdravomyslova, E., Rotkirkh, A. and Temkina, A. 2009. *Novyi byt v sovere-mennoi Rossii*. St Petersburg: Evropeiskii Universitet

Zdravomyslova, E. and Temkina, A. 2007. *Rossiiskii gendernyi poryadok: sotsiologicheskii podkhod*. St Petersburg: Evropeiskii Universitet

Zhvanetskii, M. 2009. *Izbrannoe*. Moscow: Eksmo

Zigon, J. 2011. *Multiple Moralities and Religions in Post-Soviet Russia*. Oxford: Berghahn Books

Zimbardo, P. 2007. *The Lucifer Effect: How Good People Turn Evil*. London: Random House

Zinov'ev, A. 1978. *The Yawning Heights*. London: Bodley Head

Index